Leo Strauss and Islamic Political Thought

In this book, Rasoul Namazi offers the first in-depth study of Leo Strauss's writings on Islamic political thought, a topic that interested Strauss over the course of his career. Namazi's volume focuses on several important studies by Strauss on Islamic thought. He critically analyzes Strauss's notes on Averroes's commentary on Plato's *Republic* and proposes an interpretation of Strauss's theologico-political notes on the *Arabian Nights*. Namazi also interprets Strauss's essay on Alfarabi's enigmatic treatise *The Philosophy of Plato* and provides a detailed commentary on his complex essay devoted to Alfarabi's summary of Plato's *Laws*. Based on previously unpublished material from Strauss's papers, Namazi's volume provides new insights into Strauss's reflections on religion, philosophy, and politics and their relationship to wisdom, persecution, divine law, and unbelief in the works of key Muslim thinkers. This work presents Strauss as one of the most innovative historians and scholars of Islamic thought of all time.

Rasoul Namazi is an assistant professor of political theory at Duke Kunshan University, China and assistant professor of the practice of global studies at Duke University, USA. A laureate of the Raymond Aron Prize, he has held fellowships from the Committee on Social Thought, University of Chicago, and the Alexander von Humboldt Stiftung, Ludwig Maximilian University of Munich. He is the author of articles and chapters on Islamic and Western political thought published in the *Journal of Religion, Perspectives on Political Science, American Political Thought, Iranian Studies, Interpretation, Review of Politics, Renaissance & Reformation*, and *Eurorient* as well as in collected volumes.

Leo Strauss and Islamic Political Thought

RASOUL NAMAZI
Duke Kunshan University

CAMBRIDGE
UNIVERSITY PRESS

Shaftesbury Road, Cambridge CB2 8EA, United Kingdom

One Liberty Plaza, 20th Floor, New York, NY 10006, USA

477 Williamstown Road, Port Melbourne, VIC 3207, Australia

314–321, 3rd Floor, Plot 3, Splendor Forum, Jasola District Centre, New Delhi – 110025, India

103 Penang Road, #05–06/07, Visioncrest Commercial, Singapore 238467

Cambridge University Press is part of Cambridge University Press & Assessment,
a department of the University of Cambridge.

We share the University's mission to contribute to society through the pursuit of
education, learning and research at the highest international levels of excellence.

www.cambridge.org
Information on this title: www.cambridge.org/9781009101936

DOI: 10.1017/9781009105118

First published 2022
First paperback edition 2023

A catalogue record for this publication is available from the British Library

Library of Congress Cataloging-in-Publication data
NAMES: Namazi, Rasoul, 1982– author.
TITLE: Leo Strauss and Islamic political thought / Rasoul Namazi.
DESCRIPTION: 1. | New York : Cambridge University Press, 2022.
| Includes bibliographical references and index.
IDENTIFIERS: LCCN 2021059222 (print) | LCCN 2021059223 (ebook)
| ISBN 9781009098700 (hardback) | ISBN 9781009105118 (ebook)
SUBJECTS: LCSH: Islamic philosophy – Greek influences.
| Strauss, Leo – Political and social views. | Fārābī – Criticism and interpretation.
| Averroës, 1126–1198 – Criticism and interpretation.
CLASSIFICATION: LCC B744.3 .N36 2022 (print)
| LCC B744.3 (ebook) | DDC 181/.07–dc23/eng/20211207
LC record available at https://lccn.loc.gov/2021059222
LC ebook record available at https://lccn.loc.gov/2021059223

ISBN   978-1-009-09870-0   Hardback
ISBN   978-1-009-10193-6   Paperback

To Heinrich Meier

I have read that in some Italian pictures Plato is represented holding in his hand the *Timaeus* and Aristotle his *Ethics*. If a pupil of Maimonides or of the Islamic philosophers had found pleasure in representations of this kind, he might have chosen rather the inverse order: Aristotle with his *Physics* or *Metaphysics* and Plato with his *Republic* or *Laws*.

– Leo Strauss

Contents

Preface

In recent years, there has been a considerable increase of interest in the thought and writings of Leo Strauss, now recognized as one of the most influential and controversial thinkers of his generation. A rising awareness of the importance of Strauss's commentaries on a variety of authors can be observed: his contributions to the study of the history of ancient and modern political thought, as well as Jewish figures, are generally recognized as being worthy of discussion and are debated even by those who have serious reservations about Strauss's claims and general perspective. Strauss's studies on medieval Islamic political philosophy, however, have received a rather limited response from scholars of Islamic political thought: many studies on Islamic thought are written in complete disregard of Strauss's scholarship on the subject. Those few writings that discuss Strauss's ideas, on the other hand, range from brief and very dismissive comments to a few critical but interesting discussions, a few sympathetic short but valuable essays, and detailed studies that are intellectually very rich and informative but which focus on aspects of Strauss's intellectual production other than Islamic political thought proper. This limited reception of Strauss's contribution to the study of Muslim philosophers is not consonant with the unique position medieval Islamic political thought occupies in Strauss's intellectual biography. It was because of the discoveries Strauss made while studying medieval Islamic philosophy that he was guided toward classical Greek philosophy: his studies on Maimonides pointed him back toward Alfarabi, and through Alfarabi Strauss was guided back toward Plato, as well as to a new understanding of Jewish thinkers. It is therefore not surprising that Strauss once called "Arabic political philosophy" his "specialty."[1] The same preoccupation with Islamic thought left an undeniable mark on Strauss's writings on modern philosophers and hence – as can be seen in his later writings, unpublished notes, and course transcripts – Strauss remained highly interested in Islamic thought until the end of his life. If we consider the judgment of the scholars who are knowledgeable about Strauss's intellectual biography that medieval Islamic philosophy played a major role in his thought, it is surprising that very few studies discuss Strauss's works on Islamic philosophy in much detail. One can therefore say, to borrow an apt expression, "there is room for inquiry here."[2]

This volume tries to fill this gap in the literature by focusing on this aspect of Strauss's thought in a comprehensive fashion. The result will not only reveal a better understanding of the role played by Islamic political thought in Strauss's writings but also introduce the unique perspective of one of the most original historians of philosophy on Islamic thought. There is much talk in academia about the need to open the discipline of philosophy to "non-Western" thinkers, such as Islamic philosophers. One of the prerequisites for such inclusion would be to treat the writings of these thinkers not only as objects of historical study but also as works still relevant to contemporary philosophical and politico-religious debates. Strauss was among those who entered into dialogue with the writings of Islamic figures as products of remarkable thinkers addressing universal questions. His writings can therefore help us in furthering the inclusion of these works in the discipline of philosophy and treating them with the seriousness they require.

The audience addressed in this volume consists of two main groups. First are those readers who have some familiarity with Strauss's writings and would like to know specifically about his writings on Islamic thought. My deepest desire, and I hope not a vain one, is that these

---

[1] Leo Strauss and Eric Voegelin, *Faith and Political Philosophy: The Correspondence Between Leo Strauss and Eric Voegelin, 1934–1964*, ed. Peter Emberley and Barry Cooper (Columbia: University of Missouri Press, 2004), 12 (Letter to Eric Voegelin on February 13, 1943).

[2] Daniel Tanguay, *Leo Strauss: An Intellectual Biography*, trans. Christopher Nadon (New Haven: Yale University Press, 2011), 53; Rémi Brague, "Athens, Jerusalem, Mecca. Leo Strauss's 'Muslim' Understanding of Greek Philosophy," *Poetics Today* 19, no. 2 (Summer 1998): 235–59; Georges Tamer, *Islamische Philosophie und die Krise der Moderne: Das Verhältnis von Leo Strauss zu Alfarabi, Avicenna und Averroes* (Leiden: Brill, 2001), 35–36; Makram Abbès, "Leo Strauss et la philosophie arabe. Les Lumières médiévales contre les Lumières modernes," *Diogène* 226, no. 2 (2009): 117–41.

readers, after having reread the texts discussed here "forty times" without gaining complete clarity about them, by chance encounter this volume and find that it helps them discover, at least in part, the purposes of these writings of Strauss. The second group of potential readers consists of those fellow scholars of Islamic thought who, despite their erudition, and perhaps because of the fault of our teachers, might not have been introduced to Strauss's works and his contributions to their discipline. Counting on the openness expected in scholarship, and believing in the duty of sharing one's meaningful discoveries with one's friends, this volume intends to introduce them to Strauss's unique approach to the study of Islamic philosophy. My aim is not to "convert" anybody to "Straussianism" – whatever this ambiguous label may mean – or to convince anyone that Strauss was right on every point. In general, I believe that both deference and hostility in dealing with the ideas of an important thinker result in weak scholarship. Rather than these two unscholarly passions, curiosity has been the primary motive in my study of Strauss, a curiosity I hope my readers come to share.

The following volume consists of an introduction, four chapters, and four appendices. The Introduction provides a panoramic view of Strauss's thought, with a special emphasis on his interest in Islamic political thought. This summary presentation will focus on what I call the four pillars of Strauss's intellectual project: (1) Reason and Revelation; (2) Ancients and Moderns; (3) The Theologico-Political Problem; and (4) Esotericism. All these themes have a direct relationship to Strauss's writings on Islamic thought and his biographically documented interest in the writings of the Falāsifa. This summary presentation is followed by a critical assessment of previous studies on Strauss's interest in Islamic thought, divided into two groups. The objective of this critical assessment is, first of all, to discuss some of the common misconceptions regarding Strauss's writings on Islamic philosophy in those writings that are mainly critical of his scholarship. The second objective is to show that, despite some very important studies on Strauss's scholarship on Islamic thought, there is a significant gap existing in the scholarship, which this volume tries to remedy by engaging in a careful, intensive interpretation of Strauss's writings, correspondence, and other surviving material, as well as by presenting and interpreting two transcripts on Islamic thought that were not published by Strauss.

Chapter 1 is dedicated to the interpretation of a recently discovered, unpublished typescript by Strauss on Averroes's commentary on Plato's

Republic.[3] Strauss only published a single brief text discussing Averroes in some detail. However, from his published writings on Islamic philosophy and his surviving notes, one can infer that he has read Averroes's works with considerable care.[4] In this transcript, available as Appendix A and composed sometime after 1956, Strauss underscores the conflict between philosophy and Islam in Averroes's commentary on Plato's *Republic*. The transcript consists only of short notes and, therefore, to reveal its message, it needs to be interpreted in the context of Strauss's other writings. Strauss's interpretation of Averroes is based on the idea that Averroes must have been aware of the incompatibility of Islamic revelation with the best regime of Plato. Unlike other scholars, who are mainly preoccupied with Averroes's access or lack thereof to a reliable translation of Plato's *Republic*, Strauss argues that the deficiencies of Averroes's commentary do not mean that Averroes lacked access to Plato's *Republic*; he claims that such apparent deficiencies might be intentional and significant for understanding Averroes's views. Strauss's transcript is discussed first in this volume because it is not only significant for understanding his interpretation of Averroes's commentary but also provides a good introduction to the specifics of Strauss's approach to the study of Islamic philosophy.

Chapter 2 of this study is dedicated to the interpretation of another transcript found among the Leo Strauss Papers, also included in this volume as Appendix B. Entitled "1001 Nights," the transcript contains detailed notes on many of the stories included in the Calcutta II version of the *Arabian Nights*.[5] For several generations, scholars of the *Arabian Nights* have directed their attention mainly toward questions regarding the sources and origins of the stories included in the *Arabian Nights*, as well as the study of their strictly formal characteristics. When not engaged exclusively with the literary study of the *Arabian Nights*, most scholars tend to read this remarkable document of Arabic thought to obtain information about the common mentalities and beliefs of the medieval and

---

[3] Leo Strauss Papers, box 18, folder 17, Special Collections Research Center, University of Chicago Library.

[4] Steven Harvey, "The Story of a Twentieth-Century Jewish Scholar's Discovery of Plato's Political Philosophy in Tenth-Century Islam: Leo Strauss' Early Interest in the Islamic Falāsifa," in *Modern Jewish Scholarship on Islam in Context: Rationality, European Borders, and the Search for Belonging*, ed. Ottfried Fraisse (Berlin and Boston: De Gruyter, 2018), 223n14; Tamer, *Islamische Philosophie und die Krise der Moderne*, 47n24.

[5] Leo Strauss Papers, box 20, folder 2, Special Collections Research Center, University of Chicago Library.

early modern Islamic societies. Unlike many of these studies, Strauss has offered a remarkable theologico-political interpretation of this famous Arabic text. In his notes, composed sometime after 1959, Strauss concentrates exclusively on the teachings of the stories included in the *Arabian Nights*, and reads the text as a coherent, carefully crafted whole rather than as an anthology of unconnected tales. A table of concordance of the stories discussed in Strauss's transcript and in common editions of the *Arabian Nights* is provided as Appendix C. As in the case of the transcript discussed in Chapter 1, Strauss's transcript on the *Arabian Nights* consists of brief notes of an often enigmatic character. The points Strauss discovers in the *Arabian Nights* are therefore accessible only by having the text of the *Arabian Nights* as well as Strauss's complete writings in view. This is the method I have followed to present Strauss's intentions in the transcript for readers who otherwise would perhaps not be able to derive the full benefits of reading Strauss's notes.[6]

A detailed analysis of Strauss's first substantial commentary on a writing of Alfarabi, titled "Fârâbî's *Plato*," is provided in Chapter 3.[7] This rather obscure, yet fundamental writing of Strauss contains some of his most important ideas about Alfarabi, his relationship with Plato's philosophy and religion, Alfarabi's view on esotericism, and what he later calls zetetic philosophy.

A detailed examination of Strauss's interpretation of Alfarabi's summary of Plato's *Laws* is the subject of Chapter 4.[8] Strauss's complex article on Alfarabi's summary, which complements his earlier "Fârâbî's *Plato*," has received minimal attention.[9] The original manuscript of Strauss's article, found among the Leo Strauss Papers, can substantially

---

[6] An earlier version of this chapter was published as Rasoul Namazi, "Politics, Religion, and Love: How Leo Strauss Read the Arabian Nights," *Journal of Religion* 100, no. 2 (2020): 189–231. I have made substantial additions to the previous version and entirely revised it for this volume. The table of concordance is also entirely revised on the basis of the identification of Strauss's own copy. I would like the University of Chicago Press for giving me permission to use the paper as the basis of the chapter in this volume.

[7] Leo Strauss, "Fârâbî's Plato," in *Louis Ginzberg: Jubilee Volume on the Occasion of His Seventieth Birthday*, ed. Saul Lieberman, Alexander Marx, Shalom Spiegel, and Solomon Zeitlin (New York: The American Academy for Jewish Research, 1945), 357–93.

[8] Leo Strauss, "How Fārābī Read Plato's Laws," in *What Is Political Philosophy? And Other Studies* (Glencoe: Free Press, 1959), 134–55.

[9] Daniel Tanguay, "How Strauss Read Farabi's Summary of Plato's 'Laws,'" in *Leo Strauss's Defense of the Philosophic Life: Reading "What Is Political Philosophy?,"* ed. Rafael Major (Chicago: University of Chicago Press, 2013), 98–116. See also Joshua Parens, *Metaphysics as Rhetoric: Alfarabi's Summary of Plato's "Laws"* (Albany: State University of New York Press, 1995).

improve our understanding of this text and provide the opportunity for a more detailed commentary: the paragraphs of this manuscript are numbered, and contain headings that are absent in the published version of the article.[10] My interpretation of this article will take these aspects of the original manuscript, as well as Strauss's other writings and correspondence on Alfarabi and his course transcripts, into account. The paragraph headings of the manuscript are provided as Appendix D.

[10] Leo Strauss Papers, box 22, folder 1, Special Collections Research Center, University of Chicago Library.

Acknowledgments

This occasion of the publication of my first book presents an opportunity to acknowledge long overdue as well as recent debts of gratitude. I was first introduced to the thought and writings of Leo Strauss by Pierre Manent, my teacher for many years. In his famous Friday seminar at Ecole des Hautes Etudes en Sciences Sociales on Boulevard Raspail, many gathered to experience something that would stay with them for years. Nathan Tarcov gave me the opportunity to go to the University of Chicago as a Richard Schiffrin Research Fellow at the Leo Strauss Center. He was my magnanimous host for two years as I worked on Strauss's unpublished writings and manuscripts. In Chicago I was acquainted with many colleagues, among them Nasser Behnegar, Daniel Doneson, Steven Lenzner, Ralph Lerner, Christopher Lynch, Gayle McKeen, Robert Pippin, James T. Robinson, Bernhardt L. Trout, and Stuart Warner. Their friendship and knowledge have contributed much to my research. I should here particularly mention Svetozar Minkov, whose unsparing and wise advice has been essential during these years. While working on this project I have also benefitted from the excellent guidance of Joshua Parens and his deep knowledge of Jewish and Islamic thought. The association with the Leo Strauss Center also brought me into contact with Charles E. Butterworth, my guide to the world of the Falāsifa, and a model of worldliness and scholarship. While in Chicago, I also met Heinrich Meier, who generously supported my desire to come to Munich and to continue work on this project. So much of what is good about this book owes its existence to his deep knowledge of Strauss's thought and writings and his detailed comments on the manuscript. The stay in Munich also provided me with the opportunity to discuss different aspects of this book with Eric Buzzetti,

Yashar Jeirani, Hannes Kerber, Marco Menon, and Alexander Orwin all of whom gave me thoughtful feedback. Peter Ahrensdorf, famous for his liberal spirit, unsparingly advised me every step of the way. Jenny Strauss Clay kindly provided information that proved essential to the improvement of this study. Michael Kochin helped me with Hebrew transcriptions and Clifford A. Bates with Greek ones. Kelly Burch and Alex Knepper made many suggestions for the improvement of the manuscript. I have been blessed by the most supportive editor, Beatrice Rehl. It has been a privilege working with her. I thank Nicola Maclean of Cambridge University Press and Preethi Sekar for preparing the manuscript for publication. I am grateful to the abovementioned people, the anonymous reviewers for their suggestions and comments, and some others who might have slipped my faulty memory. I am grateful to the Leo Strauss Center, Alexander von Humboldt Stiftung, and Carl Friedrich von Siemens Stiftung for supporting my research stays in Chicago and Munich. All errors and shortcomings remain the sole responsibility of the author.

Last and first – a wise man would say – I owe special thanks to my wife Pantea Khanjari, who has lived patiently with my ten-thousand-fold poverty. She has been my faithful companion during these years of constant moving from one continent to another, helping me every step of the way. She was the original audience for many of the ideas found in this book. I hope this book proves that her patience was not in vain.

Note on Citations

All citations to Leo Strauss's writings, if available, are to the most accessible English translations. When applicable, I have also provided the volume and page numbers of the German edition of Strauss's collected writings. The following abbreviations are used:

A   Followed by page and line numbers of Averroes, *Commentary on Plato's "Republic,"* trans. Erwin I. J. Rosenthal (Cambridge: University of Cambridge Oriental Publication, 1956).

AN   Followed by volume and page numbers of Malcolm C. Lyons, Ursula Lyons, and Robert Irwin, *The Arabian Nights: Tales of 1,001 Nights*, 3 vols. (London: Penguin Books, 2010).

D   Followed by page numbers of Alfarabi, "Le Sommaire du Livre des 'Lois' de Platon," ed. Thérèse-Anne Druart, *Bulletin d'études orientales* 50 (1998): 109–55.

GS I   Leo Strauss, *Gesammelte Schriften. Band 1. Die Religionskritik Spinozas und zugehörige Schriften*, ed. Heinrich Meier and Wiebke Meier, 3rd ed. (Stuttgart and Weimar: J. B. Metzler, 2008).

GS II Leo Strauss, *Gesammelte Schriften. Band 2. Philosophie und Gesetz – Frühe Schriften*, ed. Heinrich Meier and Wiebke Meier, 2nd ed. (Stuttgart and Weimar: J. B. Metzler, 2013).

GS III Leo Strauss, *Gesammelte Schriften. Band 3. Hobbes' politische Wissenschaft und zugehörige Schriften – Briefe*, ed. Heinrich Meier and Wiebke Meier, 2nd ed. (Stuttgart and Weimar: J. B. Metzler, 2008).

SNA   Followed by page and paragraph numbers of Strauss's notes on
        Averroes's commentary on Plato's *Republic*, here Appendix A.
SNAN   Followed by page and paragraph numbers of Strauss's notes on
        the *Arabian Nights*, here Appendix B.

Introduction

Before identifying, in this introduction, the specific gap regarding Strauss's scholarship on Islamic thought in the secondary literature, it is worth presenting, briefly, Strauss's intellectual biography in its connection with his interest in Islamic political thought. To this end, this introduction will provide a brief, panoramic discussion of the major questions at the heart of Strauss's intellectual odyssey by focusing on what one might call the four pillars of Strauss's philosophical project: (1) Reason and Revelation, (2) Ancients and Moderns, (3) The Theologico-Political Problem, and (4) Esotericism. This will be done while emphasizing the Islamic aspect of Strauss's thought, of course, by relying on the vast existing literature on Strauss's thought, to which I owe much. One obvious point which must nonetheless be articulated explicitly is that this presentation does *not* presume to be an exhaustive introduction to the work of Leo Strauss. Such introductions have been attempted by other scholars, to which I invite curious readers to turn by consulting the footnotes.

STRAUSS'S TURN TOWARD THE FALĀSIFA

Leo Strauss was born to an observant Jewish family in Kirchhain, Hessen, Germany on September 20, 1899. After graduating from gymnasium in 1917, he served briefly in the First World War in the German army; after the war, he began his studies at the University of Hamburg, where he conducted his doctoral dissertation under the direction of Ernst Cassirer on *The Problem of Knowledge in the Philosophical Teaching of F.H. Jacobi* (1921).[1] It is worthwhile to pause to examine this early scholarly effort. Although the dissertation was never published in full by Strauss, one would expect to hear much about Jacobi in Strauss's later writings.[2] But this is precisely what does not happen. Particularly significant, however, is that one can identify some of the key components of the whole of Strauss's thought, in a nascent state, already present in his doctoral dissertation. Friedrich Heinrich Jacobi (1743–1819), a German philosopher whose name is closely bound with the coining of the term "nihilism" and his role in the famous controversy on pantheism (*Pantheismusstreit*), played an important role in the formation of German philosophy through his attack on the pedigree of Spinoza's philosophy and the figure of Gotthold Ephraim Lessing. The story begins with the controversial reception of Spinoza in Germany as an atheistic philosopher, but it took a 1785 publication by Jacobi to transform the debate on the reception of Spinoza in Germany into a full-fledged intellectual crisis, to which luminaries like Kant, Goethe, and Herder, among many others, contributed.[3] The controversy concerned above all the status of the Enlightenment as a project founded on the authority of reason, which claimed to provide an effective foundation for moral and religious

[1] The German original is available in GS II:237–93. For the extract of the dissertation in English see Leo Strauss, "The Dissertation (1921)," in *Leo Strauss: The Early Writings (1921–32)*, trans. Michael Zank (Albany: SUNY Press, 2002), 53–61. For the French translation see Leo Strauss, "Le problème de la connaissance dans la doctrine philosophique de Fr. H. Jacobi (I)," trans. Hans Hartje and Pierre Guglielmina, *Revue de Métaphysique et de Morale* 99, no. 3 (1994): 291–311; Leo Strauss, "Le problème de la connaissance dans la doctrine philosophique de Fr. H. Jacobi (II) b) Les formes données de la connaissance," trans. Hans Hartje and Pierre Guglielmina, *Revue de Métaphysique et de Morale* 99, no. 4 (1994): 505–32.

[2] If I am not mistaken, Jacobi is only mentioned twice in Strauss's later writings: once in Spinoza's *Critique of Religion* and once in the 1964 Preface to the English translation of the same book: Leo Strauss, *Spinoza's Critique of Religion*, trans. Elsa M. Sinclair (New York: Schocken Books, 1965), 16, 204 (GS I:31, 260). One should, of course, also mention the prominent place occupied by Jacobi in Strauss's introductions to the writings of Mendelssohn. See Leo Strauss, *On Moses Mendelssohn*, ed. Martin D. Yaffe (Chicago and London: University of Chicago Press, 2012), (GS II:467–605). See also Leo Strauss, "Notes on Philosophy and Revelation," in *Leo Strauss and the Theologico-Political Problem*, ed. Heinrich Meier, trans. Marcus Brainard (Cambridge: Cambridge University Press, 2006), 178.

[3] Friedrich Heinrich Jacobi, *The Main Philosophical Writings and the Novel "Atwill,"* trans. George di Giovanni (Montreal: McGill-Queen's University Press, 1994), 173–251. A lively and authoritative account of the controversy is Frederick C. Besier, *The Fate of Reason: German Philosophy from Kant to Fichte* (Cambridge, MA: Harvard University Press, 1987), 44–109. See also Steven B. Smith, *Reading Leo Strauss. Politics, Philosophy, Judaism* (Chicago: University of Chicago Press, 2006), 67–71.

judgments and beliefs. In his explosive writing, Jacobi gives the account of his dialogue with Lessing and claimed that Lessing was a follower of Spinoza – a controversial claim because of the atheistic connotations attached to Spinoza's name. Jacobi saw the association with Spinoza as the convincing evidence for the rejection of *Aufklärung* and its rational basis. He claimed that the rationalist Enlightenment, represented in the philosophy of Spinoza, undermines the foundations of religion, morality, and thought, and inevitably leads to atheism, immorality, denial of the existence of God, relativism, and skepticism regarding the basic premises of every system of thought; or, in one word, to nihilism. Facing the impotence of reason for establishing the foundations of thought, morality, and religion, Jacobi saw only one solution: a leap of faith out of nihilism brought about by the rationalism of the Enlightenment and instead founding one's life and thought on faith through a return to orthodoxy and Christianity. Strauss wrote his dissertation on this controversial figure with all the concomitant issues related to this early interest, such as his later concern with the crisis of modern rationality and the conflict between Reason and Revelation.

After his doctoral dissertation, Strauss spent some time in Freiburg, Giessen, and Marburg. At the University of Freiburg, he came under the influence of Edmund Husserl and the young Martin Heidegger, before being employed from 1925 to 1932 at the Academy of Jewish Research in Berlin (Akademie für die Wissenschaft des Judentums) as a research assistant, where he worked (1925–28) on his first book, *Spinoza's Critique of Religion* (1930). What precise role Jacobi's ideas play in Strauss's mature philosophical approach has been an object of controversy which cannot be dealt with here in detail.[4] Two things, however, are rather clear. First, his doctoral dissertation on Jacobi led Strauss to Spinoza, and his study

---

[4] John G. Gunnell, "Strauss before Straussianism. Reason, Revelation, and Nature," *The Review of Politics* 53, no. 1 (1991): 53–74; Susan Meld Shell, "Taking Evil Seriously: Schmitt's 'Concept of the Political' and Strauss's 'True Politics,'" in *Leo Strauss: Political Philosopher and Jewish Thinker*, eds. Kenneth L. Deutsch and Walter Nicgorski (New York: Rowman and Littlefield, 1994), pp. 175–93; David Janssens, "The Problem of the Enlightenment: Strauss, Jacobi, and the Pantheism Controversy," *The Review of Metaphysics* 56, no. 3 (2003): 605–31; Smith, *Reading Leo Strauss*, 65–83; Rodrigo Chacón, "On a Forgotten Kind of Grounding: Strauss, Jacobi, and the Phenomenological Critique of Modern Rationalism," *The Review of Politics* 76, no. 4 (2014): 589–617; Corine Pelluchon, *Leo Strauss and the Crisis of Rationalism: Another Reason, Another Enlightenment*, trans. Robert Howse (Albany: State University of New York Press, 2014), 31–57; Benjamin Lazier, *God Interrupted: Heresy and the European Imagination between the World Wars* (Princeton and Oxford: Princeton University Press, 2008), 73–139.

on Spinoza already manifests two pillars of Strauss's thought – to which I shall turn shortly. Second, as we shall see, it is not difficult to see at least a certain "family resemblance" between Strauss's major intellectual concerns and issues at the heart of Jacobi's controversy, although one should be careful not to take Jacobi's rather radical positions for Strauss's complex views, which seem to elude any kind of simple identification. In our discussion of Strauss's pillars of thought, the reader is strongly advised to remain vigilant of remaining satisfied with these short descriptions; there is much debate and many contradictory ideas about Strauss's final thoughts on any of the four following issues, the debates which are well represented in the more general studies.[5]

(1) Reason and Revelation. In his study on Spinoza, Strauss is concerned with the truth of Spinoza's critique of revealed religion and its defensibility from the philosophical point of view; he shows that Spinoza in particular and the Enlightenment's rationalist critique of religion in general did not succeed in presenting a definitive refutation of the claims of Biblical religion and revelation. Strauss claims that Spinoza's critique of religion is based on presuppositions which are vulnerable to the religious position which consistently founds itself on faith and questions the availability of its religious knowledge to human reason. Spinoza's efforts, therefore, in showing the contradictory character of the Scripture, are vulnerable to an orthodox counterattack which relies on the idea of an unfathomable, omnipotent God who is not bound as such to the rules and limitations of nature. Strauss claimed that the victory of modern rationalism over the revealed religion is more the effect of propaganda and rhetoric, "laughter and mockery," than real philosophic and rational arguments. Spinoza and his followers, Strauss concluded, instead of relying on real rational refutation, overcame revealed religion without meeting its most unassailable defenses: all they did was "to 'laugh' orthodoxy out of a position from which it could not be dislodged by any proofs supplied by Scripture or by reason."[6] The idea, according to which the claims of revealed religion are not as weak as its rationalist modern opponents have pretended them to be, and that one cannot easily imagine an

---

[5] For a good overview of the major debates on Strauss's legacy and thought and bibliography see Michael Zuckert and Catherine Zuckert, *The Truth about Leo Strauss: Political Philosophy and American Democracy* (Chicago and London: University of Chicago Press, 2006), 58–80, 228–69; Michael Zuckert and Catherine Zuckert, *Leo Strauss and the Problem of Political Philosophy* (Chicago: University of Chicago Press, 2014), 311–38.

[6] Strauss, *Spinoza's Critique of Religion*, 28–29 (GS I:50–51).

effective refutation of a coherent religious perspective founded on faith in an omnipotent and unfathomable god, occupies a special place in Strauss's intellectual biography. It is reflected in the idea of an irreconcilable opposition between reason and faith, also represented by the conflict of Reason and Revelation, philosophy and religion, or Athens and Jerusalem. Strauss often claimed that this opposition cannot be overcome by any "Thomistic" synthesis of Reason and Revelation. He did not tire of repeating that in every synthesis of this kind, "however impressive, one of the two opposed elements is sacrificed, more or less subtly but in any event surely to the other." He also stated that neither of these two antagonists "has ever succeeded in really refuting the other" and they both remain contending representatives of two opposed camps.[7]

(2) Ancients and Moderns. Strauss's dissatisfaction with Spinoza's philosophy and his modern successors was only the first step in his journey from modern philosophy toward premodern thinkers. This is reflected in his lifelong enterprise of renewing what he, imitating the language of the seventeenth-century literary debate, sometimes calls "the quarrel between the ancients and the moderns," the debate which seemed to have been undoubtedly decided in the favor of the moderns.[8] The idea of the superiority of the moderns to the ancients as reflected in the concept of progress is one of the most cherished ideas of modern thought and modern man: the belief in the gradual advance in all fields of human life, from technology and politics to arts and philosophy. The fact that even today, what is considered "new" automatically acquires a positive connotation manifests the still-living universal attachment to the idea of progress. Strauss was, however, skeptical of the superiority of our thought to that of the premodern thinkers or ancients, and he shows this in many of his writings.[9] In his *Thoughts on Machiavelli*, for instance, his major writing

---

[7] Leo Strauss, *Natural Right and History* (Chicago: University of Chicago Press, 1953), 74–75; Leo Strauss, "Progress or Return?," in *The Rebirth of Classical Political Rationalism: An Introduction to the Thought of Leo Strauss*, ed. Thomas L. Pangle (Chicago: University of Chicago Press, 1989), 270.

[8] Leo Strauss, "On the Basis of Hobbes' Political Philosophy," in *What Is Political Philosophy? And Other Studies* (Glencoe: Free Press, 1959), 172; Leo Strauss and Karl Löwith, "Correspondence between Karl Löwith and Leo Strauss Concerning Modernity," *The Independent Journal of Philosophy* 4 (1988): 106 (Letter to Karl Löwith on August 15, 1946, GS III:661); Susan Meld Shell, ed., *The Strauss-Krüger Correspondence: Returning to Plato through Kant* (Cham: Palgrave Macmillan, 2018), 47 (Letter to Gerhard Krüger on December 12, 1932, GS III:414).

[9] Strauss, "Progress or Return?"; Leo Strauss, "How to Study Medieval Philosophy," *Interpretation: A Journal of Political Philosophy* 23, no. 3 (1996): 321–38.

on the one he considered to be the originator of modern political philosophy, Strauss investigates the legitimacy of Machiavelli's break with the
premodern "Great Tradition" and his founding of "the Enlightenment"
and inquires whether the Enlightenment deserves its name or "whether
its true name is Obfuscation."[10] Elsewhere, he goes even so far as to claim
that "the perfect political order, as Plato and Aristotle have sketched it,
is the perfect political order" and that it is "*morally-politically* the most
reasonable and most pleasing."[11]

Strauss's dissatisfaction with the modern critique of revelation, and
his doubts about the legitimacy of the modern project as a whole, did
not immediately lead him to what he later on called classical political
philosophy, as it is found primarily in the writings of Xenophon, Plato,
and Aristotle. If seen primarily through his publications, Strauss's interest in the ancients appears relatively late, as his first publication on a
classical philosopher is the 1939 essay "The Spirit of Sparta or the Taste
of Xenophon."[12] Strauss seems to have initially entertained the idea of
a return to premodern thought through Maimonides, one of Spinoza's
antagonists discussed in *Spinoza's Critique of Religion,* as well as
through other Jewish medieval thinkers. In this period, the premodern
thought of Greek philosophers appears more as a resource for understanding medieval Jewish thought. Apart from this Jewish orientation
in Strauss's research, his writings after his book on Spinoza also have a
modern component, reflected in his studies on Thomas Hobbes.[13] Even
in these studies, Greek philosophy occupies a marginal place as a probable source of some of Hobbes's ideas. In a letter, Strauss depicts his dual
research program during this period in the following way:

My studies of Spinoza's *Theological and Political Treatise* have shown me a connection between the theological and political problem. These studies have led me
to Spinoza's Jewish medieval predecessors, especially Maimonides, on the one
hand, and Hobbes' political science on the other hand. During the pursuit of
these sources, I formed the plan to make 1. the political science of Hobbes and

---

[10] Leo Strauss, *Thoughts on Machiavelli* (Glencoe: Free Press, 1958), 173.

[11] Strauss and Löwith, "Correspondence between Karl Löwith and Leo Strauss Concerning
Modernity," 107 (Letter to Karl Löwith on August 15, 1946, GS III:662), 113 (Letter to
Karl Löwith on August 20, 1946, GS III:669).

[12] Leo Strauss, "The Spirit of Sparta or the Taste of Xenophon," *Social Research* 6, no. 4
(1939): 502–36; Brague, "Athens, Jerusalem, Mecca," 238.

[13] Leo Strauss, *The Political Philosophy of Hobbes: Its Basis and Its Genesis,* trans. Elsa
M. Sinclair (Chicago: University of Chicago Press, 1952); Leo Strauss, *Hobbes's Cri-
tique of Religion and Related Writings,* trans. Svetozar Minkov and Gabriel Bartlett
(Chicago: University of Chicago Press, 2011).

2. the theory of prophecy in Jewish and Islamic philosophy of the Middle Ages the subject of my future studies .... After finishing my book on Spinoza, I was charged by the Akademie [für die Wissenschaft des Judentums] to analyze Gersonides' *Wars of the Lord.* I started with an analysis of Gersonides' teaching on prophecy. The research on his sources led me from Maimonides to Islamic philosophers, of whom I studied several in Arabic manuscripts – and made me realize that the connection between medieval Jewish and Islamic teaching on prophecy and Plato's *Statesman* and *Laws* had not yet been thoroughly evaluated.[14]

In this remarkable passage, apart from the double research program, what is particularly significant is the last remark about "the connection between medieval Jewish and Islamic teaching on prophecy and Plato's *Statesman* and *Laws*," because it points to what seems to have been the key moment in Strauss's engagement with Islamic political philosophy, as well as his whole intellectual project: Strauss's encounter, in 1929 or 1930, with a passage in Avicenna's treatise *On the Divisions of the Rational Sciences* to the effect that the treatment of prophecy and divine law is contained in Plato's *Laws.*[15] This statement of Avicenna was first mentioned in the essay entitled "Maimonides's Doctrine of Prophecy and Its Sources" which was originally written in 1931 and was later included in the 1935 *Philosophy and Law.*[16] Interestingly for understanding Strauss's particular interest in this passage and his knowledge of Arabic, he claims that he has also checked the Arabic original of Avicenna's treatise.[17] It therefore seems that it was Avicenna primarily who among the Muslim philosophers first caught Strauss's attention.[18] But it is also significant that after mentioning this statement of Avicenna, and interpreting it as a hint toward a unique way of looking at the phenomenon of

[14] Harvey, "Leo Strauss' Early Interest in the Islamic Falāsifa," 222 (Letter to Cecil Adler on November 30, 1933); Tamer, *Islamische Philosophie und die Krise der Moderne*, 59–60; Leo Strauss, "A Giving of Accounts," in *Leo Strauss, Jewish Philosophy and the Crisis of Modernity*, ed. Kenneth Hart Green (Albany: State University of New York Press, 1993), 462–63; Shell, *The Strauss-Krüger Correspondence*, 18–19 (Letter to Gerhard Krüger on June 26, 1930, GS III:382–83).

[15] Heinrich Meier, "How Strauss Became Strauss," in *Reorientation: Leo Strauss in the 1930s*, eds. Martin D. Yaffe and Richard S. Ruderman (New York: Palgrave Macmillan US, 2014), 17–18; Harvey, "Leo Strauss' Early Interest in the Islamic Falāsifa," 221. I will discuss Avicenna's statement in more detail below (pp. 33–35, 163–64).

[16] Leo Strauss, "Maimunis Lehre von der Prophetie und ihre Quellen," *Le Monde Oriental* 28 (1934): 99–139; Leo Strauss, *Philosophy and Law. Contributions to the Understanding of Maimonides and His Predecessors*, trans. Eve Adler (Albany: State University of New York Press, 1995), 122 (GS II:112). The former was actually published in 1935.

[17] Strauss, *Philosophy and Law*, 152n57 (GS II:112n57); Harvey, "Leo Strauss' Early Interest in the Islamic Falāsifa," 221n7.

[18] Harvey, "Leo Strauss' Early Interest in the Islamic Falāsifa," 220.

prophecy, Strauss traces the idea not to Avicenna himself, but rather to Alfarabi, and explicitly mentions Alfarabi's summary of Plato's *Laws* as the key writing for establishing this fact.[19] In any event, we seem to have a very precise piece of evidence on Strauss's first contact with Islamic political philosophy.

(3) *The Theologico-Political Problem.* Avicenna's statement, and Strauss's concern with it, opens the way for introducing another pillar of Strauss's thought: the theologico-political problem. This aspect of Strauss's thought, which one can describe as the problem or question which in a way envelopes all other parts of Strauss's intellectual biography, has many different aspects with different degrees of complexities; it will therefore be discussed in different contexts in this book and each time, by considering it through the lens of different texts under discussion, it will be seen in a different light. Here I shall only discuss this theme by pointing to the break brought about by Strauss's turn toward Islamic political philosophy. As was shown above (pp. 4–5), in his dissertation on Jacobi and his first book on Spinoza, Strauss tends to study the question of the relationship between Reason and Revelation through epistemological-philosophical lenses. Avicenna's statement, however, led Strauss to a very different view of this relationship, which can be described precisely as theologico-political, that is, looking at religion through a *political* lens: "the science that deals thematically with prophecy is *politics*" because "the aim of prophecy is political."[20] This view approaches the relationship between Reason and Revelation as akin to the relationship between "Philosophy and Law," the title of Strauss's important book in this period. What "Law" is here meant is of course torah in Judaism and sharī'a in Islam, but this does not help us understand what Strauss found particularly worthy of attention in them. The significance of law in Strauss's work can be understood by a look at a rather obscure dialogue of Plato, entitled *Minos*, the dialogue which Strauss describes as the introduction to Plato's *Laws*.[21] *Minos* deals with the question "What is Law?" and there Socrates gives a perplexing answer to this question: "Law ... wishes to be the discovery of what is."[22] Now, it is rather clear that what law means here is not what we usually mean; therefore, Strauss interprets this statement by Socrates as "law is philosophy," or that it

---

[19] Strauss, *Philosophy and Law*, 125 (GS II:115).

[20] Strauss, *Philosophy and Law*, 122 (GS II:111).

[21] Leo Strauss, "On the Minos," in *Liberalism Ancient and Modern* (Chicago: University of Chicago Press, 1995), 65.

[22] Plato, *Minos* 315a.

pretends to be something akin to philosophy.[23] This view of the law is explained in *Philosophy and Law* as follows:

[The] Islamic and Jewish philosophers of the Middle Ages are ... guided ... by the *primary, ancient* idea of *law* as a unified, total regimen of human life ... they are pupils of *Plato*.[24]

To put it differently, through Avicenna's statement, Strauss has found a way to recover the classical understanding of the law as a theologico-political whole, which is *the* alternative to philosophy. This law has a claim to being the complete knowledge of the whole, the knowledge also desired by philosophers, and by making a claim to this knowledge, the law intends to organize human life as a whole on the basis of that knowledge. It is political in the most fundamental sense of the term, as the "total regimen of life." It is also significant that in this statement of Strauss, one sees the justification of Strauss's return to the ancients and the crucial importance of Plato for understanding theologico-political problem.[25]

After the publication of *Philosophy and Law* in 1935, Strauss's study on Thomas Hobbes appeared in 1936,[26] but it was only more than ten years later that he published another book, a substantial study on Xenophon in 1948.[27] In the period from 1935 to 1945 – when he published his major study on an exclusively Islamic subject, "Fârâbî's Plato"[28] – apart from occasional book reviews, Strauss published eight studies of different lengths in journals and collective volumes: Three of these texts discuss mainly medieval Jewish thought,[29] one of them is

---

[23] Leo Strauss, *1959 Course on Plato's Laws Offered at the University of Chicago*, ed. Lorraine Smith Pangle (Chicago: Leo Strauss Center, 2016), 30 (Session 2, January 8, 1959).

[24] Strauss, *Philosophy and Law*, 73 (GS II:61).

[25] See also Leo Strauss, "Some Remarks on the Political Science of Maimonides and Farabi," in *Leo Strauss on Maimonides: The Complete Writings*, ed. Kenneth Hart Green, trans. Robert C. Bartlett (Chicago and London: University of Chicago Press, 2013), 277 (GS II:126).

[26] Leo Strauss, *The Political Philosophy of Hobbes: Its Basis and Its Genesis* (Oxford: Clarendon Press, 1936); Strauss, *The Political Philosophy of Hobbes*, 1952, (GS III:3–193).

[27] Leo Strauss, *On Tyranny: Including the Strauss-Kojève Correspondence. Corrected and Expanded Edition*, eds. Victor Gourevitch and Michael Roth (Chicago: University of Chicago Press, 2013).

[28] Strauss, "Fârâbî's Plato."

[29] Leo Strauss, "On Abravanel's Philosophical Tendency and Political Teaching," in *Isaac Abravanel: Six Lectures*, eds. John Brande Trend and Herbert Loewe (Cambridge: Cambridge University Press, 1937), 95–129; Leo Strauss, "On Abravanel's Philosophical Tendency and Political Teaching," in *Leo Strauss on Maimonides: The Complete Writings*, ed. Kenneth Hart Green (Chicago: University of Chicago Press, 2013), 579–615

dedicated prominently to Maimonides as well as to Alfarabi,[30] a short article is mainly on Alfarabi,[31] one other discusses the question of esotericism in general,[32] and two studies are dedicated to classical Greek political philosophy.[33] Significantly, it is only in one of these publications, "The Spirit of Sparta or the Taste of Xenophon," in which there is no trace of Islamic political thought. That Islamic political thought is foremost in Strauss's mind can be seen also in what he says as a justification for putting aside his project on Hobbes's critique of religion which, judging from the surviving material, was in its advanced stages.[34] Strauss writes that he has "placed Hobbes on the back burner for now, in order to first gain clarity about the history of Platonism in the Islamic and Jewish middle ages." He then calls Alfarabi an "astounding" figure and describes him as a key figure for opening a new perspective on Platonism in general and for understanding Plato himself.[35]

(4) Esotericism. Contemporaneous with Strauss's deeper engagement with Islamic political thought as a way toward classical Greek philosophy, we can also observe a further fundamental change in his thought brought about by his discovery of esotericism, the fourth pillar and one

(GS II:195–233); Leo Strauss, "The Literary Character of the Guide for the Perplexed," in *Essays on Maimonides*, ed. S. W. Baron (New York: Columbia University Press, 1941), 37–91; Leo Strauss, "Literary Character of the Guide for the Perplexed," in *Persecution and the Art of Writing* (Glencoe: Free Press, 1952), 38–95; Leo Strauss, "The Law of Reason in the Kuzari," *Proceedings of the American Academy for Jewish Research* 13 (1943): 47–96; Leo Strauss, "The Law of Reason in the Kuzari," in *Persecution and the Art of Writing* (Glencoe: Free Press, 1952), 95–142.

30 Leo Strauss, "Quelques remarques sur la science politique de Maïmonide et de Fârâbî," *Revue des Etudes Juives* 100 (1936): 1–37; Strauss, "Some Remarks on the Political Science of Maimonides and Farabi," 275–314 (GS II:125–67).

31 Leo Strauss, "Eine vermißte Schrift Farâbîs," *Monatsschrift für Geschichte und Wissenschaft des Judentums* 80, no. 1 (1936): 90–106; Leo Strauss, "A Lost Writing of Farâbî's (1936)," in *Reorientation. Leo Strauss in the 1930s*, trans. Martin D. Yaffe and Gabriel Bartlett (New York: Palgrave Macmillan, 2014), 255–65 (GS II:167–79).

32 Leo Strauss, "Persecution and the Art of Writing," *Social Research* 8, no. 4 (1941): 488–504; Leo Strauss, "Persecution and the Art of Writing," in *Persecution and the Art of Writing* (Glencoe: Free Press, 1952), 22–38.

33 Strauss, "The Spirit of Sparta or the Taste of Xenophon"; Leo Strauss, "On Classical Political Philosophy," *Social Research* 12, no. 1 (1945): 98–117; Leo Strauss, "On Classical Political Philosophy," in *What Is Political Philosophy? And Other Studies* (Glencoe: The Free Press, 1959), 78–95.

34 These were published posthumously. See Strauss, *Hobbes's Critique of Religion and Related Writings*, (GS III:263–74).

35 Shell, *The Strauss-Krüger Correspondence*, 78–79 (Letter to Gerhard Krüger on December 25, 1935, GS III:450); Strauss, *Hobbes's Critique of Religion and Related Writings*, 14.

of the most fundamental aspects of his thought. In view of Strauss's growing interest in Islamic thought in this period, it is not surprising to see that the discovery of esotericism has a direct relation with his studies on Islamic political thought. But let us first say a few words about Strauss's understanding of esotericism.

In the first essay of his famous book on esotericism, *Persecution and the Art of Writing*, Strauss begins his discussion by reminding us of one of the most fundamental principles of a modern liberal regime, namely: freedom of public discussion.[36] With the totalitarian regimes implicitly in mind, Strauss remarks that this freedom is under attack in recent times and is being "suppressed." People are under "compulsion" to coordinate their speech with the views held by the government. Strauss asks us to consider the effects of "that compulsion, or persecution" on the way people write about politics and society. Although state persecution of dissenting views has a long history, even the most radical forms of persecution in history have not succeeded in fully eliminating free thought and heterodoxy. In other words, there have always been people who have entertained heterodox ideas, even under the harshest forms of persecution and oppression. This uncontroversial claim of Strauss is followed by a controversial one, according to which persecution cannot prevent even the *expression* of heterodox thought. Here Strauss is not speaking about *samizdat* or other clandestine forms of writings in oppressive regimes. What Strauss is suggesting is that in oppressive and illiberal societies where heterodox thinkers are persecuted, writers have always found ways to communicate their heterodox ideas in writing without incurring the danger of persecution, that is, not in clandestine writings, but those writings which are in principle available to the general public. They succeeded in doing this, Strauss claims, by "writing between the lines"; by developing "a peculiar technique of writing," a "peculiar type of literature" in which the heterodox truth is presented exclusively "between the lines."[37] These writings contain two different messages: one exoteric, which is available to all readers, and one esoteric, which is concealed from all but those who know how to read "between the lines," those who know about the esoteric style and techniques of reading used in the texts. Strauss believes that esoteric authors did not simply conceal their views in their writings by lying, but rather that they hid their genuine, heterodox teaching from a certain group of readers while simultaneously

---

[36] Leo Strauss, *Persecution and the Art of Writing* (Glencoe: Free Press, 1952), 22–24.
[37] Strauss, *Persecution and the Art of Writing*, 1952, 22–25.

making them available to a select few. In other words, Strauss claims that both exoteric and esoteric teachings exist *simultaneously* in their published writings, and that there are specific techniques to decipher these writings. Strauss believes in the existence of *esoteric techniques* which are used by some writers; techniques which, if they are familiar to the reader, can help him decipher these esoteric writings. These techniques are, according to Strauss, employed by different authors throughout the ages to hide the esoteric teaching of their writings from the general reader and to reveal it only to those who know these techniques. Such readers are the real addressees of the author's esoteric teaching. Strauss mentions many different esoteric techniques of writing and reading in his studies including repetition,[38] omission,[39] center,[40] contradiction,[41] mentioning things once or several times,[42] putting words in the mouth of someone else,[43] numerology,[44] misquotation,[45] intentional mistakes,[46] allegory,[47] and so on – some of which will be discussed in this volume later on.

For Strauss, esoteric writers conceal their views and practice esotericism for different reasons. Many of them conceal their views simply to protect themselves from persecution.[48] Some other "earlier type of writers" practiced esoteric writing because of their belief in the existence of truths, dangerous truths, which should not be communicated to the many simply because they would do harm to the established social order.[49] This form of esotericism, Strauss claims, is found among those philosophers who belonged to a tradition of premodern Enlightenment.[50] Those thinkers thought that some truths must be kept secret from the many.[51] While

---

[38] Leo Strauss, *Xenophon's Socratic Discourse: An Interpretation of the Oeconomicus* (Ithaca: Cornell University Press, 1970), 125–26.

[39] Strauss, *Thoughts on Machiavelli*, 31.

[40] Strauss, "Fârâbî's Plato," 368–69.

[41] Strauss, "Literary Character of the Guide for the Perplexed," 71.

[42] Strauss, *Thoughts on Machiavelli*, 135–36.

[43] Strauss, *Persecution and the Art of Writing*, 1952, 36.

[44] Strauss, *Thoughts on Machiavelli*, 52; Leo Strauss, "Niccolò Machiavelli," in *History of Political Philosophy*, eds. Leo Strauss and Joseph Cropsey, 3rd ed. (Chicago: University of Chicago Press, 1987), 311.

[45] Strauss, *Thoughts on Machiavelli*, 125.

[46] Strauss, *Thoughts on Machiavelli*, 317n58.

[47] Leo Strauss, "The Origins of Political Science and the Problem of Socrates," *Interpretation* 23, no. 2 (1996): 162–63; Strauss, *Xenophon's Socratic Discourse*, 185–86.

[48] Strauss, *Persecution and the Art of Writing*, 1952, 33–34.

[49] Strauss, *Persecution and the Art of Writing*, 1952, 34–36.

[50] Leo Strauss, "On a Forgotten Kind of Writing," in *What Is Political Philosophy? And Other Studies* (Glencoe: Free Press, 1959), 221–22.

[51] Strauss, *Persecution and the Art of Writing*, 1952, 110–11.

in the first type of esotericism, the philosopher practices it to avoid perse-cution, in this second case he practices esotericism to protect society from doubts and radical questionings which are dangerous for the stability of a well-ordered society. There is another kind of esotericism – one that, as we shall see, is very important for the study of Strauss's own writings – which is practiced for *pedagogical* reasons. In this type of esotericism, philoso-phers embrace obscurity and refrain from conveying their true teachings directly, not because of fear of persecution nor to protect society from dangerous and unsettling ideas, but to educate their students and to train future philosophers. This type of esoteric writing demands the active par-ticipation of the reader: the reader cannot remain the passive audience of the written text but must work his way through the arguments on his own, face the contradictions in the text and other esoteric devices, and discover for himself the unwritten statements or the esoteric teaching of the writer.[52]

In what concerns the relationship between Strauss's turn toward Islamic thought and esotericism, one must say that dating Strauss's discovery of esotericism is not as simple as it might seem, and there has been a debate about the origins or the dating of Strauss's discovery of esotericism. There are two early unpublished writings on esotericism found among Strauss's papers: "Exoteric Teaching" was written sometime in December 1939; the second, which seems to be contemporaneous with the first, is a series of notes for a lecture titled "Persecution and the Art of Writing."[53] These two writings seem to be Strauss's first attempts to elucidate the concept of esotericism independently of any specific historical text, and thus they can be distinguished from other published esoteric studies of Strauss. Those other writings, mainly written from the early 1940s, apply Strauss's eso-teric hermeneutics to the writings of thinkers like Xenophon, Maimonides, Judah Halevi, Greek political philosophers, and Alfarabi.[54] But who is discussed in these two early writings? In "Exoteric Teaching" Strauss avoids discussion or even naming any medieval Jewish or Islamic thinker and mainly discusses Lessing and Schleiermacher and refers to Aristotle,

---

[52] Strauss, *Persecution and the Art of Writing*, 1952, 36–37.

[53] Leo Strauss, "Exoteric Teaching," in *Reorientation. Leo Strauss in the 1930s*, eds. Hannes Kerber, Martin D. Yaffe, and Richard S. Ruderman (New York: Palgrave Mac-millan, 2014), 275–87; Leo Strauss, "Lecture Notes for 'Persecution and the Art of Writ-ing,'" in *Reorientation: Leo Strauss in the 1930s*, eds. Hannes Kerber, Martin D. Yaffe, and Richard S. Ruderman (New York: Palgrave Macmillan, 2014), 293–304.

[54] Strauss, "The Spirit of Sparta or the Taste of Xenophon"; Strauss, "The Literary Char-acter of the Guide for the Perplexed"; Strauss, "The Law of Reason in the Kuzari"; Strauss, "On Classical Political Philosophy," 1945; Strauss, "Fârâbî's Plato."

Leibniz, Zeller, Kant, Ferguson, Rousseau, and Jacobi.[55] Strauss's lecture notes also only mention Western thinkers, including Cervantes, Lessing, Hobbes, Spinoza, Leibnitz, Montesquieu, Descartes, Bacon, Aristotle, Plato, Cicero, and Xenophon. Interestingly, Strauss claims that in his lecture he wishes to speak mainly of ancient and medieval esotericism, but no medieval writer is named.[56]

If we only had access to these early writings, we would have to conclude that Strauss discovered esotericism through the study of a few classical Greek and European writers.[57] However, there exists another earlier source of information about the discovery of esotericism by Strauss, namely his private correspondence. As can be deduced from his letters to Jacob Klein, Strauss's discovery of esotericism happens around January 1938, that is, nearly two years before the two abovementioned texts. Between January 1938 and November 1939, Strauss sends forty-two letters to Klein, among them sixteen letters discuss esotericism at some length.[58] From the letters we can deduce that Maimonides is the key writer

[55] Hannes Kerber, "Strauss and Schleiermacher on How to Read Plato: An Introduction to 'Exoteric Teaching,'" in *Reorientation. Leo Strauss in the 1930s*, eds. Martin D. Yaffe and Richard S. Ruderman (New York: Palgrave Macmillan, 2014), 203–4.

[56] Strauss, "Lecture Notes for 'Persecution and the Art of Writing,'" 297.

[57] Chiara Adorisio, "Some Remarks on Leo Strauss's Philosophical-Political Reading of Medieval Islamic and Jewish Philosophers," in *La Philosophie Arabe à l'étude / Studying Arabic Philosophy. Sens, Limites et Défis d'une Discipline Moderne: Meaning, Limits and Challenges of a Modern Discipline*, eds. Jean-Baptiste Brenet and Olga L. Lizzini (Paris: Vrin, 2019), 78.

[58] Jacob Klein (1899–1978) was a Russian-American philosopher and interpreter of Plato who was one of Strauss's closest friends. A student of Heidegger, Klein taught at St. John's College in Annapolis where Strauss was resident scholar at the end of his life. Strauss-Klein correspondence in available in Leo Strauss, *Gesammelte Schriften. Band 3. Hobbes' politische Wissenschaft und zugehörige Schriften – Briefe*, eds. Heinrich Meier and Wiebke Meier, 2nd edition (Stuttgart-Weimar: J. B. Metzler, 2008), 544–87. The following letters discuss esotericism – major writers mentioned in the letters are indicated in the parenthesis: January 20, 1938 (Maimonides, Plato, Aristotle, Alexander of Aphrodisias, Themistius, Proclus, Alfarabi, Averroes), February 16, 1938 (Maimonides, Averroes, Alfarabi, Voltaire, Nietzsche), July 23, 1938 (Maimonides, Nietzsche), October 15, 1938 (Plato, Herodotus), October 20, 1938 (Plato, Herodotus), November 2, 1938 (Herodotus, Thucydides, Plato), November 27, 1938 (Plato, Herodotus, Thucydides, Xenophon), December 2, 1938 (Maimonides, Aristotle, Xenophon, Plato, Thucydides, Sophocles), December 12, 1938 (Plato, Aristophanes), February 16, 1939 (Xenophon, Aristotle, Plato, Maimonides), February 28, 1939 (Plato, Xenophon), July 25, 1939 (Xenophon, Thucydides, Herodotus, Plato), August 7, 1939 (Xenophon), August 18, 1939 (Xenophon, Plato, Cervantes,), October 10, 1939 (Plato, Aristotle, Hesiod, Homer, Shakespeare, Parmenides, Thales), November 22, 1939 (Xenophon, Maimonides, Plato). For a discussion of these letters see Laurence Lampert, "Strauss's Recovery of Esotericism," in *The Cambridge Companion to Leo Strauss*, ed. Steven B. Smith (Cambridge: Cambridge University Press, 2009), 63–93.

who guides Strauss to his discovery of esotericism, and the application of esoteric reading to other writers happens *after* the discovery of the esoteric Maimonides.[59] The discovery of the esoteric Maimonides, however, has a prehistory which must be taken into account, an episode which is prior to the 1938 correspondence with Klein. But before going further back, an important point should be mentioned: in his letters of January 20 and February 16, 1938, that is, the first two of Strauss's esoteric letters, Alfarabi is mentioned alongside Maimonides and their connection is emphasized. In the first letter, Strauss writes that, for Maimonides, the crucial question was not the createdness or eternity of the world – according to Strauss, Maimonides, contrary to his explicit claims, believed in the eternity of the world. Strauss claims that for Maimonides the crucial question was whether the ideal legislator must be a prophet. Strauss writes that Maimonides, again in an esoteric way, denied this necessity, "as Farabi had before him and Averroes did in his own time."[60] As we shall see, one cannot disregard this connection between Maimonides and Alfarabi. It is true that in the subsequent letters, Alfarabi and Averroes disappear, but so does Maimonides. In other words, even in Strauss's private correspondence, Alfarabi remains crucial for the study of Strauss's discovery of esotericism and is somehow connected with Maimonides.[61]

Considering the importance of Maimonides for Strauss's discovery of esotericism, to trace his discovery of esotericism one must follow his writings on Maimonides, which predate his correspondence with Klein. Strauss discusses Maimonides in his 1930 *Spinoza's Critique of Religion*, but that study does not show any awareness of or even interest in the question of esotericism in Maimonides's works. In that book, words like *esoteric*, *esotericism*, *exoteric*, and *exotericism* are absent, and Strauss calls Maimonides "a believing Jew," while after his discovery of esotericism he writes that "Maimonides in his beliefs was *absolutely* no Jew."[62]

---

[59] Lampert, "Strauss's Recovery of Esotericism," 63. Heinrich Meier here speaks of "a whole series of philosophical supernovas." See Strauss, *Gesammelte Schriften. Band 3*, xxxiii.

[60] Strauss, *Gesammelte Schriften. Band 3*, 545 (Letter to Jacob Klein on January 20, 1938).

[61] See also Rémi Brague's comment that Maimonides and Alfarabi are the only authors who are present in all of what Brague calls three periods of Strauss's scholarship. Rémi Brague, "Leo Strauss et Maïmonide," in *Maimonides and Philosophy: Papers Presented at the Sixth Jerusalem Philosophical Encounter, May 1985*, eds. Shlomo Pines and Yirmiyahu Yovel (Dordrecht: Springer, 1986), 247.

[62] Strauss, *Spinoza's Critique of Religion*, 163–64 (GS I:213); Strauss, *Gesammelte Schriften. Band 3*, 550 (Letter to Jacob Klein on February 16, 1938), 751 (Letter to Gershom Scholem on December 15, 1963).

It is therefore after his book on Spinoza and in Strauss's subsequent writings on Maimonides that one must look for the discovery of esotericism. "Maimonides' Doctrine of Prophecy and Its Sources" (originally written in 1931), which was reprinted as the third chapter of *Philosophy and Law* (1935) in a revised and abbreviated form, is properly speaking Strauss's first independent study of Maimonides's writings: in his previous studies, Strauss mainly concentrated on the points of contrast between Spinoza and Maimonides, but in this study he provides a discussion of Maimonides's understanding of prophecy by tracing it to the writings of his Muslim predecessors, mainly Alfarabi and Avicenna.[63] Strauss argues that Maimonides followed his Muslim teachers and that they provided him with fundamental principles of his thought. Apart from his reference to Maimonides's Muslim predecessors, another significant aspect of this essay for Strauss's intellectual biography is that this text shows the first signs of realization of the importance of esotericism. Strauss here claims that the medieval Enlightenment of Maimonides and his predecessors was essentially esoteric, while the Enlightenment of the modern philosophers was essentially exoteric.[64] Now, in Strauss's essay it is not entirely clear what Maimonides's esoteric teaching is. However, one has a feeling that Maimonides's thought is not entirely orthodox: for instance, Maimonides argues for the superiority of the prophet to the philosopher because the prophet has access to the supernatural knowledge which is inaccessible to the philosopher. However, this claim is followed by an important qualification: the prophet's superiority is founded on the contribution of the faculty of imagination. But as Strauss mentions, the critique of imagination is one of the major themes of Maimonides's *Guide for the Perplexed*.[65] Be that as it may, this line of inquiry does not seem to lead to a definitive and conclusive distinction between Maimonides's esoteric and exoteric teachings in Strauss's book.

Strauss's next study on Maimonides, "Some Remarks on the Political Science of Maimonides and Farabi" (1936), highlights more forcefully than before the importance of Alfarabi for understanding Maimonides's thought: here Strauss begins by speaking of Maimonides's "Muslim masters" and of the profound agreement between Jewish and Muslim thought. He believes that an adequate understanding of medieval Jewish philosophy is only possible by beginning from Alfarabi's Platonism, and he therefore declares his intention to show the influence of Alfarabi's philosophy

[63] Strauss, *Philosophy and Law*, 102, 113 (GS II:88, 99).
[64] Strauss, *Philosophy and Law*, 102 (GS II: 89).
[65] Strauss, *Philosophy and Law*, 106 (GS II:92).

on Maimonides.[66] This growing importance of Alfarabi is concomitant with the awareness of the existence of esotericism in Maimonides's writings: Strauss reminds us that Maimonides's *Guide for the Perplexed* is an "esoteric book" in which Maimonides has "concealed his thought." Maimonides, Strauss claims, expresses his thought only by "allusions"; one must therefore read his book with "particular attention" to discover his esoteric teaching.[67] Maimonides does not convey his thoughts explicitly but through signs, which suffice for one "who will understand," for an attentive and duly instructed reader. One of the main qualifications of the knowledgeable reader is that he knows Alfarabi's writings.[68] This essay contains a remarkable number of passages in which the importance of esotericism is mentioned: Strauss does not speak only of the esotericism of Maimonides and Alfarabi, but also of Avicenna, *Ikhwān al-safā* (Brethren of Purity), and even of Plato.[69] Concerning Maimonides's esoteric teaching, two points seem rather obvious: Strauss points to the "philosophic" reason for Maimonides's silence on "the origins of the Torah," including its possible "natural" origin, and also ends the essay by emphasizing Maimonides's agreement with Plato on the question of providence – the same Plato who just was said to have subscribed to "the dogma of particular providence ... only because of its political utility."[70]

It is not surprising that Strauss's "Some Remarks" is contemporary with one of his few writings dedicated specifically to Alfarabi, namely "A Lost Writing of Farâbî's" written sometime in 1935 and published in 1936. This scholarly essay claims that some passages commonly thought to be from Alfarabi's *Enumeration of the Sciences* actually belong to the

---

[66] Strauss, "Some Remarks on the Political Science of Maimonides and Farabi," 276–77, 279 (GS II:125–26, 129).

[67] Strauss, "Some Remarks on the Political Science of Maimonides and Farabi," 290 (GS II:137).

[68] Strauss, "Some Remarks on the Political Science of Maimonides and Farabi," 298–99 (GS II:144–45).

[69] Strauss, "Some Remarks on the Political Science of Maimonides and Farabi," 305, 308, 308n99, 309, 309n102 (GS II: 150, 152, 152n99, 153, 153n102). Regarding the secret esoteric society of Ikhwān al-safā, I believe Strauss's owes the information to Paul Kraus who was working on Jābir ibn Hayyān, Ismāʿīlism, and related esoteric movements. See Paul Kraus, *Jābir ibn Hayyān. Contribution à l'histoire des idées scientifiques dans l'Islam. Vol. 1. Le corpus des écrits jabiriens* (Cairo: Mémoires de l'Institute d'Égypte, 1943), lv, lxiv; Paul Kraus, *Jābir ibn Hayyān. Contribution à l'histoire des idées scientifiques dans l'Islam. Vol 2. Jabir et la science grecque* (Cairo: Mémoires de l'Institute d'Égypte, 1942), 222, 316. See also Strauss, "Some Remarks on the Political Science of Maimonides and Farabi," 279n7 (GS II:128n7).

[70] Strauss, "Some Remarks on the Political Science of Maimonides and Farabi," 299, 312 (GS II: 145, 156).

first part of a trilogy of Alfarabi which includes *Attainment of Happiness*, *Philosophy of Plato*, and *Philosophy of Aristotle*. This essay is perhaps Strauss's strongest statement about the essential importance of Alfarabi for understanding Maimonides's writings. To make his claim more powerful, Strauss cites a letter from Maimonides in which he recommends Alfarabi's writings exclusively and describes them as "pure flour."[71] For Maimonides, the works of Alfarabi surpass any other, even those of Avicenna, who was put side by side with Alfarabi in Strauss's previous writings on Maimonides. Strauss concludes his essay with a remarkable statement about the importance of Alfarabi:

At the beginning of this epoch of the history of philosophy there stands not just any "predecessor," but the towering spirit who laid the ground for the later development and set down its limits by making his task the revival of Platonic-Aristotelian philosophy as philosophy proper.[72]

Strauss's subsequent writings on Maimonides go in the same direction and link Alfarabi and esotericism: "The Place of the Doctrine of Providence According to Maimonides" (1937) proclaims the existence of "the secret teaching of the *Guide*" and indicates Maimonides's agreement with Alfarabi regarding the exoteric character of the doctrine of divine rewards and punishment. These exoteric doctrines are not true, but necessary for the welfare of the political order.[73] "On Abravanel's Philosophical Tendency and Political Teaching" (1937) incarnates the fruits of Strauss's radical leap by speaking of "Maimonides and his teachers" who borrowed the idea from Plato's *Laws* that Law contains beliefs addressed to the vulgar which are not true but are useful and necessary for the well-being of the political community. Maimonides has made, Strauss claims, this distinction known in a "disguised way, partly by allusions, partly by the composition of his whole work," methods which are recognizable only to readers of his writings who are philosophers and which are inaccessible to nonphilosophers. For instance, Strauss

[71] Strauss, "A Lost Writing of Farâbî's (1936)," 264–65 (GS II:175–76). For the context of this article see Steven Harvey, "Leo Strauss's Developing Interest in Alfarabi and Its Reverberations in the Study of Medieval Islamic Philosophy," in *The Pilgrimage of Philosophy: A Festschrift for Charles E. Butterworth*, eds. René M. Paddags, Waseem El-Rayes, and Gregory A. McBrayer (South Bend: St. Augustine's Press, 2019), 67–68.

[72] Strauss, "A Lost Writing of Farâbî's (1936)," 265 (GS II:176).

[73] Leo Strauss, "The Place of the Doctrine of Providence According to Maimonides," in *Leo Strauss on Maimonides: The Complete Writings*, ed. Kenneth Hart Green, trans. Gabriel Bartlett and Svetozar Minkov (Chicago: University of Chicago Press, 2013), 315n3, 322 (GS II:180n3, 186).

implicitly argues that Maimonides, contrary to his exoteric statements, actually did not believe in *creatio ex nihilo*.[74]

Considering the points in the previous paragraph, one might consider the possibility that Strauss's discovery of esotericism happens sometime around 1936 when he was working on "Some Remarks," that is, about two years even before his 1938 esoteric correspondence with Klein. In any event, the centrality of Maimonides in his connection with Alfarabi and other Falāsifa in Strauss's thesis on esotericism seems undeniable.

The period beginning with the discovery of Avicenna's statement in the Berlin library culminates in the 1945 publication of "Fârâbî's *Plato*." Between this major study exclusively dedicated to a Muslim philosopher who Strauss called "the starting point of philosophy" and the 1957 "How Fārābī Read Plato's *Laws*," which is Strauss's last major study on an Islamic figure, there is a relative silence on Islamic political philosophy in Strauss's writings.[75] It is true that from time to time, Alfarabi and Averroes appear on the scene, but they tend to disappear rather swiftly. How can one explain this relative silence? Did Strauss lose interest in Islamic philosophy in this period? I believe the silence can be partly explained by two points. First, there is the incomplete state of the available material for the study of Islamic political philosophy in this period.[76] An example is Alfarabi's summary of Plato's *Laws*. Already in 1937, explaining the importance of Alfarabi's work, Strauss claims that "only the full understanding of its true meaning would enable us to understand adequately the medieval philosophy," and advertises the publication of this work "in the near future by Dr. Paul Kraus."[77] This hope only materialized fifteen years later in 1952, by someone else, Francesco Gabrieli; two years later, Strauss began writing his interpretation on Alfarabi's summary.[78] The same thing happened with Alfarabi's *Philosophy of Plato*, which was

---

[74] Strauss, 585–86 (GS II:200–1).

[75] Shell, *The Strauss-Krüger Correspondence*, 79 (Letter to Gerhard Krüger on December 25, 1935, GS III:450).

[76] For the historical context and the state of scholarship in this period see Muhsin Mahdi, *Alfarabi and the Foundation of Islamic Political Philosophy* (Chicago: University of Chicago Press, 2001), 3–6; Joshua Parens, "Escaping the Scholastic Paradigm: The Dispute Between Strauss and His Contemporaries About How to Approach Islamic and Jewish Medieval Philosophy," in *Encountering the Medieval in Modern Jewish Thought*, eds. James A. Diamond and Aaron W. Hughes (Leiden: Brill, 2012), 203–28; Harvey, "Leo Strauss's Developing Interest in Alfarabi," 61–62.

[77] Strauss, "On Abravanel's Philosophical Tendency and Political Teaching," 581n4, 583 (GS II:196n4, 198).

[78] Alfarabi, *Compendium Legum Platonis*, ed. Francesco Gabrieli, Plato Arabus (London: Warburg Institute, 1952).

published in 1943, and Strauss's interpretation in 1945.[79] This point also explains the importance of Strauss's notes on Averroes's commentary on Plato's *Republic*, published and interpreted here for the first time: in several of his writings, Strauss refers to the importance of this work, and shows his interest in the modern edition of this work in 1937: "The more reliable Hebrew translation is being edited by Dr. Erwin Rosenthal."[80] This edition only appeared in 1956, and presumably, shortly afterward, Strauss began composing his notes on it. Even very late in his life Strauss remained interested in this writing of Averroes, and commented on his student's, Ralph Lerner, superior English translation.[81]

The second point which explains this period concerns Strauss's collaboration with Arabists, particularly with Paul Kraus, and later on with Muhsin Mahdi. Strauss worked closely with Kraus while in Paris (1931–32) on the edition and translation of Alfarabi's summary of Plato's *Laws* as well as reading Alfarabi's *Book of Religion*.[82] Shortly after Kraus's death in

---

[79] Alfarabi, *De Platonis philosophia*, eds. Richard Walzer and Franz Rosenthal, vol. 2, Plato Arabus (London: Warburg Institute, 1943).

[80] Leo Strauss, "Cohen and Maimonides," in *Leo Strauss on Maimonides*, ed. Kenneth Hart Green (Chicago: University of Chicago Press, 2013), 221 (GS II:428); Strauss, "Some Remarks on the Political Science of Maimonides and Farabi," 278n5, 295n59 (GS II:127n5, 142n59); Strauss, "The Place of the Doctrine of Providence According to Maimonides," 321n18 (GS II:184n18); Strauss, "Literary Character of the Guide for the Perplexed," 91n156; Strauss, "On Abravanel's Philosophical Tendency and Political Teaching," 581n4 (GS II:196n4).

[81] Averroes, *Commentary on Plato's "Republic,"* trans. Erwin I. J. Rosenthal (Cambridge: University of Cambridge Oriental Publication, 1956); Averroes, *On Plato's "Republic,"* trans. Ralph Lerner (Ithaca: Cornell University Press, 1974), ix. The existence of this edition seems to owe much to Strauss's initiative. See the comment by E. I. J Rosenthal: "I must acknowledge my debt to Dr. Leo Strauss with regard to the influence of Plato on Islamic 'political' philosophy, by his first drawing my attention eight years ago to Averroes' paraphrase on Plato's 'Republic.'" Erwin I. J. Rosenthal, "Maimonides' Conception of State and Society," in *Moses Maimonides*, ed. Israel Epstein (London: Soncio Press, 1935), 191n1. I owe this reference to Tamer, *Islamische Philosophie und die Krise der Moderne*, 60n6.

[82] Muhsin Mahdi, "The Editio Princeps of Fârâbî's Compendium Legum Platonis," *Journal of Near Eastern Studies* 20, no. 1 (1961): 15; Joel L. Kraemer, "The Death of an Orientalist: Paul Kraus from Prague to Cairo," in *The Jewish Discovery of Islam: Studies in Honor of Bernard Lewis*, ed. Martin Kramer (Tel Aviv: Moshe Dayan Centre for Middle Eastern and African Studies, 1999), 209. In 1932–33, Strauss was registered for courses at École Pratique des Hautes Études under Louis Massignon on Nasr ibn Muzahim's *Waq'at Ṣiffīn* and Simon van den Bergh on philosophy and theology of Averroes. In 1933–34, he attended Massignon's course on the first religious struggles in Islam according to Abu Hanifa Dinawari, a course on Qur'ān 36, and Paul Kraus's course on the Mu'tazila. See Timothy W. Burns, "The Place of the Strauss-Kojève Debate in the Work of Leo Strauss," in *Philosophy, History, and Tyranny: Reexamining the Debate*

1944, Louis Massignon suggested to Strauss to contribute to the efforts in giving some order to Kraus's unfinished projects and unpublished manuscripts. Strauss tried to track the material related to his collaboration with Kraus on Alfarabi's summary in 1946 as he had done previously in 1936,[83] but it seems that he was either unsuccessful then, or the incomplete state of the project dissuaded him from working on his interpretation right away. Strauss's knowledge of Arabic language is questioned; the existing evidence as well as Strauss's own statement that "I can read Arabic philosophical texts without difficulty, what Professor Gotthold Weil can attest to," however, speaks against this conjecture.[84] Be that as it may, Strauss as a person seems to have been too careful a scholar to publish on Arabic writings without collaboration of an Arabist. In this regard, his acquaintance with Mahdi, who could check Strauss's translations from Arabic in his essay on Alfarabi's summary of the *Laws*, was helpful for persuading him to return to Islamic political thought. Mahdi was also instrumental, as we shall see, in Strauss's interest in the *Arabian Nights*; but Mahdi's monumental efforts in editing many of Alfarabi's writings in 1960s seem to have borne fruit rather late for Strauss to take much benefit from.[85]

---

between Leo Strauss and Alexandre Kojève, eds. Timothy W. Burns and Bryan-Paul Frost (Albany: State University of New York Press, 2016), 18n9. For Strauss's appreciation of Massignon see Heinrich Meier, *Carl Schmitt and Leo Strauss: The Hidden Dialogue*, trans. J. Harvey Lomax (Chicago and London: University of Chicago Press, 2006), 127 (Letter to Carl Schmitt on July 10, 1933).

[83] Kraemer, "The Death of an Orientalist: Paul Kraus from Prague to Cairo," 208–9; Mahdi, "The Editio Princeps of Fârâbî's Compendium Legum Platonis," 15n55. For the biographical details of the relationship between Kraus and Strauss see Eugene Sheppard, *Leo Strauss and the Politics of Exile: The Making of a Political Philosopher* (Waltham: Brandeis University Press, 2006), 82.

[84] Strauss, *Gesammelte Schriften. Band 3*, 709 (Letter to Gershom Scholem on December 7, 1933); Harvey, "Leo Strauss' Early Interest in the Islamic Falāsifa," 223–26. Gotthold Weil (1882–1960) was a prominent Arabic and Hebrew scholar. There is also notebook in German and Arabic in Strauss's handwriting in Leo Strauss Papers, box 20, folder 14, Special Collections Research Center, University of Chicago Library. As the Arabic terms are translated into German and the notebook itself is made in Germany, I believe the notebook must be very early. I could not date the notebook precisely nor could I identify the text at the basis of Arabic terms, but the marginal notes seem to refer to a specific Arabic edition's or perhaps a manuscript's page and line numbers. See also a letter written to Muhsin Mahdi by Strauss on September 27, 1954, transcribed in Chapter 4 of this volume, where Strauss writes some words in Arabic characters.

[85] Strauss, "How Fārābī Read Plato's Laws," 1959, 134n1; Muhsin Mahdi, "Years of Chicago: Forming a Soul," *Alif: Journal of Comparative Poetics*, no. 29 (2009): 176; Charles E. Butterworth, ed., *The Political Aspects of Islamic Philosophy: Essays in Honor of Muhsin S. Mahdi* (Cambridge, MA: Harvard University Press, 1992), 383ff.

Considering these points, it would be a mistake to believe that Strauss gradually lost interest in the Falāsifa: the fact that he ended what he considered one of his most important works by speaking of the importance of Abū Bakr Muhammad ibn Zakariyyā al-Rāzī, and that he began his last book by Avicenna's statement, which he discovered forty years before, show his continuing interest in Islamic political thought up until his passing.[86]

LITERATURE ON STRAUSS'S STUDY
OF ISLAMIC THOUGHT

After this summary presentation of Strauss's thought and interest in the Falāsifa, I now turn toward the scholarly reactions to Strauss's writings on Islamic thought. One basic characteristic of the reactions to Strauss's writings on Islamic philosophy, apart from some remarkable exceptions, is that they are either entirely dismissive or mainly hostile. Regarding the dismissive reactions, two examples, already brought up by Steven Harvey, suffice: in Majid Fakhry's popular 2002 book on Alfarabi, the Muslim philosopher who Strauss and his followers tried so much to revive, there is no mention of Strauss in the whole book. If there was some way to ignore Mahdi and Butterworth's translations of Alfarabi, it seems certain that they would not appear in the book either, as is the case of their own studies on the subject.[87] The same treatment can be seen in the chapter dedicated to Alfarabi in *Cambridge Companion to Arabic Philosophy* by David Reisman, who does not mention any writing by Strauss or anyone influenced by his thought, even Mahdi.[88] Now, if one considers the amount of published scholarly writings, it is understandable that one cannot know and read every scholarly publication. But there are cases in which one simply cannot remain wholly unaware of some authors and publications: whatever one might think of Mahdi's scholarship, he

---

[86] Strauss, *On Tyranny*, 309 (Letter to Alexandre Kojève on May 29, 1962); Leo Strauss, *Socrates and Aristophanes* (New York and London: Basic Books, 1966), 314; Leo Strauss, *The Argument and the Action of Plato's Laws* (Chicago: University of Chicago Press, 1975), 1.

[87] Majid Fakhry, *Al-Farabi, Founder of Islamic Neoplatonism: His Life, Works and Influence* (Oxford: Oneworld Publications, 2002).

[88] David Reisman, "Al-Fārābī and the Philosophical Curriculum," in *The Cambridge Companion to Arabic Philosophy*, eds. Peter Adamson and Richard C. Taylor (Cambridge: Cambridge University Press, 2005), 52–71. See Harvey, "Leo Strauss' Early Interest in the Islamic Falāsifa," 234n48.

certainly was considered one of the foremost authorities in the study of Alfarabi; someone who discovered, edited, and commented on many of his writings for the first time. To ignore Mahdi's whole intellectual production requires an effort.

Those writings which do not completely ignore Strauss's contribution can be mainly divided into two groups. The first group consists of writings which are, with a single notable exception, highly critical of, and even hostile toward, Strauss's contribution to the study of Islamic philosophy. In the second group are writings which are mainly, but not entirely, sympathetic to Strauss's scholarship on Islamic political thought. Let us discuss these two groups separately:

First Group. In this group one should first mention Dimitri Gutas, whose very critical assessment of several approaches to the study of Islamic philosophy, including that of Strauss and his followers, is presented in an article which is considered one of the most influential in the field of Islamic philosophy written in the past two decades.[89] In his article, Gutas tries to deal with the relative lack of interest in Islamic philosophy among "historians of philosophy in general and ... scholars of Arabic and Islamic studies in particular."[90] Gutas finds the main source of this neglect to be the scholars of Islamic philosophy themselves: "historians of Arabic philosophy, have failed to present the subject to our colleagues." They have failed to do so because they have followed three mistaken and pernicious approaches in their studies, namely "orientalist," "mystical/illuminationist," and "political" approaches. Next, Gutas begins discussing what is wrong in each of these approaches, one after another, although it seems that the first approach, "orientalist," lacks prominent representatives in the scholarship of the past hundred years and Gutas confesses that it "has weakened considerably in recent decades." It appears that this approach is only mentioned first by Gutas so that its "orientalist" ideas and prejudices can be subsequently attributed to the representatives of the two other approaches as contemporary "reincarnations" of orientalism.[91] There are ideas in Gutas's critique of the orientalist approach with which one cannot reasonably disagree; in fact, many of them are borrowed by Gutas from Mahdi's critique of

---

[89] Dimitri Gutas, "The Study of Arabic Philosophy in the Twentieth Century: An Essay on the Historiography of Arabic Philosophy," *British Journal of Middle Eastern Studies* 29, no. 1 (2002): 5–25.

[90] Gutas, "The Study of Arabic Philosophy in the Twentieth Century," 5.

[91] Gutas, "The Study of Arabic Philosophy in the Twentieth Century," 8.

orientalism.[92] But before everything else, a general observation is in order: many of the ideas which Gutas ascribes to Strauss seem to be the result of unfamiliarity with Strauss's writings. His article does not refer to any writing by Strauss, and in view of many misrepresentations of Strauss's thought, it does not seem that Gutas has actually read any of them, at least not carefully enough. I do not wish to go point by point mentioning Gutas's misrepresentations, partly because this has been already done by others, and partly because the following study is addressed to readers like him who might want to acquire some familiarity with Strauss's writings on Islamic philosophy so as to have a better understanding of his point of view.[93] I therefore just limit my assessment to five critical points about Gutas's article:

(1) Gutas claims that Strauss follows the orientalist conception of Islamic philosophy as being "invariably" about the conflict between religion and philosophy; that, according to Strauss and his followers, "all of Arabic philosophy" is about this problem.[94] Strauss certainly found the conflict of religion and philosophy to be a very important subject for his own intellectual pursuits, and focused part of his studies on it. But such a general judgment attributed to Strauss by Gutas about many centuries of the intellectual production of hundreds, if not thousands, of thinkers in any period of any civilization would be simply absurd. And of course Strauss never claimed such a thing about Islamic philosophy, and Gutas does not adduce any evidence that he did.[95] Gutas has to speak in such categorical terms ("invariable," "all of") because if he had said the same thing in qualified terms his critique would become moot.[96] This can be

---

[92] Gutas, "The Study of Arabic Philosophy in the Twentieth Century," 8n6; Muhsin Mahdi, "Orientalism and the Study of Islamic Philosophy," *Journal of Islamic Studies* 1 (1990): 73–98.

[93] Harvey, "Leo Strauss' Early Interest in the Islamic Falāsifa"; David Wirmer, "Arabic Philosophy and the Art of Reading: I. Political Philosophy," in *La Philosophie Arabe à l'étude / Studying Arabic Philosophy. Sens, Limites et Défis d'une Discipline Moderne: Meaning, Limits and Challenges of a Modern Discipline*, eds. Jean-Baptiste Brenet and Olga L. Lizzini (Paris: Vrin, 2019), 179–250. A curious case is a passage from Oliver Leaman which Gutas quotes but gives us the impression that it is from Strauss (see footnote 36: "Cited from").

[94] Gutas, "The Study of Arabic Philosophy in the Twentieth Century," 20.

[95] This seems, surprisingly, to be a rather common misunderstanding about Strauss. See also Oliver Leaman, *An Introduction to Classical Islamic Philosophy* (Cambridge: Cambridge University Press, 2004), 210; James E. Montgomery, "Leo Strauss and the Alethiometer," in *Renaissance Averroism and Its Aftermath: Arabic Philosophy in Early Modern Europe*, eds. Anna Akasoy and Guido Giglioni (Dordrecht: Springer, 2013), 303.

[96] Gutas, "The Study of Arabic Philosophy in the Twentieth Century," 19.

seen in his claim that the issue of the relationship between religion and philosophy for Islamic philosophers was "a very minor subject of concern, and only at certain times and in certain places."[97] In other words, even he himself confesses that this subject has been of some importance for certain Islamic thinkers, although he tries to devalue its place. Gutas would have seen the mistaken character of his devaluation if he had paid enough attention to the reason why even one other opponent of Strauss's approach, Oliver Leaman, who is referred to and criticized in Gutas's article, might have been forced to give a prominent place to this issue in his introductory work on Islamic philosophy: that two of the towering figures of Islamic philosophy, al-Ghazali and Averroes, cared so much about this question as to write two major controversial treatises on this question, shows its undeniable importance.[98] Again, this does not mean that this subject was the *only* concern of Muslim philosophers throughout history. It would be ridiculous if anyone claimed that it was. If Strauss found this point particularly important, it was for his own intellectual preoccupations. Like any other scholar, Strauss cared for some subjects and focused on them, while he did not have the same interest in other subjects and therefore ignored them. To focus on this subject, contrary to what Gutas claims, is not a mark of orientalism or "anti-Islamic" prejudices, just as Strauss's interest in the same problem among Jewish and European thinkers is not proof of his "anti-Semitic" or anti-Christian prejudices.[99] This can be seen also in a related objection to Strauss made by Leaman: he claims that the Straussian esoteric reading of the Muslim philosophers, which leads to the idea that these philosophers were concerned with the conflict of Islam and philosophy, proves the Straussians' orientalist biases, because this would mean that "the philosophers in the Islamic world could not really be thought of as philosophers just like philosophers everywhere else."[100] The unfounded character of this orientalist accusation is obvious: Strauss was interested in question "in Christendom and the Islamic world alike," and therefore "it does

---

[97] Gutas, "The Study of Arabic Philosophy in the Twentieth Century," 13.

[98] Gutas, "The Study of Arabic Philosophy in the Twentieth Century," 13; Al-Ghazali, *The Incoherence of the Philosophers. A Parallel English-Arabic Text*, trans. Michael E. Marmura (Provo: Brigham Young University Press, 2000); Averroes, *Tahafut Al-Tahafut (The Incoherence of the Incoherence)*, trans. Simon van den Bergh, 3rd reprint edition (London: Gibb Memorial Trust, 2008).

[99] Gutas, "The Study of Arabic Philosophy in the Twentieth Century," 21.

[100] Oliver Leaman, "Orientalism and Islamic Philosophy," in *History of Islamic Philosophy*, eds. Oliver Leaman and Seyyed Hossein Nasr (London: Routledge, 2001), 1146.

not seem useful to characterize an attitude as Orientalist if it is equally applicable to the Occident."[101]

Furthermore, contrary to what Gutas claims, Strauss does not subscribe to "the biased orientalist attitude that philosophy could not thrive in 'Islam' because of the intrinsically anti-rationalist nature of the latter."[102] The charge is quite unbelievable: if Strauss truly believed that philosophy cannot "thrive in 'Islam'" there would not have been a "Straussian" approach to the study of Islamic philosophy! This leads us to another general point: calling everything one finds wrong in some scholar's approach "orientalist" creates a strange confusion. Orientalism is usually understood as a term describing the prejudices of some scholars of non-Western, mainly Arabic thought and society; these scholars have described Arabic culture and society as inferior to their Western counterparts. Calling someone like Henry Corbin, who was so enamored with Islamic thought and Islamic philosophy "orientalist," does not make much sense. Calling Strauss an "orientalist," while he has been even considered thoroughly a student and follower of Alfarabi and Muslim philosophers, makes even less sense. Strauss was so taken with Alfarabi that one can reasonably claim that he went well beyond the existing evidence, exaggerating Alfarabi's philosophical importance.[103] In fact, attributing, repeatedly, orientalist ideas and prejudices to Strauss, along with similar curious statements such as that Strauss "did not know Arabic philosophy" in Gutas's article feels like something other than healthy scholarly disagreement, and they should be safely disregarded as serious intellectual objections.[104]

---

[101] Muhammad Ali Khalidi, "Orientalisms in the Interpretation of Islamic Philosophy," *Radical Philosophy* 135 (2006): 27.

[102] Gutas, "The Study of Arabic Philosophy in the Twentieth Century," 21.

[103] Brague, "Athens, Jerusalem, Mecca"; Shell, *The Strauss-Krüger Correspondence*, 78–79 (Letter to Gerhard Krüger on December 25, 1935, GS III:450).

[104] Gutas, "The Study of Arabic Philosophy in the Twentieth Century," 20. See the similar curiously hostile attitude toward Joshua Parens, Muhsin Mahdi, David Wirmer, Christian Jambet, and Charles Butterworth in Dimitri Gutas, "Fārābī's Knowledge of Plato's 'Laws,'" *International Journal of the Classical Tradition* 4, no. 3 (1998): 405–11; Dimitri Gutas, "Review of Muhsin Mahdi, Alfarabi and the Foundation of Islamic Political Philosophy (Chicago: University of Chicago Press, 2001).," *International Journal of Middle East Studies* 35, no. 1 (2003): 145–47; Dimitri Gutas, "On the Historiography of Arabic Philosophy: Postscript 2017," in *La Philosophie Arabe à l'étude / Studying Arabic Philosophy. Sens, Limites et Défis d'une Discipline Moderne: Meaning, Limits and Challenges of a Modern Discipline*, eds. Jean-Baptiste Brenet and Olga L. Lizzini (Paris: Vrin, 2019), 37–45; Dimitri Gutas, *Avicenna and the Aristotelian Tradition: Introduction to Reading Avicenna's Philosophical Works* (Leiden and Boston: Brill, 2014), 143n45; Dimitri Gutas, "On Translating Averroes' Commentaries," *Journal of the American Oriental Society* 110, no. 1 (1990): 92–101.

(2) Gutas claims that according to Strauss "all Arabic philosophy until Averroes is seen as having a political framework," the view which Gutas argues is based on "very flimsy evidence."[105] Again this idea, attributed to Strauss, is not exact; Strauss does not claim that "all Arabic philosophy" has a political framework, be it before or after Averroes. He is more concerned about how Alfarabi presents philosophy in a political framework and how his conception of prophecy as a political phenomenon is transmitted to Avicenna and Maimonides. On this subject, I can only refer to the discussion of the statement by Avicenna in this introduction and in the following chapters.

(3) Gutas is very critical of Strauss's thesis on esotericism, but like some other points in Gutas's paper, it is not very clear what Gutas is disagreeing with. That esotericism was an important phenomenon and has very deep and documented intellectual sources in Islamic philosophy is even conceded by Gutas.[106] What seems to be problematic for Gutas is that Strauss has applied his valid and well documented observations about the existence of esotericism to, again, "all Arabic philosophy." As in the previous cases, Strauss does no such thing. He certainly does not apply esotericism to every author, but to some specific authors like Alfarabi and Maimonides, who both discuss this issue. In other words, contrary to Gutas's claim, Strauss never speaks in such general terms as that "all" writers were esoteric writers, but rather concentrates on specific texts: for instance, Alfarabi's preface to his summary of Plato's *Laws* contains such esoteric ideas, and it is therefore legitimate to be concerned with the question of esotericism in his writings. Furthermore, if Gutas was familiar with Strauss's commentary on Alfarabi's summary of Plato's *Laws*, as well as his other writings on this question, he would have known that Strauss does not claim that "philosophers never say explicitly what they mean out of fear of persecution." Strauss

---

[105] Gutas, "The Study of Arabic Philosophy in the Twentieth Century," 22–23.

[106] Gutas, "The Study of Arabic Philosophy in the Twentieth Century," 19–20. See also Wirmer, "Arabic Philosophy and the Art of Reading," 191–92. That esotericism is a common feature of Islamic philosophy is often admitted. See for instance Leaman, *An Introduction to Classical Islamic Philosophy*, 220, 222. Leaman is also critical of Strauss's approach but his critique is much subtle: he seems to have a different understanding of Alfarabi's esoteric techniques and doctrines. As a whole, one can say that his view of Strauss's works is much more nuanced and constructive than Gutas's. See Leaman, *An Introduction to Classical Islamic Philosophy*, 222–23. In the meantime, the minor aspect of Leaman's critique in his earlier writing should be distinguished from his later very critical article in which he also uses the term "orientalism" for describing Strauss's ideas. See Leaman, "Orientalism and Islamic Philosophy."

actually claims the reverse: by relying on Alfarabi's statements at the
beginning of his summary, Strauss claims that philosophers sometimes
very openly say what they mean.[107] Moreover, persecution is neither
the only reason for practicing esotericism, nor is it the most important
one for Strauss. Strauss also cares much about pedagogical esotericism,
as well as esotericism practiced for the sake of the protection of society, the types of esotericism to which Gutas does not refer at all. I
will not speak more in detail about the question of esotericism, first
because the *historical* question of esotericism, as we shall see, is not
directly related to the subject of this volume. More importantly, this
question has been discussed in an exhaustive fashion in a remarkable
volume by Arthur M. Melzer, who has provided a detailed discussion
of esotericism and created an online appendix which includes hundreds
of statements from different authors in all periods of history referring
to esotericism. Melzer's most important contribution consists of showing how widespread are the statements about esotericism in the writings of different figures throughout history. I believe he has managed
to provide sufficient evidence to prove that esotericism has been an
undeniable historical fact, and that throughout the centuries, different
writers believed in the existence of esoteric doctrines in a large variety
of traditions: mystical, philosophical, political, theological, kabalistic,
gnostic, and the like. Melzer's book also contains an interesting section
on some common esoteric techniques, as well as historical evidence for
their existence, the techniques which scholars have always found objec-
tionable in Strauss's writings.[108]

(4) Gutas's paper presents itself as a diagnostic of the study of Islamic
philosophy, and tries to suggest a way to make the discipline more attractive to the scholars of other fields. His solution, however, does not seem
to be to the purpose. Gutas seems to be concerned that the scholars of
other fields who are "philosophically minded," reading the writings
of Corbin, Strauss, and their followers, might find Islamic philosophy
"philosophically insignificant."[109] Gutas seems to believe that his own
approach would not give that impression, and would actually establish
the image of Muslim thinkers as serious philosophers in their own right.

---

[107] Gutas, "The Study of Arabic Philosophy in the Twentieth Century," 20; Strauss, "How
Fārābī Read Plato's Laws," 1959, 136–37.
[108] Arthur M. Melzer, *Philosophy between the Lines: The Lost History of Esoteric Writing*
(Chicago: University of Chicago Press, 2014), 299–322. For the online appendix see
http://press.uchicago.edu/sites/melzer/index.html
[109] Gutas, "The Study of Arabic Philosophy in the Twentieth Century," 10, 12, 18.

The facts, however, do not correspond to Gutas's claims. If one thing distinguishes Strauss's approach from all the other alternatives, including Gutas's own, it is the seriousness with which the writings of the Falāsifa are treated. They are read in an intensive fashion which has no comparable example in the writings of other scholars, who are obsessed exclusively with antiquarian details like the availability of original Greek works to Muslim philosophers. One fundamental principle of Strauss's approach, as it can also be seen in his notes on Averroes, published and interpreted in this volume, is that the reader of medieval philosophy should not "look *down*" on the author under discussion and must begin with the healthy point of departure that "the philosopher studied by the historian of philosophy is a man by far superior to his historian in intelligence, imagination, subtlety."[110] Such a perspective would produce philosophically far superior results than the approach advocated by other historians of Islamic philosophy, who seem always prejudiced against the access of Islamic philosophers to original works, and constantly tend to underestimate the philosophic competence of the Falāsifa, by imagining intermediary sources and presupposing misunderstanding of texts and Greek ideas. In the case of Gutas himself, this can be seen in his own article, where he accuses Straussians of conducting their research "as if the Arabic philosophers had recourse to the same Greek texts of Aristotle and Plato as ours," in total disregard of what Gutas describes as "historical and philological factors which conditioned the Arabic philosophers' understanding of the Greek philosophical tradition" such as "translators' misunderstandings, scribal errors, extrapolations, exegetical additions and elaborations that accumulated over the twelve centuries and more that separate classical Greek philosophy and the beginning of Arabic, and the semantic and connotative range of Arabic terms and expressions that were current at the time of each Arabic philosopher."[111] The same perspective, as we shall see when we get to the secondary literature on Alfarabi's summary of Plato's *Laws*, is found in Gutas's rather severe review of Joshua Parens's book, and then in an essay, where Gutas claims that Alfarabi's summary is not based on Plato's *Laws,* but rather on a summary of it, perhaps the lost Arabic translation of Galen's *Synopsis*

---

[110] Strauss, "How to Study Medieval Philosophy," 322. For a good example of this approach, which is rejected out of hand by Gutas, "The Study of Arabic Philosophy in the Twentieth Century," footnote 41 see also Charles E. Butterworth, "Translation and Philosophy: The Case of Averroes' Commentaries," *International Journal of Middle East Studies* 26, no. 1 (1994): 19–35.

[111] Gutas, "The Study of Arabic Philosophy in the Twentieth Century," 21–22.

of Plato's Laws.[112] As we shall see, Gutas's hypothesis goes even against Alfarabi's own claim that he has read Plato's *Laws*. Moreover, Gutas's hypothesis means that Alfarabi was such an incompetent and unknowledgeable thinker that he could not distinguish between Plato's dialogue and a summary of it. How can one consider this perspective an evidence for the philosophic worth of Alfarabi's writings? In a similar fashion, in another hostile review, Gutas claims that any study of Averroes's commentaries on Aristotle's *Poetics* must always "take into account the decisive influence which the garbled Arabic translation of the *Poetics* and earlier Arabic commentaries had on Averroes' understanding of the text," which would again decrease the philosophic value of Averroes's commentaries.[113] Such claims do not seem like a remarkable vote of confidence for Islamic philosophers' high intellectual status. This point was also made in clear fashion by Mahdi in the article to which Gutas refers:

> One of the strangest criticisms that continues to be made by some of the representatives of the older, historical and philological tradition of Islamic studies in the West has to do with the validity of attempts to think or rethink the thoughts of a philosopher such as Alfarabi, Avicenna, or Averroes. This means that one can treat their thought historically, biographically, sociologically, and so forth – that is good scholarship. But to think philosophically when dealing with the works of these philosophers, that is said not to be scientific. This view makes no sense, of course. Without thinking theologically, one cannot understand fully the thought of a theologian; without thinking aesthetically, one cannot understand fully the work of a poet or a literary critic, and generally any important work of art; similarly, one can do all the historical or philological or sociological research he wishes, without being able to get to the core of a philosophic work.[114]

If one was in the habit of accusing others of orientalism, reducing the study of Islamic philosophy only to editing manuscripts, pointing to the real or imaginary poor understanding of Greek originals on the part of Muslim philosophers, and the enterprise of explaining everything by establishing lines of influence, the enterprise which reduces Islamic philosophy to a mere appendix of Greek thought, is more deserving of the accusation of orientalism than Strauss's approach, which treats Islamic philosophers as thinkers of the same rank as Plato and Aristotle.[115] But I believe we should not

---

[112] Gutas, "Fārābī's Knowledge of Plato's 'Laws'"; Dimitri Gutas, "Galen's Synopsis of Plato's Laws and Fārābī's Talḫīṣ," in *The Ancient Tradition in Christian and Islamic Hellenism: Studies on the Transmission of Greek Philosophy and Sciences*, eds. Remke Kruk and Gerhard Endress (Leiden: Research School CNWS, 1997), 101–19.

[113] Gutas, "On Translating Averroes' Commentaries," 92.

[114] Mahdi, "Orientalism and the Study of Islamic Philosophy," 93.

[115] Khalidi, "Orientalisms in the Interpretation of Islamic Philosophy," 28.

commit the same mistakes, and the temptation of dealing with differences of approach by recourse to such charged terms should be resisted.

(5) I also find Gutas's whole project of eliminating competing approaches in favor of a unitary, mainly historical and philological approach, advocated by Gutas himself, unreasonable. One does not have to be a Straussian, Corbinian (or Gutasian for that matter), to find their approaches useful, in the same way that one can appreciate Karl Marx or Aristotle's writings without being a Marxist or an Aristotelian. In the same vein, the following study is not an apology for Strauss or an effort to convert people to "Straussianism" (whatever that may be). It would have achieved its goal if it only persuades scholars of any approach that Strauss's writings on Islamic philosophy have something of value in them too, from which they can benefit for their own intellectual interests, which might be completely different from Strauss's. In the same fashion, I do not deny that other approaches, including those of Corbin or Gutas, are also valuable, and one can learn something of importance from them without agreeing completely with everything they say. They can at the very least play the role of a dialectical opponent. I am not completely convinced, for instance, that emphasis on the religious character of Islamic philosophy, disregarding the distinction between the rational and supra-rational, and including mystics and Sufis alongside Alfarabi and Averroes in the tradition of Islamic philosophy, characteristic of Corbin's writings and those of other scholars, is correct.[116] I also find the philologic-historical approach *detached* from a philosophic perspective on the writings of Muslim philosophers harmful for the discipline. But I cannot but appreciate the alternative scholarly approaches, and would not wish their practitioners all convert to one single approach; this would considerably impoverish the intellectual debate and reduce the healthy diversity in the field of Islamic philosophy.

Moving from Gutas's critique of Strauss, among the critical reactions to Strauss's interest in the Falāsifa, I believe Georges Tamer's is a noteworthy one.[117] His study is a thorough and intelligent reading of Strauss's writings and reflects, contrary to other critiques of Strauss, a good knowledge of and engagement with the primary sources. Tamer's approach, as a whole, is scholarly and constructive. When he makes critical remarks, he tries to create a constructive dialogue by referring

---

[116] See my brief comments in Rasoul Namazi, "Illuminationist Texts and Textual Studies: Essays in Memory of Hossein Ziai," *Iranian Studies* 53, nos 5–6 (April 14, 2020): 1–4, and Butterworth's chapter mentioned in the review.

[117] Tamer, *Islamische Philosophie und die Krise der Moderne.*

to relevant studies on Islamic philosophy. His specific points are also worthy of attention, to which I refer in this book whenever relevant to the discussion. I do not agree with his general perspective and conclusions, but as it is not still available to English-speaking readers, I will try to give a general description of his study.[118] This short summary does not of course cover all aspects of Tamer's work, but only emphasizes those points which I find particularly significant for the subject of this book.

Tamer finds Strauss's interest in Islamic philosophy already present in his first book on Spinoza, where the Averroistic critique of religion is discussed.[119] This would mean a much earlier turn toward the Falāsifa, in 1925–28, when Strauss was writing *Spinoza's Critique of Religion*.[120] Tamer finds a particularly significant idea in this early engagement, the idea which he believes to be a constant element of Strauss's thought until the end, and which englobes his whole approach to Islamic philosophy: Strauss's Averroistic interest in the political function of religion as an instrument for education of the multitude, which is dominated by irrationality and impervious to reason. In this view, and in contradistinction to what Strauss considers to be the Epicurean critique of religion, religion is not seen as a natural, spontaneous, and irrational product of the human psyche, but rather a political institution founded by intelligent men as a code of law to regulate social life. Tamer believes that this view of religion is also Strauss's own, which he borrowed from Averroes: Tamer, who deems Strauss an atheist like his models (Alfarabi, Avicenna, Averroes, etc.), nonetheless notes that Strauss believed that religion should not be refuted or destroyed, but preserved and used politically. In Tamer's view, Strauss's critique of modernity has a direct relationship with this view of religion: in his diagnostic, Tamer claims, Strauss finds the origin of the crisis of modernity in its failure to integrate religion as an instrument of order into society by discrediting it and weakening public morality. Strauss's critique of Carl Schmitt, in Tamer's eyes, consisted precisely of

---

[118] A translation of his book is set to appear by SUNY Press in the future.

[119] Tamer, *Islamische Philosophie und die Krise der Moderne*, 41–47; Strauss, *Spinoza's Critique of Religion*, 47–49, 101 (GS 1:77–79, 145).

[120] This would also coincide with Eugene R. Sheppard's suggestion that Strauss was introduced to Islamic philosophy in the period 1924–25: Sheppard, *Leo Strauss and the Politics of Exile*, 33. See also the comment by E. I. J Rosenthal in 1935: "I must acknowledge my debt to Dr. Leo Strauss with regard to the influence of Plato on Islamic 'political' philosophy, by his first drawing my attention eight years ago [i.e. ca. 1927] to Averroes' paraphrase on Plato's 'Republic.'" Rosenthal, "Maimonides' Conception of State and Society," 191n1.

remaining in the horizon of liberal secularism and not turning to religion as an effective political phenomenon.[121] It is in this perspective that Tamer tries to understand Strauss's esotericism: the philosopher is advised to say the truth about religion and its unfounded claims *only* esoterically, and exoterically he should employ "noble lies" so he does not undermine healthy myths necessary for the common good.[122] Like many other readers, Tamer has also difficulties with Strauss's esoteric interpretations and finds them unconvincing and far-fetched. He also raises some rather common objections against Strauss: that his interpretations of Alfarabi are based on the supposition that Alfarabi knew Plato's writings, which Tamer is skeptical about. This leads Tamer to the belief that Avicenna's statement, rather than to Plato's *Laws*, actually refers to a pseudepigraphic treatise which was in circulation during this time under the title of "Plato's Laws."[123]

I find two aspects of Tamer's thesis of particular importance: First, his claim about Avicenna's statement, and second, the political teaching which he ascribes to Strauss. I am not entirely convinced by either of these, but I find them both worthy of attention. In what concerns Tamer's objections to Strauss's interpretation of Avicenna's statement, two points are important. Here is Avicenna's statement, in Mahdi's translation, at the heart of the controversy:

Of this science, the treatment of kingship is contained in the book by Plato and that by Aristotle on the regime, and the treatment of prophecy and the Law is contained in their two books on the laws.[124]

Tamer mentions that this reading is based on a Gotha manuscript, while in the Constantinople version there is a variant in which rather than "their two books on laws" (kitābāhumā al-mawḍū' fī nawāmīs) it reads "two books on laws" (kitābān fī nawāmīs).[125] In other words, in the Constantinople version, 'two books on the laws' are *not* attributed explicitly to Plato and Aristotle.[126] Tamer prefers the Constantinople reading because, he claims, even in Arabic sources, there is no mention of a (pseudo-) Aristotelian book on laws. Mahdi, on the contrary, speaks

[121] Tamer, *Islamische Philosophie und die Krise der Moderne*, 93.
[122] Tamer, *Islamische Philosophie und die Krise der Moderne*, 327–28.
[123] Tamer, *Islamische Philosophie und die Krise der Moderne*, 58–87.
[124] Avicenna, "On the Divisions of the Rational Sciences," in *Medieval Political Philosophy: A Sourcebook*, eds. Ralph Lerner and Muhsin Mahdi, 1st edition (New York: Free Press of Glencoe, 1963), 97.
[125] Strauss, *Philosophy and Law*, 152n57 (GS II:112n57).
[126] Tamer, *Islamische Philosophie und die Krise der Moderne*, 64–65.

in a footnote of "the two books given in the bibliographies of Aristotle's writings, which bear the same titles as the two works by Plato."[127] Tamer thinks that Mahdi was mistaken: "Aristotle did not write such a book, and no such title can be found among the pseudo-Aristotelian Arabic translations."[128] I believe Mahdi is not referring to Arabic bibliographical sources, but rather to the list of Aristotle's writings in Diogenes Laertius who attributes "Extracts from Plato's Laws, in three books," and more importantly, "Four books of Laws" to Aristotle.[129] Tamer goes on to make another point, which is the real basis of his criticism; the question of the pseudo-Aristotelian book on the laws is not essential to his point. He reads Avicenna's statement as effectively referring to a writing by Plato on the laws, but not the genuine version of Plato's *Laws* which we are familiar with and to which Strauss refers. Tamer mentions that there were "three" books with the title "Plato's Laws" existing in this period: a pseudo-Platonic treatise which dealt with superstitious practices,[130]

---

[127] Avicenna, "On the Divisions of the Rational Sciences," 97n2.

[128] Tamer, *Islamische Philosophie und die Krise der Moderne*, 65.

[129] Diogenes Laertius, *Vitae* V.22, V.26. Regarding the attribution of a pseudepigraph on the laws to Aristotle I should also mention two supplementary points: At the end of the *Nicomachean Ethics*, Aristotle seems to promise a discussion of *nomoi* and legislation in another writing of his (1181b12ff.). The Arabic translation of *Ethics* has survived and contains these passages: Aristotle, *The Arabic Version of the Nicomachean Ethics*, eds. Anna Akasoy, Alexander Fidora, and Douglas Morton Dunlop (Leiden: Brill, 2005), 580. On this basis alone, even without knowledge of Diogenes Laertius's bibliographical information, Muslim thinkers might have believed that just as in the case of Plato's *Laws*, there is also a discussion of *nawāmīs* in Aristotle's writings, presumably in a treatise coming after the *Nicomachean Ethics*. Diogenes Laertius's report about a book specifically on laws by Aristotle seems to correspond to Aristotle's announcement at the end of the *Nicomachean Ethics*. One should also consider the possibility that our knowledge of the pseudo-Aristotelian writings in Arabic might be incomplete, and that just as in the case of Diogenes Laertius, there was perhaps such a work on laws attributed to Aristotle in Arabic sources. Furthermore, it is interesting that in his *Tahdhīb al-akhlāq wa-taṭhīr al-aʿrāq*, Ibn Miskawayh quotes a passage on *nomos* (nāmūs) and sharīʿa from Aristotle's *Nicomachean Ethics*: "The highest law [nāmūs] is from God (blessed and exalted is He!), the ruler is a second law on His behalf, and money is a third law. The law of God [nāmūs allāh] (exalted is He!), i.e., the Law [sharīʿa], is the model for all the other laws." In Ibn Miskawayh, *The Refinement of Character*, trans. Constantine K. Zurayk (Beirut: American University of Beirut, 1968), 103; Rémi Brague, *The Law of God: The Philosophical History of an Idea*, trans. Lydia G. Cochrane (Chicago: University of Chicago Press, 2007), 116–17. The original passage, different from Ibn Miskawayh's quotation, is Aristotle, *Nicomachean Ethics* 1134a26ff.

[130] Strauss knew this work: Strauss, "The Law of Reason in the Kuzari," 123. See also Liana Saif, "The Cows and the Bees: Arabic Sources and Parallels for Pseudo-Plato's Liber Vaccae (Kitab al-Nawamis)," *Journal of the Warburg and Courtauld Institutes* 79, no. 1 (2016): 1–47.

another, second pseudo-Platonic treatise which actually deals with religious law and prophecy, and a third book, which Tamer describes as the "translation of the work summarized by Alfarabi."[131] Tamer believes that Avicenna is actually referring to the second pseudo-Platonic work rather than the genuine Plato's *Laws*. One should not, however, overlook the fact that Tamer also means that the genuine *Laws* of Plato was not accessible to Arabic readers, and that Alfarabi's summary of Plato's *Laws* is actually a summary of another writing, probably Galen's lost summary of Plato's *Laws*.[132]

The question of the existence of an Arabic translation of Plato's *Laws* and related issues will be dealt with in detail when we turn to Strauss's interpretation of Alfarabi's summary of Plato's *Laws* in Chapter 4 of this book. I should only mention one point about Tamer's claim on Avicenna's statement: although it is possible that Strauss was mistaken in identifying Avicenna's reference, the alternative, that Avicenna is indeed referring to the genuine writing of Plato, remains also a possibility. It is true that Plato's *Laws* is not about, in Islamic terms, prophecy and sharī'a, but it is not difficult to see how Muslim thinkers could have seen an overlap between the Platonic depiction of Zeus–Minos–Dorian laws and the Islamic idea of Allah–Muhammad–sharī'a. In other words, the idea of a divine lawgiver, his messenger or a bringer of divine laws, and his detailed laws regulating different aspects of political society, is easily transferable from Plato's Greek context to a Muslim context; this can clearly be seen in Ibn Miskawayh's reading of the *Nicomachean Ethics*.[133] To wit, in the absence of concrete proof which contradicts Strauss's reading of Avicenna's statement, his interpretation remains a possibility and safe from Tamer's objections. I should here emphasize that certitude about the Muslim philosophers' lack of access to Plato's *Laws* is the main reason why Tamer has difficulty with Avicenna's statement. If one questions that certitude, which I will do later on, one has to begin thinking about the reasons why Muslim philosophers might have thought that Plato's dialogue is relevant to their specific theologico-political situation. This directly leads to ideas similar to Strauss's.

I also find Tamer's general claim – that is, ascribing a *teaching* of a highly political as well as secretive character *to Strauss* – unconvincing.

---

[131] Tamer, *Islamische Philosophie und die Krise der Moderne*, 67–68.
[132] Tamer, *Islamische Philosophie und die Krise der Moderne*, 65, 65n22. Tamer is here following Gutas. See Tamer, *Islamische Philosophie und die Krise der Moderne*, 65n22.
[133] On this question see also Brague, *The Law of God*, esp. 117–18. See also footnote 129 above.

A proper assessment of Tamer's claim, however, requires an independent discussion addressing many specific interpretative points in Strauss's writings, which would go beyond the main subject as well as the limitations of the current study. I will limit my comment only to what I believe is the major source of misunderstanding among Strauss's readers, which has given rise to the attribution of many contradictory and controversial political teachings to Strauss by very different scholars, including Tamer. To begin with, this specific view of religion, as an instrument of political control which responds to the conflict of theory and praxis and the insurmountable divide between the philosophers and the many, is of classical origin rather than an exclusively Averroistic doctrine. Strauss finds an example of this view in a passage from Aristotle, in which he writes of the mythical ideas about the gods which were introduced by the ancients "with a view to the persuasion of ordinary people and with a view to its use for legal purposes and for what is advantageous."[134] Following Saint Augustine, who traces this idea to certain Stoics, Strauss uses the term "civil theology" for describing this view of religion, but he also emphasizes that "this view is not peculiar to Aristotle" but is an idea found in other classical writers, including Plato, who also "affirms the dogma of particular providence only because of its political utility."[135] This civil religion was later transmitted to thinkers like the Falāsifa, Maimonides, and many philosophers of modern times including Machiavelli, Spinoza, and Rousseau. Strauss does nothing but document this tradition, as others have done.[136] What Tamer considers Strauss's personal view is only what Strauss claims to be a historically documented understanding of religion among many thinkers throughout history. In fact, in a recently published lecture, in which Strauss speaks of the classical philosophers' understanding of religion in its relationship with politics, when speaking in his own name Strauss begins to state his doubts about the effectiveness as well as desirability of such a false public religion in modern liberal regimes.[137]

---

[134] Aristotle, *Metaphysics* 1074b1–5 (C. D. C. Reeve translation).

[135] Augustine, *The City of God* IV.27; Strauss, "Some Remarks on the Political Science of Maimonides and Farabi," 312 (GS II:156); Leo Strauss, "'Religion and the Commonweal in the Tradition of Political Philosophy.' An Unpublished Lecture by Leo Strauss," eds. Svetozar Minkov and Rasoul Namazi, *American Political Thought* 10, no. 1 (2021): 97.

[136] See e.g. Ronald Beiner, *Civil Religion: A Dialogue in the History of Political Philosophy* (Cambridge: Cambridge University Press, 2011).

[137] Strauss, "Religion and the Commonweal," 110–11.

To go from Strauss's historical description of civil religion and explanation of its underlying ideas, such as the divide of the philosophers and the many, to Tamer's claim that these historical observations are in fact Strauss's recipe for resolving the crisis of modernity, requires a considerable leap which cannot be easily made. Tamer has in fact here encountered a problem which has a long pedigree among Strauss's readers who, rejecting the primary impression of Strauss as a historian of thought, consider him a thinker with a specific political teaching. In this regard, one should first mention a rather fundamental point in Strauss's whole corpus, even including the material surviving from his courses and lectures which are of more occasional character: compared to many other scholars of his generation, Strauss did not advance any specific political project or practical plan of action. To attribute a specific project to Strauss on the basis of existing evidence would be very difficult, if not impossible. Strauss rarely, if ever, speaks in his own name, but rather writes in the form of commentaries on the writings of other thinkers and on specific historical texts. Other readers, facing the descriptive character of Strauss's writings, the absence of writings by Strauss in the form of a straightforward "treatise" containing his views in an accessible fashion, yet still in search for Strauss's own teaching, were forced to find a positive teaching behind Strauss's scholarly and historical writings. They had recourse to the idea that the historical character of Strauss's writings is only a façade used for conveying an esoteric teaching underneath; that Strauss speaks in his commentaries through esoteric techniques. To establish such a thesis one must naturally begin applying all those controversial methods of esoteric reading to Strauss's own writings, with all the controversial issues concomitant with such an enterprise.[138] Tamer is aware of this tendency among some of Strauss's commentators, and he objects to this method by writing that "Leo Strauss must be taken seriously [*Ernst*], i.e., at his word and the unfortunate guesswork around his esoteric, not explicit thoughts must be avoided."[139] Hence the difficulty in establishing Tamer's thesis by referring to Strauss's explicit statements.

This does not mean that Tamer would have been more successful in establishing his thesis if he would have attempted an esoteric reading of Strauss's writings. In fact, to claim that Strauss has an esoteric thesis which

---

[138] See the same difficulty in Shadia Drury's treatment of Strauss: Zuckert and Zuckert, *The Truth about Leo Strauss*, 117ff.

[139] Tamer, *Islamische Philosophie und die Krise der Moderne*, 24–27, 35, but cf. 267n7.

recommends the establishment of a civil religion would be unpersuasive: for any esoteric teaching to be successful, the principal requirement is to *not present it as an esoteric teaching*. Every noble or base lie is only effective if it is *not* presented as a lie. In view of Strauss's deliberate and emphatic association of himself with historical writings on the idea of civil religion, esotericism, and noble lies, one cannot imagine that Strauss was unaware that such an association would weaken the chances of success of a project of civil religion in his time or in the future. Strauss finds an esoteric teaching according to which religion is only a salutary myth in the writings of Plato and Alfarabi; but neither of these thinkers spoke on this subject exoterically and in public. Plato did not question the divine origin of the Dorian Laws, nor did Alfarabi question basic Islamic tenets openly. The ideas that Tamer attributes to Strauss, such as the elitist view of knowledge, functionalist view of religion, and such are, on the contrary, presented in Strauss's writings in a very straightforward and nonesoteric fashion. How could Strauss have seriously believed that he can go on to present a religious teaching to the public while at same time discrediting all belief in such a religious teaching openly in his writings, which are also accessible to the same audience?[140]

Before moving on from Tamer's thesis, I would also like to mention two supplementary points which would help the readers of this study, as well as prevent them from looking for Strauss's specific political teachings: the first point concerns what might have led Tamer and other scholars, and might still persuade his other readers, to conclude that Strauss is not wholly impartial toward the political ideas that he ascribes to other thinkers. I believe this is mainly born out of one of Strauss's most important hermeneutical principles: that the task of a historian above all is to make the best case for the ideas advanced in the text he is commenting on. The historian should not presuppose beforehand that those ideas are wrong if they do not correspond to his own views. For the sake of historical exactitude, Strauss advises the historian that no "prejudice in favor of contemporary thought, even of modern philosophy, of modern civilization, of modern science itself" should "deter him from giving the thinkers of old the *full* benefit of the doubt."[141]

---

[140] On the difficulties of an esoteric reading of Strauss in more detail see Zuckert and Zuckert, *The Truth about Leo Strauss*, 115–55; Melzer, *Philosophy between the Lines*, 107–11. What is unsatisfactory in the Zuckerts' discussion is that they seem to deny the existence of esoteric writing in Strauss's own works, which, as we shall see, is not the case. See also Peter Minowitz, *Straussophobia: Defending Leo Strauss and Straussians against Shadia Drury and Other Accusers* (Lanham: Lexington Books, 2009).

[141] Strauss, "How to Study Medieval Philosophy," 325.

Following the same approach, Strauss always tried to adhere to what he called "*the* principle of criticism," that in treating a thinker seriously means to "take him at his strength." He therefore, not only avoided the straw man fallacy, but presented the best possible case for each view, even sometimes exaggerating the strengths of a position with which he ultimately disagreed.[142] This approach, which has much merit from a scholarly perspective, might give us the impression that Strauss actually agreed with the ideas of the authors he is discussing and presenting. But Strauss wrote commentaries and taught courses on a wide range of philosophers, theologians, and thinkers of all persuasions. It is not difficult to find passages in all of these writings and transcripts in which Strauss gives a rather sympathetic view of the ideas of the texts he is discussing: not only Xenophon, Plato, or Alfarabi, but also Judah Halevi, Machiavelli, Hobbes, Hegel, Marx, Heidegger, and even Max Weber find positive treatments in Strauss's writings and courses. It is as indefensible to attribute what Strauss says about Plato or Alfarabi to Strauss himself as to do so in the case of Strauss's claims about Halevi (an antiphilosophic thinker), Machiavelli (the founder of modern thought), Weber (the father of sociological positivism), or Heidegger (the originator of radical historicism).

The second point which must be considered is Strauss's specific approach to the relationship between philosophy and politics. Strauss was very suspicious and critical of the role of philosophy in practical politics, and used as his model Plato, whose method he described in these terms:

Plato composed his writings in such a way as to prevent for all time their use as authoritative texts. His dialogues supply us not so much with an answer to the riddle of being as with a most articulate "imitation" of that riddle. His teaching can never become the subject of indoctrination. In the last analysis his writings cannot be used for any purpose other than for philosophizing. In particular, no social order and no party which ever existed or which ever will exist can rightfully claim Plato as its patron.[143]

Strauss did not, of course, write dialogues, but he employed a variety of techniques for creating a sort of dialogue in his texts, behind which he

---

[142] Leo Strauss, "Jerusalem and Athens: Some Preliminary Reflections," in *Studies on Platonic Political Philosophy*, ed. Thomas L. Pangle (Chicago: University of Chicago Press, 1983), 168; Leo Strauss, *1963 Spring Course on Vico Offered at the University of Chicago*, ed. Wayne Ambler (Chicago: Leo Strauss Center, 2016), 59 (Session 3, October 7, 1963); Heinrich Meier, *Leo Strauss and the Theologico-Political Problem*, trans. Marcus Brainard (Cambridge: Cambridge University Press, 2006), 16.

[143] Leo Strauss, "On a New Interpretation of Plato's Political Philosophy," *Social Research* 13, no. 3 (1946): 351.

stands without taking a definite stance on the ideas advanced. In his writings, everything seems preliminary. It is often difficult to say who is talking in the text; an idea stated on one page is rejected in the next and it is replaced by another in the next chapter. It is therefore not surprising that there are sharp disagreements among Strauss's readers even about his views on the most prominent aspects of his thought.[144] It seems that just like Plato, anyone who tries to provide an exposition of Strauss's views "can easily be refuted and confounded by passages in [his writings] which contradict his exposition."[145] Strauss himself disappears in his commentaries; it is even an exaggeration to say that his voice is less "audible than that of the writers he discusses"; he seems entirely absent.[146] His writings resemble mazes which, once in a while, one believes one has escaped, codes which one believes one has eventually cracked; but in the end it is difficult to find Strauss's own personal views. Strauss followed these methods precisely to avoid the attribution of a specific political teaching to him. Strauss is often described as an anti-modern thinker, and there is certainly a very critical aspect in his treatment of modern political thought. His general view on the modern liberal regimes, especially on the American regime and its founding principles and documents is, however, a controversial issue. This issue has also been studied many times by Strauss's scholars, who have tried to discover Strauss's view of the modern liberal American regime, which seems entirely incompatible with Strauss's preference for ancient political thought; the main difficulty is that, despite his critical views, Strauss seemed to have appreciated the American regime because of its free institutions and achievements.[147] Such questions regarding Strauss's thought are many and certainly complex. As we shall see, the general skeptical philosophic approach which Strauss recommends in some of his writings makes it even doubtful that a straightforward answer to them is easy to provide.

Second Group. The writings of the scholars who have sympathetic views of Strauss's scholarship on Islamic philosophy are few but also of high quality. Some of these writings deal mainly with the biographical aspects of Strauss's interest in Islamic philosophy: as an example, we

---

[144] For an overview of some debates see Zuckert and Zuckert, *Leo Strauss and the Problem of Political Philosophy*, 311–38.

[145] Strauss, "On a New Interpretation of Plato's Political Philosophy," 16.

[146] Leo Strauss, *What Is Political Philosophy? And Other Studies* (Glencoe: Free Press, 1959), 265; Strauss, *Gesammelte Schriften. Band 3*, 545 (Letter to Jacob Klein, 20 January 1938); Lampert, "Strauss's Recovery of Esotericism," 64.

[147] For a good summary of difficulties see Zuckert and Zuckert, *The Truth about Leo Strauss*, 58–80.

can mention two articles by Steven Harvey, to which we referred previously.[148] Also important is another paper by Rémi Brague which emphasizes the importance of Islamic thought in Strauss's intellectual project.[149] A general intellectual biography of Strauss by Daniel Tanguay is another important work which emphasizes the central importance of Alfarabi in Strauss's scholarship.[150] A more substantial and very valuable contribution by Joshua Parens is a collection of articles on different aspects of Strauss's writings on medieval political philosophy.[151] Despite the importance of these contributions, from which I have greatly benefitted and to which I refer whenever suitable, the current study has a different character and deals with Strauss's contribution to the study of Islamic philosophy in a way which is different from these thought-provoking studies. This will be discussed in the next section, dealing with the aim of this volume.

THE AIM OF THIS STUDY

As we saw, much of the resistance to Strauss's writings in general and to his studies on Islamic philosophy in particular are born out of strong disagreement with the scholarly worth of his thesis on esotericism, as well as suspicions about Strauss's motives regarding the practice of esoteric writing and reading in his own works. On the question of esotericism as a historical phenomenon and esoteric reading as a legitimate and scientifically justifiable method of historical research, as was said before, I cannot say much in this study, and refer readers to other detailed discussions.[152] In what is of concern for this study, I

---

[148] Harvey, "Leo Strauss' Early Interest in the Islamic Falāsifa"; Harvey, "Leo Strauss's Developing Interest in Alfarabi."

[149] Brague, "Athens, Jerusalem, Mecca."

[150] Tanguay, *Leo Strauss. An Intellectual Biography*. See also Tanguay, "How Strauss Read Farabi's Summary of Plato's 'Laws.'"

[151] Joshua Parens, *Leo Strauss and the Recovery of Medieval Political Philosophy* (Rochester: University of Rochester Press, 2016). See also Parens, "Escaping the Scholastic Paradigm."

[152] I should only add that although I find such discussions of immense importance, I do believe that Strauss's esotericism is yet to receive the philosophic treatment which it deserves and there are some fundamental aspects of Strauss's thesis which remain mostly unexplored. What I am pointing at will be discussed implicitly here in Chapter 3, dedicated to interpretation of Strauss's essay titled "Fārābī's *Plato*." I postpone a more satisfactory treatment to a later study which I hope to finish in the future. In the meantime, a good treatment of this question can be found in the following: Heinrich Meier, "The History of Philosophy and the Intention of the Philosopher. Reflections on Leo Strauss," in *Leo Strauss and the Theologico-Political Problem*, trans. Marcus Brainard (Cambridge: Cambridge University Press, 2006), 53–75.

should only mention a specific point: as was said previously, Strauss's thesis on esotericism does not concern itself exclusively with protective esotericism, which has as its objective the protection of philosopher against persecution, nor is it only about esotericism practiced for the sake of shielding society against the so-called "dangerous truths."[153] This is while these two types of esotericism, because of the commonsensical aspect of the first and controversial character of the second, have received the lion share of attention in the literature. I believe, however, that the third kind of esotericism, namely pedagogical esotericism, has a much more fundamental importance for Strauss. This should have been obvious for those readers in search of Strauss's esoteric political teaching, because speaking of esotericism, Strauss explains that those two types of esoteric writing which exist for the sake of the protection of the philosopher and the protection of society were composed exclusively in societies in which "an era of persecution" reigned and where "freedom of inquiry, and of publication of all results of inquiry" were "not guaranteed as a basic right."[154] Such societies are fundamentally different than the contemporary liberal societies in which Strauss wrote. On the basis of this observation, Strauss addressed as clearly as possible, the obvious issue: "one may very well raise the question of what use it [esotericism] could be in a truly liberal society."[155]

Strauss's answer to this question is based on his view of philosophy and the philosophic life: Strauss subscribed strongly to the idea of philosophic life in which philosophy is not meant as a set of doctrines or teachings but rather a way of life dedicated to the search for truth. In this view, education plays a central role, because to teach philosophy is not to transmit ideas or teachings from the teacher to the student, but rather to train the student to philosophize on his own. This mainly happens in a one-on-one conversation between the philosopher and potential candidates for pursuing the philosophic life, depicted beautifully in Socratic dialogues.[156] But in the absence of philosopher-teachers who, according to Strauss, come very rarely in history, it is their writings which play the role of intermediary. Pedagogic esoteric writing has the function of imitating the dialogue between philosopher and a student

---

153 Strauss, "On a Forgotten Kind of Writing," 221.
154 Strauss, *Persecution and the Art of Writing*, 1952, 32, 36.
155 Strauss, *Persecution and the Art of Writing*, 1952, 36.
156 Leo Strauss, *The City and Man* (Charlottesville: The University of Virginia Press, 1964), 53; Brague, "Athens, Jerusalem, Mecca," 244.

of philosophy who follows the esoteric clues of the writer in the search of the esoteric teaching of the text. According to Strauss, the esoteric writers had recourse to the most complex forms of the art of writing to *intentionally* make their teaching only accessible to a select group of close, careful, determined, and untiring readers, who are their real students. It is through thinking out the problems, contradictions, half arguments, slight changes in the enumerations, repetitions, and such esoteric clues that the student is trained in the ways of philosophic thinking.[157]

Regardless of what one might think of Strauss's historical claims about the esoteric character of the writings of past philosophers, Strauss himself followed, as we shall see in the commentaries of this book, such a procedure in his writings. Strauss is an exceedingly careful writer who demands of us to read him with care – a demand that, if not met, would not reveal the most important messages contained in his writings. One of Strauss's most careful readers once confessed that if one reads Strauss's writings "as one reads a treatise," their contents will be "guarded by seven seals." A conventional reading of Strauss's works "provides us with a few arid generalizations that look like oases in a sandy desert."[158] This judgment about the difficulties of Strauss's writings is not limited to the sympathetic readers of Strauss: commenting on one of Strauss's perhaps less complex writings, James E. Montgomery confesses that, although "Strauss writes, on the whole, clear English and at first blush seems not to pose the reader any problems of verbal impenetrability," he has found it "it easier to read Derrida and Foucault, for example, than to read Strauss," that "even after repeated reading," Montgomery has found it "very difficult to understand the ideas which inform what it is that he seems to be saying."[159] If one reads many of Strauss's carefully-crafted writings as one reads ordinary and straightforward academic texts, they would provide one only with a few generalizations which lack the complexity of his observations and statements which are only dis-covered through an intensive esoteric reading of his texts. Taking into account the complexities of Strauss's art of writing requires a different way of reading and a different way of presenting his writings. What is

---

[157] Strauss, *Persecution and the Art of Writing*, 1952, 35–37; Strauss, *The City and Man*, 54; Arthur M. Melzer, "On the Pedagogical Motive for Esoteric Writing," *The Journal of Politics* 69, no. 4 (2007): 1023.

[158] Allan Bloom, "Leo Strauss: September 20, 1899–October 18, 1973," *Political Theory* 2, no. 4 (1974): 390.

[159] Montgomery, "Leo Strauss and the Alethiometer," 287–88, 298.

above all necessary is to pay attention to the complexities and subtleties of Strauss's writings and his meticulous style.

Because of the mostly negative reception of Strauss's scholarship, explaining this aspect of Strauss's writings has fallen mostly on the shoulder of scholars more sympathetic to Strauss's general intellectual project. Aware of the esoteric aspect of Strauss's writings, these scholars have produced important commentaries through reading Strauss in the meticulous way that he read others.[160] There is also a need for such commentaries, specifically on Strauss's writings on Islamic political thought, which this volume wishes to satisfy. The rare studies that do pay attention to Strauss's writings on Islamic thought, mentioned as the second group, while being very valuable contributions, are deficient in some respects: to begin with, these studies do not take into account several important unpublished manuscripts and only concentrate on Strauss's published writings. Apart from the light that these unpublished writings shed on Strauss's published works on Islamic thought, in these manuscripts, one finds Strauss's reflections on a variety of texts on which he never published anything. Consequently, a proper presentation, interpretation, and understanding of these writings are necessary if we are to have an adequate picture of Strauss's interest in Islamic thought. Furthermore, and more importantly, the dominant trend among Strauss scholars has been to emphasize Strauss's writings on European thought and Judaism. This is particularly the case in the discussion of Strauss's writings on Islamic thought, which tend to be read mainly through the lens of scholars' own concern with Jewish thought. This, of course, is understandable in view of the fact that Strauss scholarship has been for a long time plagued by controversial issues which kept most scholars away from Strauss in general, and few people who, because of their training, background, and connection with the Straussian "school," showed interest in Strauss's writings tended to concentrate either on the larger picture or only reacted to Strauss's writings as far as they had an overlap

---

[160] Among the most important examples is the following collection of essays: Rafael Major, ed., *Leo Strauss's Defense of the Philosophic Life: Reading "What Is Political Philosophy?"* (Chicago and London: University of Chicago Press, 2013). For other notable examples see Meier, *Carl Schmitt and Leo Strauss*; Meier, *Leo Strauss and the Theologico-Political Problem*; Heinrich Meier, *Political Philosophy and the Challenge of Revealed Religion*, trans. Robert Berman (Chicago and London: University of Chicago Press, 2017); Ying Zhang, "The Guide to The Guide: Some Observations on 'How To Begin To Study The Guide of the Perplexed,'" *Interpretation: A Journal of Political Philosophy* 46, no. 3 (2020): 533–65.

with their own intellectual projects. Understandable as the generalist approach to Strauss's writings is, there is a place to concentrate exclusively on Strauss's writings on Islamic philosophy. These writings also have an internal coherence which justifies their treatment independently of European and Jewish thought. In view of these points, the present study concentrates on Strauss's works on medieval Islamic thought while taking into account two recently discovered transcripts, interpreted in the first two chapters of this volume. In my interpretation of Strauss's writings, as can be seen above all in the third and fourth chapters of this volume, I will pay close attention to the esoteric character of Strauss's works and take the details of his writing into account.

Averroes between Platonic Philosophy
and the Sharī'a

Surveying Leo Strauss's writings as a whole, one receives the impression that in view of the great diversity of his intellectual production – writings which mainly consist of commentaries on authors as different as Xenophon and Edmund Burke, Thucydides and Alfarabi, Maimonides and John Locke, Judah Halevi and Machiavelli – Strauss was an author with a surprising variety of interests and intellectual projects. His writings are so diverse that they seem to resist any kind of categorization under a single heading. Strauss, however, once famously spoke about the internal unity of his writings and intellectual project as a whole: in the 1964 preface to the German edition of *The Political Philosophy of Thomas Hobbes,* he claims that throughout the years "the theologico-political problem has ... remained *the* central theme" of his whole intellectual odyssey, the problem which most clearly gives unity to the plurality of his writings.[1] Yet it would be a mistake to believe that this statement of Strauss clarifies the basic aspects of his thought to the common reader. In fact, the common reader and the more initiated are in the same boat in this regard. There are no straightforward answers regarding what the theologico-political problem actually is, in what sense it is the main axis of Strauss's writings, and even what Strauss's position is on this problem.

Let us for the moment concentrate on what the theologico-political problem is. Strauss also refers to "theologico-political" as a general term in a footnote of his 1935 book *Philosophy and Law,* a statement which

---

[1] Leo Strauss, "The 1965 Preface to Hobbes Politische Wissenschaft," *Interpretation: A Journal of Political Philosophy* 8, no. 1 (January 1979): 1 (GS III:8); Meier, *Leo Strauss and the Theologico-Political Problem,* 3ff.

might provide us with clarifying information on the meaning of this term. In this footnote, rather than referring to the "theologico-political problem," Strauss speaks first of the "theologico-political treatise" (in scare quotes) and then clarifies the meaning of these scare quotes by speaking of "the theologico-political treatises of the seventeenth century, especially those of Hobbes and Spinoza."[2] In this way, Strauss draws our attention to a rather obvious point: the term "theologico-political" is borrowed from the title of Spinoza's famous book and is employed for characterizing a series of similar writings – the most impressive examples being those of Spinoza and Hobbes. In other words, for Strauss, the "theologico-political treatise" is a specific genre of writings appearing in the early modern period. It seems that the main theme of such treatises, as Strauss understands them, is explained by the subtitle of Spinoza's treatise, the subtitle which claims that through his book the author intends to show that the "freedom of philosophizing" is compatible with and even contributes to "piety" and the "peace of the republic."[3] From Spinoza's statement one can therefore conclude that the theologico-political problem is about the problematic relationship between the element of philosophy and two other elements, namely religion and politics. This preliminary hypothesis points to two other common issues at the center of Strauss's thought: (a) The irreducible conflict or eternal tug-of-war between Reason and Revelation or "Jerusalem and Athens," and (b) the clash of politics and philosophy, or more concretely, the conflict between the city and the philosopher. The theologico-political problem seems to be the synthetic formulation of these two problems: it synthesizes the conflict of Reason and Revelation with the clash of philosophy and politics.

The theologico-political problem has several levels of meaning, consisting of outer and deeper ones. At its most basic level, it points to the fact that religion and politics, in their relationship with philosophy, are two sides of the same coin. For Strauss, philosophy and philosophers are above all concerned with one fundamental question: How should one live? This amounts to asking the question of the best way of life. As man is a political animal living with other human beings in a political

---

[2] Strauss, *Philosophy and Law*, 138n2 (GS II:31n2).

[3] The full title is as follows: "Theological-Political Treatise Containing several discourses which demonstrate that freedom to philosophize may not only be allowed without danger to piety and the stability of the republic but cannot be refused without destroying the peace of the republic and piety itself": Benedict de Spinoza, *Theological-Political Treatise*, trans. Jonathan Israel and Michael Silverthorne (Cambridge: Cambridge University Press, 2007).

community, and because this question is addressed and answered by the authoritative traditions of political societies, the theologico-political problem is essentially a political question.[4] But it is also a theological question in that, in all premodern societies, the most authoritative tradition that answers this question is the religious tradition of those societies. In other words, political society is essentially a theologico-political institution.[5] Because for Strauss free thought and critiques of common authoritative answers are the most distinctive characteristics of philosophy, and because he did not believe in the possibility of a synthesis of Reason and Revelation, he therefore argued for the strict separation of religion from philosophy and claimed that there is always a fundamental tension between the two. Philosophy not only calls any authoritative answer into question, but also provides its own answers to the question of the best way of life; therefore, according to Strauss, philosophy necessarily enters into conflict with the sacred tradition of the community and with the theologico-political front as a whole.[6] In other words, the conflict of philosophy and politics is a subsidiary aspect of the conflict of Reason and Revelation, but at the same time, religion and politics somehow form a common front. The perfect manifestation of this synthesis of religion and politics is the concept of law, or more precisely the divine law (*theios nomos*); hence the title of Strauss's book, *Philosophy and Law*, is the theologico-political problem expressed in other terms.[7] Judaism and Islam, the religions of law (torah and sharīʿa) rather than Christianity, the religion of faith, are the manifestation of this close connection between religion and politics. Furthermore, it is in Judaism and Islam that philosophy is entirely in its element, where the theologico-political problem exists in its purest form.[8]

---

[4] Strauss, "Fârâbî's Plato," 366; Leo Strauss, "Reason and Revelation (1948)," in *Leo Strauss and the Theologico-Political Problem*, ed. Heinrich Meier, trans. Marcus Brainard (Cambridge: Cambridge University Press, 2006), 146.

[5] Modern society differs from premodern society in this respect because its authoritative tradition is not religious. Strauss saw the recovery of the premodern perspective, which is the world of "the natural understanding, the natural world, or the world of common sense," as distinguished from our philosophic and scientific world, as the proper starting point of inquiry. The element of the natural world of the city is religion. Strauss, *Natural Right and History*, 77–81, 83ff.

[6] Strauss, *Natural Right and History*, 74–75; Strauss, "Jerusalem and Athens," 149–50; Strauss, "Progress or Return?," 246; Strauss and Voegelin, *Faith and Political Philosophy*, 78 (Letter to Eric Voegelin on February 25, 1951).

[7] Meier, *Leo Strauss and the Theologico-Political Problem*, 7.

[8] Strauss, *Persecution and the Art of Writing*, 1952, 9–10; Strauss, "How to Study Medieval Philosophy," 333–34.

Concern with the theologico-political problem, especially from the point of view of the conflict of philosophy and religion, is not a novel issue in the intellectual history of the West. This issue, viewed from the perspective of Islamic philosophy, immediately reminds one of the Averroistic controversy, a European phenomenon occupying the minds of many authors for several centuries. The Averroistic controversy and Strauss's engagement with the theologico-political problem seem rather close; they belong to each other. But considering these obvious affinities, a question comes to mind: If the theologico-political problem is the axis of Strauss's oeuvre, and considering the special place of Islam and Islamic philosophy in Strauss's thought and writing, why did Strauss never write anything substantial on Averroes or Averroism? It is true that Strauss was preoccupied with Averroes in several of his writings, found his works essential for understanding the classical conception of natural right, and looked at the Averroism of the Renaissance as one of the central elements of modern political philosophy, inaugurated by Machiavelli.[9] However, apart from short discussions, Strauss did not publish an independent study on Averroes's ideas.[10] What can explain this absence in Strauss's writings?

AVERROES AND THE THEOLOGICO-POLITICAL PROBLEM

Averroes occupies a unique place in the history of Western philosophy. Although the writings of many Islamic medieval philosophers were mostly unexplored in the West until the beginning of the twentieth century, Averroes has been a major figure in Europe since the Middle Ages, and the phenomenon of Averroism has been a part of the common European intellectual heritage for centuries. During this time, one of the most enduring and widely held views of Averroes has been that he was a fierce enemy of every religion. As Strauss indicates, this view was partially rejected by the classic nineteenth-century study by Ernest Renan, in which Renan questioned what he called "la légende d'Averroès." Renan tended to depict Averroes's rationalism and Islamic beliefs as two independent elements that do not directly conflict. Founding his view

---

[9] Strauss, *Thoughts on Machiavelli*, 175, 202–3, 303n24, 333n64; Leo Strauss, "What Is Political Philosophy?," in *What Is Political Philosophy? And Other Studies* (Glencoe: Free Press, 1959), 41; Strauss, "Niccolò Machiavelli," 314; Strauss, *Spinoza's Critique of Religion*, 47–49 (GS I:76–79); Strauss, *Natural Right and History*, 158ff.

[10] Strauss, *Philosophy and Law*, 81–89 (GS II:69–75).

of Averroism on this strategy of separation, Strauss observes, Renan succeeded in transforming Averroes into "a loyal, and even a believing, Muslim."[11] Renan shared, however, the basic presuppositions of historicism, and therefore saw in each system of thought the reflection of the prejudices and common beliefs of a historical period – the perspective which made his claim about Averroes's independence from the religious presuppositions of his time untenable.[12] In the generation after Renan, Léon Gauthier, although a critic of Renan, followed essentially the same path.[13] Gauthier's main claim was based on the idea that Islam is a religion without substantial doctrinal content. In Gauthier's eyes, this characteristic of Islam gave Averroes considerable latitude in avoiding a direct clash between philosophical ideas and Islamic beliefs. Gauthier saw therefore Averroes's philosophy as "un rationalisme sans réserve" which was wholly compatible with traditional Islamic beliefs.[14] Other scholars avoided Gauthier's unsatisfactory half-measures and fully embraced historicism by claiming that Islamic philosophy is a manifestation of Islamic ideas in the language of Greek philosophy. From this perspective, there cannot be a conflict between the philosophy of Falāsīfa in general – or with Averroes's philosophy in particular – on the one hand, and Islamic beliefs on the other.[15]

---

[11] Strauss, *Persecution and the Art of Writing*, 1952, 27; Ernest Renan, *Averroès et l'Averroïsme: Essai Historique*, 3rd edition (Paris: Michel Lévy Frères, 1866), 164, 293, 297.

[12] Renan, *Averroès et l'Averroïsme: Essai Historique*, v–vii.

[13] Léon Gauthier, *La Théorie d'Ibn Rochd (Averroès) sur les Rapports de la Religion et de la Philosophie* (Paris: Ernest Leroux, 1909), 177ff. This did not escape the attention of Strauss: Strauss, *Persecution and the Art of Writing*, 1952, 27n6; Strauss, *Philosophy and Law*, 143n19 (GS II:19).

[14] Léon Gauthier, "Scolastique musulmane et scolastique chrétienne," *Revue d'Histoire de la Philosophie* 2 (1928): 253; Gauthier, *La Théorie d'Ibn Rochd*, 108. The harmonizing solution is understandably popular among Averroes's readers; after all this is what Averroes advertises in his own name. See Majid Fakhry, "Philosophy and Scripture in the Theology of Averroes," *Medieval Studies* 30 (1968): 78–89; Oliver Leaman, "Is Averroes an Averroist?," in *Averroismus im Mittelalter und in der Renaissance*, ed. Friedrich Niewöhner and Loris Sturlese (Zurich: Spur, 1994), 9–22; Diego R. Sarrió, "The Philosopher as the Heir of the Prophets: Averroes's Islamic Rationalism," *Al-Qanṭara* 36, no. 1 (2015): 45–68.

[15] See August Ferdinand Mehren, "Etudes sur la Philosophie d'Averroès concernant son rapport avec celle d'Avicenne et Gazzali," *Le Muséon* VII (1888): 618; Max Horten, *Die Hauptlehren des Averroes nach seiner Schrift: Die Widerlegung des Gazali* (Bonn: Marcus und Webers Verlag, 1913), iv; Asìn Palacio, "El Averroismo teologico de Santo Tomas de Aquino," in *Homenaje a D. Francisco Codera en su jubilación del profesorado: Estudios de erudición oriental*, ed. Eduardo Saavedra (Zaragoza: Escar, 1904), 272. See also Muhsin Mahdi, "Averroes on Divine Law and Human Wisdom," in *Ancients and*

It is not an exaggeration to say that the problem of the conflict between Islamic philosophy and Islamic tenets today is a rather outmoded subject of study and is not as much addressed in the literature as it was in the past. This lack of interest in the study of the conflictual relationship between philosophy and religion is not limited to scholars of Islamic philosophy. Speaking about the lack of interest in the strict distinction between philosophy and religion in Western thought, and the predominant tendency to harmonize and to reconcile them, Strauss observed that "we do not like the suggestion that we have to make an irrevocable choice between two things which for all we know are both of supreme goodness or beauty." According to Strauss's diagnosis, scholars feel that a strict separation between Reason and Revelation would lead to the "suggestion that all our actions or thoughts may ultimately be based on a *blind* choice, on a leap into the dark." Strauss sees here a kind of psychological urge at work which tries to save us from the unpleasant feeling of "humiliation," of the sharp distinction which "offends human nature." This psychological urge has led to efforts of harmonization and synthesis, which "allow us to believe that we are the masters of the situation."[16] The lack of interest in this subject today may be also traced to the recent transformation of religion into a vehicle of self-expression and cultural identification, which is essentially different from a highly intellectual understanding of religion as a system of orthodox doctrines and beliefs which can be fruitfully compared with a specific system of philosophical doctrines. As we shall see, Strauss saw no difficulty in making such radical but fruitful comparisons between philosophical doctrines and religious beliefs.

Moderns: Essays on the Tradition of Political Philosophy in Honor of Leo Strauss, ed. Joseph Cropsey (New York and London: Basic Books, 1964), 114–17; Michel Allard, "Le Rationalisme d'Averroès d'après une étude sur la création," *Bulletin d'études orientales* 14 (1952): 7–9. As examples of more recent approaches see Anna Akasoy, "Was Ibn Rushd an Averroist? The Problem, the Debate, and Its Philosophical Implications," in *Renaissance Averroism and Its Aftermath: Arabic Philosophy in Early Modern Europe*, ed. Anna Akasoy and Guido Giglioni (Dordrecht: Springer, 2013), 321–47; Oliver Leaman, *Averroes and His Philosophy* (Oxford: Clarendon Press, 1988), 179–97.

[16] Leo Strauss, "Jerusalem and Athens (1946)" (The New School for Social Research, November 1946), 2. I am familiar with this unpublished typescript thanks to Heinrich Meier who shared it with the participants of his course entitled "Jerusalem and Athens" given at Ludwig Maximilian University of Munich in 2018 and at the University of Chicago in 2020. Strauss's lecture was presented on November 13, 1946, when he spoke in the General Seminar at the New School for Social Research in New York. See Meier, *Leo Strauss and the Theologico-Political Problem*, xvi.

More specifically among contemporary scholars of Islamic philosophy, the lack of interest in the question of the conflict between philosophy and religion has also a supplementary cause: the awareness and critique of some problematic aspects of Western scholarship on Islam. Many feel that preoccupation with the problem of Reason and Revelation comes too close to the biased views sometimes expressed in the writings of the older generation of scholars, who claimed that there is something fundamentally antirationalist in the Muslim mind which cannot separate itself from religious beliefs. There is much truth to this critique of so-called Orientalism: it is unfortunately not difficult to find examples of such views in the writings of some of the luminaries of the study of Islamic philosophy in the West.[17] Studies documenting a conflict between Islamic philosophy and Islam seem like a close relative of such biased views, and one might believe that they provide raw material for claiming that there is something particularly irrational in Islamic civilization. Although one is justified in being wary of drawing wrong conclusions from the study of the conflict of Islamic philosophy and religion, however, Strauss's lack of interest in this problem in the writings of Averroes is not related to this critique.[18] But if the absence of a substantial discussion of Averroism in Strauss's writings cannot be explained by fear of decisionism, new perspective on religion as a source of identity, or the problem of orientalism, how can one explain it? One should consider two points.

First, the question of the conflict between Averroes's philosophical views and traditional Muslim doctrines in particular, as well as to religious ideas common to the so-called Abrahamic religions in general, is mainly studied by scholars through the lens of some metaphysical views

---

[17] The classic text of this approach is of course Edward Said's book on "Orientalism." Edward Said, *Orientalism: Western Conceptions of the Orient* (London: Penguin Books, 2003). Said provides ample evidence for the existence of such biases. For a moderate and sympathetic examination of this phenomenon see Mahdi, "Orientalism and the Study of Islamic Philosophy."

[18] As I explained in the Introduction, Strauss's writings, as far as I can see, show no sign of bigotry or bias toward Muslim thinkers. Everywhere one can observe a deep appreciation for the philosophical talents of Muslim philosophers in his writings. In fact, Strauss has a much higher regard for Islamic philosophy than Christian philosophy, and for him even Jewish philosophy is in a sense highly dependent on Islamic philosophy. See Strauss, "Eine vermißte Schrift Farâbîs"; Strauss, *Persecution and the Art of Writing*, 1952, 11, 21, 95–97; Clark A. Merrill, "Leo Strauss's Indictment of Christian Philosophy," *The Review of Politics* 62, no. 1 (2000): 77–105. As we saw, this has not prevented several scholars from accusing Strauss of having orientalist biases. See also Mohammad Azadpur, "Is 'Islamic Philosophy' Islamic?," in *Voices of Change*, ed. Vincent Cornell and Omid Safi, vol. 5 (Westport: Praeger, 2007), 23–41.

attributed to Averroes. Examples include the idea of the unicity of the intellect for all human beings and the eternity of the world. In the Muslim world, the adherence of Greek philosophers to the idea of the eternity of the world was seen as incompatible with the Muslim belief that the world was created; the Greek understanding of the divine as mostly a passive being which plays very little part in the world differed from the active conception of the Islamic god who punished and rewarded believers for their actions and was fully aware of the smallest things happening in the world. Similarly, the mainly intellectual Greek understanding of the after-life did not correspond to the Islamic conception of the bodily rewards and punishments in the afterlife. These and similar issues were promi-nently emphasized in the writings of those who had important objections to Muslim Aristotelians, most famously in the writings of al-Ghazali. Now, Strauss avoided this field of speculative philosophy throughout his intellectual career and instead concentrated on practical or, more pre-cisely, political philosophy. One explanation for this is to view Strauss's approach as a result of some personal choice or division of academic labor: his field was simply not speculative philosophy, and therefore he avoided the discussion of Averroism, which was mainly studied from the perspective of speculative philosophy. It is unclear, however, whether Strauss's practical orientation does not have some philosophical justifica-tion. For instance, Strauss sometimes claims that political philosophy is more fundamental than speculative philosophy, hence his bewildering claim that political philosophy is properly speaking the first philosophy par excellence.[19] In other words, Strauss's outward lack of interest in speculative philosophy seems to have deep theoretical roots and cannot be explained as a simple division of academic labor. What might better explain Strauss's lack of interest in the traditional debate on Averroism is the fact that Strauss tended toward an understanding of philosophy which is at its core fundamentally skeptical, a zetetic enterprise free of definite theoretical positions and doctrines.[20] His preoccupation with the conflict between philosophy and religion was therefore bound to be less about doctrines and differed from the usual treatment of the Averroistic controversy as a mainly speculative debate about the adherence of phi-losophers to specific metaphysical doctrines and their compatibility with religious beliefs.

---

[19] Strauss, *The City and Man*, 20.
[20] Strauss, "Fârâbî's Plato," 393; Strauss, "The Law of Reason in the Kuzari," 105n29; Strauss, "Reason and Revelation (1948)," 146, 148.

Second, the practical orientation of Strauss's perspective should be considered alongside Strauss's view of Islam as a religion of law. Strauss saw the primacy of law as the most distinctive characteristic of Islam (and Judaism). In the case of Islam, he looked at sharīʿa or Islamic Law, a law regulating men's private and public lives alike, as the most prominent aspect of Islam which must be taken into account while discussing the theologico-political problem. Islam, being a religion of law, has a decisively political character, and this means that, although adherence to a set of doctrines or beliefs has some importance, the law and its political character are decidedly more prominent. The theoretical effects of this distinctive characteristic of Islam can be seen in the apologetics of the Muslim philosophers against the traditional accusations of heresy and apostasy. Reading these apologetical writings, one often receives the impression that the debate between the philosophical and anti-philosophical parties is a mainly hair-splitting affair without clear lines of demarcation between the two camps. Philosophers always found some subtle interpretation of the philosophic ideas that sounded compatible with some interpretation of Islamic orthodoxy. What particularly contributed to and helped the apologetic enterprise of the philosophical party was the fact that the Islamic belief system itself is rather ambiguous on major abstract, theoretical questions at the heart of the controversy, leaving considerable room for harmonizing philosophy with some understanding of Islam. From the point of view of purely theoretical questions, the rather limited and ambiguous character of Islamic dogma made the conflict between Islamic beliefs and Greek philosophy less pronounced than, for instance, the conflict between Greek philosophy and Christianity. On the contrary, the conflict became more pronounced when the questions became more practical and touched on the precepts of the Islamic Law. It is one thing to claim that some subtle interpretation of the eternity of the world is compatible with some understanding of the Qur'ān, but quite another to, following Plato, advise that women should wrestle naked alongside men in the best regime![21]

---

[21] This seems to be Averroes's suggestion: Averroes, *On Plato's "Republic,"* 59 (Rosenthal 54.17). For another example see Averroes's discussion of the practical effects of the belief in the bodily character of the afterlife. Averroes, *Tahafut Al-Tahafut*, 359–62 (Bouygues 581–84). Significantly, it is here, when a theoretical question has practical effects, that one encounters difficulties in justifying Averroes's supposedly orthodox religious beliefs. See Leaman, *Averroes and His Philosophy*, 94–96. Tamer has also observed this relationship between Averroes and Strauss: Tamer, *Islamische Philosophie und die Krise der Moderne*, 47–48.

The prominence of law or the practical aspect of Islam would have a further consequence: if law is much more prominent in Islam than its dogmas, and if the conflict between philosophy and Islam is more pronounced in practical philosophy than in metaphysics or psychology, it makes more sense to address the theologico-political problem through a study of Islamic *political* philosophy. In other words, this perspective justifies more intensive engagement with Islamic political philosophy and what Falāsīfa said and thought about politics. This path of inquiry is precisely the one followed by Strauss in his studies on Islamic philosophy, in which he concentrated exclusively on Islamic political philosophy rather than on more speculative aspects of the writings of Muslim thinkers. In the case of Averroes also, the precedence of practical philosophy should lead to an increase in importance of Averroes's political writings, more specifically his most comprehensive statement on political philosophy, namely his commentary on Plato's *Republic* (hereafter, *Commentary*). That this perspective is also shared by Strauss is confirmed not only by his lack of interest in participating in the Averroistic controversy but also from a recently discovered transcript which shows his interest in the political philosophy of Averroes: it seems that Strauss actually planned to write a study on Averroes's *Commentary*, but for some reason, partly discussed in the Introduction of this volume, did not.

Interestingly, this writing of Averroes is particularly suitable for the study of the theologico-political problem in Islamic philosophy from the point of view of practical philosophy, because Plato's *Republic* at least *seems* to be a radical political project.[22] Averroes's *Commentary* is the meeting place of a law-oriented revelation and a highly radical politico-philosophic project in the shape of a utopia. The presence of conflict between these two is nowhere more likely than here, because the *Republic* is itself Plato's most radical political work: unlike the other substantial political statement of Plato, namely the *Laws*, which mainly appears like a conservative political project with subtle philosophic undertones, the *Republic* is, or at least seems to be, consciously and conspicuously a radical project, so radical that even the literary participants of the dialogue themselves occasionally attest to the bewildering nature of Socrates's suggestions: when Socrates argues that women, whose Greek traditional

---

[22] Strauss claimed that Plato's *Republic* is not actually a practical proposal but rather a complex work which intends to raise doubts about the desirability as well as practicability of a best regime. The *Republic* is meant to convey "the broadest and deepest analysis of political idealism ever made." Strauss, *The City and Man*, 127.

virtue was to not be even heard, should begin exercising and ruling alongside men and wrestle naked the interlocutors express their unease.[23] The
view of women in Islamic Law was not much different from that of the
Greeks, and one can therefore imagine similar reactions from the Muslim
readers of the dialogue. In other words, commenting on Plato's dialogue,
Averroes was not confronted with abstract ideas about the heavenly bodies or the faculties of the human soul, but with concrete considerations
dealing with the practices of daily life under an Islamic regime, which
from the orthodox perspective touch and clash with many well-known
precepts of Islamic Law. Surely there are also more abstract ideas in the
Republic and in Averroes's commentary on it – for example, the reli-
giously correct conception of the invisible beings and the moral status
of divine commands – which can be discussed from the point of view of
Islamic orthodoxy. But because of the legalistic character of Islam and
the ambiguous character of many of these issues in Islamic theology and
scripture, the most crucial aspects of Averroes's *Commentary* prove to be
those which touch on different aspects of Islamic Law, and this seems to
be one of the reasons why Strauss decided to comment on this particular
writing of Averroes.

With these considerations in mind, let us turn toward Strauss's interpretation of Averroes's *Commentary*. This interpretation is found in a
transcript of a collection of notes; until now no attempt has been made to
present its content.[24] In what follows, Strauss's notes will be interpreted
in an effort to reconstruct his understanding of Averroes's *Commentary*.
It is fortunate that this unique transcript has survived, as its content is

---

[23] Helen P. Foley, "Women in Greece," in *Civilization of the Ancient Mediterranean*, ed.
Michael Grant and Rachel Kitzinger, vol. 3 (New York: Scribner, 1988), 1302; Plato,
Republic 452a–c, 473c.

[24] These notes are found in Leo Strauss Papers, box 18, folder 17, Special Collections
Research Center, University of Chicago Library. References to Strauss's transcript are
here identified by SNA, followed by the page and paragraph numbers of the transcript. I
have greatly benefited from Ralph Lerner's excellent translation of *Commentary*. References to *Commentary* are identified by A, followed by Rosenthal's page numbers, also
indicated in the margins of Lerner's translation. Strauss's transcript cannot be precisely
dated, but as it refers to the page numbers of Rosenthal's 1956 edition, it must have been
written sometime after 1956. A passage also (SNA 6.14) seems to refer to Muhsin Mahdi's book on Ibn Khaldūn, published in 1957. Strauss might have even composed these
notes close to his death – we know that shortly before his death he read the transcript
of Lerner's translation of Averroes. See Averroes, *On Plato's "Republic,"* ix; Muhsin
Mahdi, *Ibn Khaldūn's Philosophy of History: A Study in the Philosophic Foundation of
the Science of Culture* (London: G. Allen and Unwin, 1957). Ralph Lerner generously
showed me Strauss's annotations on the manuscript of his translation.

of interest not only for understanding the evolution of Strauss's engagement with the theologico-political problem, but also for understanding Averroes's political philosophy. Scholars have paid very little attention to this writing of Averroes, although a reliable edition has been available for more than fifty years: since the publications of the 1956 Hebrew-English edition of E. I. J Rosenthal and the 1974 excellent English translation by Ralph Lerner, very few in-depth scholarly studies have been written on any aspect of this unique writing. Therefore, to borrow an expression of Averroes, "there is room for inquiry here": Strauss's transcript may help us become aware of many aspects of Averroes's treatise which are ignored in the literature.[25] One must bear in mind, however, that the interpretation of these notes is bound to be tentative, as well as selective. It is tentative because our source for Strauss's interpretation of Averroes's *Commentary* is a series of brief notes clearly produced for Strauss's own use: in most cases the notes are ambiguous and many of them are highly obscure. What I present as Strauss's meaning is based on my understanding of Strauss's larger project as well as these ambiguous remarks. This interpretation will be selective as well, because Strauss mentions many points in his notes, and they cannot all be discussed and interpreted in this chapter. I will therefore concentrate primarily on a few particularly prominent themes on which Strauss's perspective seems easier to establish.

---

[25] Although Averroes's *Commentary* is a substantial treatise, there has been no book-length study addressing many aspects of it. The most substantial effort at addressing different aspects of this treatise remains a study by Charles Butterworth: Charles E. Butterworth, "Philosophy, Ethics, and Virtuous Rule: A Study of Averroes' Commentary on Plato's 'Republic,'" *Cairo Papers on Social Science* IX (1986): 1–95. See also Charles E. Butterworth, "The Political Teaching of Averroes," *Arabic Sciences and Philosophy* 2 (1992): 187–202; Charles E. Butterworth, "New Light on the Political Philosophy of Averroes," in *Essays on Islamic Philosophy and Science*, ed. George F. Hourani (Albany: State University of New York Press, 1975), 118–27. Muhsin Mahdi, another star student of Strauss, has also dedicated a short study in French to this writing of Averroes, which draws attention to different aspects of the treatise while avoiding a substantial discussion of them. Muhsin Mahdi, "Alfarabi et Averroès. Remarques sur le commentaire d'Averroès sur la République de Platon," in *Multiple Averroès: Actes du Colloque International Organisé À l'Occasion du 850e anniversaire de la naissance d'Averroès*, ed. Jean Jolivet and Rachel Arié (Paris: Les Belles Lettres, 1978), 91–101. A more recent study by Catarina Belo addresses the question of women in Averroes's *Commentary*: Catarina Belo, "Some Considerations on Averroes' Views Regarding Women and Their Role in Society," *Journal of Islamic Studies* 20, no. 1 (December 6, 2008): 1–20. Another notable contribution is Christopher Colmo, "Wisdom and Power in Averroes' Commentary on Plato's Republic," *Maghreb Review* 40 (2015): 308–18.

APPROACHING ISLAMIC PHILOSOPHY

Before turning to Averroes's *Commentary* Strauss begins his notes by discussing the correct approach to the study of Islamic medieval philosophy. As these preparatory remarks form a major part of Strauss's unique approach to the study of Islamic medieval philosophy, this is where we should begin before turning to Strauss's notes on the *Commentary* proper. Strauss's question is: "How to approach Islamic (political) philosophy?" This question shows the overriding importance of methodological considerations of the interpretative work for Strauss. It is in a certain way 'easy' to answer a question like this, and as Strauss explains elsewhere, this question is often answered by some general observations about the importance of scholarly thoroughness, exactness, attention to detail, and so on.[26] Although these are very sound suggestions as far as they go, one must say that they are not enough; one needs more constructive suggestions to study medieval philosophy. Strauss therefore answers this question by invoking two points. The first is that we should not approach Islamic philosophy "from a modern point of view" (SNA 1.1). What Strauss is driving at is that the scholar of Islamic political philosophy should not *look down* on his subject matter, and should avoid following the common presumption of modern philosophical progressivism, which treats the views of the past primarily as cultural artifacts and takes for granted that modern insights are superior to the insights of the past thinkers. In other words, the student of medieval Islamic philosophy must have a keen historical sense. A modern scholar is always tempted to study the works of the past as containing knowledge inferior to the knowledge available to us. However, if he or she remains faithful to sound historical scholarship, he should not have any prejudice in favor of contemporary thought. For instance, in the progressive perspective, the knowledge of a twelfth-century philosopher ultimately relies on ideas about nature and politics which are wholly inadequate and false. This old philosopher is believed to have been stuck in obsolete Aristotelian science and adheres to a nonegalitarian political order incompatible with modern scientific and democratic beliefs. However true these observations might be, to acquire a truly historical knowledge of past thinkers one must abstract from one's modern presuppositions and try to understand that thinker on his own terms. To acquire a genuine historical understanding requires us to avoid trying to understand a philosopher better than he understood himself and instead to try to understand an earlier

[26] Strauss, "How to Study Medieval Philosophy," 321.

philosopher *exactly* as he understood himself. Any other approach would significantly distort our vision and would thwart a genuine understanding of the thinker. In other words, Strauss invites us to approach the works of Islamic philosophers philosophically and avoid treating them as the relics of some refuted system of thought, works only of purely *historical* interest. This methodological point is particularly crucial for scholars of Islamic philosophy because, as Strauss explains, scholars of Christian medieval philosophy already tend to believe in the philosophic relevance of their subject, while scholars of Islamic (and Jewish) philosophy show a particular tendency to treat medieval works as only of antiquarian interest.[27]

The second point Strauss mentions is that one should not interpret Islamic political philosophy through the lens of Christian medieval thought: one should not approach it "from the point of view of Christian scholasticism," for example, "assuming that Averroes is [an] Islamic Thomas Aquinas" (SNA 1.1). Islamic philosophy has its own distinctive characteristics. To understand the major distinguishing characteristics of Islamic philosophy, one must first address what Strauss considers a very common misconception: Islamic philosophy, still to a majority of scholars, "seems to be a combination of Aristotle and Neo-Platonism" (SNA 1.1). In other words, historians of Islamic philosophy often argue that there is an undeniable affinity between Neo-Platonism and Islamic thought. However, this understanding of Islamic philosophy as a form of Neo-Platonism is not as obviously true as one might believe. Let us take the example of Alfarabi, often called *the* founder of Islamic Neo-Platonism, who, supposedly more than any other thinker, is responsible for injecting Neo-Platonic ideas into Islamic philosophy.[28] It is true that some of Alfarabi's writings contain doctrines which can be called Neo-Platonic, and in fact he explicitly refers to perhaps the most important source of Neo-Platonic ideas in Islamic thought, namely the apocryphal *Theology of Aristotle*, which he introduces as a genuine work of Aristotle.[29] However, in his authoritative exposition of Aristotle's

---

[27] Strauss, *Persecution and the Art of Writing*, 1952, 8.
[28] For Alfarabi and Neo-Platonism see Parens, *Metaphysics as Rhetoric*, 17–29; Miriam Galston, "A Re-Examination of al-Farabi's Neoplatonism," *Journal of the History of Philosophy* 15, no. 1 (1977): 13–32; Fakhry, *Al-Farabi, Founder of Islamic Neoplatonism*; Henry Corbin, *Histoire de la Philosophie Islamique* (Paris: Gallimard, 1986), 226; Majid Fakhry, *A History of Islamic Philosophy* (London: Longman, 1983), 120.
[29] Alfarabi, "The Harmonization of the Two Opinions of the Two Sages. Plato the Divine and Aristotle," in *The Political Writings: "Selected Aphorisms" and Other Texts*, trans. Charles E. Butterworth (Ithaca and London: Cornell University Press, 2001), 155 (Fauzi 16a).

philosophy, Alfarabi does not even mention this Neo-Platonic work. Furthermore, Alfarabi's *"Philosophy of Plato* shows no trace of Neo-Platonism" (SNA 1.1). It is on this basis that Strauss, and some others, have questioned the idea that Alfarabi believed in the authenticity of *Theology* and subscribed to a Neo-Platonist reading of Plato.[30] But why does Alfarabi present this apocryphal work, which he supposedly knew to be inauthentic, as a genuine work of Aristotle? To answer this question, one must bear in mind that Alfarabi refers to this work to refute what he describes as the "base and reprehensible presumption about Aristotle" according to which "Aristotle is of the opinion that the world is eternal." Alfarabi reports that according to his adversaries, Aristotle, unlike Plato, does not believe that "the world is generated and has a maker." In response to this accusation, Alfarabi claims that whoever consults Aristotle's *Theology* will no longer doubt the compatibility of Aristotle's philosophy with traditional Islamic beliefs.[31] Other instances in which obvious Neo-Platonic themes and ideas are presented are found in those political writings of Alfarabi that enumerate 'the opinions' which the citizens of the virtuous regime must have. In other words, in Alfarabi's writings, classic Neo-Platonic ideas are to be found not in philosophic writings proper, but rather in those works which can be described as exoteric defenses of philosophy, or in political works describing the *beliefs* expected of the multitude of the virtuous city.[32]

But if, according to Strauss, Neo-Platonism is not the major characteristic of Islamic philosophy, what is? Strauss here draws our attention to the fact that Alfarabi "is much closer to Cicero than to Plotinus" because he tends to present his philosophy in a radically political framework. In other words, contrary to metaphysical Neo-Platonism, Alfarabi's philosophy is highly political.[33] Strauss is here taking a position very much against the scholarly consensus: to look at the politics of Falāsīfa as an appendage of speculative philosophy was and remains a rather common

---

[30] Strauss, "Fârâbî's Plato," 359; Paul Kraus, "Plotin chez les Arabes. Remarques sur un nouveau fragment de la paraphrase arabe des Énnéades," *Bulletin de l'Institut d'Egypte* 23 (1941): 269ff., 270n1; Mahdi, *Alfarabi and the Foundation of Islamic Political Philosophy*, 34, 47–48; Galston, "A Re-Examination of al-Farabi's Neoplatonism," 15ff.; Parens, *Metaphysics as Rhetoric*, 17ff.; Strauss and Voegelin, *Faith and Political Philosophy*, 16 (Letter to Eric Voegelin on May 9, 1943).

[31] Alfarabi, "The Harmonization of the Two Opinions of the Two Sages," 153, 155 (Fauzi 15b, 16a–b).

[32] Strauss, "Some Remarks on the Political Science of Maimonides and Farabi," 286 (GS II:134); Strauss, "Fârâbî's Plato," 391.

[33] See also Mahdi, *Alfarabi and the Foundation of Islamic Political Philosophy*, 56.

view among the scholars of Islamic political thought.[34] Connected to the political character of Islamic philosophy, according to Strauss, is "the great importance of political philosophy" in its Platonic rather than Aristotelian version, for Muslim philosophers. For Strauss this is an "obvious difference from Christian scholasticism," because when Christian thinkers paid attention to political philosophy, they tended to follow Aristotle rather than Plato, and while Plato's radically political works (*Republic* and *Laws*) occupied a prominent place in the thought of Islamic (and Jewish) philosophers, Aristotle's *Politics* occupied that position for Christian thinkers.[35] This interest in Platonic political philosophy is, according to Strauss, due and "connected with [the] difference between Islam and Christianity." Islam, like Judaism, is a religion of law, while Christianity is the religion of belief or dogma.[36] Islam reveals itself to its followers mainly as law, as a *political* phenomenon. This law or sharīʿa is given by God to men through a prophet, and this is why Islamic philosophers look at Plato's political science as "the clue to the understanding of *sharia*" and also interpret "the prophet as philosopher-king."[37] This kind of political philosophy is wholly alien to and "radically different from Aristotle's *Politics*," which speaks more about regimes than about laws. This is also why in Alfarabi's enumeration of sciences, the Islamic science of jurisprudence (*fiqh*) and dialectical theology (*kalām*) are presented "as appendages to political science." They are seen as prominently political in character.[38]

---

[34] Cf. Strauss, *Persecution and the Art of Writing*, 1952, 9 with Patricia Crone, *Medieval Islamic Political Thought* (Edinburgh: Edinburgh University Press, 2005), 169; Erwin I. J. Rosenthal, "The Place of Politics in the Philosophy of Al-Farabi," *Islamic Culture* 29 (1955): 158; Richard Walzer, "Platonism in Islamic Philosophy," in *Greek into Arabic* (Cambridge, MA: Harvard University Press, 1962), 246; Parens, "Escaping the Scholastic Paradigm," 214ff.; Galston, "A Re-Examination of al-Farabi's Neoplatonism," 16. This view is also traditionally attributed to Plato himself. See Charles H. Kahn and Glenn R. Morrow, "Foreword," in *Plato's Cretan City: A Historical Interpretation of the Laws*, ed. Charles H. Kahn (Princeton: Princeton University Press, 1993), xxv.

[35] Strauss, "Cohen and Maimonides," 218 (GS II:425–26); Strauss, "How to Study Medieval Philosophy," 335; Mahdi, *Alfarabi and the Foundation of Islamic Political Philosophy*, 35–37.

[36] Strauss, *Persecution and the Art of Writing*, 1952, 9–10; Strauss, "How to Study Medieval Philosophy," 333.

[37] Strauss mentions (SNA 1.1) that Avicenna's remark on Plato's *Republic* and *Laws* points toward this aspect of Islamic philosophy. For a detailed discussion of Avicenna's statement see the Introduction of this book.

[38] Alfarabi, "Enumeration of the Sciences," in *The Political Writings: Selected Aphorisms and Other Texts*, trans. Charles E. Butterworth (Ithaca and London: Cornell University Press, 2001), 80 (Mahdi 107); Strauss, "Fârâbî's Plato," 372.

One last basic characteristic of Islamic philosophy is the absence of a tradition of natural law, which has played a central role in Christian tradition. The question of the relationship between Islamic political philosophy and the idea of natural law is one of the most subtle aspects of Strauss's thought, which we cannot fully explore here. We should, however, bear in mind that in his complex article on Judah Halevi, Strauss distinguished two camps: those who believe in the existence of natural law or related concepts like "rational commandments," "moral law," and "the law of reason" on the one hand, and those who do not subscribe to this view and only accept the existence of *endoxa* or "generally accepted opinions" (*mashhūrāt*) on the other. In the former group Strauss identifies Thomas Aquinas in Christianity, Muʿtazilī theologians in Islam, and Halevi in Judaism, while Marsilius of Padua, the Falāsīfa, and Maimonides belong to the second group. Now, what is significant is that according to Strauss, there is a direct link between subscribing to the doctrine of natural law and being a believer. When Strauss adds the short remark that in Islamic philosophy there was "no Roman law and Cicero" he is referring to the idea developed elsewhere that the "Stoic natural law teaching is the basic stratum of the natural law," the tradition which "affected Roman law" and "became an ingredient of the Christian doctrine." According to Strauss, the Stoic doctrine of natural law and its Thomistic heir are alien to the perspective of the Falāsīfa because they presuppose acceptance of divine providence.[39] In other words, the Falāsīfa do not belong to the camp of believers in revelation. This therefore explains what Strauss considers the distinctive character of Islamic philosophy and separates it from Christian Scholasticism and Thomas Aquinas in particular, to whom Strauss refers explicitly. According to Strauss, the Falāsīfa did not pursue a project of harmonization or synthesis of Reason and Revelation, which he considered impossible and only a recipe for the subordination of philosophy

[39] Strauss, "The Law of Reason in the Kuzari," esp. 95–98, 104–5, 139–41; Leo Strauss, "Marsilius of Padua," in *History of Political Philosophy*, 3rd edition (Chicago: University of Chicago Press, 1987), esp. 276, 292; Leo Strauss, "On Natural Law," in *Studies in Platonic Political Philosophy*, ed. Thomas L. Pangle (Chicago: University of Chicago Press, 1983), esp. 141–42; Strauss, *Natural Right and History*, 153–64. See also Strauss, *Persecution and the Art of Writing*, 1952, 10–11. For clarifying the opposition of the two camps, Strauss refers to the sixth chapter of Maimonides's *Eight Chapters*; Strauss, "The Law of Reason in the Kuzari," 96n4; Moses Maimonides, "Eight Chapters," in *Medieval Political Philosophy: A Sourcebook*, ed. Joseph C. Macfarland and Joshua Parens, trans. Joshua Parens, 2nd edition (Ithaca and London: Cornell University Press, 2011), 203–5. This point became clear to me by the comment of one of the anonymous reviewers, to whom I am most grateful.

to religion. In this regard, among others, Strauss is a firm believer in the "philosophic intransigence of the *falāsifa*" which made them immune to the temptation of falling victim to "the absurd intermixing of a νομος-tradition with a philosophical tradition."[40]

APPROACHING AVERROES'S COMMENTARY

Strauss now turns to Averroes's *Commentary*. How should one read it? The first point that is often raised concerns Averroes's access to the text of Plato's *Republic* itself. This question is raised because in his commentary, discussing different aspects of Plato's dialogue, Averroes makes additions which are not entirely faithful to Plato's text, omits some of the ideas present in the *Republic*, or through his editorial comments deviates from his Platonic source. In other words, Averroes's *Commentary* is not exactly a simple summary or commentary on a Platonic work, but rather a complex construction containing Averroes's own ideas as well as those borrowed from different sources, including Plato, Aristotle, and Alfarabi. The most notable aspect of the deviations from Plato's text is the fact that Averroes transforms Plato's work into a treatise by abstracting from the poetic setting of the dialogue and its several participants.[41] Facing this characteristic of Averroes's work, scholars have raised questions about the sources available to Averroes, including his access or lack thereof to an Arabic translation of the *Republic*.[42] Examining the discrepancies

---

[40] Strauss, *Natural Right and History*, 74–75; Strauss, "Reason and Revelation (1948)," 148–50, 157; Strauss, "Notes on Philosophy and Revelation," 171–72; Strauss, *Persecution and the Art of Writing*, 1952, 11; Shell, *The Strauss-Krüger Correspondence*, 39 (Letter to Gerhard Krüger on November 17, 1932, GS III:406).

[41] Averroes himself refers to this aspect of his work. See A 21.4 and 105.13ff.

[42] Franz Rosenthal, who is among those who Strauss probably has in mind here, explicitly denies that there ever existed anything close to a faithful Arabic translation of any Platonic work: Franz Rosenthal, "On the Knowledge of Plato's Philosophy in the Islamic World," *Islamic Culture* 14 (1940): 393; Franz Rosenthal, "Addenda," *Islamic Culture* 15 (1941): 396–98. See also Erwin I. J. Rosenthal, "Introduction," in *Averroes' Commentary on Plato's "Republic"* (Cambridge: University of Cambridge Oriental Publication, 1956), 12–13. For a good summary of the discussion on the existence of Plato's *Republic* in Arabic see David Reisman, "Plato's Republic in Arabic: A Newly Discovered Passage," *Arabic Sciences and Philosophy* 4 (2004): 263–300. Although Reisman provides a remarkable passage from Plato in Arabic which not only preserves the dialogic form but also includes the names of Glaucon and Adeimantus, Reisman is skeptical that a complete translation was ever made (p. 269). I am grateful to Alexander Orwin who drew my attention to this article. See also Alexander Orwin, *Redefining the Muslim Community: Ethnicity, Religion, and Politics in the Thought of Alfarabi* (Philadelphia: University of Pennsylvania Press, 2017), 15–18. For some additional evidence for the

between Averroes's *Commentary* and Plato's *Republic*, Strauss addresses two hypotheses: (a) the Arabic translation of the *Republic* available to Averroes was faulty; (b) the more radical claim that Averroes did not have access to the text of the *Republic* at all, but rather to a summary of or a commentary on the dialogue. Although the second hypothesis (b) is more commonly accepted among scholars, Strauss brings forward a much more convincing counterargument to refute it: Strauss draws our attention to the fact that "Averroes says that he summarized the *Republic* because he didn't have access to the *Politics*; this implies that he did have access to the *Republic*" (SNA 1.3, A 22.4–5). In other words, those who deny Averroes's access to the text of *Republic* go against the express testimony of Averroes himself, whom we have no reason to disbelieve.[43] The first claim (a) is more difficult to address: We don't have Averroes's translation of *Republic*, but according to Strauss, "we have no right to assume that it was bad or unintelligible" (SNA 1.3).[44] But Strauss moves further than this and makes a more radical and perhaps more substantive claim: One reason, or perhaps *the* reason, why modern scholars often assume the inferior quality of the Greek sources available to Muslim philosophers, is that these scholars find some aspects of Muslim commentaries

existence of an Arabic translation of Plato's *Republic* see Galen, *Galeni Compendium Timaei Platonis aliorumque dialogorum synopsis, quae extant fragmenta*, ed. Paul Kraus and Richard Walzer (London: Warburg Institute, 1951), 35ff. For more on Plato's writings in general and the *Laws* in particular, see Chapter 4 of this study.

[43] As we shall see in Chapter 3 of this study, this is an argument used originally by Paul Kraus for Alfarabi's access to Plato's *Laws*. See Paul Kraus's letter to Leo Strauss on May 28, 1936 quoted in Mahdi, "The Editio Princeps of Fârâbî's Compendium Legum Platonis," 6n23. As we shall see, like Rosenthal in the case of Averroes's *Commentary*, Dimitri Gutas has also argued that Alfarabi's commentary on Plato's *Laws* was not based on Plato's text, to which Alfarabi did not have access, but was rather based on Galen's summary of *Laws*. This is despite Alfarabi's explicit assertion that he had access to at least the first nine books of the *Laws*. Gutas, "Fārābī's Knowledge of Plato's 'Laws,'" 408; Alfarabi, "Summary of Plato's Laws," in *The Political Writings, Volume II: Political Regime and Summary of Plato's Laws*, trans. Charles E. Butterworth (Ithaca and London: Cornell University Press, 2015), 173 (Druart 152). See also Mahdi, "The Editio Princeps of Fârâbî's Compendium Legum Platonis," 4–6 and a view similar to Gutas in Shlomo Pines, "Aristotle's Politics in Arabic Philosophy," *Israel Oriental Studies* 5 (1975): 150–60.

[44] It is true that, unfortunately, not even a single Arabic translation of a Platonic dialogue has survived in its entirety; however, a study of Arabic translations of the Greek works which have survived often show the remarkable fidelity of the translators even to the nuances of the original Greek. For instance, the Arabic translation of *Nicomachean Ethics* is described by its modern editors as "a remarkable performance, showing nearly everywhere a firm grasp of the intricacies of the thought of Aristotle." Aristotle, *The Arabic Version of the Nicomachean Ethics*, 2.

incompatible with what these scholars believe they know about Greek philosophy. In case of Averroes, they judge what the latter says with "a view to *our* understanding of the *Republic*." Given our own understanding of the *Republic*, we are tempted to read some comments of Averroes and 'digressions' from the text of the *Republic* as results of misreading or faulty translation. However, Strauss claims, we should first ask ourselves whether "*we* understand the *Republic*." It is entirely possible that our own understanding of Plato's *Republic* is inferior to that of this Muslim thinker from many centuries ago.[45] One here sees the importance of Strauss's remark about the importance of fostering a genuine historical sense in the study of Islamic philosophy. Many such problems can be avoided by forgoing the common modern lack of appreciation for thinkers of the past.

Strauss claims that if, after examining all other possibilities, we finally arrive at the conclusion that what Averroes attributes to Plato is entirely different from what Plato actually says in the *Republic*, and if we do not find a way to explain the discrepancy by attributing it to Averroes's potential superior understanding of Plato, "this need not be due to incomprehension on his part or on the part of the translator of the *Republic*" (SNA 2.4). It is possible that Averroes's departures from Plato are *by design*; that is, he might be intentionally presenting an erroneous picture of Plato. This possibility points toward one of the most controversial aspects of Strauss's thought, namely the question of esotericism. Strauss elsewhere claims that one of the most useful techniques available to a writer who wishes to hide his heterodox thoughts is to put them in the mouth of someone else. According to Strauss, this technique can take several forms: sometimes the esoteric writer employs this technique by composing literary works in which some disreputable fictional character acts as the mouthpiece of the author.[46] There are other instances in which the author conveys his own thoughts through pseudo-historical works or

---

[45] Strauss here (SNA 2.3) provides an example from Alfarabi: Alfarabi makes an enigmatic statement in his summary of Plato's dialogues according to which, philosophers, princes, and legislators must combine the ways of Socrates and Thrasymachus in their dealings with the elect and the multitude. This statement, which might at first appear as a result of a misunderstanding of Plato's *Republic*, for Strauss is in fact based on a deep understanding of the role of rhetoric in Plato's philosophy: Alfarabi, "The Philosophy of Plato," in *Philosophy of Plato and Aristotle*, trans. Muhsin Mahdi (Ithaca: Cornell University Press, 2001), 66–67 (Rosenthal and Walzer 22); Strauss, "Fârâbî's Plato," 383; Strauss, "Some Remarks on the Political Science of Maimonides and Farabi," 303n81 (GS II:158); Strauss, "How Fārābī Read Plato's Laws," 1959, 153–54. See also A 61.1ff.

[46] Strauss, *Persecution and the Art of Writing*, 1952, 36.

even, like Machiavelli, voices many of his own views by using historical figures and the characters of Livy's *History*.[47] One of the most interesting examples of this technique is the use of form of commentary itself. While the most common medium of transmitting one's philosophical thoughts is the treatise, commentary can provide the esoteric writer with a defensive shield behind which he can hide, while conveying his own thoughts by using another author as his mouthpiece. In such pseudo-commentaries and "in the guise of a historical account" the esoteric writer "avails himself ... of the specific immunity of the commentator, or of the historian, in order to speak his mind concerning grave matters." Now, Strauss is suggesting that Averroes might have used a commentary on Plato's *Republic* as an instrument of conveying his own unorthodox thoughts safely to the reader. It is therefore not surprising that elsewhere and alluding precisely to Averroes's *Commentary*, Strauss describes Averroes as the "commentator who after all was more than a mere commentator."[48] In these notes, Strauss does not refer explicitly to esotericism, but as we shall see, he certainly believed that Averroes writes esoterically and must be read 'between the lines.' In Strauss's interpretation of *Commentary*, the question of esotericism and the theologico-political problem meet and form the perspective through which he interprets this work. He approaches *Commentary* as a work intended to be read between the lines, containing heterodox ideas incompatible with, and critical of, the reigning beliefs of the time. In this perspective, Averroes's diversions from the teachings of the *Republic* might be due to Averroes's practice of esoteric writing, through which he tries to hide his deepest, most unorthodox insights from most readers, while also revealing them to some others who know how to discern them. Averroes may 'in the guise of a historical account' pretend to be 'a mere epitomist of a Greek text' and yet transmit his own thoughts about different subjects by putting those thoughts in the mouth of Plato. To put it differently, Strauss writes that Averroes may "*use* Plato, he may hide behind Plato, for presenting unorthodox views of the sharia" (SNA 2.4).[49]

---

[47] Strauss, *Thoughts on Machiavelli*, 42.

[48] Strauss, "Fârâbî's Plato," 374–77, 374n43.

[49] Strauss gives here an example of this kind of esoteric writing found in Alfarabi's remarks on the seventh book of Plato's *Laws*. In Alfarabi's summary, we observe that the seventh chapter is supposed to explain the content of the seventh book of Plato's *Laws*. However, one will not find anything resembling the content of this chapter in Plato's *Laws*. This chapter contains a startling discussion about the successors of a supposedly divine legislator, which brings the Islamic idea of Muhammad as the 'Seal of the

Strauss's perspective on *Commentary* here is above all opposed to Rosenthal's: While Rosenthal claims that "Averroes was a convinced Muslim for whom the absolute authority and superiority of the *Sharīʿa* as prophetic revealed Law was an article of faith which shaped his thought and determined the mode of his expression," Strauss thought the issue is in fact more complex.[50] One should first begin by asking why a twelfth-century Muslim imam, judge, and scholar might decide to write a commentary on Plato's *Republic*, the work of a pagan philosopher, in the first place. To put it differently, we may rightly ask here about the status of Greek pagan philosophy in Muslim thought. This is the first question which any study of Averroes's *Commentary* must address and constantly keep in sight. To begin with, Strauss reminds us that Plato's regime presents itself as the best city, "the perfect community" (SNA 2.6). But the major characteristics of this city are communism, equality of the sexes, and the rule of philosophers, none of which are Islamic or even entirely compatible with the well-known precepts of Islamic Law, the sharīʿa. Furthermore, if Plato's regime is the perfect community for Averroes, the radically different Islamic *umma* cannot be perfect (SNA 2.6). One can even go further: Strauss claims elsewhere that on the basis of faith in revelation, one must conclude that sharīʿa and divine law render political science entirely superfluous. God through his Law has already shown men the way to organize their political life in the most perfect manner and to found the most perfect community. There is therefore no need to seek recourse to reason and science to discover the perfect community.[51]

To summarize, Strauss draws our attention to the fact that Averroes's interest in Plato's *Republic* should not be taken lightly, and that we should not assume his ignorance of the theologico-political problem. However, Strauss also remains open to the idea that "perhaps Averroes does not identify himself with Plato" (SNA 2.6). Averroes might have

---

Prophets' to mind. For Strauss, this discrepancy seems to be not due to Alfarabi's access to inferior manuscripts of Plato's *Laws*, but rather to Alfarabi's awareness of the differences between Islam and Plato's philosophy and his decision to *rewrite* Plato's dialogue to fit the new context brought about by a new revealed religion. Alfarabi may have tried to protect himself by ascribing his own heterodox ideas to the dead Plato, as a way to respond to "the problem of *Islam*" (SNA 2.4). If this can be the case for Alfarabi, it can also be the case for Averroes. Strauss, "How Fārābī Read Plato's Laws," 1959, 143–44. For a more detailed discussion see Chapter 4 in this book.

[50] Rosenthal, "Introduction," 15.

[51] Strauss, "Some Remarks on the Political Science of Maimonides and Farabi," 282 (GS II:131); Leo Strauss, "Maimonides' Statement on Political Science," in *What Is Political Philosophy? And Other Studies* (Glencoe: Free Press, 1959), 157.

even used the occasion of writing a commentary on Plato to philosophize on his own. These remarks lead Strauss to conclude that the most important issues regarding *Commentary*, including Averroes's access to manuscripts, his knowledge of Plato's *Republic*, and above all his intention in this work, cannot be decided before we arrive at an adequate understanding of *Commentary* by itself (SNA 1.5). It is therefore necessary to turn to *Commentary*. It is important here to be conscious of the transformation at work in Strauss's interpretation: what he accomplishes by his critical remarks on the common perspective on Averroes's work is to overcome the historical preconceptions which stand in the way of a truly philosophical treatment of Averroes's *Commentary*. In other words, scholarly obsession with historical questions like Averroes's access to translations and summaries must be superseded to make a truly philosophical approach to the work possible.[52]

THE PROBLEM OF THE UNIVERSAL SOCIETY

Averroes commences his summary proper of the *Republic* by observing that Plato begins his discussion of how virtues are brought about with the virtue of courage. But right away Averroes distances himself from Plato and speaks in his own name ("We say" [A 25.10]). As Strauss remarks, it seems that Averroes intends to announce his independence from Plato by showing that "he will speak first in his own name before permitting Plato to speak" (SNA 3.10): *Commentary* is as much a work of Averroes as it is a presentation of Plato's ideas. Averroes says in his own name that there are two ways in which the knowledge of first principles, the final cause, and the virtues in general are brought about in the human soul. First, through rhetorical and poetical arguments, the way which is above all appropriate for the multitude, i.e., the ordinary citizens of the virtuous city who have been educated in the exercise of virtues since their childhood. This method is neither appropriate for the education of the few elect individuals capable of attaining knowledge through demonstrative speeches, nor for those who are not citizens of the virtuous city.

---

[52] This is Strauss's favorite approach in his other commentaries too: see the discussion of the authenticity of Plato's dialogues in Strauss, *The City and Man*, 55; Strauss, *Persecution and the Art of Writing*, 1952, 31; Strauss, *Socrates and Aristophanes*, 3; Leo Strauss, *On Plato's Symposium*, ed. Seth Benardete (Chicago: University of Chicago Press, 2001), 11. Similar points are made regarding the authenticity of Xenophon's *Athenian Constitution* in Leo Strauss, *1963 Winter Course on Xenophon Offered at the University of Chicago*, ed. Christopher Nadon (Chicago: Leo Strauss Center, 2016), 160 (Session 7).

The second method by which knowledge is brought about in the soul of human beings is coercion. The first method is not used in the case of enemies, foes, or other nations who are not good and human. In its relation to foreign nations, the virtuous regime exclusively uses the second method: coercion, chastisement, or more precisely, war (A 26.3–5). Fostering the virtue of courage is a preparation for the art of war.

The question of courage is especially important for Averroes's understanding of the relationship between Islam and philosophy, because courage above all concerns war, and war touches one of the most important aspects of Islamic Law, namely the holy war (*jihād*). As Strauss puts it, "one of the great issues between philosophy and law is religious war, and this is connected with the problematic character of a *universal* society" (SNA 9.20).[53] "That Averroes makes these remarks as a Moslem" or more precisely that he sees this question relevant to his particular Islamic theologico-political situation, is shown by the fact that Averroes finds it relevant in this context to mention "our divine Law," i.e. the sharī'a. He seems to divide the sharī'a into two parts: the part that is like what is also found in human laws, and the part which is different from human laws. The part that proceeds like human laws leads human beings toward God in two ways: "speeches" and compulsion (A 26.16–19). According to Strauss, by mentioning "speeches" in general, Averroes "leaves it open" whether Islam leads the elite to the speculative truth by means of demonstration. It is possible that "speeches" include only poetical and rhetorical speeches; then demonstration is excluded. Averroes explains that the multitude is incapable of attaining knowledge through demonstrative speeches, and therefore what they are taught through poetical and rhetorical speeches is not properly speaking knowledge but rather beliefs: "knowledge of the speculative truth by rhetorical and poetic argument is in fact ignorance of the speculative truth. It certainly is not knowledge but belief which is affected by rhetorical and poetical arguments" (SNA 5.13).

Before concluding his own remarks on courage, and just when he wants to turn to Plato's discussion of this issue, Averroes adds that,

---

[53] In 1936, Strauss develops this point by remarking that "*falasifa* attribute greater value to courage than did Plato and Aristotle." According to Strauss, this orientation of the Falāsīfa is partly due to "the missionary tendency which is inherent in a universal religion," i.e., Islam, which commanded a holy war of civilization, an idea absent from the thought of Plato and Aristotle. Strauss, "Some Remarks on the Political Science of Maimonides and Farabi," 295n59 (GS II:156–57). In this regards, see also the letter to Paul Kraus on May 17, 1936 quoted in Strauss, *Hobbes's Critique of Religion and Related Writings*, 15n41 (GS III:XXIIIn41).

according to some writing of Alfarabi, this account of courage, the one which puts courage in the service of the holy war, is also what *Aristotle* asserts about the wars of the virtuous city. It therefore seems that this 'Aristotelian' account of courage, which incidentally is in harmony with the Islamic view, is different from Plato's account. But what is Plato's view? Averroes explains that for Plato, courage is *not* intended for the war of civilization. For Plato, it is only on account of some necessity that the art of war and courage are practiced. In other words, according to Strauss's understanding of Averroes, "Plato implicitly or explicitly rejects the war of civilization and the holy war" (SNA 6.14). Plato's un-Islamic view should therefore be distinguished from that of Aristotle, or rather that view which Averroes, relying on some unknown writing of Alfarabi, attributes to Aristotle. Averroes ascribes Plato's view to the idea that only a part of humanity – for Plato, the Greeks – is disposed to perfection, above all to theoretical perfection. If Plato was right, this amounts to saying that civilizational warfare, which intends to spread perfection to other nations through war and compulsion, must be rejected as a misguided enterprise. But Averroes takes issue with Plato's view of the capacities of the barbarians. While the Greeks are most disposed by nature to wisdom, Averroes claims that some men in Andalus, Syria, Iraq, and Egypt are gifted too – though he is conspicuously silent about the Arabs of Arabia proper.[54] Moreover, Averroes argues that even *if* the Greeks are particularly gifted in wisdom and intellectual virtues, other nations *might perhaps* be said to be gifted in nonintellectual virtues, and since it is fitting that everyone obtains as much human perfection as is compatible with what is in his nature, these nations may be subjected by conquest to discipline in those virtues. However, Averroes seems to take back with one hand what he gives with the other by adding that perhaps the existence and establishment of other virtues are also dependent on the development of wisdom, and perhaps if wisdom is absent in some nations, other virtues also tend to be absent. In other words, Strauss thinks that Averroes draws our attention to the question of "whether the highest development of the other virtues does not depend on the corresponding development of wisdom" (SNA 6.14).

Averroes backs away from these dangerous waters and claims that indeed many nations are disposed to receive training in nonintellectual virtues. In any case, the issue remains: excellence in these virtues requires

---

[54] Strauss here refers to Ibn Khaldūn (SNA 6.14). For a probable source of this remark (or vice versa) see Mahdi, *Ibn Khaldūn's Philosophy of History*, 199n5.

extensive education from childhood. Therefore, only little children who
have not been corrupted by the nonvirtuous regimes and by the faulty
education of their cities are apt to be trained in the virtues. But perhaps
one can say that even the older generation is not beyond hope: those who
have been brought up in regimes close to the virtuous regime can acquire
the virtues to some extent. All these qualifications prepare the ground
for Averroes's final claim: If in a given case education in virtues proves
impossible, "the people concerned must be killed or else enslaved, i.e.
treated like irrational animals" (SNA 7.14, A 27.21–24). This brings the
problematic character of Averroes's treatment of war to the fore: apart
from wars of necessity, which are mainly defensive, the only kind of war
of which Averroes seems to approve is a war of civilization, which is
ultimately dependent on the natural conditions of the enemies. While the
holy war must be waged against all mankind (according to the Prophet,
against the reds and the blacks [A 46.19–20]), the war of civilization is
only legitimate where the natural conditions of the defeated permit their
education in excellence. In other words, Strauss claims, "Averroes argues
on the premise that the purpose of the war of civilization is to spread
wisdom" (SNA 7.16). Averroes's many qualifications lead to the conclusion that in many or perhaps most cases, a war of civilization is unwarranted, and in practice wars are mainly for the sake of necessity, "not
conversion to the true religion but treating the conquered like irrational
animals" (SNA 7.15).

The problems of the holy war and the universal society appear again
when Averroes begins discussion of the size of Plato's best city (A 46.1ff).
Plato considered one thousand warriors sufficient for his virtuous city.
But Averroes claims that the size and number of citizens of the best city
must vary according to the time, the place, and the neighboring nations.
The number of warriors that Plato believed to be sufficient was in accord
with his time, and Averroes claims that Plato did not make the number
to be unalterable. Plato would have admitted as *we* do, Averroes claims,
that this number is not sufficient for a city that intends to wage a universal holy war with all the inhabitants of the earth. The incompatibility of
Plato's small city with the requirements of the universal holy war leads
Averroes to suggest another possibility: a virtuous community consisting of many smaller communities, each having a limited size. This view,
Averroes reminds us, is not that of Plato but rather of Aristotle, and
Averroes believes that it is undoubtedly the true opinion (A 46.22). In
other words, following the Islamic perspective, "Averroes demands a
universal society," consequently, he demands a society which is capable

of waging war against the whole of mankind. This leads to a retraction of Averroes's previous agreement with Plato and, Strauss writes, "brings the *conflict* between Plato and Islam into the open" (SNA 7.19). What prevents this conflict from becoming an unqualified conflict between Islam and philosophy is that Averroes claims to have found a view compatible with sharīʿa in Aristotle. The problem is that one does not know where to find this supposedly Aristotelian view in the writings of Aristotle. In other words, a doubtful reference to Aristotle is all that stands between philosophy as an un-Islamic science and philosophy as an Islamic science.[55]

Before leaving the question of holy war, it is also worth noting another relevant passage to which Strauss draws our attention: Averroes reports that according to Plato, the guardians must punish those guardians who do not obey the sharīʿa (A 41, 6–7). Now, while it is in itself remarkable to see here that for Averroes even Plato's virtuous city has a sharīʿa (see also A 44.23), it is also interesting that Averroes's Plato did not believe that wisdom could be brought about by compulsion, while he thought adherence to the sharīʿa could. If it is so, Strauss claims, "this means that for Plato wisdom is radically different from the *sharia*." It is therefore no wonder that Plato does not approve of the war of civilization or holy war, and it is tempting to conclude with Strauss that here we see a difference between Plato and Averroes, for whom the holy war for the sake of spreading wisdom is a legitimate enterprise (SNA 7.18). However, we tried to show the qualified nature of Averroes's view of the holy war, the account which must keep us cautious in passing this judgment. After all, Strauss thought that Averroes sometimes uses Plato as a mouthpiece: for Strauss, at times Averroes "says in a disguised way in his own name what he makes Plato say explicitly" (SNA 10–11.23).

---

[55] By asking: "To what Aristotelian work does he refer? A genuine work of Aristotle?" (SNA 8.19) Strauss seems to be reminding us of Alfarabi's reference to the pseudo-Aristotelian *Theology*. What is particularly interesting in Averroes's claim is that there *are* passages in Aristotle which come close to some of the things Averroes is attributing to him. But these passages are found in Aristotle's *Politics* (see 1256b24–26, 1325a10–15, 1327b30–33), the work which Averroes claims he has not had access to, and which, according to a wide scholarly consensus, was never translated into Arabic! See Pines, "Aristotle's Politics in Arabic Philosophy"; Rémi Brague, "Note sur la traduction arabe de la Politique d'Aristote. Derechef, qu'elle n'existe pas," in *Aristote politique: Études sur la Politique d'Aristote*, ed. Pierre Aubenque (Paris: Presses Universitaires de France, 1993), 423–33. Mahdi seems skeptical of this consensus and Strauss had his own doubts: Mahdi, *Alfarabi and the Foundation of Islamic Political Philosophy*, 34–35.

PERVASIVENESS OF THE THEOLOGICO-POLITICAL

To show that the conflict of philosophy and sharīʿa is not a limited issue in *Commentary*, Strauss follows his meticulous study of the text by keeping this question at the center of his interpretation. The theologico-political problem raises its head again in Averroes's discussion of the limits of warfare. Averroes reports that according to Plato, men engaged in war should not enslave those who are of their kind and speak a common language; they should not even call these enemies unbelievers, but rather those who have gone astray. This opinion of Plato, Averroes reminds us, is at variance with what many bringers of sharīʿa assert (A 60.3–4). This example is especially important because, unlike in previous cases, Averroes here only observes the contradiction between sharīʿa and the teaching of Plato and does not refer to any opinion of Aristotle compatible with sharīʿa. In other words, Strauss explains, Averroes does not pass any judgment on Plato's opinion that "*racial and linguistic unity [should] override religious diversity.*" Averroes "merely *notes* the disagreement between Plato and many prophets" without taking a side and at the same time avoids the cover provided by a recourse to some pseudo-Aristotle (SNA 8.20, 9.20).

This issue introduces us to one of the major aspects of Strauss's notes: he observes that Averroes follows a peculiar method for pointing to the conflict between Platonic philosophy and sharīʿa. Apart from cases in which he introduces a fictitious Aristotelian alternative to Plato's un-Islamic views, Averroes sometimes glosses over the presence of a conflict; he presents Plato's clearly un-Islamic opinions but "does not polemicize against Plato" or does not even point out the conflict (SNA 9.21). In other words, Averroes uses different methods for pointing to the confrontation of Greek philosophy and Islamic Law: he may directly tell the reader about such a conflict, but he may also merely plant the question in the reader's mind. It is true that Averroes calls the perspective of the sharīʿa "the indubitable truth" (A 46.22) but in view of the difficulties presented, one must confess perplexity about Averroes's final position in this conflict. What *is* Averroes's position on the theologico-political problem? Strauss believes that Averroes sheds some light on this question when he discusses the education of the guardians by music (A 29.13ff). Strauss explains that the question of education by music "concerns the use of untruth, of untrue fables" (SNA 9.21). According to Averroes, the citizens owe their knowledge about speculative and practical things to arguments. These arguments are of two major kinds: demonstrative on the one hand, and dialectical, rhetorical, and poetical on the other.

Education by music is education by the second kind of speeches, mostly by poetic and rhetorical speeches, i.e., speeches which are lower in rank and less scientific than demonstrative speeches. In other words, the education of the young is through unscientific speeches, which only *imitate* the truth. However, not every imitation is equal to another: some are closer to the original and some are remote from it. Averroes claims that the education of the best city must be based on imitations which are most close to the original (A 30.6). Still, one wonders whether this kind of education brings the many closer to the truth because, as Strauss remarks, "the vulgar cannot help taking the representations as the truth and hence the vulgar is in fact led toward the untruth" (SNA 9.21).

We can say that Averroes, reporting Plato's view, does not approve of using what he describes as untrue and base stories; yet this does not mean that he disapproves of the untrue but noble stories, or rather "noble lies"; as such, untrue stories are necessary for educating the many, who are not capable of learning the truth (SNA 9.22). Next, we receive more information about the types of stories which are conducive to courage and those which give birth to fear. Averroes claims that according to Plato fear should not be ascribed to *prophets* and chiefs, but Averroes reports that according to Plato much laughter should not be ascribed to the *righteous* and the chiefs. One must conclude with Strauss that "there is no danger that prophets be presented as given to laughter as distinguished from fear, to say nothing of weeping" (SNA 10.23).[56] Furthermore, the guardians must be exhorted to always tell the truth. However, the chiefs can and should lie to the citizens, because untrue stories are necessary for the education of the vulgar, who are incapable of knowing the truth itself. In fact, we learn that "[n]o bringer of a nomos is to be found who does not make use of invented stories, for this is something necessary for the multitude to reach their happiness" (A 32.22–24, SNA 11.24). In the

---

[56] The question of laughing and weeping, or rather comedy and tragedy, and their relationship with philosophy, is one of Strauss's most complex observations which seems to have Nietzschean origins but is also attributed to the Socratic school. What here seems to be Strauss's meaning is to draw our attention to the close relationship between morality, seriousness, and tragedy on the one hand, and philosophy, playfulness, and comedy on the other. See Strauss, *The City and Man*, 61; Strauss, *Socrates and Aristophanes*, 140, 312; Leo Strauss, *Xenophon's Socrates* (Ithaca: Cornell University Press, 1972), 170; Strauss, *Gesammelte Schriften. Band 3*, 743 (Letter to Gershom Scholem on November 22, 1960); Strauss and Voegelin, *Faith and Political Philosophy*, 90 (Letter to Eric Voegelin on June 4, 1951); Friedrich Nietzsche, *Beyond Good and Evil. Prelude to a Philosophy of the Future*, trans. Walter Kaufmann (New York: Vintage Books, 1989), 42 (aphor. 30); Plato, *Laws* 803b.

same vein, Averroes claims that happiness should not be represented to the many as a reward for virtuous actions, nor suffering as punishment for vicious actions. Happiness should rather be represented as the health of the soul, its survival and eternal life. Averroes does not explain if suffering should *also* be represented as the privation of the last two.[57]

According to Averroes's report, Plato says that the guardians should not be frightened by the horrifying stories about the afterlife, "i.e. there must not be presentations of hell as little as of demons and of the devil" (SNA 10.23). Here Averroes makes the cryptic remark "*in his own name*" that "women's songs" should be kept from the guardians, those songs which depict death as an evil (A 32.2).[58] This point touches one of the most interesting aspects of Averroes's *Commentary*, which Strauss has clearly in mind. In one of his early writings, Strauss attributes the importance of courage for Falāsīfa to two things. The first, which was mentioned before, is the universalistic character of Islam. Strauss also attributes the importance of courage to "the polemic against 'superstitious' menaces which are inherent in a universal religion that is thereby popular."[59] Furthermore, in a later writing of his, Strauss refers to Averroes as "the commentator who after all was more than a mere commentator" and who "directly attacks the teaching of the *Republic* concerning the life after death."[60] These passages together make it clear that the main superstition which Strauss has in mind is the belief in the afterlife. Although in the notes under discussion, Strauss does not refer to or discuss the specific passages of Averroes's

---

[57] As we shall see in the Chapter 3 of this volume, Strauss draws our attention to the "heretical" view found in Alfarabi's *Political Regime* according to which the souls of the wicked dissolve into nothing, and only those of the virtuous are immortal. Strauss, "Fârâbî's Plato," 372; Alfarabi, "Political Regime," in *The Political Writings, Volume II: Political Regime and Summary of Plato's Laws*, trans. Charles E. Butterworth (Ithaca and London: Cornell University Press, 2015), 72 (Najjar 83); Ibn Tufayl, *Hayy Ibn Yaqzān: A Philosophical Tale*, trans. Lenn Evan Goodman (Chicago: University of Chicago Press, 2015), 100 (Gauthier 13–14).

[58] For the significance of the "women's songs" see Alfarabi's remark about "senseless ravings and old wives' tales" quoted in Ibn Tufayl, *Hayy Ibn Yaqzān*, 100 (Gauthier 14); Shlomo Pines, "Limitations of Human Knowledge According to Al-Fārābī, Ibn Bājja, and Maimonides," in *Collected Works of Shlomo Pines*, ed. Moshe Idel and W. Z. Harvey, vol. 5 (Jerusalem: Magnes, 1997), 404. As we shall see in the Chapter 3, Strauss refers to this famous passage elsewhere. See Strauss, "Fârâbî's Plato," 372; Strauss, *Thoughts on Machiavelli*, 175; Meier, *Political Philosophy and the Challenge of Revealed Religion*, 66n80.

[59] Strauss, "Some Remarks on the Political Science of Maimonides and Farabi," 296n59 (GS II:157).

[60] See Strauss, "Fârâbî's Plato," 376n43. See also Strauss, "On Natural Law," 142: "certain Islamic Aristotelians [asserted] that the only divine punishment is the loss of eternal felicity."

Commentary to which he refers in his two other writings, it is worth mentioning them. In the first passage (A 62.11–13) Averroes summarizes the qualities of the philosopher as described in the *Republic*. When Socrates reaches the virtue of courage, he claims that a true philosopher "believes that death is not something terrible" (*Republic* 486b1–2). Averroes gives a different justification of the philosopher's courage by claiming that for "one who has no courage will be unable to despise the nondemonstrative arguments on which he has grown up, and especially if he has grown up in these cities." What Strauss believes Averroes is driving at becomes clearer by the second passage in Averroes's *Commentary* to which Strauss refers. This second passage (A 105.14–25) is where Averroes explains why he has not summarized the content of the tenth book of the *Republic*, where Plato's theory of the immortality of the soul, "the argument by which he explains that the soul does not die," is presented. Plato's story which depicts "the bliss and delight that await the souls of the happy and the just, and what awaits the souls of the tormented," Averroes claims, is "of no account, for the virtues that come about from them are not true virtues." Averroes does not believe that such untrue stories are even necessary to a man's becoming virtuous, because we see many people who "albeit devoid of these stories, are not less well off than those possessing [these] stories." I believe the most important statement connecting Averroes's two passages in Strauss's mind comes next, when Averroes mentions that these stories about the fate of the virtuous and the nonvirtuous in the afterlife are "stories that over which the ancients had already disputed; and Plato was troubled thereby." In other words, according to Strauss, Averroes accuses Plato of lacking the necessary courage which has led him to fall victim to "the nondemonstrative arguments on which he has grown up."[61]

There are other cases in which Averroes insensibly moves from reporting Plato's views to discussing claims which can be described as his own. For instance, Averroes, reporting Plato's criticism of physicians and judges, says that the virtuous city does not need the art of judges. Strauss believes that these comments are Averroes's own, because in this context Averroes also refers to the cities of his own time and questions the beneficial character of the art of adjudication, i.e., *fiqh* or Islamic jurisprudence. Perhaps to diminish the radical character of his remark, Averroes only allusively refers to "our time and the past" and gives us the impression of

---

[61] See also Heinrich Meier, *On the Happiness of the Philosophic Life: Reflections on Rousseau's Rêveries in Two Books*, trans. Robert Berman (Chicago: University of Chicago Press, 2016), 54–55.

speaking only about the corruption of the contemporary cities (A 37.15–20, SNA 12.26). Strauss finds the same criticism of *fiqh* and sharī'a in the discussion of inferior and corrupted regimes: Averroes explains that if the true philosopher-king is not available, an *inferior* regime can be founded on the basis of the laws legislated by the true king; these laws must be applied by a successor who is expert in jurisprudence, i.e., *fiqh*. Averroes also imagines the possibility of a dual system of rule, in which an imperfect king rules in conjunction with an expert in jurisprudence, and claims that this kind of inferior regime actually exists in contemporary Muslim cities (A 81.1–8). That sharī'a and *fiqh* are inferior instruments of rule is also implied when Averroes mentions many legislators who have erred by legislating highly particularized or detailed laws, in contradistinction to more general laws (A 47.8–19, SNA 12.26).

There are other instances in which, according to Strauss, Averroes's view is rather ambiguous; in these cases, Averroes limits the purpose of his commentary to simply planting questions in the mind of the reader. For example, Averroes reports, at some length, Plato's view about the elimination of people born with incurable defects. According to Plato, Averroes claims, people who are unfit to benefit the city because of incurable defects should be killed, or they may commit suicide. Averroes remarks on the controversial character of Plato's suggestion by introducing two groups of people: those who argue against this proposal, and those who agree with it. However, he refrains from deciding the matter explicitly, or as Strauss has put it, "his decision is obscure" (A 38.16–17, SNA 12.29). A similar ambiguity exists in the case of the actualization of the best regime: Averroes explains that the best city requires the existence of philosophers, and philosophers in their turn must have been brought up in a virtuous city. It therefore seems that the actualization of the best city is in fact impossible. However, Averroes claims that philosophers can appear in current cities, and if they rule for what he calls *an infinite time*, the best regime would emerge (A 63.3–5). Regardless of what Averroes's claim means for understanding his view of the eternity *a parte post*, it seems that for him "[the] best regime [is] not in existence now nor was it ever in existence under Islam," including even in the early Islamic period. In fact, it seems that for Averroes "our time" in contradistinction to *Plato's time* is that of decay and corruption (SNA 14.42, 11.25; A 35.11–12, 35.19–20).

A more sensitive issue that receives the same ambiguous treatment is the question of prophecy: at the beginning of his book Averroes divided the Muslim sharī'a into two parts: human and divine (A 26.17–19). He gives us the impression that only the human part of the sharīʿa is common to all laws. This points to a larger issue that Averroes calls attention to and at the same time expertly avoids addressing: the relationship between prophecy and philosophy (A 61.17–19). It seems that for Averroes, the qualifications of the perfect legislator are exactly the same as the qualifications of the philosopher (A 60.21ff); even "Lawgiver" (i.e., bringer of sharīʿa) is equated with the philosopher (A 61.14–16). But what can the gift of prophecy add to the already excellent qualities of the philosopher-king? It seems that for Averroes, only a prophet can prescribe the divine aspect of the sharīʿa, i.e., the laws concerning religious matters, namely temples, prayers, sacrifices, and offerings. However, later on, he claims that the divine aspect of *nomos* – the laws concerning temples, prayers, sacrifices, and offerings, or more generally those laws which regulate men's relationship with God – as Strauss puts it – is also common to "all *nomoi* and *shariai*" (SNA 12.27, A 47.23–28). In other words, one can speak of many 'divine' laws (see also A 41.6–7 and 44.23). As these religious laws and regulations are common to all the laws and are presumably found in every city, Strauss concludes that for Averroes there is "no excess of *sharia* beyond reason and nature" (SNA 13.37).

Strauss also observes that Averroes is not consistently reserved about the contradiction between Plato's philosophy and the traditional order of Muslim communities in his time: sometimes he is surprisingly outspoken and does not avoid taking controversial positions without any recourse to convenient silences or fictitious references. The most remarkable example of these cases is the discussion of equality of the sexes in the *Republic*. Averroes writes that in Plato's city, women engage in the same activities as men; they practice the art of war, take part in government, and might acquire wisdom. Averroes knows this is not what happens in the cities of his time. In these cities, women are merely confined to procreation and are put in the service of their husbands. Averroes believes contemporaries and the sharīʿa regarding women are in error, and considers it as "self-evident" that because women are not trained in human virtues in these cities, they come to resemble plants, are a burden upon men, and are the cause of poverty in contemporary cities (A 54.9ff). Averroes observes also the difference between the laws of Plato and the sharīʿa of his time regarding the community of women (A 55.11–15), consanguineous intercourse (A 56.11–13), nakedness of women (A 54.17) and private property (A 42.9), and does not refrain from approving of these measures. One must add that the remarkable radicalism of Averroes's speech is also attested to by the fact that in this context he accepts (Strauss: "without any polemics") that the virtuous city must remain fixed in size forever (SNA 13.35; cf. A 56.23 with A 46.22–23; see also A 57.6, 79.24–25).

AVERROES, REASON, AND REVELATION

Strauss's notes on Averroes's *Commentary* are a perfect example of how fruitful his meticulous observations are; it is difficult to deny that Strauss's reading of Averroes's work through the lens of the theologico-political problem helps us acquire a better perspective on Averroes's work. Regardless of how much we are persuaded by Strauss's more general thesis about the conflict of Reason and Revelation or the esoteric art of writing, any serious reader of Averroes's *Commentary* is bound to read this work differently after encountering Strauss's observations. In other words, there is an un-Straussian case to be made for reading Averroes as Strauss reads him: the points of conflict between what Averroes says in his commentary and Islamic orthodoxy, as they become manifest through Strauss's observations, are so prominent that only a prior uncritical attachment to the idea that Averroes was and must have been a simple orthodox Muslim can persuade us to ignore many curious aspects of Averroes's *Commentary* as they concern Islamic Law. But Strauss's notes are also interesting for those readers who are more curious about the presence of particularly 'Straussian ideas' in these notes. Among these specifically Straussian themes, the most prominent in these notes is the question of the conflict between Reason and Revelation. Consequently, I will mention three points which are of interest regarding Strauss's thesis about the conflict of Reason and Revelation.

The first point concerns Averroes's discussion of Plato's theology. In his commentary, Averroes refers to Plato's criticism of untrue and base tales, but replaces Plato's examples of such stories with the tales common in his own time. One example which Averroes brings up is that God should not be said to be the cause of good *and* evil (A 30.26). God is wholly good, and evil ought to be attributed only to other causes, for example to demons or Iblis. However, this also creates certain problems: a guardian believing in the existence of such supernatural beings will be soft-hearted and timorous. It is therefore advisable to trace evil to matter, darkness or privation – Strauss believes that this means, for Averroes, teaching "omnipotence" is not a part of the education of the best city (SNA 10.22). This point is of particular importance because according to Strauss, faith in revelation stands or falls with the belief in divine omnipotence and it is because of the incompatibility of belief in divine omnipotence and philosophy that Strauss denies the possibility of philosophers believing in revelation. "There cannot be faith in God that is not faith in our being *absolutely* in the hands of God, and this means that is not faith in God's *omnipotence*, and therefore in the possibility of *miracles*." In fact, Strauss goes so far as to say that "all philosophers deny divine omnipotence."[62] In this regard, it seems that Strauss has found what he considered to be the major point of contention between philosophers and believers in Averroes's *Commentary*, and in his view, Averroes has positioned himself squarely in the camp of philosophers.

The second point appears in Strauss's comments on Averroes's discussion of the Platonic doctrine of the noble lie. Averroes says in his own name that the multitude must be taught by imitation of the truth, but an imitation which is close to the truth; yet he makes Plato say more directly and in a less orthodox manner that the sharīʿa teaches by fictitious stories, because "if the *sharia* represents true happiness by imaginary happiness and the first principles by political principles, the bringer of the *sharia* must use fictitious stories" (SNA 10–11.23). What is true of the sharīʿa is also true of human rulers and especially philosopher-kings. Averroes tells us that lying does not befit God's rulership (A 32.13–14), but he also adds that human rulers must lie to their subjects, because the multitude are incapable of knowing the truth. In other words, these untrue stories are designed to fill the gap between the knowledge of the philosopher-king and the vulgar. But if God is a ruler, Strauss observes, "the distance between God and the most intelligent human beings is infinitely greater than the distance between the most intelligent human rulers and their human subjects." Therefore, the divine ruler is as much in need of fictitious stories as the human ruler and sharīʿa must contain untrue stories appropriate for the vulgar. As Strauss puts it, "if God is a ruler, he *must* lie–or if he does not lie he is not a ruler" (SNA 11.24). These ambiguous remarks seem to refer to one of the most important aspects of Strauss's thought: the argument of natural theology. This argument

---

[62] Strauss, "Reason and Revelation (1948)," 158, 166, 169; Strauss, "Jerusalem and Athens (1946)," 14; Strauss, "Notes on Philosophy and Revelation," 169; Strauss, "Jerusalem and Athens," 166. See also Strauss, *Spinoza's Critique of Religion*, 28 (GS I:50); Leo Strauss, "On the Interpretation of Genesis," in *Jewish Philosophy and the Crisis of Modernity*, ed. Kenneth Hart Green (Albany: State University of New York Press, 1997), 360. See also Strauss, *The Argument and the Action of Plato's Laws*, 150 as well as the discussion of divine omnipotence in Strauss's comments on Plato, *Laws* 896e in Leo Strauss, *1971–72 Course on Plato's Laws Offered at St. John's College*, ed. Lorraine Smith Pangle (Chicago: Leo Strauss Center, 2016), 587 (Session 26).

occupies a decisive place in Strauss's engagement with the claims of revelation.[63] At its most basic level, the argument of natural theology aims to refute the claims of revelation through demonstrating the impossibility of revelation. In order to do so, Strauss begins with the concept of a god as the most perfect being. This most perfect being, as it is known from experience, proves to be the wise man, the philosopher. According to Strauss, this view of man gives us an indirect access to the most perfect being simply. In other words, one begins by the most perfect human being and develops an analogy which acts as the instrument of evaluating the claims of revealed religion. For instance, if the most perfect human being is characterized by his self-sufficiency, a god must also be a self-sufficient being who consequently would not be dependent on or concerned with men's worshipping him, in the same way that the wise man would not care for the praise and approval of others.[64] In these notes also, it seems that Strauss is referring to such an analogy at work in Averroes's *Commentary*. Although he does not develop the idea in detail, it seems that according to Strauss, Averroes draws our attention to the fact that the complete truthfulness of God is incompatible with the wisdom expected from a perfect being as it is reflected in the recourse of the philosopher to the noble lie in his dealing with vulgar.[65]

---

[63] The argument of natural theology is not prominently discussed in Strauss's writings, and our knowledge of it is owed mainly to three lectures. The first lecture entitled "Reason and Revelation" was given at the Hartford Theological Seminary on January 8, 1948. See Strauss, "Reason and Revelation (1948)." The second lecture entitled "The Mutual Influence of Theology and Philosophy" was first published in January 1954 in Hebrew and in 1979 in the English original: Leo Strauss, "The Mutual Influence of Theology and Philosophy," *The Independent Journal of Philosophy* 3 (1979): 111–18. The third source is an untitled lecture on Plato's *Euthyphro* published posthumously: Leo Strauss, "An Untitled Lecture On Plato's Euthyphron," ed. David Bolotin, Christopher Bruell, and Thomas L. Pangle, *Interpretation: A Journal of Political Philosophy* 24, no. 1 (1996): esp. 14. Interest in Strauss's treatment of natural theology is mainly due to the writings of Heinrich Meier and those influenced by his scholarship. For a good introduction to this question, with references to Meier's writings, see Marco Menon, "Leo Strauss and the Argument of Natural Theology," *Etica and Politica* 18 (2016): 573–89. See also Strauss, *Gesammelte Schriften*. *Band* 3, 732 (Letter to Gershom Scholem on January 16, 1953), 755 (Letter to Gershom Scholem on November 5, 1966).

[64] Cf. "So in other words, love is based on need. Yes, that is the axiom underlying both Plato and Aristotle. Love is based on need. Therefore a being which has no need cannot love. That is the great difference between Plato and Aristotle on the one hand, and the Bible, that the Bible recognizes a kind of love which comes from abundance and not from need." Strauss, *1959 Course on Plato's Laws*, 295 (Session 11, February 19, 1959).

[65] See also the following remark: "The first principle and the second principles (i.e., God and the angels) must be represented by their analogues in the political principles [i.e., as rulers issuing commands]" (SNA 9.21; square brackets are in the original).

While the first and second points, as they appear in Strauss's notes, seem to point in the direction of a rejection of the claims of revelation by Averroes, the third point seems to point in the opposite direction. Before turning to Plato's *Republic*, Averroes prefaces his work with an introduction in which the subject of the book is discussed. According to Averroes, the practical science the *Commentary* deals with is divided into two parts: scientific and practical. The first part is found in Aristotle's *Nicomachean Ethics*, while the second half is discussed in Aristotle's *Politics* as well as in Plato's *Republic*. Averroes claims that because Aristotle's *Politics* is not yet available to him, he intends to dedicate his summary only to the second part of the practical science as far as it is presented in Plato's *Republic*. But to prepare the reader for his discussion of the second part of the practical science, Averroes also intends to give a summary of the first part of it, on which the second part is founded. However, in the survey of the first part, which we expect to be *wholly* based on Aristotle's *Ethics*, Strauss writes, Averroes "uses, and even explicitly refers to Plato's *Republic*"; in fact, in this summary of the first part Aristotle is not even mentioned (A 22.27, 23.31; SNA 3.9). Strauss claims that, contrary to the impression Averroes gives at first, for Averroes "the *Republic* contains the two parts of practical science." This is particularly important because in this part of the book, Averroes does not even pretend to be only a commentator of some Greek book, but rather a transmitter of what he believes to be the truth about practical science. Consequently, he identifies himself with the teaching of the *Republic* as whole. This must be taken into account when later on Averroes gives us the impression of being a 'mere epitomist' because, Strauss writes, a complete adherence to the teaching of the *Republic* "would imply a complete break with Islam" (SNA 3.9). One is here forced to ask: in view of the many un-Islamic points that Strauss observes in *Commentary*, does Strauss think that Averroes has broken with Islam? The first and the second points seem to confirm this claim. However, there is a third point in Strauss's notes whose significance is not easy to establish. Commenting on a passage in which Averroes divides the Islamic sharīʿa into divine and human parts (A 26.16–19), Strauss writes that according to Averroes, the truly divine part of the sharīʿa is not found in Plato: "only the lower part of the divine law is covered by the *Republic*." In this passage, Averroes implies that the truly divine part of the sharīʿa, unlike the part which resembles the human laws, does not lead men toward truth by speeches or compulsion, but rather by other methods. Strauss suspects that "the specifically divine ways leading men to God are not speech and war but silence and peaceful action." Strauss continues his comments by observing that "practical science (i.e., philosophy) is perhaps not able to understand those parts of the divine law which have no analogy in human law" (SNA 5.12). Strauss's meaning here is not entirely clear: When referring to "silence" is he pointing toward mysticism and the supra-rational?[66] Does he mean that Averroes believed in the possibility of the supra-rational and that he asserted philosophy *per se* is incapable of addressing the supernatural? If this is Strauss's meaning, he seems to be pointing to the reason-revelation impasse by saying that for Averroes, the truly divine part of the sharīʻa is outside the reach of Plato or even philosophy. But it is also possible that Strauss means that only theoretical philosophy is the appropriate branch of philosophy for addressing the nonpractical questions. In other words, Strauss attributes to Averroes the idea that only theoretical philosophy, in contradistinction to practical philosophy, is capable of dealing with (and perhaps refuting) the fundamental claims of revealed religions (see SNA 2.7) – but why then does Strauss equate "practical science" with the whole of philosophy in his notes? Unfortunately, based on Strauss's remarks, it is not possible to conclude what his last word is, but it is nonetheless important to keep these points in mind while reading his notes on Averroes's view of revelation and reason.

---

[66] See also: "Aristotle himself admits that there is something higher than reason or *logos* or *ratio* and he calls that *nous*, *intellectus*, the understanding, as distinguished from reason. Now, could there not be an intellect, a mental perception, without *logos*, without reason, a mental perception which, as it were, shatters all *logos* and all *nomos* or law? Then, from this point of view, the perfection of man would not consist in any activity, in any work, as Aristotle puts it, but in a certain suffering, in a certain way of being affected: *pathos* as distinguished from [praxis?], in an experience of *the* principle, of the [inaudible]. So from this point of view the highest to which man can raise cannot be achieved by an ascent, by a methodic ascent from the primary seeing to the principles but, as it were, a sudden interruption, a sudden appearance of – a sudden presence or a sudden call: *nous* without *logos*. Now this – what I try to describe – is generally known by the name of mysticism, but in a wide sense where it also would include the Biblical revelations, something which transcends the work of the *logos*." "One can say this–that is, I believe true of Plato and Aristotle in the same way as a whole–no *nous*, intelligence, without *logos* and no *logos* without *nous*. These go together .... *Nous* without *logos* is mysticism." Leo Strauss, *1963 Spring Course on Aristotle's Nicomachean Ethics Offered at the University of Chicago* (Chicago, 1963), Session 3, April 9, 1963 and Session 15, June 6, 1963. See also Strauss, *Gesammelte Schriften*. Band 3, 701 (Letter to Gershom Scholem on August 2, 1933). See also this curious statement: "[m]ysticism is one form in which philosophy can appear" in Strauss, *On Tyranny*, 275 (Letter to Alexander Kojève on April 22, 1957) and also Strauss, *Persecution and the Art of Writing*, 1952, 111n46. Can one speak of a specific Straussian doubt about the religious character of Islamic mysticism?

2

Politics, Religion, and Love

How Leo Strauss Read the Arabian Nights

It is difficult to find any non-Western work of literature that has had more of a lasting effect on Western thought than the *One Thousand and One Nights* (in English more commonly called the *Arabian Nights*, hereafter *Nights*). Since its introduction to Western readers in 1704 by Antoine Galland, this work has captured the imagination of its Western readers unlike any other intellectual product of the Arabic language. The *Nights* not only has played a key role in shaping the Western image of the East, but has also contributed to the West's self-understanding.[1] In one of its most popular editions, namely that of the British Arabist Richard Francis Burton, the *Nights* comprises sixteen volumes and contains more than four hundred stories of various lengths and complexities. Facing such a writing, which even in its least monumental recensions consists of so many intricate and mysterious stories of an uncanny character, coming from a culture and society worlds apart from anything European, Western readers were bound to react in many different ways: from treating it as a source of rather scandalous entertainment, to highly scholarly approaches which read it as a source of all kinds of information, literary, poetical, religious, and political. When Galland first introduced the *Nights* to French audiences, it was mainly calibrated to the tastes of the eighteenth-century French salons; but this does not mean that Galland saw his translation only as a source of entertainment. He also considered

---

[1] Robert Irwin, "Preface," in *The Arabian Nights and Orientalism: Perspectives from East and West*, eds. Yuriko Yamanaka and Tetsuo Nishio (London: I.B. Tauris, 2006), viii.

it as having a public function, a sort of popular manual addressed to French readers in which they could find valuable information about the foreign world of Islam. The turn to the *Nights* as a source of information really began, however, at the beginning of the nineteenth century, with the increasing turn of Europeans toward the "oriental" countries, the foundation of several institutions for the study of oriental languages, and the development of the field of orientalism. One can clearly observe this considerable change of perspective in the translations of Edward William Lane and Burton. Their translations both contain an enormous number of footnotes, often reflecting questionable orientalist prejudices, which are meant to provide information and insights into different aspects of the Muslim world. The supplementary material added to Lane's translation was believed to be so important from the scholarly perspective that it was even published as a separate book, titled *Arabian Society in the Middle Ages*.[2]

Today, we are far from such Orientalist naiveté, and we no longer look, at least not uncritically, for the real East in the *Nights*. The stories of the *Nights* are still considered a valuable source of information, though mainly with regard to specific aspects of medieval Muslim societies which are not represented in traditional sources. Contrary to our contemporary interests, medieval writings are mainly concerned with the lives of the more prominent classes – the political elite and administrators, military figures, religious scholars, famous scientists, philosophers, Sufis, and mystics find a prominent place in these writings. On the contrary, the ordinary and private lives of the lower classes, little merchants, the underworld of petty thieves, criminals, their mentalities, beliefs, prejudices; more broadly speaking the social history of these societies, is not addressed in the literature of the period, and our interest in them can find its material more readily in the *Nights*.[3] There has also been some interest in the more intellectual aspects of the *Nights*, for instance in its religious as well as political

---

[2] Edward William Lane, *Arabian Society in the Middle Ages: Studies from the Thousand and One Nights*, ed. Stanley Lane-Pool (London: Chatto and Windus, 1883).

[3] A powerful argument for this view is Robert Irwin, *The Arabian Nights: A Companion* (London: Allen Lane-The Penguin Press, 1994), 6. See also Irmeli Perho, "The Arabian Nights as a Source for Daily Life in the Mamluk Period," *Studia Orientalia Electronica* 85 (2014): 139–62. For a criticism of this view see Mahdi's third interpretative essay in Muhsin Mahdi, *The Thousand and One Nights* (Leiden: Brill, 1995), 164–81.

aspects.[4] What is significant, however, is that even these scholarly writings on the *Nights* treat it more as a *mirror*, or *reflection* of mentalities, historical facts, events, prejudices, and beliefs. In other words, they presuppose that what they find valuable in the *Nights* is not *intentionally* put there; their existence is more due to the impact of the context in which these stories were written and read. The contextualist view of texts, ideas, schools of thought, and even whole philosophical systems, is of course neither new nor rare. Major classic writings, philosophical ideas, religious thinkers, and the like, are often considered a reflection of their historical context, born out of the beliefs and practices of their milieu. Plato has been read as being representative of the ideas common among the pro-Spartan, anti-democratic elite of Athens; writings of Muslim philosophers have been considered a reinterpretation of distorted Greek ideas through the lens of the Muslim beliefs, which the Muslim thinkers shared with their nonphilosophic contemporaries; John Locke's *Second Treatise of Government* has been interpreted as the reflection of the point of view of the rising English bourgeoisie to which Locke belonged. But this is not the only perspective brought to bear on classic writings and the thought of the thinkers of the past. Plato's *Republic*, Ibn Tufayl's *Ḥayy ibn Yaqẓān*, and Locke's *Two Treatises of Government* are also read, even mainly, for their theoretical worth, as products of remarkable *authors* who thought deeply about specific subjects, sometimes disagreeing with, sometimes approving of, the common ideas of their societies, composing their writings with a specific *intention* in mind. These authors, it is widely supposed, wrote their works to convey a specific teaching to the reader, and they expected the reader to employ his efforts to discover that teaching. One can then legitimately ask: why the *Nights* is not read in the same way?

---

[4] Duncan B. MacDonald, "From the Arabian Nights to Spirit," *The Muslim World* 9, no. 4 (October 1, 1919): 336–48; Robert Irwin, "Political Thought in 'The Thousand and One Nights,'" *Marvels and Tales* 18, no. 2 (2004): 246–57; Yuriko Yamanaka, "Alexander in the Thousand and One Nights and the Ghazālī Connection," in *The Arabian Nights and Orientalism: Perspectives from East and West*, eds. Tetsuo Nishio and Yuriko Yamanaka (London and New York: I.B. Tauris, 2006), 93–115; Nabil Matar, "Christians in The Arabian Nights," in *The Arabian Nights in Historical Context: Between East and West*, eds. Saree Makdisi and Felicity Nussbaum (Oxford: Oxford University Press, 2008), 131–53; Muhsin J. Al-Musawi, *The Islamic Context of The Thousand and One Nights* (New York: Columbia University Press, 2009); Bruce Fudge, "Underworlds and Otherworlds in The Thousand and One Nights," *Middle Eastern Literatures* 15, no. 3 (December 1, 2012): 257–72. See also a very useful and regularly updated bibliography on the *Nights* by Ulrich Marzolph: wwwuser.gwdg.de/~umarzol/arabiannights.html.

The specific, and rather common, approach to the *Nights* as mainly a reflection of ideas, rather than a writing with a specific intention, is partly born out of a difficulty regarding the authorship of this work. The *Nights* is often described as a "book without an author." Galland already refers to this idea in the preface of his translation:

The name of the author of such a great work is unknown; but presumably it is not all by a single hand; for how can we believe that a single man had the imagination fertile enough to suffice for so many fictions?[5]

Lane, for his part, went against Galland's view and claimed that the *Nights*, which he translated, was composed by one or perhaps a maximum of two authors in Mamluk Egypt, sometime at the beginning of the sixteenth century or shortly before. He hypothesized that the stories have probably a more ancient origin, but he claimed that one or two authors must have rewritten the stories, added new material, and arranged them according to their *purpose*.[6] This view was severely criticized by Burton in his translation, who could not believe "how the distinguished Arabist came to such a conclusion."[7] Burton was convinced that the *Nights* does not have a single author, but rather many authors, presumably holding different views; authors who added new stories and revised the older ones during a long period of time. Burton's view is now considered the correct one and the idea of a single authorship for the *Nights* is generally rejected.[8] The prominence of this view leads us, however, to a very important exception which goes against the consensus: Muhsin Mahdi (1926–2007), a prominent scholar of Islamic thought and one of the most important scholars who dedicated a great part of his intellectual efforts to the *Nights*. Mahdi's scholarship was mainly focused on the study of

---

[5] "On ignore le nom de l'auteur d'un si grand ouvrage; mais vraisemblablement il n'est pas tout d'une main; car comment pourra-t-on croire qu'un seul homme ait eu l'imagination assez fertile pour suffire à tant de fictions ?" My translation. Antoine Galland, *Les Mille et Une Nuits: Contes Arabes* (Paris: Le Normant, 1806), I: xxix.

[6] Edward William Lane, *The Thousand and One Nights, Commonly Called, in England, The Arabian Nights' Entertainments* (London: Charles Knight and Co., 1839), I: xii–xiv.

[7] Richard F. Burton, *The Book of the Thousand Nights and a Night* (London: Burton Club, 1885), X: 92.

[8] Apart from Lane, another notable exception is Marie Lahy-Hollebecque, *Le Féminisme de Schéhérazade: La Révélation Des Mille et Une Nuits* (Paris: Radot, 1927). She claims that the *Nights* has a single author, a feminist one no less. Lahy-Hollebecque's position was, however, more based on her view of the *Nights* as a feminist writing. As we shall see, the more important opposing view, held by Mahdi, is more scholarly and is based on the study of manuscripts.

Islamic political thought and the writings of Alfarabi. His interest in the *Nights*, a work which was for centuries in Arab and European countries considered a "low" kind of literary entertainment suitable primarily for less sophisticated readers, does not fit as a matter of course, and is in need of some explanation.[9]

How Mahdi began working on the *Nights* can be summarized as follows: before the publication of Mahdi's critical edition of the *Nights* in 1984, there were four main Arabic editions of the *Nights*, called Calcutta I (published 1814 and 1818), Breslau or Habicht (published 1824–43), Būlāq I (published 1835), and finally Calcutta II or Macnaghten (published 1839–42). None of these editions were scholarly, and there was much doubt and obscurity regarding their provenance and authenticity. The situation began to change at the end of the nineteenth century, when an orientalist by the name of Hermann Zotenberg published an essay on Galland's translation of the *Nights*. Zotenberg's essay in turn attracted the attention of Theodor Nöldeke, one of the most prominent scholars of Islam. The idea was born that a critical edition of the *Nights* is a necessity for the advance of scholarship.[10] The project was picked up at the beginning of the twentieth century by Duncan B. Macdonald (1863–1943), who began working on the manuscripts of the *Nights* and announced his project to publish a critical edition of Galland's manuscript, collating it with other surviving manuscripts.[11] The project did not bear fruit before Macdonald's death, and it was Mahdi who began working on it in 1959, with the results being published, after fifteen years of painstaking effort

---

[9] In his *Kitāb al-Fihrist*, Ibn al-Nadīm, the Arab bibliographer, describes the *Nights* as "truly a coarse book, without warmth in the telling." Ibn al-Nadīm, *The Fihrist: A Tenth Century AD Survey of Islamic Culture*, trans. Bayard Dodge (New York: Columbia University Press, 1970), II: 713–14. For Mahdi's biography and bibliography see Butterworth, *The Political Aspects of Islamic Philosophy: Essays in Honor of Muhsin S. Mahdi*, 7–9, 383–401; Mahdi, "Years of Chicago. Forming a Soul"; Charles E. Butterworth, "In Memoriam: Muhsin S. Mahdi," *The Review of Politics* 69, no. 4 (2007): 511–12.

[10] Hermann Zotenberg, "Notice sur quelques manuscrits des Mille et une nuits et la traduction de Galland," *Notice et extraits des manuscrits de la Bibliothèque nationale et autres bibliothèques* 28 (1888): 167–320; Theodor Nöldeke, "Review of 'Histoire d''Alâ al-Dîn ou la Lampe merveilleuse' by Hermann Zotenberg," *Wiener Zeitschrift für die Kunde des Morgenlandes* 2 (1888): 168–73.

[11] Duncan B. MacDonald, "Lost MSS. of the 'Arabian Nights' and a Projected Edition of That of Galland," *Journal of the Royal Asiatic Society of Great Britain and Ireland* (January 1911): 219–21; J. Jermain Bodine, "Magic Carpet to Islam. Duncan Black Macdonald and the Arabian Nights," *The Muslim World* 67, no. 1 (January 1, 1977): 1–11.

and hard work, only in 1984: the critical edition of the *Nights* based on the oldest surviving manuscripts.[12]

It is not an exaggeration to say that Mahdi's edition of the *Nights* remains one of the most important developments in the study of this classic Arabic writing. Mahdi was, however, more than a simple editor. As remarkable as his philological talents were, Mahdi had a philosophic perspective which remains an exception among the Arabists. Mahdi's scholarly edition was accompanied by a remarkable theoretical perspective on the text. In order to understand Mahdi's general view of the *Nights*, we should mention some technical but nonetheless unavoidable points. The manuscripts of the *Nights* are divided into two main branches: the "Syrian," famously used by Galland, and the "Egyptian," which is the basis of other editions, most importantly of the so-called Calcutta II. The Syrian manuscripts are considerably shorter and contain only about forty stories told in 282 nights. This is while the Egyptian editions go up to 1,001 nights, giving the impression that they are "complete" while the Syrians are often described as "incomplete." Mahdi challenged this view. He claimed that the original work (the so-called mother source) of the *Nights* was produced sometime in the thirteenth or perhaps fourteenth century in Syria. In Mahdi's view, Galland's "incomplete" manuscript is a copy of that original work, perhaps going through an intermediary stage. Galland's shorter manuscript, Mahdi claimed, is a rather faithful reproduction of the original work and contains practically all the original stories. In Mahdi's view, the other Egyptian manuscripts are not faithful to the original work and contain later additions. Mahdi tried to show in his detailed study that, under pressure to provide the complete version of the text as advertised by the title of the work, Arab copyists began adding stories to the collection. This process of adding stories was later continued and accelerated with the rising interest of Europeans in the *Nights*. Already, Galland himself, because of his obsession with finding the complete version of the *Nights*, began adding stories to his translation without explaining their provenance: these additional stories did not actually belong to the manuscript of the *Nights* which Galland had in his possession, but were rather from unrelated writings as well as oral traditions which were transcribed with the assistance of a Maronite Christian

---

[12] Muhsin Mahdi, *The Thousand and One Nights: From the Earliest Known Sources: Vol. 1. Arabic Text* (Leiden: Brill, 1984); Muhsin Mahdi, *The Thousand and One Nights: From the Earliest Known Sources: Vol. 2. Critical Apparatus: Description of Manuscripts* (Leiden: Brill, 1984).

called Hanna. This process of addition continued in the next generation by people like Dom Denis Chavis, Michel Sabbāgh, and Mordecai Ibn al-Najjār, who even forged manuscripts, mainly for financial gain, and fabricated stories to provide a "complete" version of the *Nights*. Mahdi saw Galland and his followers as responsible for creating so much confusion about the textual history of the *Nights*, whose most faithful version, Mahdi claimed, is Galland's own manuscript, which Mahdi edited.[13]

On the basis of his research, Mahdi was persuaded that the *Nights*, as it is found in the authentic sources, is a carefully designed writing with a definite author.[14] In his view, the Syrian version of the *Nights* is not an unintelligent compilation of disparate stories haphazardly put together by many editors from previous older sources, but a carefully crafted whole designed by an author, "a consummate storyteller" with a specific intention.[15] Mahdi clearly distinguished between the authentic version of the *Nights*, produced by the original author, and later Egyptian versions, which were produced by copyists "who missed what he was after and thought that the book was like a hole in the ground in which one could dump one story after another regardless of their styles, structures, or contradictory aims." According to Mahdi, these later scribes "disfigured the book and produced the confusing text" found in later recensions.[16] Mahdi even claimed that the author of the authentic *Nights* specifically refrained from including more stories in his rather modest collection because that would have created insurmountable difficulties regarding the relationship between King Shahriar and Shahrazad, two antagonists of the frame story.[17] Even the anonymity of the author finds an explanation in Mahdi's mind: it is due to the specific character of the *Nights* as a "subversive work meant for adults who had lost their innocence." The author of the *Nights* has decided to "veil" his identity in order to not take responsibility for a writing which Mahdi considered truly radical.[18] Mahdi wrote interpretative essays on the *Nights* born out of his specific

---

[13] Mahdi, *The Thousand and One Nights*, 1–87; Mahdi, *The Thousand and One Nights: Vol. 1: Arabic Text*, v–ix; Irwin, *The Arabian Nights*, 54ff.

[14] Mahdi, *The Thousand and One Nights*, 140–42. It should be mentioned that Mahdi's position on the authorship of the *Nights* is sometimes ambiguous. He often speaks of the "author" as well as "authors" without explaining how these two ideas should be reconciled. See Mahdi, 142, 163. In this regard, Mahdi's judgment is a detailed elaboration of Lane's view on the basis of philological research.

[15] Mahdi, *The Thousand and One Nights*, 7–8.

[16] Mahdi, *The Thousand and One Nights*, 163.

[17] Mahdi, *The Thousand and One Nights*, 49.

[18] Mahdi, *The Thousand and One Nights*, 37.

approach to this work, in which he tried to explain the teaching contained in the stories.[19]

Mahdi's interpretation of the *Nights* as a work written by an author with definitive, coherent, and specific intention goes against the most common contemporary approaches as reflected in recent scholarship. When not read as a resource for the study of popular beliefs, practices, and mentalities of the people living in the context in which the stories were written, like other historical texts, the *Nights* has been investigated and dissected by the instruments of historical criticism and studied from an exclusively literary approach. Considered an expression of creative genius, akin to a collage, the *Nights* is often treated as a variety of stories with a variety of origins finding their source and prototypes in Persian, ancient Indian, Mesopotamian, and ancient Egyptian cultures. The attention of scholars has therefore been mainly directed toward questions regarding the sources and origins of the stories, as well as the comparative folk-narrative study of the purely formal characteristics of the stories, narrative motifs, and tale-types. In this perspective, the *Nights* is today studied "not so much as an individual work of literature but rather as a phenomenon comprising various manifestations in different forms of creative expression."[20] From this perspective, it would be difficult to attribute a definite intention to the author or speak about *the* teaching of the *Nights*, precisely because it is thought that there is not a single author behind the whole work: there cannot be a coherent message in this book because we are not dealing with a unified whole, but rather a compilation of disparate stories – ones that have been frequently added and transformed by narrators over the centuries.

LEO STRAUSS AND THE *ARABIAN NIGHTS*

Mahdi's specific approach to the *Nights* distinguishes itself from common contemporary scholarship on the *Nights*. It has, however, a close predecessor that seems to have had a definitive impact on Mahdi's perspective, although there are important differences between the two. This

---

[19] Mahdi, *The Thousand and One Nights*, 127–81. The first essay is a reprint of Muhsin Mahdi, "Remarks on the 1001 Nights," *Interpretation* 3, nos. 2–3 (1973): 157–68.

[20] Ulrich Marzolph and Richard van Leeuwen, *The Arabian Nights: An Encyclopedia* (Santa Barbara: ABC-CLIO, 2004), xxiv; Ulrich Marzolph, "The Arabian Nights in Comparative Folk Narrative Research," in *The Arabian Nights and Orientalism: Perspectives from East and West*, eds. Tetsuo Nishio and Yuriko Yamanaka (London: I.B. Tauris, 2005), 25–46.

interpretation is found in a transcript by Leo Strauss entitled "1001 Nights," found among his surviving papers. Before turning to this interpretation, let us say a few words about the transcript itself. Mahdi mentions that he began working on the project of editing the *Nights* by the advice of Nabia Abbott and Strauss, "my former teachers."[21] It is reported that Mahdi gifted to Strauss the six volume German translation of the *Nights* while recovering from heart surgery. These volumes, still in existence, are inscribed in Mahdi's hand, reading: "For Leo Strauss. On his sixtieth birthday. Cynthia and Muhsin Mahdi." The date mentioned is "Chicago, [19]59."[22] Later, on September 27, 1960, Strauss writes to Seth Benardete that he is "reading ... the *1001 Nights*" and he describes the work as an equivalent of Aristophanes's plays "under Islam."[23] A few months later, Strauss again writes to Karl Löwith that "I plan to read it [Gadamer's *Truth and Method*] as soon as I am through with my most pressing work (which includes the *1001 Nights*)."[24] The relationship between the *Nights* and Aristophanes's works seems to have been particularly important for Strauss, as again on January 24, 1961 he writes to Peter H. von Blanckenhagen that "in my free time I am reading *1001 Nights* which has much in common with Aristophanes, as you can imagine."[25] Strauss's interest in the *Nights* is also reflected in a published essay and three-course transcripts. Most significantly, in his course on Montesquieu's *Persian Letters*, Strauss says:

And now if one would think of this beautiful document of despotism which he [Montesquieu] surely knew, I think, and which I have no doubt some of you

---

[21] Mahdi, *The Thousand and One Nights: Vol. 1: Arabic Text*, vii.

[22] I owe the anecdote to Charles E. Butterworth. Jenny Strauss Clay provided me with essential information about Strauss's copy. I am grateful to both. The edition used by Strauss is the German translation of the Macnaghten or Calcutta II recension by Enno Littmann. Enno Littmann, *Die Erzählungen aus den Tausendundein Nächten. Vollständige Ausgabe in Sechs Bänden. Zum ersten Mal nach dem arabischen Urtext der Calcuttaer Ausgabe vom Jahre 1939 übertragen von Enno Littmann. Einleitung von Hugo von Hofmannsthal*, 6 vols. (Leipzig: Insel-Verlag, 1953). It is the same version famously translated by Richard Burton and translated recently by Malcolm and Ursula Lyons. Malcolm C. Lyons, Ursula Lyons, and Robert Irwin, *The Arabian Nights: Tales of 1,001 Nights*, 3 vols (London: Penguin Books, 2010). Here the Lyons translation is used; references to the *Nights* are identified by AN, followed by volume and page numbers.

[23] Seth Benardete Papers, SB 04–05, The New School Archives and Special Collections.

[24] Strauss, *Gesammelte Schriften. Band 3*, 685 (Letter to Karl Löwith on December 13, 1960).

[25] Leo Strauss Papers, box 4, folder 2, Special Collections Research Center, University of Chicago Library.

know, the Arabian Nights, in which there is so much shown of humanity and virtue—and also of vice, I admit. But what is the point in the Arabian Nights, simply stated? I think that the whole story shows the terrible character of despotism. These stories are all told in order to save the life of an innocent human being. She tells the stories in order to keep the sultan curious, and the continuation the next night is the only way she can save herself. So there is no doubt that Montesquieu meant this seriously.[26]

It seems that sometime between the end of 1959 and the beginning of 1961, Strauss read the German translation of the *Nights* and composed his notes.[27] Mahdi, for his part, went on to edit his edition of the *Nights* and also wrote several commentaries on the book, one of them just after Strauss's death. These essays can be considered thoughtful applications of Strauss's historic-philosophic approach to the critical edition of the *Nights*. Mahdi's interpretation is not, however, a simple elaboration of Strauss's. In fact, there are fundamental differences between Strauss's and Mahdi's approach to the *Nights*. Strauss pays much attention to parts of the book that Mahdi later describes as inauthentic additions to the original work by thoughtless Arab editors, misguided European scholars, and unscrupulous manuscript fabricators. In contrast to Mahdi, who limited his essays to the Syrian version of the *Nights*, Strauss based his notes on the Calcutta II version, as translated by Enno Littmann. This version contains more stories than any other recension of the *Nights* and, before Mahdi's groundbreaking edition, was widely considered to be the original and "complete" version of the book, the claim strongly contested by Mahdi. In fact, Mahdi's main claim is that whoever studies the larger editions "with care" and "from beginning to end finds no connection

---

[26] Leo Strauss, *1966 Spring Course on Montesquieu Offered at the University of Chicago*, ed. Thomas L. Pangle (Chicago: Leo Strauss Center, 2014), 75 (Session 5, January 18, 1966); Strauss, "Jerusalem and Athens," 148; Leo Strauss, *1967 Course on Nietzsche Offered at the University of Chicago*, ed. Richard Velkley (Chicago: Leo Strauss Center, 2015), 7 (Session 1); Leo Strauss, *1971–72 Course on Nietzsche's Beyond Good and Evil Offered at St. John's College*, ed. Mark Blitz (Chicago: Leo Strauss Center, 2014), 6 (Session 1, October 6, 1971).

[27] Strauss's notes are found at Leo Strauss Papers, box 20, folder 2, Special Collections Research Center, University of Chicago Library. References to Strauss's transcript are identified by SNAN, followed by the page and paragraph numbers of the transcript. The transcript is provided in this volume as Appendix B. In a letter to Joseph Cropsey on August 15, 1960, Strauss writes: "As soon as feasible I shall dictate to Mr. Gildin my observations regarding the 1001 Nights and let you have a copy." Hilail Gildin (1928–2015), a student of Strauss in this period, later became a professor of philosophy at Queens College, City University of New York, and the editor-in-chief of *Interpretation: A Journal of Political Philosophy*.

between *all* the stories" included in them. Mahdi argued that such a connection can be found only in the considerably shorter Syrian version.[28]
Strauss, on the contrary, tried to find such a connection between all the
stories of the Calcutta II recension.

Strauss's interpretation can be described as the synthetic application of
three out of four main problematics of his thought to the *Nights* – the
problematics which I have previously called the pillars of his thought. In
Strauss's notes, the *Nights* is read as a carefully designed and coherent
document of the premodern Enlightenment, composed in an esoteric manner by a thinker of high rank with a specific intention and specific teaching,
dedicated to the discussion of the theologico-political problem in the multi-
religious context of medieval Islamic societies. To begin with, Strauss's
esoteric techniques of reading are perhaps nowhere less controversial than
when applied to works like the *Nights*. Strauss claimed that one of the common techniques of esoteric writing is to state one's heterodox ideas under
the guise of a storyteller, a narrator, or a mere expositor, granting a certain
immunity to the author and thereby putting a distance between oneself and
the opinions reflected in one's writing. This is the reason, Strauss claims,
for finding "in the greatest literature of the past so many interesting devils,
madmen, beggars, sophists, drunkards, epicureans, and buffoons."[29] These
characters might have been the way by which persecuted freethinkers transmitted their controversial ideas. Whatever the merits of Strauss's thesis
regarding the interpretation of different philosophical works may be, the
Nights is a literary work. It is generally admitted that literary writers often
employ rhetorical devices, such as symbolism, to convey unstated mean-
ings. Consequently, it is a common practice among scholars to pay attention to the unstated or indirectly conveyed intentions of literary works.
Furthermore, Strauss's interest in the *Nights* is closely related to another
pillar of his thought, namely the theologico-political problem, reflected in
Strauss's lifelong preoccupation with the relationship between religion and
various aspects of human life, especially politics and philosophy. As was
mentioned before, the religious aspects of the *Nights* have not escaped the
notice of its readers, as religion is omnipresent in the stories. Religion in the
Nights does not always play an uncontroversial role. Many stories depict
religious conversion, proselytism, and the struggle between the adherents
of different religions in a very prominent fashion, which above all reminds
one of another pillar of Strauss's thought, namely the conflict between

[28] Mahdi, *The Thousand and One Nights*, 140–41.
[29] Strauss, *Persecution and the Art of Writing*, 1952, 36.

Reason and Revelation.[30] In Strauss's interpretation of the *Nights*, the question of esotericism, the theologico-political problem, and the conflict of Reason and Revelation join together and form the perspective through which he interprets this work. He reads the *Nights* as a work intended to be read between the lines, containing heterodox ideas incompatible with, and critical of, the reigning beliefs of the time, and depicting the conflict of religious beliefs with the political order. Although this perspective on the *Nights* is unique and surely susceptible to criticism, it is not without precedent in the study of comparable writings. For instance, the idea that the authors of *Kalīlah wa Dimnah* and of the stories of the Brethren of Purity (Ikhwān al-Ṣafā') voiced heretical ideas and their criticism of sacred beliefs through esoteric techniques such as putting their ideas in the mouths of certain characters, and even animals, is shared by other scholars.[31]

A detailed description of Strauss's interpretation of the *Nights*, evidently, can be only provided through an interpretation of Strauss's notes, which will be the subject of this chapter, in which I will try to show how Strauss went about finding a coherent message in the edition he was reading. However, an explanation is in order: as Strauss comments on a considerable number of the stories contained in the long edition of the *Nights*, the major themes of Strauss's interpretation are presented here while focusing on some of the most revealing stories. The points Strauss discovers in the *Nights* are accessible only by having the text of the recension he has been reading as well as his other writings in view. I have therefore tried to provide an interpretation of these notes by having these two sources constantly in view, in order to present Strauss's intentions for readers who otherwise would perhaps not be able to derive the full benefits of reading Strauss's notes. As the objective is to understand Strauss through his own principles, this presentation will proceed in a purely descriptive manner. I will therefore leave the critical evaluation of Strauss's interpretation, as well as my reservations about his reading of the *Nights*, aside. Such a critical evaluation must begin by taking

---

[30] Josef Henninger, "Mohammedanische Polemik gegen das Christentum in 1001 Nacht," *Neue Zeitschrift für Missionswissenschaft* 2 (1946): 289–305.

[31] Clifford Edmund Bosworth, "The Persian Impact on Arabic Literature," in *The Cambridge History of Arabic Literature: Arabic Literature to the End of the Umayyad Period*, ed. R. B. Serjeant et al., vol. 1 (Cambridge: Cambridge University Press, 1984), 487–88; Jennifer London, "How to Do Things with Fables," *History of Political Thought* 29, no. 2 (2008): 189–212; Shatha Almutawa, "'The Death of the Body Is the Birth of the Soul': Contradictory Views on the Resurrection in Rasā'il Ikhwān Al-Safā," *Studia Islamica* 113 (2018): 56–75.

Mahdi's claim about the incoherence of the recension used by Strauss into account. Furthermore, in view of the character of Strauss's notes, the following interpretation has a tentative character and should be read in the same spirit. These notes are certainly of considerable importance because, as in the case of his notes on Averroes's commentary on Plato's *Republic*, discussed in Chapter 1, they shed light on Strauss's view of a classic writing on which he did not publish an interpretation. Strauss's notes are clearly of somewhat playful character and, again, should be read in the same spirit. I believe, however, that regardless of their place in Strauss's intellectual biography, Strauss's notes can play an important role as a model of fruitful reading of the *Nights* as a serious literary work containing essential observations on religion and politics, a reading which has few examples in the contemporary scholarship.[32] With these points in mind, let us turn to Strauss's notes.

CRITIQUE OF THE REIGNING BELIEFS

Strauss begins his notes with his famous numerological observations (SNAN 1.1). One must first explain a point about this unusual practice present in many of Strauss's writings: Strauss's interest in numerology is not related to the view that numbers have occult, divine, or mystical characters. What Strauss is interested in can be described as *conventional* numerology, that is, the idea that some writers conventionally used numbers for transmitting their message. The importance of such practices in medieval and early modern writings, especially in Islamic thought, is well-known and there is no reason to reject Strauss's observation in principle.[33] One should also bear in mind, especially when we reach Strauss's own writings discussed in the next two chapters, that Strauss tried to

---

[32] One can clearly see how Strauss benefitted from the *Nights* for reflection on classic theoretical issues and also for understanding other similar writings. For example, in a letter to Joseph Cropsey on August 12, 1960, Strauss writes the following: "Did you ever think of the possibility that there is a connection between Abraham's sacrifice of Isaac and God's jealousy? On reflection it seems obvious, but the poor one (to use an Arabism) needed the 1001 Nights." For Strauss's discussion of this issue in the *Nights* see pp. 98–99 below. For another similar example, see the connection established between the *Nights* and Shakespeare's *Othello* by Strauss, see p. 106, footnote 47. I am grateful to Hannes Kerber who drew my attention to this letter.

[33] In the case of Islamic thought it suffices to mention Abjad numerals. For a general introduction see Vincent Foster Hopper, *Medieval Number Symbolism* (Mineola: Dover Publications Inc., 2003). For a good bibliography on the use of numerology in Islam see Annemarie Schimmel, *The Mystery of Numbers* (New York: Oxford University Press, 1994), 288–90.

imitate these numerological practices in his own writings, partly in the spirit of playfulness, partly for pedagogical reasons explained in the Introduction of this book.

In his numerological observations, Strauss claims that the number 1001 in the title of the *Nights* is perhaps chosen by the author to transmit a message about the content of the work. This number is a multiple of 7, 11, and 13. The theological symbolism of the number 7 is obvious, as in Abrahamic beliefs God created everything in 6 days and took his rest on the 7th day (Genesis 1, Qur'ān 7:54, 2:29, 67:3, 71:15, 78:12). Number 11 is less obvious, but coming after 10, which represents the Law (as in Ten Commandments), it sometime stands for disobedience.[34] The number 13, particularly mentioned by Strauss in his reading of Machiavelli, also seems to have an anti-theological significance.[35] These three numbers are therefore for Strauss a kind of wink toward the theologico-political problem and the conflict of Reason and Revelation. Strauss also suggests that the book might be considered 1003 Nights – if one adds two stories told before the ones told by Shahrazad. Number 1003 in its turn is a multiple of seventeen and fifty-nine. For Strauss, the number seventeen represents nature (*phusis*), as the Greek alphabet, the original language of the study of nature, has seventeen consonants: the consonants being mute like nature are put in opposition to tradition which must be audible to be transmitted.[36] The significance of number fifty-nine is not entirely clear, but it seems that for Strauss it also represents nature.[37] These

---

[34] See "Eleven is the sin. Eleven transgresses the Ten Commandments," in Friedrich Schiller, *The Piccolomini*, Act II, Scene I.

[35] Strauss, *Thoughts on Machiavelli*, 52; Strauss, "Niccolò Machiavelli," 311. See especially the comparison with Spinoza in the latter.

[36] Nasser Behnegar, "Reading 'What Is Political Philosophy?,'" in *Leo Strauss's Defense of the Philosophic Life: Reading "What Is Political Philosophy?,"* ed. Rafael Major (Chicago: University of Chicago Press, 2013), 41n5; Leo Strauss, "How To Begin To Study The Guide of the Perplexed," in *Liberalism Ancient and Modern* (New York: Basic Books, 1968), 158; Strauss, *On Tyranny*, 275 (Letter to Alexandre Kojève on April 22, 1957). Strauss's interest in number 17 is not unprecedented and its historical importance for different ancient and medieval authors is documented by other scholars. See Kraus, *Jābir ibn Ḥayyān: Contribution à l'histoire des idées scientifiques dans l'Islam. Vol 2. Jabir et la science grecque.*, 187–303, esp. 216–17, 220–23; Lloyd Ridgeon, *Morals and Mysticism in Persian Sufism: A History of Sufi-Futuwwat in Iran* (New York: Routledge, 2010), 144.

[37] Commenting on Plato's *Laws*, Strauss writes: "The Athenian suggests then that the future city should consist of 5,040 land holders and defenders of their plots and the same number of plots. This number has the advantage that it can be divided by all numbers up to ten; in fact, it is susceptible of fifty-nine different divisions." Strauss, *The Argument and the Action of Plato's Laws*, 73, 79. The chapter dedicated to *Discourses on Livy* in Strauss's *Thoughts on Machiavelli* also consists of fifty-nine paragraphs. It should be also mentioned that fifty-nine is the seventeenth prime number. I owe these observations to Steven J. Lenzner.

numerological observations are followed by a general statement about
the content of the whole work: "The overall suggestion: refutation of the
nomos regarding inferiority of women; and: indictment of tyranny; and:
how *jealousy* of a king is appeased" (SNAN 1.1). How these three subjects, namely a critique of nomos or (religious) law, a critique of tyranny,
and a critique of "jealousy" are related will gradually become clear. But
what is particularly interesting is that these subjects prove to be, one way
or another, connected with religion: tyranny and jealousy are both divine
(SNAN 4.12, 14.39) and women represent erotic longing as a kind of
"counter-religion" (SNAN 14.39). It is therefore fitting to begin at the
beginning before turning to politics and love.

In Strauss's interpretation, the critical view of the author of the *Nights*
towards the sacred is first reflected in the frame story of the *Nights*: King
Shahriar invites his younger brother Shah Zaman to visit him. On his
way to Shahriar, Shah Zaman discovers his wife in an act of infidelity
with a kitchen boy. Enraged and jealous, Shah Zaman kills both of them
and then proceeds to visit his brother. During his visit, Shah Zaman suffers from a deep depression. He spends his time in the palace while his
brother King Shahriar goes out hunting. One day while looking out the
window, Shah Zaman sees his brother's queen in the courtyard betraying
her husband with a black slave. Surprisingly, by witnessing the misfortune of his brother, Shah Zaman's condition improves, and he informs
Shahriar about their shared affliction. Dismayed by their misfortune,
they both decide to roam the world in hope of finding someone whose
misfortune is greater than theirs. On their way, they discover a jealous
jinni, a male supernatural being. The demon's wife betrays him with men
every time the demon takes a nap on the shore (AN I 5–7). Just as in the
case of Shah Zaman, the misfortune of the demon brings joy to the jealous kings, and they return to rule their realms.

For Strauss, the major leitmotif of many of the stories in the *Nights*
is the jealousy of kings, demons, and caliphs (see SNAN 1.1, 4.12, 5.15,
10.30). The jealous beings encounter unfaithful women and, being slaves
of jealousy, their anger leads to violence. King Shahriar takes revenge
not only by killing his unfaithful wife after returning to his realm but
also takes a wife every day and kills her the next morning – until he
marries Shahrazad, who tells him stories to stay alive. For Strauss, the
lesson is that it is a dangerous thing to deceive "kings"; their jealousy
must be taken into account (SNAN 1.2). But who are "kings" and why
is jealousy so important? Jealousy is one of the traits of the biblical God,
"for the Lord, whose name is Jealous, is a jealous God" (Exodus 34:14).

Exclusiveness is the core of monotheism, therefore jealousy is *the* characteristic of the god of monotheism. There is a famous hadith that makes the same point:

Sa'd ibn 'Ubada said, "If I were to see a man with my wife, I would have struck him with the sword, and not with the flat part (side) of it." When Allah's Messenger heard of that, he said: "Are you surprised at Sa'd's jealousy? By Allah, I am more jealous than he, and Allah is more jealous than I. Because of His jealousy Allah has prohibited abomination, both open and secret. And no person is more jealous than Allah."[38]

Strauss makes this point rather forcefully: "Allah is a jealous God" (SNAN 1.4). However, he also observes that "it is not dangerous to deceive demons," as one can see how the wife of a demon has betrayed him with 570 men without the demon knowing about it (AN I 6; SNAN 1.2). In other words, the jealousy of a fantastic being does not seem to be as dangerous as that of a real being. But what do such fantastic beings represent in the *Nights*? To answer this question one must turn to the story of the merchant and the demon (AN I 10–19): in this story, a group of travelers tell stories to appease the anger of a demon. In the first story, an old man tells the demon that because his wife did not bear him any children, he took a concubine. The concubine bore him a son. The wife became jealous and through magic turned the son and the concubine into a calf and a cow, and asked her husband to sacrifice them at Eid al-Adha – a Muslim festival which symbolizes the story of God asking Abraham to sacrifice his son as an act of submission to God's command (Muslims sacrifice an animal at this ceremony in remembrance of that story). In the man's story, a young girl who possesses magic skills recognizes human beings under the shape of animals. For revenge she turns the jealous wife into a gazelle and restores the son to his human shape. The story reminds us of and clearly points to the sacrifice of Isaac by Abraham, except that here a jealous wife asks her husband to sacrifice his son, thus confirming Strauss's suspicion that in the *Nights* divine jealousy is a theme (SNAN 1.4).

The second story is told by a merchant who is accompanied by two greyhounds. He explains to the demon that the dogs are his ungrateful

---

[38] Imam Muslim, *Ṣaḥīḥ Muslim. Vol. IV*, trans. Nasiruddin Al-Khattab (Riyadh: Darussalam, 2007), 195 (Hadith 3764). For the relationship between jealousy and women in the Bible cf. Genesis 30:1 with Numbers 5:29. Exclusivity, i.e. not admitting partners, is the core of jealousy. Jealousy of God who doesn't suffer sharing our love with others, is also a common theme in Islamic mysticism. See Annemarie Schimmel, *Mystical Dimensions of Islam* (Chapel Hill: University of North Carolina Press, 2011), 39.

brothers whom he has rescued from bankruptcy several times. The three brothers together went on a journey and during the trip the narrator meets a beautiful young woman on the shore. He takes her with him onto the ship. His two brothers become jealous and throw the couple overboard. But the beautiful woman turns out to be an '*ifrita*, a she-demon who declares her faith in Islam and the Prophet. The she-demon is angry with the merchant's treacherous brothers and offers to kill them. However, the merchant tries to appease the demon's anger and asks for a more lenient punishment. The she-demon agrees to turn them into greyhounds instead of killing them (AN I 17). As Strauss observes, the "she-demon wished a greater revenge than the brother of the treacherous brothers" (SNAN 1.4). The merchant is more humane towards his fellow men than the Muslim she-demon.

By underscoring the difference between the humane punishment of the merchant and the inhuman cruelty of his fantastic religious lover, Strauss reminds us of his discussion of the "inhuman cruelty" characteristic of Biblical morality (SNAN 14.39). Strauss argued that one of the major concerns of early modern thinkers such as Machiavelli was that biblical morality legitimized, nay, made inhuman or pious cruelty a duty.[39] That what is meant by the cruelty of these supernatural beings is divine cruelty is corroborated by another story that a woman tells before the caliph: Once, she went on a journey and arrived at a city of unbelieving fire-worshippers. All the inhabitants of the city, including children and animals, have been transformed by God into stone because, as she learns later from the only surviving witness, they did not heed a mysterious voice that summoned them to convert to the True Faith of Islam. The only inhabitant of the city who was saved was the son of the king of the city. The prince was clandestinely proselytized by a Muslim woman, a servant of the king who treacherously concealed her religion (AN I 110–11; see also the story of the semi-petrified prince on pp. 105–106 below and SNAN 5.14 and 18.62).[40]

According to Strauss, jealousy and pious cruelty are not the only objects of the *Nights'* critique of religion. In this work, Strauss implies, religion in general is seen as a pernicious phenomenon. In the *Nights*, according to Strauss's reading, God is depicted as a major impediment to the good life.

---

[39] Strauss, *Thoughts on Machiavelli*, 187.

[40] The story seems inspired by the stories of many generations in the Qur'ān who also refused to heed the messengers and were consequently destroyed. See Qur'ān 6:10–11, 7:59–136.

He observes this in the dialogue of the wise vizier Shimas with the young prince Wird Khan. The dialogue is at first sight a longwinded repetition of the ideas common to the scholars of the time. However, in the middle of the uninteresting back and forth some interesting points are hidden: one is that vizier Shimas mentions that this life and the next "are at variance with one another" and therefore one living in this world will inevitably "injure his soul in the next." Prince Wird Khan approves this point by describing this world as the kingdom of an unjust king in which, as Strauss explains, "men cannot be just" (SNAN 17.58). He explains the situation of those who live in the belief in an afterlife as someone who has "fallen between two kings" (AN III 462–64). They live in an impossible situation created by the introduction of the belief in an afterlife. This view of the divine is most clearly depicted in the story of the peahen and the duck (AN I 613–21): A peacock and a peahen, looking for a place to be safe from wild animals, go to live on an island. One day a duck arrives and tells them that he is afraid of the "son of Adam." The duck has been warned of man's viciousness in a dream. The duck thinks that the son of Adam is the source of all evil and goes around warning all animals about the danger of man. However, in the end the duck is the one who is hunted by man. When the duck perishes, the peahen (a high-flying bird) says that the duck perished because he did not glorify God, and was punished for it. Strauss calls this "a female explanation of the fate of beings" (SNAN 10.30). The duck and the peahen say in fact the same thing. As Strauss explains, the story read literally would hardly make sense, as animals are killed not only by man but also by other animals. The story would make sense, then, only if it is interpreted in human terms: seen from the point of view of animals, *man is God*. The peahen unknowingly unveils the message of the duck's symbolic warning: all evil comes from God – this is why we see the duck and other animals take refuge in the protection of a lion. But the peahen also obfuscates the message of the duck by hiding the real culprit, that is, God, in whose absence all animals would live comfortably and in perfect harmony and friendship.

If the peahen was not such a high-flying bird (SNAN 8.30), she could see the real culprit. This seems to be the reason why Strauss also refers to the remarkable story of an old woman who lives in the desert. The old woman feeds on bitter water and snakes. When a traveler asks her why she lives in this earthly hell, she asks the traveler about his own country. The visitor, who is on his way to Mecca on pilgrimage, describes his hometown: in his city, everything exists in abundance and there are "such blessings as are only to be found in the Paradise which Almighty

God describes as being reserved for his pious servants." (AN II 274). The woman tells him that the "earthly" paradise of the visitor is ruled by a tyrant who if "he wants can drive you from your house and uproot you," thereby reminding us, among other things, of God's expulsion of man from the original Paradise. Then she compares this tyrant with the old rulers who governed with grace. The author completes this story by narrating the story of al-Hajjaj ibn Yusuf, the famous Muslim governor. Al-Hajjaj rebuked the demands for a more lenient rule by saying that "Almighty God has appointed me as your ruler." Strauss compares this story with Book 1, Chapter 26 of Machiavelli's *Discourses on Livy* (SNAN 14.39). Only in that chapter, which according to Strauss is specifically devoted to the phenomenon of tyranny, does Machiavelli directly quote from the Bible. Machiavelli uses a famous quotation from the New Testament (also a part of the Magnificat that is frequently sung in Church services) to describe the actions of King David – while the Biblical passage is in fact about God. Machiavelli is therefore describing actions similar to David's as being "very cruel" and the enemy to every way of life. Strauss thinks that this is Machiavelli's esoteric way of saying that God, like Philip of Macedon (also mentioned in the chapter) is a cruel and inhuman tyrant.[41] In other words, according to Strauss, the author of the *Nights* and Machiavelli look at the Biblical/Qur'ānic image of God as a violent tyrant ruling over human beings. It is therefore not surprising that Strauss sees a relationship between Aristophanes's comedies and the *Nights*. In Aristophanes's *Peace*, Tyrgaeus succeeds in bringing peace to Hellas by disinterring the goddess of peace against the explicit command of Zeus: "The just and pleasant life of ease and quiet cannot be brought about except by dethroning the gods."[42]

WISDOM, BELIEFS, AND POLITICAL THEOLOGY

What should one conclude from the critique of religion in the *Nights*? Is it the intention of the *Nights*, according to Strauss, to help men get rid of religion? Does the author think that men should live their life without religion? Strauss often argues that before Pierre Bayle, no philosopher argued for the possibility of an atheistic society; even unbelieving

---

[41] Strauss, *Thoughts on Machiavelli*, 44–49; Harvey C. Mansfield, *Machiavelli's New Modes and Orders: A Study of the Discourses on Livy* (Chicago: University of Chicago Press, 2001), 99.

[42] Strauss, "The Origins of Political Science and the Problem of Socrates," 147.

thinkers thought that some kind of religion, even in the form of a salutary myth or more precisely a "political theology," is necessary for the functioning of a decent political order.[43] The same seems to be true of the *Nights*: its teaching is rather the manipulation of beliefs in the service of a decent human life.

This point is intimated in the story of the fisherman and the *'ifrit* (AN I 19ff.). This story represents the new situation of the wise in the world of revealed religions (SNAN 3.7 end). The story depicts a poor fisherman who goes to cast his net in the river to earn his day's living. From the beginning, we suspect that he is no ordinary fisherman: he is "musical" and while casting his net sings verses about his own wisdom and his undeserved poverty (AN I 21). The fisherman catches a brass jar in his net – one with a lead seal imprinted with the inscription of Solomon. Unknowingly he opens the jar, and thereby frees a heretical demon who rebelled against Solomon and was imprisoned in the jar. During his captivity, the demon had sworn to kill the person who freed him from the jar and now plans to kill the poor fisherman. But the fisherman is very confident of his own intelligence. He apparently knows many things about religion and its powers. First, he conjures the demon by "the Greatest Name of God" to answer his questions.[44] The demon is apparently shaken and tamed by the mentioning of the Greatest Name. The fisherman benefits from the perplexity of the demon: he tricks him into returning to the jar and puts back the brass stopper imprinted with the inscription of Solomon. The fisherman seems to be a master of the art of controlling demons by using the revealed religion.

The demon begs for mercy, but the fisherman refrains from releasing him and begins to tell a story to explain to the demon why he cannot trust him. The story told by the fisherman is that of King Yunan and Duban the sage (AN I 25ff). King Yunan, whose name means "Greece,"

---

[43] Strauss, *Natural Right and History*, 198; Strauss, "The Law of Reason in The Kuzari," 115, 130; Strauss, "Religion and the Commonweal," 90. For the classical understanding of political theology see Augustine, *The City of God* IV.27. For a genealogy of the concept and its transformation see Bernd Wacker and Jürgen Manemann, "'Politische Theologie.' Eine Skizze zur Geschichte und aktuellen Diskussion des Begriffs," in *Politische Theologie und Politische Philosophie*, eds. Marie-Christine Kajewski and Jürgen Manemann, 1st ed. (Baden-Baden: Nomos Verlagsgesellschaft, 2016), 9–54.

[44] Traditionally the "Greatest Name of Allah" (al-ism al-ʼaʿẓam) is said to be hidden from ordinary men. According to a hadith, the Greatest Name of Allah is "the one which if He is called by it, He will answer": Ibn Majah, *Sunan. Vol. V*, trans. Nasiruddin Al-Khattab (Riyadh: Darussalam, 2007), 114 (Hadith 3857); Amira El-Zein, *Islam, Arabs, and Intelligent World of the Jinn* (Syracuse: Syracuse University Press, 2009), 81–82.

suffers from leprosy; there comes a sage who has studied the books of
the Greeks, the Persians, the Arabs, and the Syrians.[45] He is the master
of all the sciences and manages to cure the king with his medical knowledge and is given the most splendid rewards. The new status of the sage
arouses the jealousy of the vizier. The vizier tries to convince the king
that the sage is a dangerous individual possessing unknown powers who
might kill the king in the same way that he had cured him. The king is at
first skeptical of the vizier's claim, but the vizier tells a story to convince
him. In the vizier's story, a wicked *vizier* conspires with a female demon
to kill the prince, but the demon foolishly advises the prince to pray
to God if he wants to save himself. The prince prays, and being saved,
goes back to the king explaining how the wicked vizier wanted to kill
his son. The king kills the wicked vizier and now King Yunan, listening
to the story, is convinced that he should also kill the sage Duban. When
the sage is brought for execution he says that he is innocent and killing
him after the service he has done for the king would be like "the crocodile's reward." The king asks the sage to tell the story of the crocodile,
but surprisingly the sage refuses to do so. After unsuccessfully pleading
with the king to spare his life, the sage requests some delay for putting
his affairs in order. When the sage returns, he offers a magic book to
the king and tells him that the book will make his head speak after
it has been cut off. All that the king should do, he says, is read some
passages from the book. The sage is beheaded, but as the king tries to
open the book, he sees that the pages are stuck together. The king licks
his fingers to open the pages, but the pages had been poisoned by the
sage, and the king dies: the king "Greece" and the sage end up killing
each other.

   As Strauss mentions, nothing is said about the fate of the wicked jealous vizier, but we can assume that he inherited the kingdom. Strauss
thinks that "the wicked vizier is a prophet who denigrates his predecessors," namely the wicked viziers of the past. He has devised a plan to
destroy the foolish king ("the prophet's master") and his rival, the sage,
in a mutual destruction (SNAN 2.5). The episode reminds Strauss of the
conflict of Athens and Socrates (SNAN 3.7–8, 4.12), and how two partners who could have been beneficial to each other followed the path of

---

[45] Cf. the career of Duban with the common background of philosophers in the Islamic
world. See for instance the surviving passages from Alfarabi's autobiography in Fakhry,
Al-Farabi, Founder of Islamic Neoplatonism, 158ff.

mutual destruction.[46] The sage of the story who could not tell a story to save his own life should learn from the musical fisherman, his religious knowledge and poetic powers, or from the prince who learned the power of prayer from a demon. The fisherman is a musical sage who has learned to use the divine art of prayer and religion to imprison the demon.

Strauss observes the same teaching in another story of the *Nights*, the story of the second dervish. This dervish, who is especially religious, was transformed into a monkey by a descendant of Satan. The dervish-monkey is presented to a king who has an intelligent daughter knowledgeable about the art of magic: a princess who knows 170 charms (10 × 17). She discovers the monkey to be a prince and pledges to release him. A fierce fight between the king's daughter and the demon who has put the dervish under spell takes place. In the end, the dervish is restored to his human shape but the princess is mortally wounded and dies: the princess and the demon end up killing each other (AN I 74, 86, 88). Strauss imagines the possibility of an alliance between the princess and the heretic demon against the religious dervish and thinks that such an alliance would lead to the ruin of "the wicked vizier" and his master "the ugly negro slave" (SNAN 3–4.12; for "the ugly negro slave" see p. 106 below).

Such a fruitful alliance with a descendant of Satan would be devoid of any fanaticism. The same is true of the alliance between the fisherman and the heretic demon who rebelled against Solomon (SNAN 2.6, 3.9). The fisherman releases the demon, and the demon shows the fishermen a lake containing four kinds of fish in different colors. He tells the fisherman that he can become rich by selling the fish to a king. But when the fish are fried by the king's cook, the kitchen-wall splits open, and a young woman appears and speaks to the fish, and the fish speak to her. To find the mystery of the fish, the king asks the fisherman to take him to the lake. Near the lake, the king discovers the palace of a young prince, the lower part of whose body had been turned into stone. The prince tells the king the story behind his condition: his wife has been betraying him

---

[46] The spurious story that a king killed Socrates probably finds its origin in a misunderstanding about *archon basileus*, the Athenian magistracy dealing with the indictment against Socrates for impiety. It is mentioned in Plato, *Euthyphro* 2a3. The same spurious story is reflected in al-Kindi's anecdote about Socrates: Al-Kindi, *The Philosophical Works of Al-Kindi*, trans. Peter Pormann and Peter Adamson (Karachi: Oxford University Press, 2012), 263. Another possibility is that the story has reminded Strauss of another Socrates, "the Armenian Socrates" in Xenophon's *Education of Cyrus*, who is killed by the jealous Armenian king. See Xenophon, *Education of Cyrus* III.1.38ff; Strauss, *1963 Winter Course on Xenophon*, 370 (Session 15, February 20, 1963).

by committing adultery with a "leprous ugly black slave" who lives in a domed shrine-like hut and sleeps on cane stalks covered with rags and tatters. Although she is mistreated by the black slave, the princess humbles herself to him and praises him like a god. When the prince found out about his wife's adultery he tried to kill the black man, but only injured him. As revenge, the wife, who knows sorcery, has turned the lower part of the prince's body into stone and his subjects into the fish found in the lake. The adulterous princess lashes the prince every day and nurses the injured black slave. The king kills the black slave and forces the wife to lift the spell, thereby returning the citizens of the city to their human forms. The king also rewards the fisherman and, contrary to King Yunan and the sage, they end up helping each other.[47]

For Strauss, the alliance of the fisherman and the demon leads to rescuing the population of a city and the salvation of the prince of that city, betrayed by a woman in love with a black slave. Strauss calls the fisherman "the enemy of the fish" (SNAN 3.6). It seems that he has a passage in Alfarabi's *Philosophy of Plato* in mind in which the fish symbolize stupidity and men devoid of human intelligence are compared to "a fish with a shape like that of a man."[48] The fisherman is a philosopher, the enemy of stupidity, but he does not remain the enemy of the fish. The new fisherman-philosopher *helps* the fish by transforming them into human beings. The sage is the savior of the many in the age of revelation. Strauss also mentions that the actions of the fisherman were not possible

---

[47] In a letter to Joseph Cropsey on August 15, 1960, Strauss writes the following: "If you happen to write to [Allan] Bloom whose address is not known to us tell him that the story near the beginning of the *1001 Nights* of the fisherman and the demon (which includes the story of the prince transformed into stone) is in substance identical with the *Othello* as he reads that play." Bloom's interpretation of the *Othello* was published shortly before Strauss's letter, in March 1960. Bloom's interpretation deals naturally with the question of jealousy which is obviously essential to Shakespeare's play. What is however more significant is that Bloom strongly implies that the character of Othello is a metaphor for speaking of god. Bloom claims that Shakespeare has depicted Othello as a physically unattractive man to explain the origin of his jealousy: jealousy is disease of a being who lacks self-assurance; he knows that he is unlovable but nonetheless sees himself as deserving to be loved and therefore punishes those who do not love him like a tyrant. In Strauss's words, "God is jealous either because He is not, or does not believe himself to be, infinitely attractive" (SNAN 5.15). See also Allan Bloom, "Cosmopolitan Man and the Political Community: An Interpretation of Othello," *American Political Science Review* 54, no. 1 (March 1960): esp. 147. I am grateful to Hannes Kerber for sharing Strauss's letter with me.

[48] Alfarabi, "The Philosophy of Plato," 64 (Rosenthal and Walzer 18). I owe the reference to Nasser Behnegar. The origin of the idea seems to be Aristotle, *History of Animals* 505a33–b1 in which fish are described as animals lacking most of the sense-organs.

in the time of Socrates, namely, trusting in oaths and imprisoning demons with the Name of God: the revealed religions have given birth to new theologico-political problems as well as new *arms* (SNAN 3.7). Strauss compares the prince's adulterous wife, who had preferred to him a most ugly leprous slave, with the wicked vizier in the story told by the fisherman (SNAN 4.12). The wife is a prophet who *believes* in the beauty of the ugly slave and his attachment to him had transformed the people into fish, the dumbest of all animals.[49] The new religion marks the rise of the fortunes of the ignoble – the slave who fornicated with the queen of King Shahriar was called Mas'ūd, "the fortunate."[50]

The alliance between the sage and the irreligious demons and kings is possible if the sage learns about the power of religion and puts it in the service of the many.[51] The sage should also learn how to appease the king and the demon, and learn to charm them by his story telling, just like Shahrazad, who not only mastered medicine and philosophy but also the art of storytelling, and thereby managed to save her own life and that of her fellow women. The possibility of an alliance between kings

---

[49] This is also the message of the fantastic story of Ma'ruf the cobbler: in that story it is shown how a poor cobbler who has run away to another city from his ugly and troublesome wife starts believing his own lies that he is in fact a rich merchant and that his caravan will arrive soon with his many fantastic possessions. Only a miraculous ring can make his vain hopes a reality (SNAN 18.63).

[50] Mahdi, *The Thousand and One Nights*, 128. In a famous tradition, the Prophet states that "I was sent to the red and to the black." On the basis of this tradition, Averroes argues that Islam is intended for all mankind: Averroes, *Faith, and Reason in Islam: Averroes' Exposition of Religious Arguments*, trans. Ibrahim Najjar (Oxford: Oneworld Publications, 2001), 103–4 (Qasim 220). It is said that Muhammad, upon his triumphal return to Mecca, asked Bilal, a black African slave, to call the people to prayer. Several prominent Meccans were unhappy about this, which occasioned the revelation of 49:13: "We have created you from male and female and made you peoples and tribes that you may know one another. Indeed, the most noble of you in the sight of Allah is the most righteous of you." See also Qur'ān 30:22 and the Prophet's Farewell Address: "Indeed, there is no superiority of an Arab over a non-Arab, nor of a non-Arab over an Arab, nor of a white over a black, nor a black over a white, except by *taqwa* [piety]." Aḥmad ibn Ḥanbal, *Al-Musnad* (Beirut: Dar "Ihya" al-Turath al-'Arabi, 1993), Hadith 22978. Islam is also depicted as a lean and brown slave in the story of the Yemeni and his six slaves (AN II 83–96): in that story, the order of the brown slave girl in the enumeration is changed and she is particularly praised. The same is the case of the thin slave girl. Neither of them quotes the Qur'ān in their speeches, thus separating themselves from the four others, as if they *are* the Qur'ān and do not need to remind us of their Qur'ānic superiority (SNAN 14.38).

[51] See "language of brutes" (SNAN 1.3), "mistake of the sage" (SNAN 2.5), "the king's daughter who knows 170 [17 × 10] charms" (SNAN 14.12), "*address of Schechrazad to her king* to the effect that religion depends on government" (SNAN 15.41).

and sages is depicted, not only in the frame story of the whole work in which Shahrazad tames King Shahriar and teaches him many things but also at the end of the story of the just King Anushirvan (AN II 327). At the end of this story, Shahrazad addresses the king for the first time and approves of the opinion of "the wise men and philosophers" who said that "religion depends on the king," showing the way toward an alliance between kings and sages for the subduction of religion (SNAN 14.40).

However, one must remain prudent about the possibility of such an alliance. Strauss reminds us of the limitations of the power of wisdom in guiding human life. This is intimated in the story of Wird Khan. Before the birth of Wird Khan, his father King Jali'ad had a dream which predicted the injustice of his unborn son. The king tries to prevent the fulfillment of the prophecy by giving his son an exemplary philosophic education and asking the wise Shimas to be the vizier to his son. In the end, as Strauss explains, a twelve-year-old boy and the fear of impending invasion of enemies succeed in doing what philosophy and wise men could not do: they knock some reason into Wird Khan (AN III 503ff., SNAN 17.58). The tale depicts the impuissance of philosophy and wise counsel in controlling the tyrannical tendencies of King Wird Khan.

LOVE AND LIBERATION

According to Strauss, one of the major aspects of premodern thought is the awareness of the limits of politics.[52] He also intimates the presence of such an awareness in the *Nights*: "men cannot be just while living in this life" (SNAN 17.58). This means that the real remedy for the problem brought about by revealed religions should not be sought in the sphere of politics. But where should one discover the real remedy offered by the *Nights*? The answer seems to be in love and erotic longings. This should not sound surprising, as one can easily describe the *Nights* as a love story: love is the major theme of the whole work and is the guiding motive of many of its characters. However, Strauss gives a theologico-political twist to this observation and calls "the counter-religion of love" a recurring theme of the work (SNAN 13.39). Eroticism and love are somehow related to the *Nights*' view of religion. To explain what is meant here, let us first begin with some preliminary observations about love in the *Nights*.

---

[52] Strauss, "The Spirit of Sparta or the Taste of Xenophon," 528; Strauss, *The City and Man*, 127; Strauss, "On Classical Political Philosophy," 1959, 94; Strauss, *Natural Right and History*, 151.

Love, eroticism, and the body are depicted as the principal targets of religious thought in the *Nights*. One can see this in a group of six stories (SNAN 14.39). The first one is about an extremely religious son of the caliph who has chosen to live ascetically. He works as a bricklayer for a trifling wage, although he has a precious ruby in his pocket (AN II 213–17). The following stories prove to be a concealed criticism of the basis of the prince's mode of life: in the second story, an eminent man has met a remarkable schoolteacher who masters the Qur'ān, grammar, poetry, and philology. The narrator describes him as a man of intelligence, contrary to the common belief that schoolteachers are stupid. After a while the narrator finds the teacher in mourning. He asks him about the cause of his sadness and the teacher responds that his beloved had just died. The narrator questions him about her identity but the teacher tells him that he had never seen her: he had fallen in love only after hearing someone recite a poem about her, and recently he had heard another verse, indicating that the woman of the first poem had died. The narrator calls the teacher a fool, and Strauss describes the story as "falling in love on hearsay" (AN II 217–19, SNAN 14.39). The story reminds us of the princess who believed in the beauty of an ugly slave. In the third story, we meet yet another schoolmaster, who has surprised his guest with his knowledge of jurisprudence, grammar, and philology. At night, the guest hears a loud cry in the house and finds the teacher covered in blood and about to die. Asked what has happened, the teacher answers that his reflection about the works of Almighty God has led him to believe that all the members of the body created by God serve a purpose except the sexual organs. He has therefore cut the useless source of his erotic longings with a razor. The narrator again calls all schoolmasters foolish and Strauss describes the message as "the absurdity of asceticism" (AN II 219, SNAN 14.39). The next story describes a schoolmaster who loiters in a mosque (AN II 219–20). He cannot read or write but pretends that he does and tricks parents into sending their children to him. Although he is illiterate, he pretends that he can read the letter of a husband to his wife and tells her that her husband is dead. The story is followed by the story of a king who desires his subject's woman. When the husband suspects that the king has his eyes on his wife, he refuses to sleep with her until the king assures him that he has lost interest.[53] The next story is the fantastic story of the bird

---

[53] Cf. the story of Abu 'Isa and Qurrat Al-'Ain (AN II 239) in which Isa hides his love for the slave girl Qurrat who is offered to the caliph.

Rukh and all the incredible things told about it, followed by several stories of unhappy lovers. One of the stories is about a man who sees a beautiful woman and falls in love, but has no house to which he can invite her. He therefore goes to the house of his friend, called Muslim. The friend gives him money to buy some food, but when he returns to the house, he finds that Muslim has locked the door and is making love to the woman. When he knocks, Muslim simply grabs the food and closes the door, saying that God at the Day of Judgment will reward and repay him for the favor that he has done for him (AN II 225–27).

In the *Nights*, religion is the enemy of *eros* and erotic longings. But man is an erotic being and love is a part of his nature. Religion must therefore mutilate man's nature. The metaphorical mutilation of human nature by religion is depicted literally in the story of the hunchback: in that story, a Muslim, a Jew, and a Christian tell stories of mutilated Muslim men. Strauss remarks that the most mutilated Muslim is the one in the story told by the Muslim (SNAN 6.17, AN 189–97): the Muslim narrator has attended a gathering for recitation of the Qur'ān where the Muslim jurists were also present. After the recitation, the table is set for a feast, and on the menu, there is an almond dish. A young man among the guests whose thumbs and big toes have been cut off refrains from eating the food unless he washes his hands 120 times, reminding us of the ritual ablutions. The guests ask for the story behind his aversion to the dish. He says that he was once a poor merchant when a beautiful slave-girl of the caliph visited his shop. He fell in love and married her, but before consummating the marriage, he ate the same almond dish and forgot to wash his hands. In the bedroom and about to enjoy the union, the slave-girl smelled the scent of the dish and was repulsed by the merchant's unwashed hands. Outraged by the merchant's lack of manners, she cruelly cut the merchant's thumbs and toes as a punishment for not washing his hands after eating. The young man later took an oath to wash his hands before eating the almond dish again. Remarkably, despite the terrible punishment, the slave-girl has become the merchant's wife and they continue to live together.

Strauss finds the origin of religion's anti-erotic vision partly in the bodily dimension of erotic desires. God is noncorporeal and lacks *eros*. "God is jealous either because He is not, or does not believe himself to be, infinitely attractive, and the reason for that is his hiddenness: He Himself is the ground of His jealousy" (SNAN 5.15). However, the God of the *Nights* is not and cannot be responsible for the effects of His jealousy. In the story of the crow and the cat we see Him depicted as a mere spectator: sitting under a tree and living in peace, a cat and a crow see a leopard coming towards them. The crow flies to safety, but the cat, unable to save himself, asks for the crow's help. The crow sees a herds-man and his dogs nearby and attracts the dogs towards the tree. The leop-ard runs away and is followed by the dogs. The herdsman only observes the whole affair from afar. For Strauss, the story points to the absence of divine providence by depicting "man" as a silent observer who does not do anything, but only observes (AN I 640–41, SNAN 11.30). The effects of God's jealousy on human life therefore come about through human beings, who believe in divine punishment (SNAN 5.15, 15.50).[54]

The effects of belief in divine punishment are seen most forcefully in the story of a young man who is robbed of the pleasure of love by a loquacious barber. The story is narrated by a tailor who has been to a wedding, where he meets a limping young man. As soon as the young man sees a certain barber also attending the feast, he refuses to sit down, telling the guests that he had sworn never to stay in the same town as this barber. Asked about his story, the young man tells the guests that he was once rich and fell in love with a beautiful young woman and arranged to meet her at her home. But before going to the appointment, he decided to shave his beard, and called the barber to his house. The barber turns out to be a remarkable individual and claims to be a modest man of few words who never meddles with the affairs of others. He guesses that the young man is going to meet his lover and offers his services to smooth things over. Exasperated by the barber's meddling, the young man gets rid of him and sneaks away to the house of the beautiful woman, but, unbeknownst to him, the barber follows him. While in the woman's room, to the young man's dismay, her father unexpectedly returns home and starts punishing one of the maids for some minor infraction. The barber, who is waiting outside, hears the wailings of the maid and thinks that the father has caught the young man. He begins shouting in the street that his master is being killed in this house, thereby causing an uproar and attracting a huge crowd of people outside. The father,

---

[54] According to Strauss the same theme is discussed from a similar point of view in Aristo-phanes's *Wasps*: Philocleon is a zealous Athenian addicted to law courts and condemn-ing his fellow men. He is tricked by his son into acquitting a defendant but Philocleon is afraid of having committed a sin against the gods. For Strauss, Philocleon's addiction to law courts and his savagery against his fellow men is the result of his belief in the punitiveness of the gods. Philocleon is also an unerotic man and does not desire wine and other refined pleasures. Strauss, "The Origins of Political Science and the Problem of Socrates," 147.

hearing the barber's accusations, asks him to search the house to see for himself that he hasn't murdered anyone. Meanwhile, the young man has concealed himself in a trunk. The barber finds the trunk and leaves the house running with the trunk on his back. The young man manages to throw himself out of the trunk, but breaks his leg, and that is why he is limping – and why he cannot bear to see the barber (AN I 205–17).

Strauss pays particularly close attention to the personage of the barber: he is a busybody who is of a very low status; Strauss mentions his "cameldriver" friends to show his status (SNAN 6.17). But at the same time, this busybody barber boasts of his expertise in all aspects of occult and religious sciences: he knows the Qur'ān and the reports of the Prophet, and resembles an accomplished religious scholar, if not more. He is described as "the ruler of kings" and is proved to be a "demagogue" who successfully mobilizes common people in a revolt.[55] The barber tells the story of his six brothers and against all evidence to the contrary he boasts of his own taciturnity and politeness; he is wont to denigrate his brothers, and calls them talkative and impolite. Strauss compares the barber to the wicked vizier (the prophet) who denigrated his predecessors, and surmises that the barber's brothers were also barbers. This is why the barber is capable of performing "miracles" and brings the dead hunchback to life. In the barber's story of his six brothers, Strauss underscores the stories of the central brothers (the third and the fourth).[56] The second brother is invited to an extremely beautiful house to enjoy making love to a beautiful woman. He enters the house but is asked to endure anything at all if he wants to have his desire. He is slapped, his beard is shaved, his mustache is plucked, and his eyebrows are dyed. He is asked to dance around the house while the slave-girls and eunuchs throw objects at him. Constantly encouraged to endure everything for the union, he obeys every command. In the end, he is thrown in the middle of a crowded market stark naked and drunk – without enjoying love. The third brother is a blind beggar. He goes into a house to beg for money but goes away empty-handed. He is followed by the owner of the house. The beggar,

---

[55] Cf. "Socrates does get into trouble through a certain inbetween type of man [i.e., Strepsiades], who is *not distinguished by honesty*. Here we remind ourselves of the fact that the old juryman of the *Wasps* ... is also socially an inbetween type. Needless to say that the *demagogues* too belong to the inbetween type." Strauss, "The Origins of Political Science and the Problem of Socrates," 152–53 (italics added).

[56] The importance of the central items in an enumeration and the central passages, paragraphs or chapters is one of the common principles of Strauss's hermeneutics. For the justification of this principle see Cicero, *Orator* 50, and *De Oratore* II.313ff; Strauss, "Fârâbî's Plato," 371n35; Strauss, *Xenophon's Socrates*, 58.

not being able to see the owner of the house, joins other blind beggars who eat their food together and share their daily proceeds. They suspect that a stranger is among them and get into a fight with the owner of the house who wanted to steal their money. The fight attracts a crowd and they are all brought to the governor. Before the governor, the owner of the house pretends to be blind and accuses the others to be impostors who pretend to be blind. The governor gives some of the beggars' money to the owner of the house and keeps the rest for himself while punishing the beggars. Strauss observes that two of the brothers succeed in entering a house but the second brother is robbed of the pleasure of *love* while the third who is there to earn *money* is robbed of the money he had. Three brothers clearly belong together (SNAN 6.17).

While *eros* is the target of religious thought, it is also the way towards liberation. This is owing to the fact that for Strauss there is a link between erotic longings and philosophy: *eros* is a rebellious, even *the* most rebellious, desire. It does not obey the law and does not bend to the will of *nomos*. It is the unruliest human desire and hence *the* target of religious thought. One can easily see this in Genesis, where the first disobedience leads to consciousness about one's sexuality. *Eros* opens the way for philosophy, as the essence of philosophy is also rebellion. In fact, for Strauss, "*eros*, in its highest form is philosophy." Eros leads man away from and beyond the city and *nomos* and encourages men to disregard *nomos*. This is why there is a connection between women, wisdom, and *nomos* in the *Nights*. As Strauss explains, "refutation of the nomos regarding inferiority of women" is one of the major themes of the whole work (SNAN 1.1). Women, representing *eros* as well as wisdom, are *the* enemy of *nomos*. Elsewhere Strauss goes so far as to call "the philosophic *eros*" the *phusis* of the philosopher.[57] *Eros* and wine are also old allies. In the same way that *eros* rebels against the law, wine loosens the tongue and mind's fetters that bound it to the ancestral and the sacred.[58] This is why according to Strauss, Aristophanes's myth in *Symposium* "teaches that by virtue of *eros* man ... will approach a condition in which they become a serious danger to the gods."[59]

---

[57] Strauss, "Fârâbî's Plato," 361.
[58] The theme of wine drinking and its opposition to the sense of shame, respect for the old laws, and established order is mentioned by Strauss in his commentary on Plato's *Laws*. In the *Laws*, the search for the best laws, which are to replace the old divine laws of Crete and Sparta gets underway when the old men of the dialogue are freed from their restraints by talking about wine drinking, whereupon they engage in a "vicarious enjoyment of wine through a conversation about wine." See Strauss, *The Argument and the Action of Plato's Laws*, 19–21; Strauss, "What Is Political Philosophy?," 31.
[59] Strauss, "The Origins of Political Science and the Problem of Socrates," 150.

In the *Nights* too, *eros* is depicted as incompatible with the sense of shame and fear of God. In a story, Nur al-Din, a young man who knows that wine drinking is "a great sin, forbidden in His Book by Almighty God" (AN III 351) learns from his companions to ignore the prohibition against wine drinking. He finds it bitter at first but is told by a gracious old man (see the Devil, p. 115 below) to try it with sugar. He is next told about its uses: "it emboldens the coward and encourages copulation." When the young man returns home, he in his drunkenness strikes his father and blinds him; he leaves his parents and falls in love with a Frankish woman who can successfully pretend to be Christian to her Christian parents and abuse Islam. But at the same time, this woman kills her Christian brothers and avoids being brought back to her parents by professing Islam, and threatens the caliph with divine punishment were she, as a Muslim woman, to be separated from her lover and returned to infidels (AN III 423–24). The wine-drinking of the young Nur and his later father-beating recalls Aristophanes's *The Clouds*, where Pheidippides beats his father after going through philosophical training at Socrates's Thinkery. The wine-drinking has prepared Nur to ignore the patriarchal order and has put him on the path of falling in love with a Christian woman. The opposition between *eros* and religion can also be seen in the story of the wife of a Frankish knight who is in love with a Muslim merchant. The merchant abstains from intercourse with the Christian woman because of her religion, but she forsakes her husband and avoids being sent back to her Christian husband by professing her faith in Islam: an unbeliever converts to Islam to satisfy her desire and Islam is depicted as the handmaiden of love. One can imagine the same thing happening with Christianity in a different context (SNAN 17.55).

The most striking example of the stories that depict the transgression of the divine law in the *Nights* is that of Judar the fisherman (AN II 610–48). The fisherman is instructed by a magician to go through seven tests in order to unravel all the mysteries (AN II 625). In the first six tests, he must confront several fantastic beings who try to kill him. Each time, Judar is directed by the magician to offer himself willingly and without fear, so as to go to the next level. The magician explains to the fisherman that these fearsome beings are only images and that he should not fear them. The sixth test is to confront a black slave and to open a door by saying "Isa [Jesus], tell Musa [Moses] to open the door." The most interesting test is the seventh and last: to succeed in this test, Judar must force the phantom of his mother to strip off her clothes and allow him to look at her nakedness. Judar is instructed by the magician to ignore his mother's pleas, for if he does not he will die (AN II 624). At first Judar is hesitant as his mother tells him: "Have you a heart of stone, my son, that you would shame me by uncovering my private parts? This is unlawful." But Judar learns to ignore her pleas and succeeds in passing the test. In his comment on this story (SNAN 15.47) Strauss is probably thinking about a similar story in Herodotus's *Histories*. He explains the importance of this episode many years before in a letter to Jacob Klein.[60] In Herodotus, Candaules persuades Gyges to see his wife's nakedness (I.8.1–2). For Strauss, this represents questioning the basis of the patriarchal law. Shame and fear are the instruments by which the ancestral protects itself, and the one who questions the ancestral must first vanquish his fear and sense of shame at doing so. As Seth Benardete, following Strauss's lead, explains, "to see [human beings] naked is to see them as they are, stripped of the concealment of clothes. And laws are like clothes: they too conceal from us the way things are. All laws say that certain things cannot be seen; before certain things one must have shame."[61] The story of Judar is that of a man who learns to do away with his cowardice and sense of shame and learns to look at things as they are. However, there is one major difference between the story of Judar and that of Gyges: while Gyges sees the nakedness of a beautiful woman, Judar sees the ugliness of his mother's old and frail body. The sacred is thus seen as an ugly old woman, or as Strauss puts it, as "treacherous hags or old witches" (SNAN 5.14). The tradition seduces young men and transforms them into religious zealots, like the old treacherous woman in the story of the lady of the house who has converted the son of a king.

The story of Judar shows transgression in its brutality. However, transgression has its own charms and beauties. In fact, what leads to transgression is often attraction to beauty. We encounter the beauty of transgression in a story in which the Devil himself is depicted as an attractive, handsome old man possessing eloquence and remarkable grace; he is fond of wine, can sing Arabic poems of supreme beauty, and is apparently himself in love (AN II 777–78)! It seems that he also procures women for men (AN II 796, SNAN 15.49). But the most remarkable of the stories which depict the triumph of love over religion and the charms of transgression is the story of Nur al-Din 'Ali and Anis al-Jalis (AN I 244–78). In that story, we are introduced to a sultan in Basra "who loved

60 Strauss, *Gesammelte Schriften. Band 3*, 556 (Letter to Jacob Klein on October 15, 1938).
61 Seth Benardete, *Herodotean Inquiries* (The Hague: St. Augustine's Press, 1969), 12.

the poor, the beggars and all his subjects, distributing his wealth to those who believed in Muhammad" (AN I 244). Nur, a young man, seduces and sleeps with a slave girl intended for that sultan. Together they travel to Baghdad and have a drinking party in the garden of the caliph, and even make the pious old gardener of the caliph join them in transgression (SNAN 7.20). The gardener, who is aptly called Shaikh Ibrahim, is a strict follower of the injunction of the Prophet about wine and has not consumed wine for thirteen years, but he is persuaded by the fine casuistry of Nur to drink with them (AN I 262–63). The caliph sees the burning lights of the banquet in his garden *from afar* and at first believes that the city has been taken from him – and in a sense it has. The vizier tries to calm the caliph's anger with an excuse: he tells the caliph that Ibrahim has asked the caliph's permission to have a party in the garden to celebrate his son's circumcision. The vizier has forgotten to tell the caliph about it. The caliph thinks that he must join the party as he believes that the pious gardener is entertaining the poor and the dervishes at the gathering. But before joining the gathering, the caliph wants to observe it anonymously, so he climbs a high tree and observes the party from *above a tree*. When the caliph sees the pious gardener cup in hand, drinking and singing with a young and beautiful couple, he becomes furious over such transgressions being committed in his garden. But listening to the music and observing the graceful young man and woman, the caliph joins the party and excuses the participants (cf. AN III 351). The story perfectly describes Strauss's point about "the impotence of kings vis-à-vis love" as one of the recurring themes of the work (SNAN 15.50).

As it was previously mentioned, in his remarkable essays on the *Nights*, Muhsin Mahdi argued that a common theme cannot be found in the whole of the stories included in the large editions of the *Nights* and thought one must look for a common theme only in portions of the stories, namely the "Syrian branch" version.[62] It seems that Strauss had been trying to find such a common theme in all the stories included in the Calcutta II edition and that his notes are the result of this effort. This common theme is the theologico-political solution of the medieval enlightenment. Theoretical radicalism and practical moderation are characteristic of this solution. For Strauss, the author's radical and critical thought is clearly joined with practical moderation: although he leads

---

[62] Mahdi, *The Thousand and One Nights*, 141. In his notes, Strauss mentions about 144 stories included in the Calcutta II edition. Of these only thirty-four are included in Mahdi's edition.

the reader step by step toward his esoteric radical views, he carefully bows to the common opinions of his time at every turn. Liberation from prejudices and false opinions is reserved for those few who see through the orthodox disguise; they are taught to live like the author, a stranger in his homeland, "praising, speaking, seeing, doing things against [his] intent so as to please the prince."[63] It seems that for Strauss, the author of the *Nights* is no revolutionary; his political teaching consists of learning to live with the reigning opinions and trying to find some breathing space for the life of the mind. He does not propose the root and branch elimination of the reigning beliefs. His teaching consists only of a tactful handling of the common opinions in the interest of a decent human life. He is a private man who lives "as a member of an imperfect society which he tries to humanize within the limits of the possible."[64]

---

[63] Niccolò Machiavelli, *Discourses on Livy*, trans. Harvey C. Mansfield and Nathan Tarcov (Chicago: University of Chicago Press, 1996), 214 (III.2); Strauss, *Thoughts on Machiavelli*, 168.

[64] Strauss, *Persecution and the Art of Writing*, 1952, 17.

3

From Alfarabi's Plato to Strauss's Alfarabi

"Fârâbî's *Plato*" is an enigmatic essay.[1] It is one of only three texts that
Strauss dedicated exclusively to an Islamic philosopher, in all three cases
to Alfarabi. The other two essays, namely "A Lost Writing of Farâbî's"
and "How Fārābī Read Plato's *Laws*" had destinies which distinguish
them from "Fârâbî's *Plato*."[2] "A Lost Writing of Farâbî's," written
sometime in 1935 and published in 1936, is a rather limited essay whose
sole objective is to show that some parts of Falaquera's *Reshit Ḥokhmah*
are a summary of a trilogy of Alfarabi which includes *Attainment of
Happiness*, *Philosophy of Plato*, and *Philosophy of Aristotle*. Strauss's
claim in this text was rather modest and was bound to be become obsolete by the publication of the second part of the trilogy in 1943.[3] It therefore makes sense that Strauss never tried to republish this early essay in
his later collections. "How Fārābī Read Plato's *Laws*," this last writing
of Strauss on Alfarabi, published first in Louis Massignon's Festschrift in

---

[1] In this chapter, all numbers identified by ¶ in parentheses refer to the paragraph numbers of Leo Strauss, "Fârâbî's *Plato*," in *Louis Ginzberg: Jubilee Volume on the Occasion of His Seventieth Birthday*, ed. Saul Lieberman, Alexander Marx, Shalom Spiegel,
and Solomon Zeitlin (New York: The American Academy for Jewish Research, 1945),
357–93. "Fârâbî's *Plato*" was "written in the period from November 12, 1943, to
March 29, 1944." Meier, *Political Philosophy and the Challenge of Revealed Religion*,
46n38.
[2] Strauss, "Eine vermißte Schrift Farâbîs," 90–106 (GS II:167–76); Strauss, "A Lost Writing of Farâbî's (1936)"; Leo Strauss, "How Fārābī Read Plato's Laws," in *Mélanges
Louis Massignon*, vol. III (Damascus: Institut français de Damas, 1957), 319–44; Strauss,
"How Fārābī Read Plato's Laws," 1959.
[3] Alfarabi, *De Platonis philosophia*. This does not, of course, decrease the importance of
Strauss's claim. See Mahdi, *Alfarabi and the Foundation of Islamic Political Philosophy*,
5; Harvey, "Leo Strauss's Developing Interest in Alfarabi," 70–71.

1957, like practically all of Strauss's monographs was later included in a collection of essays in 1959. "Fârâbî's *Plato*" was neither a limited essay like "A Lost Writing of Farâbî's," nor was it republished in later collections by Strauss.[4]

"Fârâbî's *Plato*" is also enigmatic because it is a meticulous study dedicated exclusively to a very minor writing of Alfarabi, whose full title is "The philosophy of Plato, its parts, and the grades of dignity of its parts, from its beginning to its end" (hereafter *Plato*). Although Muhsin Mahdi, one of the foremost scholars of Alfarabi and Strauss's student, called the trilogy which includes this work "Alfarabi's most important philosophical work," one must confess that the importance of at least the last two parts seem to have escaped everyone else.[5] In fact, Mahdi himself ignored a detailed discussion of *Plato* in his major writing on Alfarabi. Although this writing of Alfarabi is not entirely ignored by other scholars, Strauss's essay remains the only detailed monograph on this work in the more than seven decades since the critical edition of this work became available to scholars.[6] A cursory look at *Plato* shows the reason for this lack of interest: it is a very minor treatise of less than twenty-one pages in Arabic, with obscure and perplexing content. Alfarabi's objective in this short treatise is to expound the philosophy of Plato from its beginning to its end. This rather ambitious plan is very modestly executed, because what Alfarabi mainly does is simply name the Platonic dialogues, explain their titles in rather fanciful terms, and give a very short but bewildering summary of their content, which in many cases hardly corresponds to what we find in those works. One can say that this writing of Alfarabi, even

---

[4] In this regard its fate rather resembles that of Strauss, "The Spirit of Sparta or the Taste of Xenophon." After Strauss's death, "Fârâbî's *Plato*" was included in a collection of contributions to the annual *Proceedings* and various Jubilee volumes published by the American Academy for Jewish Research. This republication reproduces the old edition of "Fârâbî's *Plato*" without any changes or revisions. See Arthur Hyman, ed., *Essays in Medieval Jewish and Islamic Philosophy* (New York: Ktav Publishing House, 1977), 391–427.

[5] Mahdi, *Alfarabi and the Foundation of Islamic Political Philosophy*, 5.

[6] This is not contradicted but rather confirmed by two other partial discussions of this work: these two discussions by Christopher Colmo are both reactions to Strauss's essay and under the influence of his monograph. See Christopher Colmo, "Theory and Practice: Alfarabi's Plato Revisited," *American Political Science Review* 86, no. 4 (1992): 966–76; Christopher Colmo, *Breaking with Athens: Alfarabi as Founder* (Lanham: Lexington Books, 2005), chapter 5. See also Christopher Colmo, "Reason and Revelation in the Thought of Leo Strauss," *Interpretation* 18, no. 1 (1990): 145–60; Steven J. Lenzner, "Strauss's Farabi, Scholarly Prejudice, and Philosophic Politics," *Perspectives on Political Science* 28, no. 4 (January 1, 1999): 194–202.

more than his references to the apocryphal *Theology of Aristotle*, confirms the low opinion of the most prominent scholars about the access
of Islamic philosophers to Greek philosophical writings: how can anyone
who had access to the dialogues of Plato believe that *Protagoras* means
"compassion" or that *Laches* means "preparation" or that *Crito* is also
called the *Apology of Socrates*?[7] In full knowledge of these major problems to which he also refers, Strauss decided to write a detailed study
on this minor writing of Alfarabi. One reason for this special attention
seems to be that this work is exclusively dedicated to the presentation
of Platonic philosophy, which was one of Strauss's constant preoccupations during his life. Strauss's other study of Alfarabi is also dedicated to
another writing of Alfarabi on Plato's *Laws*. In other words, *Plato* and
Alfarabi's summary of Plato's *Laws* are of particular interest to Strauss
because both are "historical" works on Platonic dialogues. But considering the dubious historical worth of these two writings, one cannot say
that we have a convincing explanation for Strauss's emphatic interest.
This explanation is only possible after a detailed discussion of the project
which Strauss pursues in "Fârâbî's *Plato*," the discussion which is the
subject of this chapter.

ARISTOTELIANISM, NEO-PLATONISM, AND ISLAM

"Fârâbî's *Plato*" can be described as an esoteric reading of Alfarabi's short
treatise. In other words, Strauss's essay tries to unveil the esoteric teaching of Alfarabi's treatise, which is different from what one acquires while
reading it in a nonesoteric way. Consequently, the use and discussion of
different esoteric techniques is one of the major parts of Strauss's text.
The problem of esotericism appears rather early in "Fârâbî's *Plato*," and
already at the beginning of his paper, Strauss begins to apply his esoteric
method to some of the major preconceptions about Islamic philosophy:
he begins his text by reminding us of the importance of the Falāsifa for
understanding Maimonides's *Guide for the Perplexed*.[8] This is because –
although appearances might prove misleading – Maimonides's *Guide*
"presents itself as a Jewish correction of the latter." The Falāsifa or "the

---

[7] For a recent historical discussion see Coleman Connelly, "New Evidence for the Source
of Al-Fārābī's Philosophy of Plato," in *A New Work by Apuleius: The Lost Third Book
of the De Platone*, ed. Justin Stover (Oxford: Oxford University Press, 2016), 183–97.

[8] In the introduction to *Persecution and the Art of Writing*, Strauss twice reminds us, in a
rather comical fashion, that *falāsifa* and *falsafa* are the Arabic transcription of the Greek
words for "philosophers" and "philosophy." See Strauss, *Persecution and the Art of*

philosophers" are defined by Strauss, following the scholarly convention, as "Islamic Aristotelians," and their teaching is described "as a blend of genuine Aristotelianism with Neo-platonism" and, Strauss adds, "of course, Islamic tenets" (¶ 1). This common description of Islamic philosophers – which is very much alive to this day – as well as Strauss's use of the term "Maimonides' philosophic background" (¶ 2) suggest that a critical engagement and evaluation of the common scholarly views is one of Strauss's first major concerns in this essay. Beginning with a discussion of the apparent Aristotelianism of Islamic philosophers, Strauss emphasizes one aspect of *The political governments* and its two parallels: in these writings Alfarabi treats "the whole of philosophy ... within a political framework" thus imitating Plato's *Republic* and *Laws*, rather than any writing of Aristotle (¶ 4). We might therefore suspect that to call Alfarabi an Aristotelian is not very precise. Among other things, a clear-cut separation of theoretical from practical philosophy seems absent in at least some of Alfarabi's works. But if to describe Alfarabi as a strict Aristotelian is not entirely correct, should one not also rethink Alfarabi's Neo-Platonism, as well as his adherence to "Islamic tenets"? Concerning Neo-Platonism, Strauss explains that to reconcile his Aristotelianism with this radical Platonism, Alfarabi could try to show that "the explicit teachings" of Plato and Aristotle can be reconciled.[9] This way is followed in a treatise of Alfarabi entitled *Concordance of the opinions of Plato and Aristotle* (¶ 5).

Writing, 1952, 10n4, 12n8. Such an explanation is absent in "Fârâbî's *Plato*," and the Arabic term does not appear, which probably points towards the "unhistorical" project pursued in "Fârâbî's *Plato*." This also makes the changes subsequently made significant. The addition of those two rather unnecessary footnotes brings the total of the introduction's footnotes to twenty. For the contextual reasoning behind Strauss's introductory statement on the relationship between Maimonides and Alfarabi see Harvey, "Leo Strauss's Developing Interest in Alfarabi," 73.

[9] Strauss also mentions two other methods available to Alfarabi for harmonizing Aristotelianism and Platonism: The second method is to prove that "the esoteric teaching of both philosophers are identical." The third method consists of showing that "the aim" of both Plato and Aristotle is the same. For Strauss, this third method is followed by Alfarabi in *The Philosophy of Plato and of Aristotle*, a tripartite work whose second part is dedicated to the philosophy of Plato. Strauss does not say anything about the second method. He explains, however, in the introduction to *Persecution and the Art of Writing* that, according to Alfarabi, Plato and Aristotle "have given us philosophy" as well as "the ways toward it and the way toward its introduction after it has been blurred or destroyed." According to Strauss, this agreement seems much more fundamental than any difference of doctrines. Furthermore, this concern with the revival of philosophy after its demise seems to be one of the reasons for Strauss's interest in Alfarabi in general, the founder of political philosophy in Islamic civilization. See Strauss, *Persecution and the Art of Writing*, 1952, 12.

Strauss cautions us, however, not to attach great importance to this work as a reliable source representing Alfarabi's thought. Strauss arrives at this conclusion through two points, referred to in footnote 4: First is the use of the term "opinion" in the title of the *Concordance*, which Strauss apparently understands to be the equivalent of the Greek *doxa*. In other words, the positions defended in the *Concordance* should be considered to be the "opinions" of unphilosophical character, rather than Alfarabi's own philosophical positions.[10] Second, in the *Concordance*, Alfarabi makes use of the *Theology of Aristotle* to defend the philosophers against the attacks of the orthodox theologians; in this work Alfarabi manages to harmonize Plato and Aristotle mainly by relying on the pseudo-Aristotelian *Theology of Aristotle*. Alfarabi, Strauss claims, seems to be aware of the fact that this Neo-Platonic work is falsely attributed to Aristotle. On the basis of these points, Strauss – here following Paul Kraus, who is referred to in the footnote – believes that *Concordance* is "an exoteric treatise" which cannot be relied on for discovering Alfarabi's true, esoteric teaching.[11] Supplementary arguments against the Neo-Platonic reading of Alfarabi are offered in ¶ 8, where Strauss claims that our first impression of reading Alfarabi's *Philosophy of Plato*, the impression which Strauss thinks will only be reinforced by further investigation, is that Alfarabi's view of Plato's philosophy cannot be considered Neo-Platonist: this impression is the result of the fact that Alfarabi seems to have identified philosophy with the practical art of the king, has apparently subordinated the philosophical themes of the *Timaeus* to the political subject matter of the *Republic*, and gives a particularly nonmetaphysical interpretation of Plato's writings. It therefore seems that for Alfarabi, Plato's philosophy is fundamentally political, and since Alfarabi "considered the Platonic view of philosophy the true view," Alfarabi's own philosophy is essentially political. Such a fundamentally political view of Platonic philosophy seems to be rather far from what is conventionally considered Neo-Platonic.

---

[10] See also ¶ 33: "Fârâbî's only mention of spiritual things occurs in a summary of popular opinions, or at any rate of opinions of men other than Plato."

[11] For this question see Alfarabi, *Alfarabi's Philosophy of Plato and Aristotle*, trans. Muhsin Mahdi (Ithaca: Cornell University Press, 2001), 3–6; Alfarabi, *The Political Writings: "Selected Aphorisms" and Other Texts*, trans. Charles E. Butterworth (Ithaca and London: Cornell University Press, 2001), 119–24; Galston, "A Re-Examination of al-Farabi's Neoplatonism"; Marwan Rashed, "On the Authorship of the Treatise On the Harmonization of the Opinions of the Two Sages Attributed to Al-Fārābī," *Arabic Sciences and Philosophy* 19 (2009): 43–82. For more on this debate see Harvey, "Leo Strauss's Developing Interest in Alfarabi," 80–82.

While Strauss began his discussion by describing the thought of Alfarabi and his followers as "a blend of genuine Aristotelianism with Neo-platonism and ... Islamic tenets," from this mixture "Neoplatonism" must be removed, as Aristotelianism was previously put aside. Strauss is aware of the unusual character of his view and confesses that this view of Alfarabi's philosophy goes so much against our "inherited" opinions that he is, or rather we are, "hesitant" to accept it (¶ 8). The relation of philosophy and politics in the thought of Alfarabi seems therefore in need of further investigation, the investigation we will pursue when we speak about the precise nature of philosophy in Strauss's essay. But independent of that question, we see that Strauss has thrown two of the widely held beliefs about Alfarabi into question: namely, his apparent Aristotelianism and Neo-Platonism. We should wait and see whether the third belief mentioned by Strauss, namely, Alfarabi's adherence to Islamic tenets, is also questioned. The third element is of particular importance because, more than any other aspect of Strauss's interpretation, it is related to the question of esotericism.

ALFARABI'S ESOTERICISM

Strauss's essay seems to be as much about Alfarabi as about esotericism. This is why Strauss claims that he has "made free use" of it for the introduction of *Persecution and the Art of Writing*.[12] Strauss calls Aristotelianism, Neo-Platonism, and Islamic tenets the three "heterogeneous" elements which in Alfarabi's thought are transformed into "a consistent, or intelligible, whole" through some "principle" which one might be able to grasp if one follows "the signpost" erected by Maimonides (¶ 1). This "principle" seems to be esotericism. The signpost is found in Maimonides's letter to Samuel ibn Tibbon, in which he praises Alfarabi's writings in the strongest terms, especially that book which he considered Alfarabi's most important book. That book is called by Maimonides *The principles of the beings*, but Strauss tells us that its original title is *The political governments*.[13] We therefore have a precise idea of the place one should begin the study of Maimonides's *Guide*: Alfarabi's *Political*

---

[12] Strauss, *Persecution and the Art of Writing*, 1952, 5.
[13] Fauzi Najjar, in his edition, synthesizes these two titles by calling it "Al-Siyāsa al-Madaniyya also known as The Treatise on the Principles of Being." Alfarabi, *Kitāb Al-Siyāsa al-Madaniyya, al-Mulaqqab Bi-Mabādi al-Mawjūdāt*, ed. Fauzi Najjar (Beirut: al-Maṭbáa al-Kāthūlīkiyya, 1964).

governments. Although one here expects to read a discussion of this work, right away Strauss warns us that it "would be unwise to attempt such an analysis now," because we still lack a satisfactory edition of *The political governments* and of its "two parallel works," namely *The principles of the opinions of the people of the virtuous city* and *The virtuous religious community*.[14] This very unsatisfactory explanation for refraining to provide a discussion of *The political governments*, the explanation which later on will be replaced by an esoteric explanation, does not stop Strauss from making some radical claims about this work.

Maimonides presumably preferred *The political governments* to its two other parallel presentations. Although Strauss does not pursue a study of *The political governments*, he reminds us of the fact that the proper understanding of this work "presupposes" the study of those parallel writings of Alfarabi. The reason is that the teaching contained in *The political governments* consists of "the silent rejection of certain tenets which are adhered to in the two other works" (¶ 3). For now, Strauss does not explain what he means by this statement, but one cannot ignore the fact that a tortuous line of argument, which only Strauss's rhetoric can smooth out, has led us from Maimonides's *Guide for the Perplexed* to a writing of Alfarabi which is not available for discussion, and from there to Alfarabi's parallel works and their contradictions. From the title of Alfarabi's treatise and also the description of *Plato* which Alfarabi provides at the end of *The Attainment of Happiness*, Strauss concludes that this work intends to be "a complete survey" of the philosophy of Plato. From this, Strauss concludes that if Alfarabi happens to overlook some Platonic topic in his presentation, one should conclude that Alfarabi considered that topic "either unimportant or merely exoteric" (¶ 6). We have therefore two esoteric techniques, which are supposed to help us access the true teaching of Alfarabi in his writings: as we shall see, silent rejection, which Strauss mentioned, is done through *contradictions*; this should be added to the practice of *silence* as another esoteric method. Let us begin with contradictions.

---

[14] For the English translations, see the following editions: *"The Political Governments"* = Alfarabi, "Political Regime," in *The Political Writings: Volume II Political Regime and Summary of Plato's Laws*, trans. Charles E. Butterworth (Ithaca and London: Cornell University Press, 2015), 27–97; "The Principles of the Opinions of the People of the Virtuous City" = Alfarabi, *On the Perfect State*, trans. Richard Walzer (Oxford: Clarendon Press, 1985); "The Virtuous Religious Community" = Alfarabi, "Book of Religion," in *The Political Writings: "Selected Aphorisms" and Other Texts*, trans. Charles E. Butterworth (Ithaca: Cornell University Press, 2001), 85–115.

Strauss describes the use of contradictions as "a normal pedagogic device of the genuine philosophers." He tells us that he learned this esoteric technique "from Maimonides who knew his Fârâbî" (¶ 13). This technique is used to explain the contradictions between *The political governments* and its parallel works: in *The political governments* and *The virtuous religious community*, two works in which Alfarabi expounds his own doctrine, Strauss claims, Alfarabi "pronounces more or less orthodox views concerning the life after death." This is while, in his lost commentary on the *Nicomachean Ethics*, discussing Aristotle's views, Alfarabi goes so far as to say there is no happiness but in this life, and describes the religious doctrine of life after death as "ravings and old women's tales" (¶ 17). The footnote attached to this section helps us understand better what is meant here: Strauss is following Ibn Tufayl, who claimed that Alfarabi's works are full of uncertainties because in *The virtuous religious community*, Alfarabi has claimed the souls of the wicked live on forever in infinite torments after death, a doctrine which, like Strauss, one can call "simply orthodox." What Strauss calls the "heretical" but also "tolerable" view is found in *The political governments*, where Alfarabi states that the souls of the wicked dissolve into nothing, and only those of the virtuous are immortal.[15] We therefore have here a concrete example of the discrepancies between Alfarabi's different writings, the contradictions between orthodox and heretical views that Strauss claimed is a typical concern of esoteric writers.

The second esoteric method is to simply refrain from mentioning an idea in a text as a way of showing one's disagreement. Strauss does not try to find a historical source for this esoteric technique, but mentions several specific ideas in Alfarabi's treatise which are discovered through awareness of this technique: According to Strauss, one expects that in his treatise, which intends to be "a complete survey" of the philosophy of Plato, Alfarabi mentions the doctrine of the immortality of the soul as it is presented in the *Phaedrus*, the *Phaedo*, and the *Republic*. Furthermore, as Alfarabi presents philosophy as fundamentally political, one would expect him to refer to the "ideas" of justice and of other virtues. But surprisingly, Alfarabi does not refer to any idea or the doctrine of ideas in his presentation. Similarly, the distinction between this world and the next,

---

[15] See Alfarabi, "Political Regime," 72 (Najjar 83); Ibn Tufayl, *Hayy Ibn Yaqzān*, 100 (Gauthier 13–14).

which Alfarabi mentions in his other writings, is completely absent in *Plato*. Strauss claims that Alfarabi's disregard of the distinction between this world and the next, and his silence about Plato's doctrine of immortality and ideas, show that Alfarabi "rejected" or rather considered these doctrines merely an "exoteric" part of Plato's philosophy (¶ 16).

Repetition is another esoteric technique which Strauss finds originally in Maimonides and applies to Alfarabi's treatise. According to Strauss's reading of Maimonides, repetition is a normal pedagogic device of the philosophers (¶ 23). Esoteric repetition occurs when an esoteric writer repeats an idea, enumeration, or statement in his work while making slight changes. Those who are familiar with this esoteric technique detect these slight differences, which seem negligible to the untrained reader ("the vulgar"). For instance, in the discussion of Alfarabi's view of the divine, Strauss mentions that Alfarabi uses the adjective "divine" as part of a dichotomy, the opposing element of which is "human" or "bestial." In a subsequent passage, a repetition of this dichotomy, "human" and "bestial" are the opposing poles, that is, divine-bestial is replaced by human-bestial. According to Strauss's reading, this is Alfarabi's esoteric way of intimating his usage of the term "divine": "divine" seems to be only a comparative category used for qualifying the superior alternative without any supernatural connotation (¶ 33).

Another esoteric method established through Maimonides is the importance of what appears *only once* in Alfarabi's writings. This esoteric technique is of particular importance for understanding *Plato* as a whole, because this treatise itself is a rather unique writing of Alfarabi, and one on which Strauss exclusively relies for discerning Alfarabi's true teaching. Now, considering the fact that some of the ideas expounded in *Plato* appear only in *Plato* and nowhere else, Strauss reminds us that following Maimonides's guideline, one should not attach more weight to those ideas that are repeated most often; in fact, what is only said once has much more importance and says more about the true ideas of an esoteric writer than his oft-repeated claims (¶ 20).

As we have observed, Strauss relies on Maimonides for most of his esoteric techniques. There is, however, one specific esoteric technique, which he owes to Cicero, and that is the importance of *centers* (footnote 35). Strauss claims that one of the esoteric ways of conveying an important message to the careful and select reader is to put them at the center of an enumeration (for instance: the second item of a list which includes three items) or a text (for instance in the eleventh page of a twenty-one page text or the second part of a three-part treatise). In the case of *Plato*, the importance of the whole treatise is implied by the fact that it is the second part of a tripartite work. Because *Plato* is the central part of the trilogy, Strauss considers it "the least exposed part" of the work, in which Alfarabi can be more outspoken (¶ 16). For instance, because it is the central part, in this work Alfarabi can completely drop the distinction between the happiness of this world and that of the other world, while this distinction is prominent in the first part of his trilogy. In another instance, Strauss discusses three statements which Alfarabi makes concerning the relation between philosophy and the royal art, and concludes that the second or the central statement reflects Alfarabi's true teaching. This esoteric technique is used by Alfarabi because, Strauss remarks, "the average reader," or the many who are not familiar with this esoteric method, will not consider Alfarabi's second or central statement his true teaching and similarly, will attribute as much weight to the first part of the trilogy as to its other parts (¶ 13).

One last esoteric method which, more than any other, seems important for Strauss's study of *Plato* is *commentary* itself as an esoteric technique. In Strauss's view, *Plato* is much more reliable as a source of Alfarabi's true teachings, because in this treatise Alfarabi "sets forth explicitly, not so much his own views, as the views of someone else" (¶ 17). Alfarabi is less forthcoming when he speaks in his own name, for instance in his more canonical writings, because in those writings he is explicitly taking responsibility for the content of the work. Contrary to all other scholars, who put much more weight on the works in which Alfarabi sets forth his own doctrine, Strauss relies on *Plato*, in which Alfarabi presents the doctrines of someone else. Strauss believes that this way of writing is one of the most effective techniques of esoteric writing, because in this type of writing, Alfarabi "avails himself then of the specific immunity of the commentator, or of the historian, in order to speak his mind" (¶ 20). From this, Strauss concludes that we must scrupulously avoid having recourse to other writings of Alfarabi to interpret *Plato*, and in fact for him this short treatise takes precedence over all other writings of Alfarabi. When the doctrines deduced from it are in conflict with other writings of Alfarabi, one must therefore reject those other writings.

ALFARABI AND ISLAM

In an age where religion has acquired the status of personal beliefs and of lifestyle, to question the religious beliefs of a past philosopher, let alone a

Muslim philosopher, seems a rather outmoded subject of study.[16] Strauss, on the contrary, since his early studies, shows a rather curious interest in this question, and the conflict of Reason and Revelation remained one of the major themes of his studies throughout his life. Considering the unusual character of this form of scholarship in the eyes of modern scholars, it is not surprising that some have criticized Strauss's view of Islamic philosophy precisely because he sees it through the lens of the conflict between Reason and Revelation: they have even gone so far as to question whether such an inquiry, to which someone like al-Ghazali dedicated a substantial treatise and to which Averroes responded, was really a major issue at the time.[17] Strauss's engagement with Alfarabi's esotericism is above all the reflection of his concern with the question of Reason and Revelation. If Alfarabi practices esoteric writing, it is above all because of his unorthodox religious ideas. Strauss claims that one must be aware of the peculiar situation of medieval thinkers in general and Alfarabi in particular: the Greek philosophers like Plato and Aristotle were often free to state their doctrines because they were in most cases "under no compulsion to reconcile" them with "the requirements of faith" (¶ 15). Alfarabi and his companions were in a different position and had to take precautions in stating doctrines in contradiction to Muslim beliefs.

Strauss mentions five different views of Alfarabi which he believes are stated esoterically because they are incompatible with Islam. The heterodox doctrine which, more than any other, appears to be at the center of Alfarabi's *Plato,* is that philosophy on its own is sufficient for achieving happiness. This doctrine, which Strauss attributes to Alfarabi, is rather incompatible with the primary impression one gets from reading Alfarabi's treatise. Why does Strauss have a different interpretation of *Plato?* Let us follow his argument: In his treatise, Alfarabi explains that Plato's investigations were guided by the question of the perfection of man, of his happiness. According to Alfarabi's Plato, man's perfection is inseparable from two things: a certain science and a certain way of life. Plato's investigation led to the conclusion that the desired science is provided by philosophy and the desired way of life is the result of the royal or political art. Plato also concluded that the philosopher and the

---

[16] See Chapter 1 of this volume. For a discussion of heresy in Islamic philosophy which concentrates on more outspoken figures see Sarah Stroumsa, *Freethinkers of Medieval Islam: Ibn al-Rāwandī, Abū Bakr al-Rāzī and Their Impact on Islamic Thought* (Leiden: Brill, 1999).

[17] See the discussion of this subject in the Introduction of this volume.

king are identical, and therefore these two arts are synthesized in the person of the philosopher-king. Plato defines philosophy as "the science of the essence of each of all beings," as "the art of demonstration," and therefore simply identifies the main subject and the method of philosophy as entirely different from the subject matter of political philosophy and its method. When Plato distinguishes between the science and the way of life which contribute to the perfection and happiness of man, the science which is philosophy proper is presented as a theoretical science, a science which only treats nonpolitical subjects. This science is discussed in the *Timaeus*, whereas the study of the way of life is presented as belonging to the practical art and is discussed in the *Laws*. This rather strict distinction between philosophy proper and political philosophy is called by Strauss "'the aim' of Plato" according to Alfarabi (¶ 10).

Strauss reminds us, however, that this understanding of philosophy is rather in conflict with the explicit teaching of *Plato*: the idea of philosophy as an unpolitical investigation is not compatible with the treatise under discussion because it is precisely in *Plato* that Alfarabi identifies philosophy with the royal art. First, Strauss responds that Alfarabi only identifies the "true" philosophy with the "true" royal art. He explains later on (footnote 28) that the "true philosophy" (*al-falsafa 'alā al-iṭlāq* / "philosophy *simpliciter*"), which unites both theoretical and practical perfection, is not philosophy proper, which only includes theoretical perfection. It is only in the perfect city that these two are united in the person of the philosopher-king, while in other imperfect cities, we see the royal art acting independently of philosophy. Strauss claims that even this statement is not very precise, and he continues with a discussion of three statements which Alfarabi makes concerning the relation between philosophy and the royal art (¶ 12): (1) the human being who is a philosopher (*al-insān al-failasūf* / *homo philosophus*) and the human being who is a prince (*al-insān al-malik* / *homo rex*) are the same thing. This first statement, according to Strauss, is not free of some ambiguities: the term "human being" is here explained by a reference to Aristotle, who attributes the philosopher's virtuous actions to the fact that he, as a "human being," lives together with other human beings and acts as a *mere* human being and not like a semi-divine contemplative being. It is also worthy of remark that this statement, Strauss mentions, happens to be found right at the middle of *Plato* (footnotes 27 and 35). Strauss also draws our attention to the fact that this statement is not prefaced by Alfarabi's usual claim that "Plato investigated" this question, but is rather stated without any qualification; it is only "explained" by Plato. In any event, this statement does not mean what we usually believe: Alfarabi is only saying that a philosopher cannot acquire the unpolitical science of being without first acquiring the political science of the prince, and the prince cannot acquire the royal art without first acquiring the science of the philosopher. In other words, this ambiguous statement preserves the distinction between philosophy and the royal art. (2) In his central statement on the relationship between politics and philosophy, Alfarabi claims that according to Plato, the philosopher and the king *each* attain their perfection through the exercise of one faculty. It seems that in Strauss's interpretation, each of these two attain their perfection through a different faculty, and therefore, the distinction between the science of the philosopher and the science of the prince is still present. (3) In the third statement, Alfarabi claims that the philosopher and the king have each one faculty, and these two faculties *each* provide, not only the science of the beings, but also the desired way of life. We therefore have two different faculties which provide for the one who possesses one of them, independently of other faculties, both the science of the beings and the science of way of life. In other words, in this statement, philosophy and the royal art seem to be "coextensive," because each one of them can provide what is necessary for happiness. Strauss claims, however, that this does not mean that Alfarabi identifies philosophy with the royal art: they might be coextensive and even be equally sufficient for achieving the science and the way of life necessary for the happiness, but the fundamental distinction remains: philosophy is primarily directed toward the science of the beings, and the royal art is primarily directed toward the right way of life. But if Alfarabi thinks that philosophy and the royal art are two distinct faculties, why does he "hesitate" to say so "overtly"? Why does he "blur" the distinction between the theoretical character of philosophy and the practical character of the royal art? Why does Alfarabi give us the impression that philosophy can on its own provide the science of the beings as well as the right way of life, and also wants us to think that philosophy must be supplemented by something else in order to produce happiness? Why does Alfarabi make two incompatible and contradictory claims (¶ 13)?

Strauss claims that Alfarabi's circumspection regarding the relationship between philosophy and the royal art is somehow connected with the relationship between human perfection and happiness; it therefore seems that these two are not the same. At first, it appears that for Alfarabi, philosophy provides the science of the beings, which realizes man's perfection. This perfection is distinguished from happiness by the fact that only by the addition of the royal art, which produces the right way of life, can this perfection lead to happiness. In other words, although man can achieve his perfection through philosophy, philosophy in itself is not sufficient for attaining happiness. Strauss claims that identifying the philosopher and the king has for its objective a correction of this primary impression: if the philosopher and the king are identical, it means that philosophy and the royal art are also identical, and therefore philosophy, which now also contains the royal art, can lead not only to man's perfection but also to his happiness. In other words, it seems that philosophy is now sufficient to produce happiness, and need not be supplemented by something else. Strauss does not claim that this is entirely satisfactory, because he says that Alfarabi leaves "the precise relation of philosophy to the royal art" in "doubt." Alfarabi, however, makes it "perfectly clear" in his second and central statement that "philosophy by itself is sufficient to produce happiness" (¶ 14). But what does "philosophy" mean here? Is it divorced from the royal art, or does it include it? At first Strauss seems to suggest that it is difficult to explain why Alfarabi speaks "circumlocutorily about the relation of philosophy to the royal art," although he finds it quite easy to explain why Alfarabi makes contradictory statements about "the relation of philosophy to happiness." But right away, he explains that "the identification of philosophy with the royal art," which he considered difficult to understand, is used by Alfarabi "as a pedagogic device." This pedagogic device is used by Alfarabi for leading his select readers to his deeper view. This deeper view is that only theoretical philosophy – by itself and independently of anything else, including the royal art – leads to true happiness. Strauss qualifies this true happiness as a happiness "in this life," because this is "the only happiness which is possible." This last remark is somehow connected with Strauss's reference to Maimonides: as Strauss explains, Maimonides distinguished between perfection and happiness and implies that happiness is the same thing as "eternal life" while perfection does not depend on life after death (footnote 32). But if this is Strauss's last word on the subject, it would mean that perfection is the only thing available and happiness is impossible. Or to put it differently, perfection, which is attained through theoretical science, is the only true happiness.

Strauss calls this specific understanding of happiness "the consideration of speculative sciences" and points us toward Thomas Aquinas. Aquinas has argued that this kind of happiness, which he rejects, is the one defended by Aristotle. This is the "imperfect happiness, such as can be had in this life." According to Aquinas, man's true and final happiness is attained "through knowledge of something above the human intellect," and consists of a happiness compatible with divine revelation and the idea of immortality. Strauss claims that the idea according to which true happiness consists of leisurely philosophical contemplation does not go as a matter of fact, but rather needs "some preparation and adjustment." Plato and Aristotle could openly argue for such a view because they were under no compulsion to reconcile this temporal view of happiness "with the belief in the immortality of the soul or with the requirements of faith." Medieval thinkers like Alfarabi were in a different position, and had to take the requirements of the predominant religion of their time into account. Regardless of these concessions to the ruling religion, Strauss claims that according to Averroes's report, Alfarabi believed "that man's only perfection consists of the speculative sciences," and furthermore stated that "the dictum that man becomes a separate being is 'an old women's tale,' since that which is generated and corruptible will not become eternal."[18]

Alfarabi's view of man's ultimate happiness is not the only problematic point from the religious perspective. Strauss seems even to deny Alfarabi's belief in the existence of anything supernatural (¶ 32). According to Alfarabi, philosophy as the science of the beings is above all the science of the natural beings (as distinguished from the artificial beings). But what about the supernatural beings? In his summary of the *Timaeus*, Alfarabi mentions divine beings alongside natural beings as the object of philosophy, which means that the divine things are not, strictly speaking, natural beings. In other words, the science of the natural beings seems different from the science of the divine beings. Strauss suggests two ways of reconciling these divergent statements: The first is to define the natural beings in a way that includes the divine beings. The divine beings are as natural as nondivine natural beings because they also do not owe

---

[18] This is Kalman P. Bland's translation of a passage from Averroes's *Epistle on the Possibility of Conjunction with the Intellect* (surviving only in Hebrew). Strauss refers to this passage in footnote 39. The German translation in Steinschneider's book referred to by Strauss is the following: "Diess hat Abu Nazar in seinem Commentar zur *Nicomachia* [*Nicomachica*] bewogen, anzunehmen, dass der Mensch keine andere Vollkommenheit, als die durch die speculativen Wissenschaften zu erreichende habe, und er bemerkt: die Ansicht, der Mensch werde ein separates Wesen, ist eitles Geschwätz, denn das Werdende [und] Vergehende wird kein Ewiges." See Averroes, *The Epistle on the Possibility of Conjunction with the Active Intellect by Ibn Rushd with the Commentary of Moses Narboni*, ed. Kalman P. Bland (New York: Jewish Theological Seminary of America, 1982), 85; Herbert A. Davidson, *Alfarabi, Avicenna, and Averroes on Intellect: Their Cosmologies, Theories of the Active Intellect, and Theories of Human Intellect* (New York: Oxford University Press, 1992), 70–73.

their existence to human art. This way of making sense of Alfarabi's divergent statements would also mean that in his summary of the *Timaeus*, mentioning the divine beings alongside the natural beings was simply superfluous or unnecessary. Strauss's second solution is to explain Alfarabi's statement by referring to the *Timaeus*. In that dialogue, Plato calls not only the maker of the universe and the traditional Greek gods divine, but also the universe, the heavens, and also the heavenly bodies themselves. Now, the idea of heavenly bodies as divine, a heretical position according to Muslim beliefs, is attributed by Averroes to Avicenna and his disciples; the view which, as Strauss explains elsewhere, seems to be particularly philosophical, as distinguished from "Abrahamic."[19] This would mean that by "divine" Alfarabi only means natural beings which are distinguished from other natural beings by their superior status: these divine beings are still natural, as they are bodies, or inhere in bodies. This would also mean that Alfarabi did not actually believe in the existence of supernatural or noncorporeal beings. Strauss surmises that this might explain his previous observation that Alfarabi is silent about incorporeal movers (the so-called intelligences), separate substances (i.e., beings that are not bodies and do not inhere in bodies), and about the ideas (another kind of noncorporeal beings) (¶ 32). The second way of explaining the divergent statements of Alfarabi is of course, as Strauss mentions, incompatible with other writings of Alfarabi, in which he famously refers to and discusses these incorporeal beings; but Strauss has already told us that these writings, in which Alfarabi speaks "in his own name," do not have the same status as those writings in which Alfarabi presents the ideas of someone else.

There seems to be a problem with this claim of Strauss about Alfarabi's view of the supernatural (¶ 33): in Alfarabi's *Plato* there is one mention of "spiritual things," that is, beings that are not bodies and do not inhere in bodies. But Strauss draws our attention to the fact that "things" are not exactly "beings," although he has already told us that things, being qualities, relations, or products of beings, are dependent on beings. The existence of spiritual things therefore presupposes the existence of spiritual beings, the claim which Strauss fortifies with a reference to Plato's *Apology* in which Socrates tries to refute the charge of atheism by saying that if he believes in daimonic things, he must also believe in daimons. Strauss skips a discussion of this question by saying "however this may

---

[19] Strauss, "The Law of Reason in the Kuzari," 125–26, 126n98; Strauss, "On the Interpretation of Genesis," 369.

be," but the weakness of this Socratic counter-argument is rather obvious: one can believe in "spiritual things" or daimonic things and still not believe in the existence of spiritual beings or daimons, in the same way that one can believe in the existence of divine things (places of worship, religious rituals, religious texts, etc.) without believing in the existence of divine beings or gods.[20] Furthermore, Strauss advances three other points, all of which also amount to questioning Alfarabi's belief in the existence of spiritual beings. First, Alfarabi mentions "spiritual things" only when presenting the common views of people different from Plato, the views of "the multitude." Second, in the same context Alfarabi four times mentions "divine things," three of which again are, Strauss claims, attributed to people other than Plato. In the only case in which he mentions divine things while presenting Plato's investigation, according to Strauss ("I am inclined to believe," see also "I do not know" [¶ 19]), these divine things are "identical with the science of the beings and the right way of life."[21] Third, it seems that Alfarabi uses the adjective "divine" as part of a dichotomy, the opposing element of which is human or bestial. In a subsequent passage, a similar dichotomy appears, in which "human" and "bestial" are the opposing poles. In other words, "divine" seems to be only a comparative category, used for qualifying the superior alternative without any supernatural connotation.[22]

Alfarabi claims that the rule of the philosopher is the instrument through which the philosopher achieves his own happiness and produces happiness for all other human beings who are living under his rule in the virtuous city. As the virtuous city needs to be realized in this world, the question of the legislator becomes central. Here the legislator can simply be identified as the prophet, the founder of a revealed religion, and therefore Alfarabi's view of happiness comes in line with the orthodox view: true happiness is only accessible through Revelation. Strauss draws our attention, however, to the fact that in *Plato*, contrary to *Attainment of Happiness*, the legislator is not explicitly identified with the prophet and the philosopher. Strauss claims that Alfarabi's silence on this point is

---

[20] Leo Strauss, "On Plato's Apology of Socrates and Crito," in *Studies in Platonic Political Philosophy*, ed. Thomas L. Pangle (Chicago and London: University of Chicago Press, 1983), 47; David Leibowitz, *The Ironic Defense of Socrates: Plato's Apology* (Cambridge: Cambridge University Press, 2010), 132.

[21] In four cases mentioned by Strauss, two are clearly related to Plato (15, 12, and 15, 13), one is clearly that of other people (14, 16), and one is not easy to identify (15, 6), but as it is preceded by "He [i.e. Plato] mentioned that," one can safely say it is Plato's view. This might explain why Strauss sounds less than certain about this point.

[22] The same point is made by a reference to Lessing. See footnote 97 of "Fârâbî's *Plato*."

designed intentionally to make the unwary reader identify the legislator with the prophet and, one can add, with the philosopher. This is what Strauss considers Alfarabi's "provisional solution," his exoteric teaching. He thinks, however, that Alfarabi's esoteric teaching is that the philosopher, legislator, and prophet are separate beings: the legislator and virtuous man are more closely akin, which explains why Strauss thinks that according to Alfarabi, "the function of the legislator is not the highest human perfection" (¶ 22).[23] The legislator of the best city does not have to be the prophet Muhammad, because apparently there are other "virtuous cities" founded by different legislators. What above all shows the difference between the philosopher on the one hand and the prophet and legislator on the other is what Strauss calls Alfarabi's "final solution": happiness does not require the establishment of the perfect political community, and perfect happiness is acquired through the science of beings, which is only accessible to philosophers. Considering the fact that this final solution seems incompatible with the idea of a divine legislator, it is not surprising that Alfarabi, in the guise of commenting on Platonic dialogues, denigrates the intellectual value of the science which deals with the study of Islamic Law, namely *fiqh* (¶ 18).

The most important point, however, which points toward Alfarabi's heterodoxy is his view of the immortality of the soul. Strauss claims that the absence of the immortality of the soul in Alfarabi's presentation of Plato's philosophy, the doctrine which Strauss thinks must have been mentioned in Alfarabi's short presentation of Platonic dialogues, points towards the fact that Alfarabi took this Platonic idea as an exoteric doctrine. One must bear in mind that Strauss's attention to the question of immortality has a precedent: Al-Ghazali also accused philosophers of irreligion for denying the traditional view of the immortality of the soul.[24] Furthermore, the question of immortality occupies a unique position in Strauss's essay, as shown in the epigraph of "Fârâbî's *Plato*," which is a quotation from Lessing. As this quotation points to some of the most important points mentioned in "Fârâbî's *Plato*," we shall now discuss it in more detail.

---

[23] Strauss, *Persecution and the Art of Writing*, 1952, 15n10.

[24] In this connection, see a curious report appearing in the commentary by Asclepius on Aristotle's *Metaphysics*: "a certain Panaetius is said to have had the audacity to deny the authenticity of the *Phaedo* because he denied the immortality of the soul and wanted to make of Plato a partner of this denial." František Novotný, *The Posthumous Life of Plato*, trans. Jana Fábryová (Prague: Academia Prague, 1977), 54. I owe this information to Peter Ahrensdorf.

IMMORTALITY OF THE SOUL

Lessing occupies a special place in Strauss's writings. Strauss calls Lessing one of the freest minds of modernity and from whom Strauss claimed he has learned many things, including the art of esoteric writings.[25] Considering Strauss's preoccupation with the question of esotericism in "Fârâbî's *Plato*," it is not surprising that he opens it with an epigraph from Lessing. He does not, however, explain the reasoning behind his selection of this specific epigraph. To understand the significance of this quotation, we should say a few words about the source of the epigraph, to which Strauss clearly points: *Leibniz on Eternal Punishment*, published in 1773. Lessing's text consists of three parts: in the first part, Lessing informs his readers about the existence of a hitherto unpublished preface by Leibniz to a work by the Socinian Ernst Soner. In his work, Soner attacked the doctrine of eternal punishment, and Leibniz intended to republish Soner's work while refuting his attack on eternal punishment in a preface. As Leibniz did not find the occasion to publish his preface along with Soner's work, Lessing intends to publish this brief preface for the benefit of his readers and in defense of the orthodox view of eternal punishment, which he does in the second part of his essay.

Soner had argued that eternal punishment does not correspond to divine justice because a just god would not inflict an infinite punishment for a finite sin. As God is just, therefore, eternal punishment does not exist. In his short preface, published by Lessing for the first time, Leibniz tries to refute Soner's view by arguing against the finitude of sin: the transgression of the sinner is infinite because there is an infinite afterlife in which the sinner continues to sin even after his death. This infinite sin merits an infinite punishment, and therefore a just god would punish the transgression of the sinner with eternal punishment. In the end, however, Leibniz's preface proves to be a very minor affair: as Lessing reminds us, Soner's work itself is long forgotten, and the same argument for eternal punishment has been presented in other writings of Leibniz. Shouldn't he then, Lessing asks himself, have left Leibniz's preface in obscurity? Lessing answers in the negative because his intention is to

---

[25] Strauss, "Notes on Philosophy and Revelation," 178; Leo Strauss and Karl Löwith, "Correspondence between Karl Löwith and Leo Strauss," *The Independent Journal of Philosophy* 5/6 (1988): 190 (Letter to Karl Löwith on July 17, 1935, GS III.657); Strauss, "Exoteric Teaching"; Strauss, "A Giving of Accounts," 462; Marc Buhot de Launay, "Leo Strauss et la découverte du classicisme ésotérique chez Lessing," *Les Études philosophiques* 65, no. 2 (2003): 245–59.

clarify "the attitudes and reasons which underlay" Leibniz's defense of eternal punishment.[26] Now, the simple fact that Leibniz intended to republish a practically forgotten work which argues against the orthodox doctrine of eternal punishment is worthy of remark: we know, for instance, in the case of Spinoza's writings, that one of the common ways for advertising unorthodox ideas was to republish the works containing such ideas while including some superficial refutation of those ideas supposedly to "protect" readers against dangerous perplexities.[27] We might therefore, like Leibniz's contemporaries, to whom Lessing also alludes, suspect that, contrary to first impressions, Leibniz might have been sympathetic to Soner's critique of eternal punishment. In any event, after quoting Leibniz's unpublished brief preface in the second part of his text, Lessing's job seems to be finished, but he continues making supplementary remarks in the third part of his work, in which he takes issue with one of Leibniz's detractors. In fact, it seems that Leibniz's short preface, which Lessing himself confesses is nothing new, as Leibniz has said the same thing in other works, serves as an occasion for a more important discussion. Surprisingly, Lessing tells us, he is not entirely convinced that Leibniz's argument against Soner is conclusive; he even goes so far as to say that perhaps Leibniz refrained from publishing his preface because on further reflection he also found the argument unconvincing! But if Leibniz did not find his own argument convincing, why did he present it nonetheless in his other writings? Lessing claims that a writer can propose an argument that he finds unconvincing in another place because the "same thought can have an entirely different value in another place." This is the passage which Strauss uses as the epigraph of "Fârâbî's *Plato*."

Lessing dedicates the third part of his work to a confrontation with one of Leibniz's detractors, Johann August Eberhard. According to Eberhard, Leibniz did in fact oppose the doctrine of eternal punishment, and his defense of the orthodox view must be ascribed to Leibniz's desire to acquire universal approval for his system of thought. To make his views agreeable to the orthodox readers, Eberhard claimed, Leibniz adapted them to their prejudices, one of them being their belief in eternal punishments. Lessing strongly opposes Eberhard's view of Leibniz,

---

[26] G. E. Lessing, "Leibniz on Eternal Punishment," in *Lessing: Philosophical and Theological Writings*, trans. H. B. Nisbet (Cambridge: Cambridge University Press, 2005), 43.

[27] Catherine Wilson, "The Reception of Leibniz in the Eighteenth Century," in *The Cambridge Companion to Leibniz*, ed. Nicholas Jolley (Cambridge: Cambridge University Press, 1995), 460. Cf. Lloyd Strickland, "Leibniz on Eternal Punishment," *British Journal for the History of Philosophy* 17, no. 2 (2009): 326.

but this without claiming that Leibniz really believed in this doctrine. Eberhard is mistaken because he has completely misunderstood Leibniz's art of writing: Leibniz followed, Lessing claims, the venerable tradition of ancient philosophers who "in their *exoteric* pronouncements ... tried to lead each individual along the path to truth" on which they found him.[28] In other words, according to Lessing, Leibniz does not merely practice his art of writing to gain followers or perhaps to protect himself against persecution; he also has a philanthropic intention.

Lessing concedes that Leibniz's defense of the doctrine of eternal damnation is exoteric, and that "he would have expressed himself quite differently *esoterically.*" The doctrine of eternal punishment is the exoteric formulation of a "great esoteric truth," namely that "nothing in the world is isolated, nothing is without consequences, and nothing is without eternal consequences."[29] In this regard, eternal punishment is the *consequence* of sin. If the reader is shocked that Leibniz's defense of eternal punishment has an entirely different meaning in this context and that his view is anything but orthodox, next Lessing mentions that even this view is "a mere possibility." To the question of why one should frighten people with eternal punishment which is only a mere possibility, Lessing replies: why not frighten with it, since it can only be frightening to someone who has never been earnest about the betterment of himself?[30] It therefore seems that the salutary effects of the doctrine of eternal punishment are somehow more important than its truth. In fact, in Lessing's comments it turns out that Hell does not exist, nor do the corporal punishments mentioned in Scripture! The punishments of which Scripture warns us, Lessing claims, are only the natural ones which would follow from sin; there is nothing supernatural about them. Those passages in Scripture which say otherwise exist because "the higher wisdom" considered that such extraordinary threats are necessary and recognized that it was salutary to express them purely in terms of our ordinary sensibilities, taking all its imagery from physical pain, which is more accessible to ordinary men.

Lessing claims that Leibniz's doctrine of the best possible world does not mean that all human beings will eventually attain happiness. The gradual growth in perfection applies only to the general conditions of the whole, not to all individual beings. Leibniz's presentation of his doctrine, as well

[28] Lessing, "Leibniz on Eternal Punishment," 46.
[29] Lessing, "Leibniz on Eternal Punishment," 52.
[30] Lessing, "Leibniz on Eternal Punishment," 54.

as how others understood it, seem to be much more generous towards human beings. According to Lessing, this exoteric generosity, or rather philanthropy, should not hide the fact that for Leibniz the punishment of sinners does not lead to the correction of all human beings. Just like Socrates, who also believed in eternal punishment, "at least to the extent of considering it helpful to teach it in the most unexceptionable and explicit terms," Leibniz "extends correction to those who merely witness the punishment, even if it has no effect on those who are themselves punished."[31] It seems that the threat of divine punishment is addressed to those human beings who need such frightening statements to mend their ways.

To resume, it seems that according to Lessing, Leibniz's art of writing is designed to serve two groups of readers in equal measure: to guide the astute readers toward a more profound understanding of their perfection, and to educate the vulgar with unreal threats which are more suitable to their understanding. Now, these two different forms of esotericism are also present in Strauss's essay, "Fârâbî's *Plato*." As esotericism can be practiced for different reasons, one might distinguish between protective esotericism, which has the objective of protecting the heterodox writer from persecution while guiding the potential philosophers towards the truth on the one hand, and a form of educative exotericism, which intends to replace the common unphilosophical ideas of the multitude with the truth or rather "an approximation to the truth" on the other (¶ 23). Strauss claims that Alfarabi's statements about the political aspect of philosophy should not be considered "a mere stepping-stone" in Alfarabi's argument. What Strauss means is that these statements have two functions: the first function corresponds to the defensive esotericism, which not only protects the heterodox philosopher but would also gradually lead his insightful readers to the idea that philosophy is the only way to happiness, that real happiness is only possible in this life, and that "the popular notions about the happiness of the other world" are erroneous. But the political statements have a second function, which corresponds to what we called educative esotericism. Strauss explains this by reminding us of the element which is common to both kinds of esotericism, namely the danger which philosophers' necessary membership in a political society exposes them to. But while in protective esotericism, this danger leads to the philosopher's caution in addressing the elite, in

---

[31] Lessing, "Leibniz on Eternal Punishment," 48. This passage is quoted in Leo Strauss, "How to Study Spinoza's Theologico-Political Treatise," in *Persecution and the Art of Writing* (Glencoe: Free Press, 1952), 182.

educative esotericism this danger leads to a different way of addressing "the vulgar," who seem to be as much in need of philosophers' guidance as the elite and potential philosophers. Learning how to educate the vulgar without endangering oneself was, according to Strauss's reading of Alfarabi, the result of a major turn in Plato's thought, a "correction of the Socratic attitude" (¶ 23). While Plato's teacher Socrates, because of his "moral fervor," had no other option but to either "comply" with the erroneous doctrines of his fellow citizens or to "openly challenge" them thereby risking persecution, Plato learned how to combine "the way of Socrates," appropriate for dealing with the elite, with "the way of Thrasymachus," appropriate for dealing with the vulgar. In other words, Plato, whose "moral fervor was mitigated by his insight into the nature of beings," put aside the "revolutionary" and "uncompromising" attitude of Socrates and picked up a "conservative" way of action. This "insight into the nature of beings" perhaps has led to a better understanding of what is possible in politics and what is impossible and should be avoided. Plato's conservative attitude consisted of "gradual" and step-by-step "replacement … of the accepted opinions by the truth or an approximation to the truth," a gentle and imperceptible "undermining" or the "destruction of the accepted opinions." The educative and protective esotericisms are in a sense two sides of the same coin, and both are born out of an awareness of the limits of politics, of an "insight into the nature of beings." While the protective esotericism protects the philosopher who is teaching the truth to the select few, the educative esotericism protects the philosopher who is teaching "an approximation to the truth" or "an imaginative representation of the truth" to the vulgar. Strauss describes this form of political action as "the secret kingship of the philosopher" and distinguishes it from Socrates's doctrine of the "philosopher-king who rules openly in the perfect city," giving us the impression that this was Socrates's real political program, perhaps due to his "uncompromising" and misguided "moral fervor." Plato's "secret kingship" is the middle ground between revolutionary overconfidence about the political effectiveness of philosophy, which leads to the direct participation of philosophers in the politics of the best regime, and total disregard for the political life of the city on the part of philosophers. It is the Platonic from of philosophical "philanthropy" which leads to the indirect influence of the philosopher "who lives privately as a member of an imperfect community."[32]

---

[32] Leo Strauss, "Introduction," in *Persecution and the Art of Writing* (Glencoe: Free Press, 1952), 17.

Now, it is interesting that this whole idea of educative esotericism, which guides the multitude toward salutary opinions, the idea to which Strauss points by including Lessing's epigraph, is also present in a work by Averroes, to which Strauss also refers. In "Fârâbî's *Plato*," Averroes is mentioned seven times: six times by name (¶¶ 2, 5, footnote 39, footnote 41, footnote 58, footnote 93) and once without being named (footnote 43). The last reference to Averroes is to the work in which Averroes highlights the salutary character of the doctrine of immortality as the reason for the philosophers' defense of this doctrine. Contrary to his practice of defending the philosophers against al-Ghazali's religious charges through philosophical arguments, here Averroes bases his whole apology of the philosophers on the political necessity of this doctrine. The philosophers regard immortality "as most important and believe in it most," according to Averroes, because it is "conducive to an order amongst men on which man's being, as man, depends and through which he can attain the greatest happiness proper to him." Such religious beliefs "lead towards wisdom in a way universal to all human beings" and seek "the instruction of the masses generally" while philosophy only addresses a few intelligent people who are capable of philosophizing. This also explains why the depiction of the afterlife in religion is more bodily than spiritual: such material depictions are more accessible to the real addressee of religious teachings, namely the multitude, than highly abstract spiritual depictions. Here Averroes goes so far in his defense of religious beliefs that he approves of al-Ghazali's condemnation of the people who deny such salutary beliefs, those who are determined "to destroy the religious prescriptions and to undo the virtues." Averroes joins al-Ghazali in calling such people "heretics" and will assure us that "both theologians and philosophers will no doubt kill them," but alas "they have no actual power" to do so. In any event, Averroes states that "[w]hat Ghazali says against them is right."[33]

After discussing the question of immortality, Strauss writes that he would like to discuss a third example of Alfarabi's heterodox ideas (¶ 18). It seems that the question of happiness and the immortality of the soul are the two examples already discussed. In other words, we receive another

---

[33] Averroes, *Tahafut Al-Tahafut*, 359–62 (Bouygues 581–84). For Strauss's view of the salutary effects of religious beliefs see Leo Strauss, "Notes on Lucretius," in *Liberalism Ancient and Modern* (Chicago: University of Chicago Press, 1995), 100, 105, 127, 131; Strauss, *Spinoza's Critique of Religion*, 10–11, 29–30, 47–49 (GS I:21, 50–51, 76–79). For the difficulty which Averroes's unusual method of defending philosophers' belief in the immortality of the soul creates for traditional scholarship see Leaman, *Averroes and His Philosophy*, 94–96.

indication, apart from the epigraph of the text, that the question of immortality, being the second and central example, is of particular importance. The third example is the problematic place of the religious sciences, namely Islamic jurisprudence (*fiqh*) and dialectical theology (*kalām*) in Alfarabi's thought. In *Enumeration of the Sciences*, the work in which Alfarabi "speaks in his own name," these sciences are treated as parts of political science. According to Strauss, this way of treating religious sciences seems to mean three things: First, it seems that this is Alfarabi's way of saying that Islam, as a revealed religion which is primarily a law regulating social life, comes "first into the sight of the philosopher as a political fact." Second, Strauss claims that here it seems that Alfarabi, "as a philosopher ... suspends his judgment as to the truth of the super-rational teaching of religion." Third, one receives the impression that Alfarabi is trying to make room for a revealed theology, as distinguished from the natural theology of philosophers. Now, it is surprising that these three claims about the relationship between religious science and political science in the thought of Alfarabi are presented by Strauss, through the use of colons and phrases like "in other words," as if they grow out of each other or are equivalent. It is true that Alfarabi's treatment of the question suggests that Islamic Law and its related sciences are political phenomena and are treated as such; furthermore, it is true that Alfarabi tends to discuss religious questions in a way that suggests some form of detachment; it is also true that dialectical theology for Alfarabi is a form of revealed theology; in fact, it is what dialectical theology is. But these three facts are not the same; perhaps they are somehow connected, but Strauss does not explain how. In any event, Strauss now claims that these kinds of ambiguities disappear entirely in *Plato*, and Alfarabi, through "the mouth of Plato" declares that religious sciences do not lead to man's highest perfection because these sciences cannot supply the science of the beings. Furthermore, religious knowledge in *Plato* is ranked lower than other sciences, even lower than linguistic sciences, although Strauss mentions that religious knowledge has something in common with language, because they are both specific to a particular community. To understand this whole laconic discussion, one should check two footnotes of this section. In the first footnote (41), Strauss draws our attention to the fact that, despite the low rank of the religious sciences, Alfarabi does not reject divine worship. In fact, Alfarabi recommends conformity with the laws and beliefs of the religious community in which one is brought up as a necessary qualification for the future philosopher. Strauss reminds us of the fact that here Alfarabi is following Plato, who also recommended such conformity. In other words, Alfarabi advises the philosopher to conform his acts to the common religious practices of his society while questioning, no doubt esoterically, the truth of these practices and the claims of that religion in general. Strauss claims that the full agreement of Alfarabi with Plato on this point appears after consulting three passages in Plato's *Timaeus, Seventh Letter,* and *Ion.* Looking up these passages, one finds the idea that one must accept the common religious beliefs in *Timaeus* and *Ion,* but looking up the central reference to *Seventh Letter* (330e), one comes away empty-handed. Some might claim that it cannot be an accident that exactly in providing the central reference Strauss makes a mistake; such a reader would draw our attention to the fact that the mistaken reference is in fact significant, because Plato is there explaining that the philosopher should refrain from advising a city which does not heed his advice and threatens him with death. Furthermore, perhaps a reference to Plato's works here is not even necessary: Strauss quotes from the editor of *Plato,* who has confessed that the view of divine worship presented in the work does not correspond to the Platonic view, but rather fits Alfarabi's thought very well. The agreement of Alfarabi with Plato is furthermore underscored by a reference to the *Apology,* in which Socrates claims that he only possesses human wisdom, and divine wisdom is wholly inaccessible to him. Strauss claims that *Alfarabi* interpreted this Socratic claim not as Socrates's denial of the truth of the divine wisdom, but rather as a way of specifying the modest status of his own wisdom. A reference to Averroes also clarifies that the divine wisdom meant here is the one "based on, or transmitted by, prophecy." Now this whole discussion is problematic for several reasons: First, if we accept this supposedly Farabian understanding of the Socratic thesis, it means that contrary to Strauss's earlier claim, Alfarabi did not have a negative view of the cognitive value of religious speculation; he rather simply claimed ignorance. Second, it is not clear where Alfarabi offers this interpretation of the Socratic thesis. Third, Strauss elsewhere explains that the Socratic claim of ignorance regarding divine wisdom is "a polite expression of his rejection of that wisdom."[34] In the next footnote (42), Strauss makes a rather surprising claim: although Alfarabi, through the mouth of Plato, explicitly rejects the value of *fiqh* and *kalām,* "he is completely silent about the result of Plato's examination of 'religious speculation.'" Strauss continues: "'religious speculation' may well refer to mystical knowledge of God himself." The meaning of this statement is that religious speculation is a

---

[34] Strauss, "The Law of Reason in the Kuzari," 107n33.

form of intuition independent of logical deduction and syllogism. In the Neo-Platonic view this kind of knowledge is mainly attributed to God's way of knowing things but also to "philosophers" in a mystical state. It seems that according to Strauss, Alfarabi's reticence in discussing this type of knowledge is a way of dismissing the supra-rational claims and methods of the Neo-Platonic school with which Alfarabi is often identified. So much for Alfarabi's supposed outspokenness. But one cannot say the same thing about Strauss.

One of the most impressive aspects of "Fârâbî's *Plato*," which distinguishes it from Strauss's other writings, is its unique emphasis on unbelief and irreligiosity. It is true that Strauss does not call Alfarabi an atheist, but he leaves no doubt that Alfarabi rejected Islam and considered its claims to truth entirely worthless. Now, it is true that Strauss attributes the same irreligious perspective to many other philosophers, but nowhere else do we see Strauss speaking so emphatically with an approving tone of a philosopher who he clearly depicts as an unbeliever. Here two relevant examples come to mind. Regardless of his sympathetic evaluation of Machiavelli, in *Thoughts on Machiavelli* Strauss clearly employs a condemnatory voice which has even distorted readers' understanding of Strauss's position right from the beginning.[35] "The Law of Reason in the *Kuzari*," the second example which comes close to Strauss's outspokenness about the philosophers' unbelief in "Fârâbî's *Plato*," also contains passages in which Strauss speaks with his usual balanced and ambiguous position regarding the question of Reason and Revelation.[36] Some have claimed that Strauss's outspoken and very sympathetic depiction of Alfarabi's unbelief is rhetorical. According to this view, Strauss is in a sense exaggerating this aspect of Alfarabi's thought, giving us a presentation of Alfarabi's unbelief in a "graceless and unrestrained manner" which is "remarkable for its lack of subtlety" and fails to give "moderation its due" in order to counter the common prejudice regarding Islamic philosophy as an eclectic mixture of religion and philosophy.[37] One can

---

[35] For a detailed discussion of Strauss's rhetorical strategy in *Thoughts on Machiavelli* see Meier, *Political Philosophy and the Challenge of Revealed Religion*, 23–115.

[36] For the rhetorical character of Strauss's presentation of Judah Halevi and the question of the unbelief of the philosophers cf. Strauss, "The Law of Reason in the Kuzari," 109 with Laurence Lampert, "Exotericism Embraced: 'The Law of Reason in the Kuzari,'" in *The Enduring Importance of Leo Strauss* (Chicago: University of Chicago Press, 2013), 46.

[37] Lenzner, "Strauss's Farabi, Scholarly Prejudice, and Philosophic Politics," 199ff. For an example of Strauss's radicalism on this subject in his private correspondence see Strauss, *Gesammelte Schriften. Band 3*, 706 and 707 (Letter to Gershom Scholem on December 7, 1933).

question this view of Strauss's essay, "Fârâbî's *Plato*," by referring to the fact that it seems Strauss somehow saw the situation completely differently in all his other writings, which deal with the conflict of Reason and Revelation. In all those other writings, Strauss is always more emphatic about the claims of Revelation. We should therefore say that Strauss's most authoritative observation about his intellectual context was that belief is much more in need of support than unbelief. Considering this point, one should rather say that Strauss's way of writing in "Fârâbî's *Plato*" encourages common intellectual prejudices, which tend to favor unbelief and Reason rather than belief and Revelation. Is it the reason why Strauss decided against the republication of his essay? What does it then say about Strauss's other writings, which emphatically invite us to be "open to the challenge of theology," which seem to even go so far as to depict a conflict of Reason and Revelation in which Revelation has the upper hand? Is it possible that "Fârâbî's *Plato*," this very personal and *unique* writing of Strauss, depicts more authentically Strauss's genuine positions than those *repeated* statements of his? Is it not significant that in the revised version of "Fârâbî's *Plato*" in the Introduction of *Persecution and the Art of Writing*, Strauss's most emphatic and personal statement on Alfarabi's unbelief is absent?[38]

WHAT IS PHILOSOPHY?

With his esoteric reading of *Plato*, Strauss intends to prove that Alfarabi's view of happiness and his rejection of the supernatural, prophecy, Islamic jurisprudence, and immortality of the soul mean that he cannot be considered a Muslim philosopher. Strauss is, however, aware of the fact that

---

[38] Cf. "For may one not expound, as a commentator, or as a historian, with the greatest care and without a muttering of dissent such views as he rejects as a man? May Fârâbî not have been attracted as a pupil of philosophers by what he abhorred as a believer? I do not know whether there ever was a 'philosopher' whose mind was so confused as to consist of two hermetically sealed compartments: Fârâbî was a man of a different stamp. But let us assume that his mind was of the type conveniently attributed to the Latin Averroists" (¶ 19) with "Yet could not Farabi, as a commentator, have expounded, without a muttering of dissent, such views as he rejected as a man? Could he not have been attracted, as a student of philosophy, by what he abhorred as a believer? Could his mind not have been of the type that is attributed to the Latin Averroists?" Strauss, *Persecution and the Art of Writing*, 1952, 14. See also ¶ 34 and its disappearance in the Introduction of *Persecution and the Art of Writing*. For a detailed discussion of the rhetorical aspect of Strauss's depiction of the conflict between Reason and Revelation see Meier, *Leo Strauss and the Theologico-Political Problem*, 3–29.

his claims about Alfarabi's philosophy are highly dependent on esoteric techniques of reading, and are therefore controversial. Some might claim that in *Plato*, Alfarabi is expounding the views, not of himself, but rather that of "other men" who were non-Muslim "pagans" (¶ 19). One can then explain away the problematic points in Alfarabi's exposition of Plato's philosophy by the fact that he "as a commentator, or as a historian" is bound to present the ideas of his subject faithfully without indicating his disagreement with the ideas presented in his commentary or historical work. Strauss therefore hypothesizes that Alfarabi, "as a pupil of philosophers," a faithful follower of Plato, may have disagreed with the ideas of his teachers "as a believer." But right away he rejects such a possibility by qualifying Alfarabi as a "philosopher" who cannot have been so "confused" as to at the same time subscribe to contradictory ideas: perhaps he could not have been a "philosopher" and also a "believer" at the same time. Such a contradictory stance has been traditionally ascribed to the so-called Latin Averroists: Could Alfarabi have been a Latin Averroist *avant la lettre*? But the difference between the Latin Averroists and Alfarabi is rather evident: the former expounded a heretical teaching faithfully, while Alfarabi seems rather strict about avoiding a literal presentation of Plato's ideas, which are rather tolerable from the believer's point of view. A "mere commentator of Plato" who intends to be a faithful expositor of Plato's ideas would not ignore Plato's "tolerably orthodox doctrine concerning the life after death" in his presentation, but this is precisely what Alfarabi does. According to Strauss, this "flagrant deviation from the letter of Plato's teaching" more than "any explicit statement of his" proves that he did not believe in the afterlife and that he considered the Platonic doctrine of immortality false. It would therefore mean that any statement of his in defense of immortality and life after death in his other writings, in which he speaks in his own name, must be considered "as prudential accommodations to the accepted dogma." This is also the case in what "the commentator, or historian" Alfarabi says about religious sciences, because it is difficult to see how "a believing Muslim" could have found a critique of *fiqh* in Plato's writings. In fact, Alfarabi is only a figure who exemplifies "the genuine philosopher" for Strauss, the philosopher who "can never become a genuine convert to Judaism or to any other revealed religion."[39]

---

[39] Strauss, "The Law of Reason in the Kuzari," 104–5, 105n29; Strauss, "Literary Character of the Guide for the Perplexed," 43.

Considering these points, Strauss can claim that he has proved that none of three terms applied to Alfarabi are a faithful description of his thought: he is neither a straightforward Aristotelian, nor a Neo-Platonist, nor an orthodox Muslim. He is a philosopher. But what is philosophy and who is a philosopher?

This question can be described as one of the main themes or even *the* theme of "Fârâbî's *Plato.*" Strauss repeatedly defines philosophy according to Alfarabi as the science of the essence of all beings. It is "the science of *Timaeus*," a theoretical science or art par excellence, which is fundamentally distinguished from the practical arts. It is also "the way leading to theoretical science." In other words, philosophy is the *actual* investigation of beings which leads to that science and also science itself. This definition of philosophy is also connected with what Alfarabi means by "Plato's philosophy," or what Strauss calls its "precise meaning" – the unpolitical science of the essence of all beings (¶ 11). This meaning of philosophy is not incompatible with Alfarabi's first definition of Plato's philosophy, that is, with the essentially political investigation of happiness. It is true, Strauss argues, that the philosopher, in the quest for the essence of all beings, must transcend the sphere of moral or political things, but he should also give an account of his doing so. He should justify his philosophical investigation. As the context of this investigation is the political society, the justification transforms itself to the political justification of philosophical investigation, to the question of "what is the right way of life?" This justification, which is "merely preliminary," is in a sense, Strauss claims, philosophic because "only the philosopher is competent to elaborate that question and to answer it." Despite the preliminary character of this exercise, philosophy as the quest for the truth about the whole cannot be separated from it, from the self-knowledge which grounds the need for such a knowledge and clarifies "the difficulties obstructing its discovery and its communication" (¶ 11). Here, "communication" refers to the question of esotericism. Strauss reiterates, however, that philosophic investigation and this preliminary step "do not belong to the same level" and, as Strauss mentioned before, they have "different ranks." It is even more reasonable to say that this self-knowledge is not, properly speaking, a part of philosophy and must therefore be distinguished from it. This is reflected in the fact that in *Plato*, contrary to Alfarabi's other writings, philosophy does not consist of separate theoretical and practical parts. In other words, although philosophy has a direct connection with political philosophy, which acts as a preliminary to theoretical science proper, philosophy is essentially a theoretical pursuit. This understanding of philosophy sounds rather traditional. One should not, however, conclude that Alfarabi's understanding of philosophy, or rather Strauss's understanding of it, is traditional.

The untraditional view of philosophy presented by Strauss is reflected above all in the last paragraph of "Fârâbî's *Plato*." After a dense evaluation of Alfarabi's view of the supernatural, which leads to the rather radical conclusion that Alfarabi did not believe in the existence of such beings, Strauss confesses that his observations are far from being the last word on Alfarabi's view of the supernatural or incorporeal substances. They do not "suffice" to make a definitive judgment about Alfarabi's view of these sensitive subjects. One can perhaps add that in these types of esoteric readings of the works of philosophers which Strauss pursues, this kind of uncertainty must always be expected. Strauss himself implies the same thing by saying that although "a man such as" Alfarabi "doubtless" had "definite convictions" on some subjects, it is not easy to say what these convictions were. But, surprisingly, Strauss believes that his observations "suffice" to substantiate the claim that Alfarabi's "philosophy does not stand and fall with the acceptance of such [supernatural or incorporeal] substances." What Strauss means is that these doctrines do not play a particularly important role in Alfarabi's philosophy. What is fundamental in Alfarabi's philosophy is the "spirit" in which he pursues his research, not his "convictions."[40] That spirit is what Alfarabi has in common with other philosophers, even with a "philosophic materialist," while that spirit distinguishes him from any "non philosophic believer." Philosophy, in all its forms, is therefore strictly distinguished from belief.[41] The philosophical spirit consists of pursuing the science of all beings and not the science of the various ways of life. In other words, Alfarabi's view of philosophy is "essentially and purely" theoretical and not political. Philosophy is the "way leading to" the science of all beings; it is "the actual investigation of things which leads to that science" and *not* that science itself.

This view of philosophy, which Strauss identifies with the original sense of *skepsis* (meaning speculation, inquiry, and examination but also doubt and hesitation), is rather unique. One gets the impression that,

[40] Philosophy "designates primarily, not a set of dogmas, and in particular the dogmas of the Aristotelians, but a method, or an attitude." Strauss, "The Law of Reason in the Kuzari," 105n29.
[41] "[Philosophy] is *radically* atheistic. The difference between Plato and a materialist like Democritus fades into insignificance if compared with the difference between Plato and any doctrine based on religious experience." Strauss, "Reason and Revelation (1948)," 146.

according to Strauss, science which is pursued by the philosopher is wholly beyond our grasp, and philosophy should be only considered an endless "quest for truth" without any expectation of ever achieving that truth. This seems to be why elsewhere Strauss can describe philosophy, "when one contrasts its achievement with its goal," as "Sisyphean."[42] The endlessness of the quest seems to be due to the fact that if one resists the temptation to accept any conviction which is "unevident or unproven," there will be not much left; there will always be doubts about and objections to any proposed solution. Despite the endlessness and apparently fruitlessness of this quest, Strauss finds it so valuable that he calls it the only thing which makes "life worth living." In a way, Strauss's interest in *Plato* shows his own preference for such a view of philosophy.[43] When describing Alfarabi's procedure in presenting Plato's philosophy, Strauss distinguishes it from other procedures. The first procedure which Alfarabi does not follow is that which presents the final Platonic teachings. According to Strauss, Alfarabi's procedure is not teaching oriented; this also seems to be one of the reasons why, to reconcile his Platonism with his adherence to Aristotle, Alfarabi did not try to present the identity of the esoteric doctrine of Plato and Aristotle (¶ 6). The image of Alfarabi that appears in Strauss's essay is a rather curious one: Strauss seems to be particularly interested in modeling a philosopher without any substantial philosophical doctrine or dogma, a philosopher only interested in philosophical inquiry itself. He does not seem like someone who promotes some specific doctrine, even on subjects which appear prominent in Strauss's presentation. For instance, Strauss claims that Alfarabi was an unbeliever, but Strauss does not seem to have discovered Alfarabi's specific refutation of Revelation. All that Strauss seems to care about is that Alfarabi rejects the claims of revealed religion in favor of a superior life of inquiry and zetetic philosophy. In fact, these two ideas, the rejection of Revelation and the superiority of the philosophic life, which are clearly connected, seem to be the only positive doctrines attributed to Alfarabi by Strauss.[44] It is difficult to describe precisely what this zetetic philosophy is. It can rather be described negatively, by what it is not. It is not dogmatic philosophy: dogmatic philosophy is the philosophy which

---

[42] Strauss, "What Is Political Philosophy?," 40.

[43] Strauss, *On Plato's Symposium*, 4–5; Strauss, *On Tyranny*, 196–97.

[44] This is done through a clear and, from the *historiographical* point of view, problematic abstraction from some of Alfarabi's positive doctrines. See Colmo, "Theory and Practice," 973ff.

not only presupposes that the solution for, at least, the most important questions is achievable, but also claims to have discovered it. In a sense, most philosophers, as long as we believe that they have offered definitive answers to decisive questions, have been dogmatic. Zetetic philosophy is also different from skeptical philosophy in the traditional sense of the term. Skeptics presuppose that ultimate solutions to the most important questions are beyond our reach. Zetetic philosophy seems to have something in common with dogmatism as well as with skepticism: it shares dogmatism's trust in our powers to solve the ultimate problems, but it also shares skepticism's mistrust in the given answers and entertains a rather radical dissatisfaction with them. If one looks closely, one is tempted to say that zetetic philosophy is much closer to skepticism than to dogmatism. The crucial point seems to be that zetetic philosophy keeps alive the *hope* for reaching a solution, or rather does not reject out of hand the possibility of such a solution. Whether this is entirely satisfying as a distinctive characteristic is not entirely clear. One can perhaps say that zetetic philosophy in practice is not distinguishable from skepticism: they both hardly propose any definitive answer to our questions. Zetetic philosophy does not offer a solution without in the same breath mentioning its provisional character and its deficiencies. The fact itself that according to Strauss "the questions are clearer than the answers" gives us the impression that no clear answer to those questions is achievable, and that we will always be dealing with questions. If one considers the unfinished character of the philosophy which Strauss describes as only a *description* of its *current* state, one can maintain the difference between skepticism and zetetic philosophy. But if what Strauss is pointing at is a claim about the *essential* capacities of philosophy and its *future* results, then one must say that zetetic philosophy cannot be distinguished from skepticism. Perhaps the most radical and also the most impressive depiction of this view is presented by Strauss in the following words, where the possibility of the properly philosophic knowledge, that is, demonstrative knowledge, is implicitly denied:

Philosophy is concerned with understanding reality in all its complexity. Its complexity may preclude demonstrative answers to the fundamental questions: the arguments in favor of the various incompatible answers may be inconclusive. This would not make the philosophic enterprise futile: for the philosopher, full understanding of a *problem* is infinitely more important than any mere answer. What counts from the philosophic, i.e., the theoretical, point of view, is the articulation of the *subject matter* as an articulation supplied by the argument in favor of two contradictory answers rather than the answers themselves. Philosophy in its original sense is disputative rather than decisive. Disputation is possible only for people who are not concerned with decisions, who are not in a rush, for whom nothing is urgent except disputation.[45]

One of the main differences between skepticism and zeteticism seems to be that the hopelessness, or rather dogmatic and a priori despair of skepticism, does not provide the necessary encouragement for the quest for the truth. How can one seriously bear the effort of seeking the truth if one knows beforehand that it is not achievable? Or, can one say that the activity of the philosopher finds its source of energy elsewhere? In a short paragraph (¶ 24) which Strauss calls a "conclusion" but which is actually a bridge to the next paragraphs, Strauss draws our attention to the disagreement of Alfarabi's Plato with Socrates. The distinction between perfection and happiness points to this disagreement because "happiness is not simply identical with human perfection or its exercise" but is only achieved when that perfection is accompanied by the highest pleasure. According to Strauss, Alfarabi points toward the fact that this is Plato's view and not Socrates's by writing that the Platonic dialogue which praises pleasure is "attributed to Socrates," or as Strauss puts it, "merely attributed" to Socrates. Strauss attributes Socrates's lack of interest in pleasure to his "moralism." As the status of morality is now in question, Strauss begins a discussion of the "relation of philosophy to morals" in Alfarabi's *Plato*. He explains Alfarabi's critique of the moral life or "the virtuous life" by referring to a passage in which Alfarabi writes that "the virtuous way of life is what leads to the achievement of this happiness." According to Strauss's reading, "this happiness" is here the "apparent happiness," as distinguished from the "true happiness." Strauss uses Falaquera's translation of this passage in which "this happiness" is translated as "the happiness of this world" to conclude that the true happiness, to which the virtuous way of life does not lead, is "the happiness of the other world," the happiness which is superior to the apparent happiness, to the happiness of this world (¶ 25). Here again Maimonides helps Strauss to claim that, according to Alfarabi, the virtuous way of life is in the service of "the well-being of the body" while "the well-being of the soul" is produced by philosophical contemplation "alone." If the last qualification is taken literally, it means that morality does not contribute anything to "the true happiness," "the happiness of the other world," or "the well-being of the soul." Strauss knows that these claims, which are greatly dependent on extraneous sources, are in

---

[45] Strauss, "Reason and Revelation (1948)," 148.

need of confirmation in Alfarabi's text. He should, however, confess that Alfarabi does not say what the desired way of life is; at most, Alfarabi says what "it is not," and even this is not said explicitly. What Alfarabi says explicitly is that the desired way of life is supplied by the royal art, which later on is implicitly identified with philosophy. But how can philosophy as a theoretical art be considered a practical art? This is possible, Strauss claims, "if contemplation itself is the highest form of action" (¶ 26). According to Strauss, Alfarabi's reticence on these points has led translators to misunderstand and mistranslate his writing. He attributes mistakes of translators to Alfarabi's intentional misdirection and reticence, which have an esoteric character. Strauss claims that Alfarabi "wanted to be understood by the majority of his readers in exactly the same way in which he has been understood by his modern translators." In what concerns the question of morality, the obscurity of the passages which discuss the desired way of life is designed to give the majority of the readers the impression that the desired way of life is the virtuous way of life. Alfarabi succeeds in misleading most of his readers without even making the claim that the desired way of life is the virtuous way of life by relying on a common predisposition of theirs. Alfarabi knew that the majority of his readers would miss his reticence and would read in his obscure passage a defense of morality, because Alfarabi agreed with Montesquieu that men "love morality," that "in every country in the world morality is desired," and because the majority of readers themselves identify the desired way of life with the virtuous way of life (footnote 76). Strauss is now ready to substantiate his claim that according to Alfarabi, the virtuous life is mainly in the service of the happiness of this world and the well-being of the body – the claim he previously substantiated by referring to Falaquera and Maimonides; this time he will do so by referring to Alfarabi's own writing. He finds the evidence for this claim in a passage in which Alfarabi rejects the claim of the practical arts to provide the desired knowledge and the way of life necessary for happiness. These practical arts only provide the useful, necessary things and the gainful things. The gainful things are also identical with virtuous things. If Alfarabi rejects the idea that the practical arts provide the desired way of life, and if the virtuous things are the result of the practical arts, it means that the desired way of life cannot be the virtuous way of life, because the virtuous way of life is also a virtuous thing. Moreover, the fact that virtuous things are put side by side with the gainful things means that they are all in the service of the well-being of the body and the happiness of man in this world.

Alfarabi's critique of morality is not the complete rejection of every notion of virtue and nobility. Strauss explains that Alfarabi's rejection of the virtuous way of life and his denigration of what is useful, gainful, and virtuous or noble is only a way to distinguish what is truly useful, gainful, and virtuous or noble from what the many believe to be so. Alfarabi is actually promoting the truly gainful and virtuous things, which are the philosophic life and the science of the beings, and the truly useful, which is philosophy. In other words, it seems that Alfarabi is arguing for something much less controversial, namely that the philosophic life is the truly virtuous way of life, and that the true virtues and noble things are different from those believed by the multitude. Strauss intends, however, to prevent us from concluding that Alfarabi is only making a rather banal claim, which amounts to saying that the multitude is mistaken about true morality and the virtuous life. Alfarabi's view is as radical as it can be: he refrains from identifying the desired way of life with the virtuous way of life because he does not wish to give us the impression that he wishes to replace the multitude's "lower morality" with "the highest morality," the vulgar lax moral standards with a stricter morality (¶ 30). Alfarabi believes that the virtuous way of life known to the vulgar is in fact moral, while the truly virtuous way of life which he advocates is not strictly speaking moral. What Strauss is driving at is that in morality the decisive consideration is to act morally, to do the moral action for its own sake and not for its benefits, while in the type of virtuous action which Alfarabi promotes, the virtuous action is born out of knowledge, and the virtuous action is done because reason recommends it. It may be, which is actually true in many cases, that "the conduct of moral man and that of the philosopher" are the same. But this external appearance should not lead us to confuse the truly moral action and the action of the philosopher, which is born out of knowledge. This is the reason why Alfarabi refrains from identifying the desired way of life with the virtuous way of life.

PHILOSOPHY AND HISTORY

The title of "Fârâbî's *Plato*" seems to be a reflection of the way in which Strauss refers to the edition which he is using.[46] But he also uses this expression, without the italicized "Plato," nine times.[47] One is therefore tempted

---

[46] See footnote 5.
[47] 2 × in ¶ 9, 1 × ¶ 11, 1 × in ¶ 16, 3 × in ¶ 22, 1 × in ¶ 23, 1 × in footnote 32. Strauss once mentions "Fârâbî's Platonism" (¶ 5).

to interpret the title as more than an ordinary reference to Alfarabi's treatise: Who is "Farabi's Plato" as distinguished from "Plato"? Could the title mean that "Farabi's Plato" is different from "the historical Plato"? In the same vein, the question of *Plato* as a historical work and Alfarabi as a historian is one of the major themes of Strauss's essay. Strauss draws our attention to the fact that in his short treatise on the philosophy of Plato, Alfarabi does not engage in a "historical study" of the development of Plato's thought (¶ 6). The fact that Alfarabi presents Plato's philosophy without regard to Socrates or to his other predecessors shows how much Alfarabi was not concerned with history (footnote 7). What Alfarabi is concerned with above all is Plato's "investigations," and he tries to show "the inner and necessary sequence" of those investigations by assigning to each step one Platonic dialogue. Strauss confesses that what Alfarabi says about some of the dialogues sounds "fairly fanciful." He knows that Alfarabi certainly did not have access to some of those dialogues, and his indirect knowledge of them might have been distorted by the secondary sources. But, he asserts, it is "unimportant" what Alfarabi thought about those dialogues to which he did not have access: what is more important is what he thought about Plato's philosophy as a whole, which he knew from the *Republic, Timaeus,* and the *Laws.* Strauss thinks that Alfarabi was not a "commentator" or a "historian," at least not in the ordinary sense of the term, because if he was one, we should expect him to expound with the greatest care all the doctrines of Plato. Strauss's Alfarabi is so much a nonhistorian that he even goes so far as to attribute a critique of *fiqh* to Plato (¶¶ 19, 20). If Alfarabi was "a mere commentator of Plato" who followed his teacher to the letter, he must have been almost compelled to embrace a tolerably orthodox doctrine concerning life after death. But Alfarabi does the reverse by his silence.[48]

Strauss argues that Alfarabi occupies an ambiguous position as a commentator: as a commentator, his end or objective in commenting on Plato's works seems to be to expound and explain Plato's views on different subjects. One might suppose that this end is as compatible with expounding Plato's erroneous views as with Plato's true views. In this regard, one might say that the ideal commentator that Alfarabi should have imitated is a faithful conveyer of a doctrine that he might find true or false. But this is precisely what Strauss denies. Strauss's Alfarabi is

---

[48] In this regard Alfarabi is less outspoken than Averroes, who directly rejected Plato's doctrine of immortality, thus proving himself to be more than a "mere commentator" (footnote 43). See the discussion of this issue in Chapter 1 of this volume.

far from such an ideal commentator, so much so that the reader must consider him an unreliable narrator, an unfaithful and untrustworthy commentator of Plato who must be disbelieved on every point. Strauss claims that Alfarabi presents his own controversial views precisely in those works in which he "sets forth not so much his own views, as the views of someone else" (¶ 17). Those works are precisely commentaries in which Alfarabi pretends to be a faithful conveyer of the views of someone else, to be a historian. But why would Alfarabi resort to such practices and betray the confidence of his reader who expects him, as a true commentator, to transmit the teaching of other writers faithfully and free of distortions? The obvious answer would be that Alfarabi resorts to such distortions and declares heretical ideas through "the mouth of Plato" to avoid persecution, and this is what Strauss claims (¶ 18). In other words, Alfarabi avails himself of "the specific immunity of the commentator, or of the historian, in order to speak his mind concerning grave matters" (¶ 20). This is therefore the first reason for considering *Plato* a nonhistorical work: writing a pseudo-historical commentary is an esoteric technique. Through commentary one can make heterodox claims by attributing one's ideas to the text one is explaining. In this case, *Plato* is unhistorical, because it serves as a vehicle for Alfarabi's own teaching. As radical as Strauss's claim might seem, this is not Strauss's whole or even most fundamental claim.

In a fundamental digression, Strauss makes a much more radical claim about the place of historical research and the activity of commentary in Alfarabi's thought.[49] In that digression, Strauss provides two supplementary reasons for the nonhistorical character of *Plato*. He does that by first explaining that Alfarabi deviates from the letter of Plato's teaching if "he considers that literal teaching erroneous" (¶ 21). This leads to the second reason for which Alfarabi might have presented Plato's teaching in an unhistorical fashion: Alfarabi might have believed that, for instance, the doctrine of ideas and the immortality of soul are merely exoteric teachings of Plato. In that case, Alfarabi refrains from conveying these teachings in his commentary if he believes that "Plato himself considered the doctrines in question merely exoteric." This second reason for the unhistorical character of *Plato* is obviously a rather straightforward case of esoteric reading of Plato's writings by Alfarabi. But abruptly Strauss introduces us to another, third reason for Alfarabi's deviations: Alfarabi's

---

49 "But let us return to the point where we left off" (¶ 22). This indicates that the whole preceding discussion, at least from ¶ 19 or perhaps from ¶ 13, is a digression.

"historical" writing on Plato is "not a historical work," not only because Alfarabi puts his own words in Plato's mouth to protect himself, and not only because he believed in the exoteric character of some of the literal teachings of Plato – Alfarabi also provides a historically incorrect picture of Plato's ideas, Strauss claims, because he "may" have believed that a given "Platonic teaching" is not "the true teaching" (¶ 21). To put it differently, Alfarabi does not hesitate to deviate from Plato's exoteric *or esoteric* teaching of Plato if he believes that that teaching is incorrect, and this *even if he believes Plato actually adhered to that erroneous doctrine.* We are here completely outside of the common-sensical understanding of the work of a commentator.

According to Strauss, Alfarabi, in his commentary on Plato, "presents not so much the historical Plato, as the typical philosopher." This typical philosopher, as much as he is "assisted" by his teachers, charts "his own way." It seems that according to Strauss, the end of this Platonic commentator is not so much the transmission of the historical truth, but rather the transmission of the results of his own philosophical activity. A Platonic commentator employs the form of commentary only as an instrument of philosophizing. Strauss also sees a connection between Alfarabi's unhistorical work and the historical Plato, between Plato's dialogues and the historical Socrates, and between the Platonic Socrates and the historical Egypt. Alfarabi's *Plato* is unhistorical in the same way that Platonic dialogues do not represent the historical Socrates, and in the same way that Socrates does not describe the real Egypt to his interlocutors. Regarding Socrates and Egypt, Strauss quotes (footnote 48) a Platonic passage which he revises to fit this context. But Strauss also does not quote the last part of that passage: "Socrates, you easily make Egyptian speeches – and speeches from whatever country you wish." Just after this passage, in the same dialogue, Socrates criticizes Phaedrus for this sarcastic comment by saying that men in former times were ready to hear something as long as it was true, regardless of who said it, while the people today care more about the source than the truth of the saying.

Plato, as he is presented by Alfarabi, is not "the historical Plato" but rather "Farabi's Plato," a Plato fashioned and created by Alfarabi. A true Platonist, Strauss claims, is not concerned with the historical truth but rather with the truth simply. However, considering the fact that Strauss here quotes Descartes, one must conclude that Alfarabi is here depicting a typical philosopher simply, Platonist and non-Platonist. This typical philosopher is concerned with discovering the truth on his own rather than with being the truthful conveyer of the teachings of some-body else. In this regard, there is practically no difference between com-mentary and treatise because they are both instruments in the service of the philosophic life: with the former, the philosopher philosophizes in the guise of a historical account, and with the latter, the philosopher philoso-phizes in the open. And as the activity of philosophy is fundamentally problematic and exposed to persecution, commentary is the preferred mode of philosophizing because the true philosopher does not care about being recognized as the original source of an idea. For him the truth is in the end fundamentally "anonymous." Strauss believes that for Alfarabi, or rather for every philosopher, philosophy is *the way* leading to the sci-ence of all beings rather than the science itself, "the investigation rather than the result." Alfarabi's Platonic style of commentary is the incarna-tion of that investigation which is called the philosophic life.

In any event, one must also remind oneself of the fundamentally prob-lematic character of philosophizing in the guise of a commentary: there is a kind of falsehood at the heart of the whole enterprise of pretending to convey someone else's thoughts and instead presenting one's own views. But Strauss claims that this is precisely what public speech demands: "a mixture of seriousness and playfulness" (¶ 21). It is playful for one to pretend to be commenting on the writing of an old philosopher while philosophizing on one's own. It is playful to make "fanciful remarks on the purport of various dialogues" as if one is seriously providing the summary of those dialogues. This, according to Strauss, explains some peculiarities of *Plato*: for instance, Alfarabi's Plato seems entirely with-out "philosophic predecessors," as if he was "the first philosopher," and this despite the fact that Alfarabi must have known from the sources at his disposal that this is not true – in fact, according to Strauss, Alfarabi intimates this knowledge in some of the passages of *Plato* – for instance, in his summary of the *Menexenus*. Now, Strauss's whole reading is based on an important supposition: that Alfarabi had access to the historical material which is at our disposal. Only by presupposing this access can Strauss find the absence of some doctrines in Alfarabi's presentation of Plato's philosophy intentional and therefore significant. Strauss calls this a major concern for "the historian" who studies Alfarabi's work. Strauss reminds us of "the non-historical purpose of the *Plato*," which makes such historical questions irrelevant. Alfarabi's unfamiliar descriptions of the Platonic dialogues have a "non-historical purpose"; they are perhaps meant to teach "an important philosophic truth." Strauss, here speak-ing as a "historian," argues that Alfarabi's access to the sources is not decisive because even if Alfarabi only repeated what he read in a lost epitome, he took full responsibility for the content of his own presentation.[50] Furthermore, the fact that Alfarabi decided to present his own thoughts "in the guise of a historical account" is important for understanding his view of his own "contribution" to the philosophical tradition: he subordinates the individual understanding of the philosopher to the "necessarily anonymous" character of the philosophic truth. Strauss describes Alfarabi as "a true Platonist," a Platonist who is only concerned with philosophical truth, in contradistinction to "historical (accidental) truth." He refers us here to *Protagoras* and *Charmides* (footnote 49). The passage in *Charmides* is clearly about the anonymous character of truth: Socrates explains the philosophic method by saying that "the question at issue is not who said it, but whether what he said is true or not." The reference to *Protagoras*, however, seems to have a different objective. In this part of the dialogue, Socrates asks the interlocutors to leave "odes and poetry," and instead concentrate on their search for the philosophical truth, because such discussions about the meaning of poems and the real intention of the poet Simonides, namely historical questions, are for Socrates unimportant, vulgar, and childish frivolities. Serious investigators should avoid such extraneous voices because such thinkers "cannot be questioned on what they say," and their real meaning remains elusive. Here everyone has "a different opinion about what he means, and they wind up arguing about something they can never finally decide." In other words, while the reference to the *Charmides* concerns the anonymity of the truth, the reference to *Protagoras* is about what we might call the problem of historiography. The question of historical truth, as Strauss indicates by his references, can distract us from the real philosophical questions, because when a historical truth, for instance concerning the verses of a poet, becomes the topic of discussion, people often become entangled in a useless discussion about the meaning of those verses, an

---

[50] This response partly predicts and partly reacts to the hypothesis advances by some scholars who have been unsuccessfully searching after Alfarabi's predecessors. Strauss's specific interlocutors seem to be Franz Rosenthal and Richard Walzer. See Richard Walzer, "Arabic Transmission of Greek Thought to Medieval Europe," *Bulletin of the John Rylands Library* 29 (1945): 172; Alfarabi, *On the Perfect State*, trans. Richard Walzer (Oxford: Clarendon Press, 1985), 9; Rosenthal, "On the Knowledge of Plato's Philosophy in the Islamic World." See also Rosenthal, "The Place of Politics in the Philosophy of Al-Farabi," 158; Muhsin Mahdi, "Al-Fārābī's Imperfect State," *Journal of the American Oriental Society* 110, no. 4 (1990): 691–726; Ralph Lerner, "Beating the Neoplatonic Bushes," *Journal of Religion* 67, no. 4 (1987): 510–17.

argument about something which can never be decided and only distracts one from the search for philosophical truth. This is why Strauss concludes his complex discussion of Alfarabi's view of the divine by saying that it "would be rash to maintain that the foregoing observations suffice for establishing what Farabi believed as regards any *substantiae separatae*" (¶ 34). This lack of certainty about Alfarabi's real position is later expanded to his whole philosophy, as Strauss claims that "Fârâbî doubtless had definite convictions concerning a number of important points, although it is not as easy to say what these convictions were." This again seems to be as true for Alfarabi as for any other philosopher or "man such as Fârâbî," particularly those who practice esotericism. It seems that Strauss holds the view that there is some kind of unbreachable barrier which separates the thought of people like Alfarabi from their readers and commentators, the barrier which makes every certainty about their true convictions impossible.[51] As Strauss understands it, the true task of the philosopher is to set these kinds of historical questions aside for a genuine philosophical quest. The work of commentary is not unlike philosophy itself, in which the questions are more evident than the answers. With enough care and effort, one can discover which question a philosopher tries to answer, but one might not be able to discover the answer of that author, especially if one believes there is an esoteric art of writing present in the work, the art of writing which always opens the way to a multiplicity, if not an infinity, of possible interpretations.

ON THE "INTRODUCTION" OF *PERSECUTION*
AND THE ART OF WRITING

In the preface of his 1952 work *Persecution and the Art of Writing*, the book which brought together formerly published essays from 1941, 1943, and 1948, Strauss writes that for the introduction of the whole book he has "made free use" of his "Fârâbî's *Plato*." This claim, which "has no counterpart in all his other work," sounds like an invitation to compare these two writings.[52] Strauss begins his introduction with the claim that the subject of his book falls into the province of the sociology of knowledge, and shows his dissatisfaction with this field

---

[51] See Strauss, "The Law of Reason in the Kuzari," 131n115; Friedrich Nietzsche, *Beyond Good and Evil: Prelude to a Philosophy of the Future*, trans. Walter Kaufmann (New York: Vintage Books, 1989), 16 (aphor. 10).

[52] Meier, *Carl Schmitt and Leo Strauss*, 87n112.

of study because it does not include the sociology of philosophy, which should study the relationship between philosophy as such and society as such. Strauss's book intends to remedy this gap in the scientific literature on the sociology of knowledge. To find the necessary material for the study of this new field, Strauss had to turn to other ages and lands, more precisely to the Jewish and Islamic philosophy of the middle ages. Strauss draws our attention next to the poverty of our understanding of Jewish and Islamic philosophy compared with that of Christian scholasticism. The latter is more at home in our age, while the former suffers from a grave misunderstanding which hides the tumultuous relationship between philosophy and society. Judaism and Islam, contrary to Christianity, are religions of law rather than faith; they have therefore a more pronounced political character. Islamic and Jewish philosophy as a response to this political character have concentrated on Plato's *Republic* and *Laws*, the works which made understanding of Islam and Judaism as perfect law for the political order possible. Strauss here turns to the esoteric character of the Islamic philosophers as a bridge to a summary of "Fârâbî's *Plato*" in ten paragraphs, while selectively quoting the content of his essay with some small changes: of about fifteen thousand words of "Fârâbî's *Plato*," Strauss reuses a tenth, which is about one-fourth of the whole introduction. After this summary, Strauss returns to the tension between philosophy and society in Islam and Judaism, as distinguished from Christianity. It turns out that the situation of philosophy is more precarious in Judaism than in Islam. In fact Islam is a kind of mean between Christian harmony of philosophy and religion and the radical conflict of Judaism and philosophy. Regardless of this small detail, Islamic and Jewish philosophy both suffered from and also reaped the benefits of their precarious condition. Plato's success in averting the direct conflict between society and philosophy should not blind us to its fundamental character. It is the task of the sociology of philosophy to understand this conflict.

In this same introduction, Strauss suggests that the reader should consider the "precise meaning of 'repetition'" by referring to his essay on Maimonides.[53] In "Fârâbî's *Plato*," he explains this in a rather clear statement:

As we might have learned from Maimonides, "repetition" is a normal pedagogic device which is destined to reveal the truth to those who are able to understand by themselves while hiding it from the vulgar: whereas the vulgar are blinded

---

[53] Strauss, *Persecution and the Art of Writing*, 1952, 16n12.

by the features, common to the first statement and the "repetition", those who are able to understand will pay the utmost attention to the differences, however apparently negligible, between the two statements and in particular to the "addition", made in the "repetition", to the first statement. (¶ 23)

We should therefore look at some of repetitions in Strauss's introduction and consider changes, additions, and subtractions. Through these repetitions, Strauss points toward the most important and essential points of his forgotten writing. What are these essential points? When reproducing the discussion of Plato's turn from the way of Socrates and his new approach towards politics, Strauss makes four changes: First, the fundamentally theoretical character of Platonic philosophy disappears from the repetition. Second, Plato's "insight into the nature of beings" which "mitigated" Plato's "moral fervor" and led to his critique of Socratic moralism is not reproduced and is subtracted from the repetition. This absence is, however, somehow remedied by the inclusion of a short discussion of "rational laws" in the seventh paragraph, the subject of the chapter on Judah Halevi.[54] Third, "literary productions of 'the philosophers'" (¶ 23) is now replaced by "the activity of the *falāsifa*." Fourth, the consequence of "the gradual replacement of the accepted opinions," which in "Fârâbî's *Plato*" is described as the "destruction of the accepted opinions," is dropped in the repetition. Gone also is Strauss's observation that Alfarabi's silence about Plato's doctrine of immortality means that Alfarabi considered that part of Plato's philosophy "an exoteric doctrine." What remains is that Alfarabi "silently rejects Plato's doctrine of a life after death." This is Strauss's way of pointing us to the principal historiographical claim of "Fârâbî's *Plato*" in ¶ 21, the idea of *Plato* as a nonhistorical work. In other words, Strauss guides the careful reader towards the central importance of that paragraph which might seem to have been entirely forgotten in the repetition. This point should be considered side by side with the disappearance of one of Strauss's two personal statements in "Fârâbî's *Plato*" (¶ 19: "I do not know whether there ever was a 'philosopher' whose mind was so confused as to consist of two hermetically sealed compartments: Fârâbî was a man of a different stamp.") This prepares the ground for turning to Strauss's next and last essay on Alfarabi. The essay which is one of the most difficult studies he ever wrote.

---

[54] Strauss, *Persecution and the Art of Writing*, 10–11.

4

Strauss, Alfarabi, and Plato's *Laws*

Shortly before his death in 1973, Leo Strauss planned to put together a collection of his articles dealing with very different subjects and philosophers under the title of "Studies in Platonic Political Philosophy."[1] In what sense Strauss could describe these writings as "Platonic" is not easy to explain. What seems to be rather clear, however, is that he could not call them Machiavellian, Nietzschean, or Xenophontean. That Strauss attached a particular importance to Plato's thought and writings has not eluded the attention of his readers. After all, his last major writing, or rather what he, perhaps as a Platonic gesture, left to one of his closest students to publish after his death, was a commentary on Plato's *Laws*.[2] The importance of Plato for Strauss does not mean that he published often on Plato. In fact, it was only in 1964, after more than three decades of intense study of Plato, that Strauss, a confirmed scholar well

---

[1] Leo Strauss, *Studies in Platonic Political Philosophy*, ed. Thomas L. Pangle (Chicago and London: University of Chicago Press, 1983).

[2] According to a famous ancient story (Diogenes Laertius *Vitae* III.37, Olympiodorus, *Prolegomena* VI.24) when Plato died, the *Laws* was still on wax tablets and was published posthumously by Philip of Opus, one of Plato's students, or as Strauss describes him, "a kind of [literary] executor." In his two courses on Plato's *Laws*, Strauss mentions this story three times and suggests that Plato might have explicitly decided to write *Laws* late in his life because he might have thought that a "certain subject can be properly treated only if you are old, and therefore [Plato thought] I will not write it or begin to write it until I am old." Strauss, *1971–72 Course on Plato's Laws*, 396 (Session 18); Strauss, *1959 Course on Plato's Laws*, 66 (Session 3, January 13, 1959), 397 (Session 14, March 3, 1959). Compare this with the account given by Joseph Cropsey, Strauss's literary executor, of the publication of Strauss's last book in Strauss, *The Argument and the Action of Plato's Laws*, vii–viii.

in his sixties published his first study dedicated exclusively to a Platonic dialogue.[3] Between his commentary on Plato's *Republic* and his last book on the *Laws*, Strauss published several pieces on different Platonic dialogues. But his last book on Plato's *Laws* seems to occupy a special place, although this is not obvious from the immediate reactions to it: it would not be an exaggeration to say that Strauss's *The Argument and the Action of Plato's Laws* was either coldly received by other scholars or was simply rejected by them.[4] These negative reactions were in a sense expected even by Joseph Cropsey, who in his foreword pointed to the unusual characteristics of the book, its repetitive appearance, reticent prose, and unattractive style.[5] Considering the unusual character of Strauss's last book, one is naturally led to an obvious question: why did Strauss decide to dedicate his last energies to writing a whole book of unusual character on a rather neglected dialogue of Plato? An adequate answer to this question requires a proper understanding of Strauss's commentary on the *Laws*, but to begin acquiring such an understanding, one does well to follow the signpost erected by Strauss himself. This signpost, in its conspicuousness as well as its modesty, is found right at the beginning of his book: it is a quotation from Avicenna's *On the Divisions of the Rational Sciences* which, in Strauss's translation, goes as follows: "... the treatment of prophecy and the Divine law is contained in ... the *Laws*."[6]

This statement, as Strauss explains at the beginning of his 1971–72 course on Plato's *Laws* offered at St. John's College, has preoccupied him

---

[3] Strauss, *The City and Man*, chapter II.

[4] See Allan D. Nelson, "Review of The Argument and the Action of Plato's Laws by Leo Strauss," *Canadian Journal of Political Science* 9, no. 3 (1976): 515–16; Thomas M. Robinson, "Review of The Argument and the Action of Plato's Laws by Leo Strauss," *The Classical World* 70, no. 6 (1977): 405; Trevor J. Saunders, "Review of The Argument and the Action of Plato's Laws by Leo Strauss," *Political Theory* 4, no. 2 (1976): 239–42; M. Schofield, "Review of The Argument and the Action of Plato's Laws by Leo Strauss," *The Classical Review* 28, no. 1 (1978): 170. For more positive and recent evaluations see David Bolotin, "Review of The Argument and the Action of Plato's Laws by Leo Strauss," *The American Political Science Review* 70, no. 2 (1977): 668–70; Harry Neumann, "Review of The Argument and the Action of Plato's Laws by Leo Strauss," *Journal of the History of Philosophy* 17 (1979): 81–82; Mark J. Lutz, "The Argument and the Action of Plato's Laws," in *Brill's Companion to Leo Strauss' Writings on Classical Political Thought*, ed. Timothy W. Burns (Leiden and Boston: Brill, 2015), 424–40; Clemens Kauffmann, "'Men on Horseback.' Leo Strauss über 'The Argument and the Action of Plato's Laws,'" in *Platons Nomoi: Die politische Herrschaft von Vernunft und Gesetz*, eds. Francesco Knoll and Francisco L. Lisi, vol. 100, Staatsverständnisse (Baden-Baden: Nomos-Verlag, 2017), 212–46.

[5] Strauss, *The Argument and the Action of Plato's Laws*, vii.

[6] Strauss, *The Argument and the Action of Plato's Laws*, 1.

since "about forty years ago," more precisely since 1929 or 1930, when he
"was a student of Jewish medieval philosophy and therefore also of Islamic
philosophy," reading Avicenna's popular epistle for the first time in the
Berlin National Library.[7] Avicenna's statement, which establishes a connection between Plato's *Laws*, Plato's political book par excellence, on the one
hand, and prophecy (nubūwwa) and the Islamic Law (sharī'a) on the other,
was bound to capture Strauss's attention: the statement ties all the elements
of the theologico-political problem together. What all of this means could
only become clear if we knew how Avicenna read Plato's *Laws*. If there was
no extensive discussion of Plato's *Laws* found in Avicenna's extant writings,
however, it would be helpful if the commentary of some other *faylsūf* on the
Laws were available, someone who was "considered the greatest authority
in philosophy, apart from Aristotle himself" by the "men of the competence
of Avicenna."[8] It is a piece of good luck that such a commentary exists, by
the hand of none other than Alfarabi himself: *Summary of Plato's Laws*
(hereafter *Summary*).[9] Strauss's familiarity with and interest in Alfarabi's
Summary goes back to right after his discovery of Avicenna's statement. He
worked on a German translation and emendations of Alfarabi's manuscript
with Paul Kraus in 1931–32 in Berlin.[10]

---

[7] Strauss, *1971–72 Course on Plato's Laws*, 1 (Session 1); Strauss, "A Giving of Accounts,"
     463; Meier, "How Strauss Became Strauss," 17–18. See the discussion of the controver-
     sies around Avicenna's statement in the Introduction to this volume. See also James W.
     Morris, "The Philosopher-Prophet in Avicenna's Philosophy," in *The Political Aspects
     of Islamic Philosophy: Essays in Honor of Muhsin S. Mahdi*, ed. Charles E. Butterworth
     (Cambridge, MA: Harvard University Press, 1992), 169n15 and n16.
[8] Strauss, "Fârâbî's Plato," 355, 377.
[9] The Arabic text along with a Latin translation was first published by Francesco Gabrieli.
     Thérèse-Anne Druart prepared an improved edition on the basis of new manuscripts and
     emendations suggested by Muhsin Mahdi. This edition is now available in an excellent
     English translation by Charles E. Butterworth: Alfarabi, *Compendium Legum Platonis*;
     Mahdi, "The Editio Princeps of Fârâbî's Compendium Legum Platonis"; Alfarabi, "Le
     Sommaire du Livre des 'Lois' de Platon," ed. Thérèse-Anne Druart, *Bulletin d'études
     orientales* 50 (1998): 109–55.; Alfarabi, "Summary of Plato's Laws," in *The Political
     Writings: Volume II Political Regime and Summary of Plato's Laws*, trans. Charles E.
     Butterworth (Ithaca and London: Cornell University Press, 2015), 97–175. For discus-
     sions about the title of the treatise see Mahdi, "The Editio Princeps of Fârâbî's Com-
     pendium Legum Platonis," 1n2; Alfarabi, "Le Sommaire du Livre des 'Lois' de Platon,"
     110–11. Unless otherwise indicated, all references to the *Summary* are to Druart's edi-
     tion in the following form: D page number. These page numbers are also indicated in
     Butterworth's translation, which I use for translations.
[10] See Strauss, "On Abravanel's Philosophical Tendency and Political Teaching," 1937,
     96n4; also Strauss's letter to Charles Kuentz on May 1, 1946 in Kraemer, "The Death
     of an Orientalist: Paul Kraus from Prague to Cairo," 209; Mahdi, "The Editio Princeps
     of Fârâbî's Compendium Legum Platonis," 1n1, 15; Alfarabi, "Le Sommaire du Livre
     des 'Lois' de Platon," 119.

It is safe to assume that Strauss's commentary on Plato's *Laws* is somehow influenced by Alfarabi's *Summary*. In fact, Strauss never seems to have lost interest in the *Summary*, because not only did he try to track the material related to his collaboration with Kraus shortly after Kraus's death, he also retells the famous story told by Alfarabi at the beginning of the *Summary* as an introduction to his 1971–72 course on Plato's *Laws*.[11] More importantly, two years after the publication in 1952 of Gabrieli's edition of the *Summary*, Strauss began working on an essay which later was published in Louis Massignon's Festschrift as "How Fārābī Read Plato's *Laws*" and finally, with slight modifications, as a chapter in *What Is Political Philosophy?*[12] Considering his longtime interest in Alfarabi's *Summary*, one should say that this essay, Strauss's last publication specifically dedicated to the Falāsifa, is a culmination of a project which Strauss began in the 1930s. Therefore, it seems that the only beginning, which is not arbitrary, the proper point of departure for understanding Strauss's reading of Plato's *Laws* is an analysis of his essay on Alfarabi's *Summary*. But before turning to this analysis, we should say a few words about the debate around Alfarabi's own work to bring out the specific character of Strauss's reading of the *Summary*.

---

[11] Kraemer, "The Death of an Orientalist: Paul Kraus from Prague to Cairo," 209; Strauss, *1971–72 Course on Plato's Laws*, 1 (Session 1).

[12] Leo Strauss, "How Fārābī Read Plato's Laws," in *Mélanges Louis Massignon*, vol. III (Damascus: Institut français de Damas, 1957), 319–44; Strauss, "How Fārābī Read Plato's Laws," 134–55. In this chapter, references to this essay are to the paragraph numbers (¶ paragraph number). The dates indicated on the manuscript of the essay are August 20, 1954–September 8, 1954. See the notebook in Leo Strauss Papers, box 22, folder 1, Special Collections Research Center, University of Chicago Library. All references to the manuscript of the essay, including the paragraph headings and emendations, are found in this notebook. Apart from addition of some commas, slight modified punctuations, very few grammatical revisions, replacement of a few words, some revised quotations, and slight reformulation of some sentences, the revisions which I believe do not change anything of substance in the revised edition, there are several changes in the 1959 edition which are worthy of note: (1) In the new edition the footnotes are numbered sequentially. (2) In ¶ 10 "allude to punishment in the other life" is replaced by "refer to punishment in the other life." (3) In ¶ 13 "the laws are superior to wisdom of every kind" is now in quotation marks and reads "superior to all wisdoms." (4) In ¶ 17 "eternity or creation" which was originally in single quotation marks are put in double quotation marks. (5) In ¶ 19 twice "*sharī'a*" is replaced by "revealed law." (6) In ¶ 21 "subject to the laws of Zeus" is replaced by "to whom the laws of Zeus were given." (7) In ¶ 21 "Both Zeus and Apollo used in their two laws or in the ordinances of their two *sharī'a*'s" is replaced by "Both Zeus and Apollo used in their codes or in the ordinances of their revealed laws."

DEBATE ON ALFARABI'S *SUMMARY*

Despite the availability of a reliable edition of Alfarabi's *Summary* for about seven decades, one cannot claim that it has found its place as a major source for the study of Alfarabi's philosophical views. Very few scholarly studies have been written on any aspect of this unique writing.[13] This lack of interest in Alfarabi's *Summary* is quite unusual, especially if we consider the unique place occupied by this writing of Alfarabi in Islamic philosophy as well as in the scholarship on Plato's *Laws* in general. The only other surviving commentary on a Platonic dialogue by a Muslim philosopher is Averroes's commentary on Plato's *Republic*. The difference being that the Arabic original of Averroes's commentary does not seem to have survived, and we have to rely exclusively on the Hebrew translation, with all the problems such a reliance entails. This, while we possess a reliable edition of Alfarabi's original Arabic text.[14] Furthermore, although there has been a rise of interest in Plato's *Laws* in recent decades, and despite the fact that in the antiquity and Middle Ages some ideas presented in the *Laws* attracted the attention of some thinkers, overall "the *Laws* was not subject to much interpretative activity" in antiquity.[15] Alfarabi's *Summary* occupies, therefore, a unique place in the history of the reception of Plato's *Laws*: its treatment of the whole nine books of the *Laws* has no parallel in what we know from the accounts of the commentaries written in antiquity. To resume, Alfarabi's *Summary* "is the sole extant premodern commentary on the *Laws*."[16] This lack of

---

[13] Apart from Strauss's own essay, there is one other study by Joshua Parens which treats the *Summary* as a source of philosophical ideas; but even that study is written by a scholar influenced by Strauss and his students. One can also mention the introduction by Charles E. Butterworth to his translation and another essay by Steven Harvey: Parens, *Metaphysics as Rhetoric*; Alfarabi, *The Political Writings: Volume II Political Regime and Summary of Plato's Laws*, trans. Charles E. Butterworth (Ithaca and London: Cornell University Press, 2015), 97–129; Steven Harvey, "Can a Tenth-Century Islamic Aristotelian Help Us Understand Plato's Laws?," in *Plato's Laws: From Theory to Practice*, eds. Samuel Scolnicov and Luc Brisson (Sankt Augustin: Academia Verlag, 2003), 325–30.

[14] Mahdi, "The Editio Princeps of Fârâbî's Compendium Legum Platonis," 1–2; Parens, *Metaphysics as Rhetoric*, xix.

[15] Christopher Bobonich, ed., *Plato's Laws: A Critical Guide* (Cambridge: Cambridge University Press, 2010), 1; Francesco Knoll and Francisco L. Lisi, eds., *Platons Nomoi: Die politische Herrschaft von Vernunft und Gesetz*, vol. 100, Staatsverständnisse (Baden-Baden: Nomos-Verlag, 2017), 9–20; Harold Tarrant, *Plato's First Interpreters* (Ithaca: Cornell University Press, 2000), 205.

[16] Parens, *Metaphysics as Rhetoric*, xxi.

interest in Alfarabi's *Summary*, however, is partially justified due to the uncertainty about the nature and objective of the work itself: it is not easy to discern what Alfarabi's *Summary* actually means to be. When one hears the word "summary" one imagines something like an encapsulation of a larger work. Strauss explains this problem in the central paragraph of his essay, where he describes Alfarabi's text as "a mere report of the content of the *Laws*, a simple enumeration of the subjects discussed in the *Laws*" (¶ 12). But this does not correspond, he explains, to what one actually finds in Alfarabi's *Summary*, because, as Strauss notes, Alfarabi's work appears "a pedantic, pedestrian and wooden writing which abounds in trivial or insipid remarks and which reveals an amazing lack of comprehension of Plato." Strauss's claim is based on the observation that there are "many Platonic thoughts to which Farabi hardly alludes," as well as "many contentions for which one seeks in vain in the text of the *Laws*."

Facing this characteristic of the work, traditional scholars turned to a hypothesis which came most naturally to them: if many aspects of the *Laws* are missing in Alfarabi's summary, and if there are things mentioned which cannot be found in the *Laws*, perhaps a reliable translation of Plato's *Laws* was not available to the author. This was already the hypothesis of Francesco Gabrieli, the original editor of the *Summary*: he claimed that one must suppose that there must have been intermediary sources which formed Alfarabi's understanding of Plato's *Laws*, and that Alfarabi's *Summary* is not actually based on either of the two known translation of Plato's *Laws* available at the time, but rather on some sort of compendium of Plato's *Laws*.[17] S. M. Stern agreed with Gabrieli's hypothesis in his review, and even drew the natural conclusion: if the *Summary* is based on some kind of intermediary, "then the attribution to Farabi can hardly be maintained, for it is difficult to see why Farabi should have made a compendium of a compendium."[18] The hypothesis did not receive universal acceptance, and Strauss, Muhsin Mahdi, Joshua Parens, and Thérèse-Anne Druart assumed that Alfarabi must have had

---

[17] Alfarabi, *Compendium Legum Platonis*, ix–xii. In his *Kitāb al-Fihrist*, Ibn al-Nadīm, the Arab bibliographer (d. 995/998), mentions two translations of the *Laws*, one by the famous Hunayn ibn Ishāq, and the other by a student of Alfarabi, Yahya Ibn 'Adī. See Ibn al-Nadīm, *The Fihrist: A Tenth Century AD Survey of Islamic Culture*, 2:592.

[18] S. M. Stern, "Review of R. Klibansky (Ed.), F. Gabrieli (Ed. and Tr.), Plato Arabus, Volumen III. Alfarabius: Compendium Legum Platonis. London: Warburg Institute, 1952, 21s.," *Bulletin of the School of Oriental and African Studies* 17, no. 2 (1955): 398.

access to Plato's *Laws*.[19] Even Richard Walzer, who otherwise was very much convinced that Alfarabi "learned most of the things that set him apart from his fellows" from some "putative Greek 'source' of some three centuries earlier," was in this case convinced that Alfarabi must have had access to the full text of the *Laws*.[20] One scholar who persistently maintained Gabrieli and Stern's hypothesis and went after finding Alfarabi's source was Dimitri Gutas. First, in his rather severe review of Parens's book, and then in a full essay, Gutas claimed that Alfarabi's *Summary* is not based on Plato's *Laws*, but rather on a summary of it, perhaps the lost Arabic translation of Galen's *Synopsis of Plato's Laws*.[21] Gutas bases his claim on the comparison of three different manuscripts which both overlap and differ in various aspects: through this comparison, Gutas tries to show that two of the manuscripts are actually two independent works by two different authors, one by Alfarabi and the other probably by a certain Abū-l-Faraj Ibn-aṭ-Ṭayyib. These two authors, Gutas claims, have been both summarizing either the translation of Galen's *Synopsis* or something close to it.[22] Gutas also implicitly mentions and responds to Stern's discomforting suggestion by speaking of the possibility that Alfarabi might have "doctored" his intermediary source to create a compendium of a compendium "along the explicatory and doctrinal lines customary with his" philosophy. Gutas claims that Alfarabi has "molded transmitted material to fashion his own philosophy."[23] That such suggestions require much more substantial elaboration to resolve the issue raised by Stern is not difficult to see: in the interest of consistency, one expects Gutas to take the final step and deny the authorship of Alfarabi of such a strange compendium of compendium, something which he refrains from doing.

A more substantial claim was needed to make the hypothesis of an intermediary source more consistent. It was provided in the assessment of the debate by Steven Harvey. He evaluated Gutas's textual arguments and

[19] Mahdi, "The Editio Princeps of Fârâbî's Compendium Legum Platonis," 5–6; Parens, *Metaphysics as Rhetoric*, xxx; Alfarabi, "Le Sommaire du Livre des 'Lois' de Platon," 112–13. Already in 1936, Paul Kraus rejected the hypothesis of an intermediary source. See Kraus's letter to Leo Strauss on May 28, 1936 quoted in Mahdi, "The Editio Princeps of Fârâbî's Compendium Legum Platonis," 6n23. Reportedly, Druart has changed her initial view. See Steven Harvey, "Did Alfarabi Read Plato's Laws?," *Medioevo: Rivista di storia della filosofia medievale* 28 (2003): 61n34.

[20] Alfarabi, *On the Perfect State*, 10, 356, 363, 365; Richard Walzer, *Greek into Arabic: Essays on Islamic Philosophy* (Cambridge, MA: Harvard University Press, 1962), 238.

[21] Gutas, "Fārābī's Knowledge of Plato's 'Laws'"; Gutas, "Galen's Synopsis of Plato's Laws and Fārābī's Talḫīṣ."

[22] Gutas, "Galen's Synopsis of Plato's Laws and Fārābī's Talḫīṣ," 117–18.

[23] Gutas, "Galen's Synopsis of Plato's Laws and Fārābī's Talḫīṣ," 118–19.

concluded that they are unconvincing.[24] But this did not prevent Harvey from siding with Gutas's thesis based on his own evidence. The evidence was that for him, the "*Summary* simply reads like a summary of a summary. Most conspicuously, there is no indication that the book [i.e., Plato's *Laws*] is a discussion among three people."[25] In other words, the dialogic form of the *Laws* seems completely unknown to Alfarabi. Harvey considers the nondialogic character of Alfarabi's *Summary* to be due to "the failure of a professional summarizer." He cannot entertain the idea that "a perceptive philosopher" like Alfarabi would have omitted such an important and decisive aspect of the *Laws* if he had a direct access to it.[26] In addressing Stern's conclusion implicitly, Harvey avoids Gutas's unsatisfactory solution by claiming that it "may well be that Alfarabi believed that the text upon which he commented was Plato's." He even goes so far as to consider the possibility that the so-called translations of the *Laws* on which Alfarabi might have based his *Summary* were actually themselves summaries or epitomes of the *Laws*, without Alfarabi or *even* the translators themselves being aware of that.[27] Harvey's hypothesis is perfect for arguing that Alfarabi did not have access to Plato's *Laws*, but rather to a summary of it, while avoiding saying that a serious thinker of Alfarabi's rank wrote a summary of a summary. Contrary to Gabrieli and Gutas, however, Harvey's doubts about Alfarabi's access to Plato's *Laws* do not persuade him to question the philosophic value of Alfarabi's *Summary*: he still believes that one can learn important things from Alfarabi's work about Plato's *Laws*, and has even dedicated an essay to the subject.[28] What Harvey specifically cautions us about is "that we must exercise great caution before making or accepting any arguments from silence or other such arguments."[29] This remark is specifically directed at Parens, and more importantly for our subject here, at Strauss: they both attribute much importance to what Alfarabi omits in the *Summary* as a way to discover his teaching and intention.[30]

In the introduction to his translation of the *Summary*, Charles E. Butterworth discusses Harvey's evaluation of the debate. Although he

[24] Harvey, "Did Alfarabi Read Plato's Laws?," 54–61.
[25] Harvey, "Did Alfarabi Read Plato's Laws?," 64. See also Harvey, "Can a Tenth-Century Islamic Aristotelian Help Us Understand Plato's Laws?," 323; Harvey, "Leo Strauss' Early Interest in the Islamic Falāsifa," 227n28.
[26] Harvey, "Did Alfarabi Read Plato's Laws?," 65.
[27] Harvey, "Did Alfarabi Read Plato's Laws?," 62–63.
[28] Harvey, "Can a Tenth-Century Islamic Aristotelian Help Us Understand Plato's Laws?"
[29] Harvey, "Did Alfarabi Read Plato's Laws?," 65; Harvey, "Can a Tenth-Century Islamic Aristotelian Help Us Understand Plato's Laws?"
[30] See Parens, *Metaphysics as Rhetoric*, xxiv–xxviii.

is sympathetic to Harvey's view and finds it balanced as a whole, he still seems more inclined to the view that Alfarabi had access to the text of Plato's *Laws*. Butterworth addresses the evidence raised by Harvey in support of his thesis and finds it unconvincing. The same linguistic formulas and stylistic idiosyncrasies which Harvey mentions to argue that Alfarabi is summarizing a summary, as Butterworth notes, are also present in Alfarabi's commentaries on Aristotle, and "we do know [Alfarabi] had direct access to Aristotle's treatises." Moreover, Butterworth argues that in none of his writings on Plato that have come down to us does Alfarabi mention the dialogic-form of Platonic writings.[31] Butterworth's point about the linguistic peculiarities of Alfarabi's *Summary*, I believe, effectively responds to Harvey's linguistic evidence. His claim about the dialogic-form misses, however, Harvey's main contention: Harvey is very much inclined towards Franz Rosenthal's radical claim, supported by F. E. Peters and Gerhard Endress, that "[Alfarabi] never came across a true Platonic text, no matter in what language" and that perhaps none of the medieval Arabic translations of Plato were really "verbal reproductions of an unaltered Platonic wording."[32] The evidence giving rise to these doubts and sustaining Harvey's thesis is that no medieval Arabic translation of any of Plato's writings has survived. One should, however, bear in mind that there is some evidence, even quotations in dialogic form, in medieval sources which show awareness of the dialogic character of Plato's works. Even skeptical scholars have been persuaded that there is too much evidence to suppose that all these passages come from summaries, especially those of Galen, since the only complete Galen synopsis which has survived, that of *Timaeus*, does not preserve the dialogic-form.[33] Furthermore, it is remarkable that Harvey refers to the beginning

---

[31] Alfarabi, *The Political Writings: Volume II, Political Regime and Summary of Plato's Laws*, 106–7.

[32] Harvey, "Did Alfarabi Read Plato's Laws?," 63 and 63n41; Harvey, "Can a Tenth-Century Islamic Aristotelian Help Us Understand Plato's Laws?," 322; Rosenthal, "On the Knowledge of Plato's Philosophy in the Islamic World," 411; Francis Edward Peters, *Aristotle and the Arabs: The Aristotelian Tradition in Islam* (New York: New York University Press, 1968), 169. This is still the common consensus: See Rüdiger Arnzen, "Plato, Arabic," in *Encyclopedia of Medieval Philosophy*, ed. Henrik Lagerlund (Dordrecht: Springer, 2011), 1012–16; Rüdiger Arnzen, "Plato's Timaeus in the Arabic Tradition. Legend – Testimonies – Fragments," in *Il Timeo: Esegesi Greche, Arabe, Latine. Greco, Arabo, Latino*, eds. Francesco Celia and Angela Ulacco (Pisa: Pisa University Press, 2012), 181–85.

[33] A good summary is found in Reisman, "Plato's Republic in Arabic: A Newly Discovered Passage," esp. 269–71. See also Arthur J. Arberry, "Some Plato in an Arabic Epitome," *Islamic Quarterly* 2 (1955): 86–99; Dimitri Gutas, "Plato's Symposion in the Arabic Tradition," *Oriens* 31, no. 1 (1988): esp. 40.

of the first treatise of the *Summary*, in which the dialogue between Cleinias and the Athenian Stranger is mentioned by Alfarabi, without its having any impact on Harvey's thesis. Finally, one should be careful not to attribute too much importance to the literary reading of Platonic dialogues: this approach is a recent one in Platonic scholarship.[34] Although one can adduce good arguments in favor of this literary approach, one should not assume that medieval thinkers would have agreed with them and attributed the same importance to the literary character and the dialogic-form of Plato's works, as one can observe in Averroes's comment on him "eliminating the dialectical arguments" from his commentary on the *Republic*.[35] Moreover, it is significant that a philosopher of Aristotle's caliber, who after all knew his Plato, also seems uninterested in the dialogic-form of Plato's writings, and for instance, in *Politics*, quotes the Athenian Stranger of the *Laws* as well as Socrates of the *Republic* simply as "Plato."[36]

The best evidence for the access of Alfarabi to the text of Plato's *Laws* is, as usual, the oldest one already proposed by Kraus. In a letter to Strauss, Kraus writes: "And the Nomoi paraphrase of Fārābī does not seem to me to be simply a re-edition of the galenic one. It is too unconventional for that. And besides, Fārābī himself says that he had the original under his eyes when paraphrasing it, which does not exclude the possibility that he also used the paraphrase of Galen, which was translated at his time."[37] Harvey's hypothesis, according to which Alfarabi might have

---

[34] On this change of attitude and bibliography see Gerald A. Press, "The State of the Question in the Study of Plato," *The Southern Journal of Philosophy* 34, no. 4 (December 1996): 509, 511–12; Gerald A. Press, "The State of the Question in the Study of Plato: Twenty Year Update," *The Southern Journal of Philosophy* 56, no. 1 (March 2018): 10.

[35] Averroes, *On Plato's "Republic,"* 3 (Rosenthal 21); Alfarabi, *The Political Writings: Volume II Political Regime and Summary of Plato's Laws*, 106.

[36] Aristotle, *Politics* 1261a5–11, 1265a12, 1266b4, 1271b1, 1274b9. For an exemplary list of such instances in the Aristotelian corpus see Erik Ostenfeld, "Who Speaks for Plato? Everyone!," in *Who Speaks for Plato? Studies in Platonic Anonymity*, ed. Gerald A. Press (Lanham: Rowman and Littlefield, 2000), 216n24. See also Socrates the Younger in *Metaphysics* 1036b25. The same view is found in Diogenes Laertius (*Vitae* III.52) who names Socrates, Timaeus, the Athenian Stranger, and the Elean Stranger as Plato's mouthpieces.

[37] "Und die Nomoi-Paraphrase des Fārābī scheint mir nicht einfach eine Reedition der galenischen zu sein. Dazu ist sie zu eigenwillig. Und außerdem sagt ja Fārābī selbst, dass er bei der Paraphrase das Original unter den Augen hatte, was nicht ausschließt, dass er sich auch der Paraphrase des Galen bedient hat, die zu seiner Zeit übersetzt vorlag." (Paul Kraus's letter to Leo Strauss on May 28, 1936). My translation. Original quoted in Mahdi, "The Editio Princeps of Fârâbî's Compendium Legum Platonis," 6n23. The

relied on a summary of the *Laws* without even being aware of it, is certainly possible. But it is possible like many other incredible things. I find the idea that a competent philosopher like Alfarabi and translators like Hunayn ibn Isḥāq and Yahya Ibn ʿAdī could not distinguish between a genuine work of Plato and its paraphrase right around the time and place where Greek translations were still being made hard to believe. Attaching so much worth to such an incredible hypothesis rather than more reasonable alternatives would eventually lead to further problems: this can be clearly seen in the case of a remarkable point, mentioned by Harvey too, about the preservation of the dialogic form and the interlocutors of the *Laws* in a few passages quoted by Al-Bīrūnī, born only two decades after Alfarabi's death. Facing such interesting evidence, mentioned by Harvey himself no less, instead of deducing the most natural conclusion, which would be the possibility of medieval Arabic readers having access to Plato's *Laws*, Harvey presses ahead by a supplementary hypothesis: "Could al-Bīrūnī's source have been an abridgement in dialogue form?"[38] But when an improbable hypothesis encounters difficulties which can only be dealt with by adding more supplementary hypotheses, it is time to question one's basic premises. Furthermore, although Harvey finds his denial of Alfarabi's access to Plato's *Laws* compatible with the view that one can learn something valuable from Alfarabi about Plato's *Laws*, one can reasonably doubt this. The careful reading of Alfarabi's *Summary* like the one found in Strauss's essay owes much of its legitimacy to the view that Alfarabi was a very competent student of Plato, and this presupposes reliable access to the text of the *Laws*.

These critical points do not obviously mean that all the evidence speaks in favor of Alfarabi's access to a reliable version of Plato's *Laws*. Considering the loss of many Arabic medieval writings, perhaps forever, the question of Alfarabi's access to Plato's *Laws* might never receive a definite answer. The philosophical value of Strauss's commentary also, as I shall try to show in my presentation, is not entirely dependent on

---

same argument is used by Strauss to argue for the access of Averroes to Plato's *Republic* (SNA 1. 3). Apart from the end of the *Summary* (D 152), Strauss implicitly refers to two other passages to show that Alfarabi expects the reader to have the *Laws* "at his elbow" (¶ 12): "anyone who looks into the original work on which this book is based" (D 133); "anyone who reads those chapters" (D 141). These two passages are mentioned in the footnote 6 of Strauss's essay.

[38] Harvey, "Did Alfarabi Read Plato's Laws?," 65n42. For the importance of Al-Bīrūnī's references to Plato's *Laws* see Geoffrey J. Moseley, "Arabic Support for an Emendation of Plato, Laws 666b," *The Classical Quarterly* 69, no. 1 (2019): 440–42.

the truth of his supposition that Alfarabi had access to Plato's dialogue. Regardless of what one can learn from Strauss's essay about Alfarabi, one can see that there are many interesting philosophical ideas present and developed in Strauss's interpretation of Alfarabi's *Summary* worthy of serious consideration independent of their purely historical aspect. It was necessary to address the doubts raised about this question before turning to Strauss's essay, however, because the existing scholarly consensus might give one the impression that in view of the existing evidence, the Falāsifa's lack of access to Plato's works is beyond question, and that to argue otherwise with Strauss is a sign of some unreasonable attachment to a mythological image of Falāsifa, or a romantic view of their philosophical status and activities. If the previous observations succeed in awakening a prejudice in favor of Strauss's supposition and, even more, in arousing suspicion against the powerful opposing prejudice, they have accomplished their goal.

ALFARABI'S ART OF WRITING: THE PIOUS ASCETIC

Strauss describes Alfarabi's *Summary* as consisting of a preface and nine chapters, or rather nine "speeches" (¶ 1). Elsewhere he mentions that calling a writing "a speech" or in Arabic "a *maqâla*, hints at the essentially oral character of its teaching."[39] While Alfarabi justifies his summarizing only the first nine books of the *Laws* by saying that he has seen *only* these nine books, Strauss questions Alfarabi's claim, which opens

---

[39] This remark appears in Strauss's essay on the "literary character" of Maimonides's *Guide*, in which Strauss is explaining the right manner of approaching Maimonides's book. Relying on the linguistic root of the word *maqāla* which is the same as the root of the verb *qāla* meaning "to say" or "to speak," Strauss claims that Maimonides avoids intentionally using terms such as "treatise" (*risāla*) or "book" (*kitāb*) for describing his work to imply an important point: *Guide* is a writing which tries to imitate, as much as possible, an oral conversation between a philosopher and his heterogenous audience, consisting of individuals with different capacities and concerns; it is in a sense a "Platonic dialogue" in nondialogic form. In such a conversation, the distinction between the esoteric message of the philosopher and his exoteric teaching is possible by paying attention to the intricacies of the text through esoteric techniques of reading while taking into account the multiplicity of the audience and the limitations imposed on the author by his specific historical situation. See Strauss, "Literary Character of the Guide for the Perplexed," 47; Strauss, "On a New Interpretation of Plato's Political Philosophy," 349–50; Strauss, *The City and Man*, 58–60; Strauss, "How to Study Medieval Philosophy," 336; Strauss, *The Argument and the Action of Plato's Laws*, 2, 62; Brague, "Athens, Jerusalem, Mecca," 243–44; Kenneth Hart Green, *Leo Strauss and the Rediscovery of Maimonides* (Chicago: University of Chicago Press, 2013), 147–48.

the possibility of Alfarabi declining to summarize the tenth book of the *Laws*, "Plato's theological statement *par excellence*" (¶ 1). Is it an "accident" that the correct number of the books of the *Laws* is the middle of ten and fourteen, which Alfarabi mentions as the number of the books related by others? Is it also an accident that the correct number is the number of the central paragraph of Strauss's own essay?[40]

Alfarabi's *Summary*, Strauss notes, has an un-Platonic preface, in which Alfarabi explains to the reader "how to read Plato's *Laws*." Strauss summarizes Alfarabi's initial claim as follows: "The men of judgment have observed men's natural inclination to make unwarranted generalizations." They have discovered that if they always act in a certain manner, the exceptional cases in which they deviate from their customary behavior will escape the notice of the common people because "the deviation will be thought to be a repetition" (¶ 2).[41] The term "repetition" reminds us of one of Strauss's techniques of esoteric writing; namely, paying attention to the deviations in repeated items of a writing, deviations which escape the notice of the common reader, but are of particular help to the careful reader to discover the esoteric teaching of the text.[42] One can say that the action of the men of judgment, as for instance in the case of Alfarabi, is reflected in the way they write a commentary:

[40] On the importance of the center as an esoteric technique of writing see Strauss, "Fârâbî's Plato," 368–69; Strauss, *The Argument and the Action of Plato's Laws*, 39; Strauss, *Xenophon's Socrates*, 8, 58. Strauss seems to have been right about the intentional silence of Alfarabi regarding the tenth book of the *Laws*: Brague, *The Law of God*, 118.

[41] What Strauss translates as "men of judgment" is *al-ḥukamā*. Although it has the same root (*ḥkm*) as *ḥukm*, which is often translated by "judgment" – i.e., the decision-making activity of the judges as well as rulers – *al-ḥukamā* in the writings of Islamic philosophers is commonly translated as "the wise," which is the common way of saying "the philosophers." "Men of judgment" and "man of judgment" appear four times each in Strauss's essay (3× in ¶ 2, 1× in ¶ 7 and 3× in ¶ 4, 1× in ¶ 6, respectively); *al-ḥukamā* and *al-ḥakīm* appear four times in the *Summary* (2× in D 124, 1× in D 141, 1× in D 152). See Muhsin Mahdi, "Religious Belief and Scientific Belief," *The American Journal of Islamic Social Sciences* 11 (1994): 247; Dimitri Gutas, "Classical Arabic Wisdom Literature. Nature and Scope," *Journal of the American Oriental Society* 101, no. 1 (1981): 53; Amélie Marie Goichon, "Ḥikma," in *Encyclopaedia of Islam*, ed. Th. Bianquis et al., 2nd ed., vol. 3 (Leiden: Brill, 1986), 377–78. In the republished version of his essay, Strauss has revised the previous version to add an eighth "the men of judgment" (cf. ¶ 2 in the original with the republished version). The word "wise" is never used in Strauss's essay and he goes to some length to not use it (see footnote 2). "Wisdom" is only mentioned twice by Strauss: once in an unliteral translation of a passage of the *Summary* – ¶ 13: "superior to all wisdoms" [D 125]. Literally: "superior to all wise sayings." The same word (*ḥikma*) appears only once in Alfarabi's *Summary* (D 134).

[42] Strauss, *Xenophon's Socratic Discourse*, 125–26; Strauss, "Literary Character of the Guide for the Perplexed," 63, 74; Strauss, "Fârâbî's Plato," 372.

how they repeat, omit, and deviate from their sources. The un-Platonic preface of the *Summary* is followed by the story of an abstemious pious ascetic who, Strauss remarks, "in spite of" or, "because of," his virtues, has drawn the anger of the ruler of the city and is trying to escape (¶ 3). His escape is made possible by wearing the garment of vagabonds, the guise of which, Strauss notes, it is not clear how he obtained. Did he possess them already, or has he obtained them through questionable means? The pious ascetic's probity seems to be in question, perhaps his other virtues are too. One can doubt he could have become so artistically proficient to imitate a drunkard and to play an instrument if he were strictly abstemious.[43]

One of the wise men mentioned in Alfarabi's general remark has turned out to be a pious ascetic: he "happens to be a pious ascetic" (¶ 5). One is tempted to say that to be a pious ascetic is not his necessary quality, but is something determined by his specific situation.[44] The most important characteristic of the pious ascetic is that he has established his reputation as "a man of the strictest morality and religion." Based on this reputation, no one expects him to lie, even in order to save his life. The public, which has "very severe notions of decency" (¶ 4) would not expect him to go against his reputation as a man of "probity," the man who never lies; the public does not see such moral rules as what "can safely be disregarded in extreme cases."[45] Appropriately, the pious ascetic's lying "in deed" is not considered truly a lie by the public. One might say that the pious ascetic is an ascetic in a specific sense. His asceticism is that of "a jockey, who in order to win a race must live very restrainedly."[46] He has no reservation against lying or, in Alfarabi's words, "to play a flute or to dance" or do other "extremely repugnant and base" things if they are "obligatory" and save him from "persecution," because for him "what counts is thinking and investigating and not morality."[47]

That the question of morality is one of Strauss's main preoccupations in this essay is later confirmed in ¶ 18, which deals with the issue of

[43] Mahdi, "The Editio Princeps of Fârâbî's Compendium Legum Platonis," 15n57.

[44] Strauss, "The Law of Reason in the Kuzari," 115.

[45] Strauss, "The Law of Reason in the Kuzari," 130, 139, 141. Cf. Strauss, *Socrates and Aristophanes*, 198. with Montesquieu, *The Spirit of Laws*, XXV.2 *in fine* quoted in Strauss, *1966 Spring Course on Montesquieu*, 96 (Session 5, April 11, 1966). See also Strauss, "Fârâbî's Plato," 385–86; Strauss, "Reason and Revelation (1948)," 177.

[46] Strauss, "A Giving of Accounts," 465. For the origin of the idea see Nietzsche, *On the Genealogy of Morality* III.8.

[47] For "repugnant" things see D 131.

morality in its relationship with philosophy. Strauss draws our attention first to a passage in which Alfarabi compares the legislator to a beekeeper, and the citizens with bees in the beehive. Strauss raises an issue regarding the Latin translator's understanding of this passage. The translator believes that the relationship between the beekeeper and the bees is akin to the relationship between the legislator and those citizens who are described by Alfarabi as "the wicked and the lazy," to the exclusion of others. Strauss does not believe that the translator's interpretation is as obvious as one might believe. To clarify his point, Strauss enumerates three pairs of terms ("the bees and the beekeepers," "the free and the slaves," "the way of the legislator and the right road") while specifically excluding a fourth pair consisting of "the wicked and the lazy" (Latin: "mali et otiosi homines"; Arabic: "al-ashrār wal-baṭṭālīn"). Next, Strauss puts four questions forward to clarify Alfarabi's purpose in this passage. The first question points toward the universal character of the work of the legislator, who, like a beekeeper, can only concern himself with the universal and not with the individual.[48] The second question points toward the tyrannical character of the legislative art, which, like the art of beekeeper, treats the citizens as slaves who must obey commands through force rather than persuasion. The third question clarifies the simile of legislator and beekeeper. The fourth question asks whether "there is a point of view" from which "the free" can be seen as "wicked." Strauss does not explain what that point of view might be. Perhaps one might be able to shed more light on this question if one concentrates rather on the relation between "the free" and "the lazy." Strauss invites us rather to turn to two passages in Alfarabi's *Summary* which makes clearer the issue that he has in mind:

Truly the impudent is the one who deliberates only according to himself and his happiness, and that is why he is hated by the gods, and, being hated *by the gods*, he does not benefit from the help *of the gods*; and whoever does not benefit from *their* help leaves no beautiful and pleasant trace. He then set out to describe him (*that is to say, the best prince and legislator*) and he recalled what he had to take care of; and he said that he had to focus first on the care of the body, then on the soul, then on external things, degree after degree; and he brought examples of this and he spoke of it abundantly when it was particularly useful.

---

[48] This seems to be also the purpose of footnote 13, which consists of references to seven passages: the central one implies the esoteric art of writing, which addresses each group according to their particular capacities, sometimes acting like a physician who administers medication by mixing it with appetizing food. Cf. Strauss, "Notes on Lucretius," 83–84.

This quotation, which happens to appear right in the middle of Alfarabi's *Summary*, gives two descriptions which seem difficult to synthesize.[49] The first description depicts an insolent self-centered individual who is hated by the gods while the second description concerns a man who cares about the perfection of his body and soul. Gabrieli has tried to attribute each of these two descriptions to two different individuals. Strauss's claim consists of not only pointing toward the identity of Gabrieli's two individuals but also of suppressing Gabrieli's additions in his translation by italicizing them, additions which imply the existence of providence. The individual described in this passage, according to Strauss, is a "man" who is not concerned "with things other than his own felicity." In the previous version of his essay, Strauss spoke more emphatically of the man who is not concerned "with anything except his own felicity." This man who is indifferent toward the gods and is focused on the cultivation of his body and soul seems to be the same man who can be described as "lazy."[50] What remains to be seen is how this same individual can also be described as "wicked." This seems to be explained in Strauss's immediate discussion of another passage of the *Summary*, in which Alfarabi explains the relativity of the just and the noble things ("all these things are noble and shameful in reference to something else, and not in that they would themselves be noble or shameful") in contradistinction to the objective character of the useful things characteristic of the arts. This claim has a theologico-political character too, to which Strauss implicitly refers: the noble things (see καλά in the paragraph heading of ¶ 18), belong to "the realm of opinion"; the noble things are connected with "courage, war, city" as well as "kindred things."[51] These are next

---

[49] See Strauss's remark that the *Summary* "consists of 41 pages" (footnote 1). See also Strauss's allusion to the central passages of Alfarabi's *Philosophy of Plato* in Strauss, "Fârâbî's Plato," 367n27, 371n35. In "Fârâbî's *Plato*," the term "human being" is explained by a reference to Aristotle, who explains that the philosopher's virtuous actions are due to his relation with others in his capacity as a *mere* human being, in contradistinction to his divine philosophic character.

[50] The connection which Strauss has in mind seems to come from the Latin word "otiosus," which he translates as "the lazy." The term can be understood as a description of those who benefit from *otium*, a Latin translation of the Greek *schole*, "leisure" characteristic of philosophic contemplation. See Friedrich Solmsen, "Leisure and Play in Aristotle's Ideal State," *Rheinisches Museum für Philologie* 107 (1964): 193–220; Jean-Marie André, *L'otium dans la vie morale et intellectuelle romaine des origines à l'époque augustéenne* (Paris: Presses Universitaires de France, 1966), 149–50.

[51] Like some of Strauss's other writings, such as *Thoughts on Machiavelli*, the manuscript of Strauss's essay has a heading for each paragraph, the headings which are not reproduced in the published version. The transcription is available here in as Appendix D.

described as "the high and holy" regarding which men have "fanatical disagreement."[52] One is tempted to say that the man described in these passages has a kinship with the pious ascetic, who also has a questionable relationship with morality.[53]

The story of the pious ascetic, according to Alfarabi, clarifies one of the secrets of the writings of Plato, who was famous for writing by recourse to symbols, riddles, obscurity, and difficulty or, in Strauss's words, by means of "allusive, ambiguous, misleading and obscure speech" (¶ 5; see also ¶ 18). Just like the pious ascetic, Plato sometimes deviated from his usual style and spoke frankly, which went unnoticed by the public. Although Alfarabi tells the story of the pious ascetic to clarify Plato's style of writing, Strauss notes, it seems that the parable is not entirely to the purpose: First, it is true that like the pious acetic, Plato is a "man of judgment" who took account of what is "useful," but contrary to the pious ascetic, Plato did this less in view of what is useful to himself and his own safety than in view of "what is useful for the sciences or their existence in the cities and nations." Second, "Plato was not a pious ascetic" (¶ 7). Not only the idiosyncrasies of the pious ascetic's character do not correspond to our image of Plato, also while the pious ascetic lies on occasion and in deed, Plato seems to be insincere as a matter of course and in speech. One can therefore legitimately wonder who the pious ascetic is. Regardless, what the pious ascetic and Plato have in common is that they are both "men of judgment" and that they speak the dangerous truth by surrounding it with untruth or innocent truth. It is in this manner, Strauss notes, that "Plato has written about laws."

According to Strauss, Alfarabi's purpose in his *Summary* is to extract and explain "the thoughts to which Plato has alluded in his *Laws*" or those which Plato "intended to explain" in his work (¶ 8). There seems to be a difference between alluding to a thought and intending to explain a thought, but Strauss claims that they are in fact the same: one alludes to a thought when one intends to explain it – the intention is "consummated"

My transcription of the headings was significantly improved by Heinrich Meier and Svetozar Minkov to whom I am grateful. Meier has previously transcribed the headings of *Thoughts on Machiavelli* to which, when suitable, I refer in this chapter. See Meier, *Political Philosophy and the Challenge of Revealed Religion*, 187–97.

[52] See Isaiah 57:15.

[53] In this regard, it might also be helpful to some readers to mention the epigraph of Strauss's "Persecution and the Art of Writing" from W. E. H. Lecky. See Strauss, *Persecution and the Art of Writing*, 1952, 22; Montgomery, "Leo Strauss and the Alethiometer," 289.

only by the reader who can interpret the allusions. Plato did not want to explain the truth to all men indiscriminately, so he chose to employ allusions. Alfarabi followed Plato's example in his own summary, which has a "two-fold" character: it is written for those who desire to know the *Laws* and can bear "the toil of study and meditation" on the one hand, and those who cannot bear that hardship on the other. Strauss notes, however, that Alfarabi's *Summary* is not of much use to the second group, whose desire to know the *Laws* through Alfarabi's *Summary* even turns into aversion because that desire cannot be satisfied: they cannot consummate the intention of the writer who transmits his thought through allusions. Strauss, however, continues to speak of the "two-fold meaning" of Alfarabi's work, as if the *Summary* is not exclusively addressed to that specific group of elite readers and has something for the more ordinary reader too. This point is clarified by comparing Alfarabi's style of writing enigmatically to "men on horseback" (¶ 8).

The metaphor of man on horseback, with its multiple facets, appears in several writings of Strauss, with different connotations. As Strauss intimates elsewhere, the metaphor finds its original source in Xenophon and is also reflected in Machiavelli, and Jonathan Swift's *Gulliver's Travels*. In Xenophon's *Cyropaedia*, a certain Chrysantas, a companion of Cyrus, speaks of his desire to be a centaur, a half-man, half-horse creature who synthesizes human prudence and brachial dexterity with the speed and the strength of a horse. Centaurs can attack with strength and take flight with speed. But in view of the limitations of the centaur as an indivisible whole who cannot enjoy the human nor equine-specific goods to the full, Chrysantas opts rather for becoming a knight, a man on horseback. A rider is independent of his ride because they both are capable of existing independent of each other. The rider can benefit from human and equine goods at the same time, enjoying the eyesight and hearing of a man as well as those of a horse.[54] The superiority of the man on horseback to the centaur seems to be the core of this metaphor in Strauss's eyes. But how this should be understood is a complex issue and can at least take two or three different forms. To begin with, there is the fact that the man on horseback is a divisible whole; the rider can dismount the horse when necessary. The flexibility of the man on horseback consists of being able to mount and dismount the horse at will, and to react to different needs adequately. Commenting on the passage in Xenophon's *Cyropaedia*, Strauss interprets the man on horseback as reflecting a unity consisting of reason and

[54] Xenophon, *Cyropaedia* IV.3

sub-reason, rational and sub-rational.[55] It does not seem that the relation between these two elements is simply one of the rational part ruling over the irrational, the relation of which one can describe as a simplistic form of Platonism. Two parts, rather, seem to play different complementary roles, and contribute to the perfection of the whole synthesis. In other words, there seems to be a form of cooperation between the rider and the horse in which both parts have a specific function. In theologico-political terms, this is reflected in Machiavelli's teaching that Chiron is a model of perfect synthesis of law and force. Machiavelli recommends using both man and beast in our actions, which Strauss understands as Chiron replacing God. More clearly elsewhere, Strauss claims that in the Machiavellian perspective *"imitatio Chironis* replaces *imitatio Christi,"* half-beast half-man replaces half-god half-man.[56] That this dichotomy and its political lesson apply also to Alfarabi is shown by the fact that Strauss, in his earlier writings, has spoken of Alfarabi replacing the "divine-human" dichotomy with the "human-beast" dichotomy, and has named Alfarabi as the founder of a tradition followed by Machiavelli which proposes a "secular alliance between philosophers and princes friendly to philosophy," an alliance between the high and the low.[57]

Furthermore, if one understands the rational rider as depicting the wise, and the irrational horse as the many, the metaphor can be seen as the illustration of a cooperation between the philosopher and the many: this republican form of the alliance is depicted in Machiavelli's story of Carmignuola, the Italian general who dismounts his cavalry to defeat the enemy, with the cavalry representing the aristocracy and the infantry standing for the people.[58] More abstractly, the message is to defeat the

---

[55] Strauss, 1963 *Winter Course on Xenophon*, 299 (Session 12).

[56] In a letter to Seth Benardete, Strauss writes: "Will you be so kind as to reread the passage on Chirone in *Principe* ch. 18 – I have the impression that the half-man half-beast with its two natures who taught the ancient princes, has been replaced, *nei tempi moderni*, by *uno mezzo Dio e mezzo uomo* with his two natures who teaches modern princes, i.e., Chiron replaces again Christ. Hence *imitatio Chironis* replaces *imitatio Christi*. Question: are not the 'reasonable horses' of *Gulliver* IV really *centaurs*, and hence the lesson of *Gulliver* in this respect [is] identical with, and derived from, Machiavelli? Can you, with the library at your disposal, reconsider *Gulliver* IV with a view to this question: do these horses have any traits reminiscent of the Centaurs (I have in mind some rather subtle suggestions)?" I am grateful to Svetozar Minkov who drew my attention to this letter and transcribed it for me. See also Meier, *Political Philosophy and the Challenge of Revealed Religion*, 82–83, 190 (the heading for II.21).

[57] Strauss, "Fârâbî's Plato," 391–92; Strauss, *Persecution and the Art of Writing*, 1952, 15; Meier, *Political Philosophy and the Challenge of Revealed Religion*, 44–45.

[58] Machiavelli, *Discourses on Livy*, 171 (II.18); Strauss, *Thoughts on Machiavelli*, 159; Mansfield, *Machiavelli's New Modes and Orders*, 246–47.

supernatural forces by founding the political order on "the low but solid ground" of this-worldly goods.[59] Another form of the relation between the rider and the horse is reflected in the twofoldness of the speech of the perfect man, the twofoldness which depicts the "unity of knowledge and communication of knowledge."[60] In a sense, the perfect man or philosopher is a mixture of these two elements as they are present in his twofold speech. The twofoldness corresponds to two different audiences, the elite and the many. The elite is the interlocutor of the human side of the philosopher's speech, while the many is the addressee of the equine part. To be able to synthesize the human and the equine part is in a way the essence of the so-called Socratic turn and its accompanying art of esoteric writing. It is a testimony to the richness of this metaphor that here the horse can also be interpreted as reflecting the unruliness of reason, while the man represents moderation. The man on horseback depicts then the rule of moderation over wisdom, the lesson being that wisdom cannot "be divorced from moderation," which Strauss considered to be the essence of the Socratic turn, separating the Socratic school from the Pre-Socratic philosophers.[61] Through an allusion to "the horse-drawn Parmenides," Strauss describes these pre-Socratic predecessors as those who follow the "*logica equina*" and cannot lie, even nobly.[62] The thought is born out of the poem which begins with Parmenides depicting himself as being drawn by mares toward the sun, and speaks of the impossibility of saying what is not, that is, of lying. Parmenides and his companions are drawn by their unruly equine reason toward the truth. But the deeper truth is that wisdom divorced from moderation cannot "bring to light" something which "cannot be illumined by the sun."[63] That which the sun cannot bring to light can be seen only in the darkness of the cave, "the world of common sense."[64] The Parmenidean perspective, which can be depicted by the image of a centaur and not man on horseback, is also present in Swift's *Gulliver's Travels*, where a race of

---

[59] Strauss, *Natural Right and History*, 196, 247.

[60] Strauss, *Thoughts on Machiavelli*, 290.

[61] Strauss, *The Political Philosophy of Hobbes*, 1952, xvi; Strauss, *Natural Right and History*, 123.

[62] Strauss, *Persecution and the Art of Writing*, 1952, 23.

[63] Parmenides, Diels-Kranz 28.B1.1–30, 28.B2.7–8; Strauss, *Thoughts on Machiavelli*, 290.

[64] Strauss, *Natural Right and History*, 79, 123; Svetozar Minkov, *Leo Strauss on Science: Thoughts on the Relation between Natural Science and Political Philosophy* (Albany: State University of New York Press, 2016), 57. See also Strauss, "What Is Political Philosophy?," 32; Strauss, "On Classical Political Philosophy," 1959, 92; Meier, *Political Philosophy and the Challenge of Revealed Religion*, 44–45.

centaurs called Houyhnhnms, living in a dystopian island, are incapable of lying and are alien to all human refinements: they cannot tolerate a human being in their midst.[65]

ALFARABI'S *SUMMARY* AND THE PROBLEM OF ISLAM

If Alfarabi's *Summary* is as allusive and enigmatic as Plato's *Laws*, one might reasonably ask what the justification of Alfarabi's esoteric commentary on a Platonic esoteric writing might be. The justification, Strauss notes, is found in the fact that Plato's allusions "which were intelligible to some of Plato's contemporaries are not equally intelligible to men of the same type among Fārābī's contemporaries" (¶ 9). Strauss does not explain what has brought about this change, but rather moves to another question: how to discover Alfarabi's allusions. One way to discover them is to find what remains "unsaid" in the *Summary*, what is "the most important subject" which is not mentioned.[66] Strauss here has recourse to his other writing on Alfarabi, which he has commented on several years before. In that work, as it was explained in Chapter 3 above, Strauss claims, Alfarabi implies that "the necessary and sufficient condition of happiness, or man's ultimate perfection, is philosophy" (¶ 9). Now, Strauss claims that the *Summary* is silent about philosophy and that the words "philosophy," "philosopher," and their derivatives are absent in it. This claim is partially true, because in fact the word *falsafa* and its derivatives do not appear in the *Summary*, although more common Arabic words for designating philosopher (*ḥakīm*) and philosophy (*ḥikma*) do appear. It is rather more significant that the words philosophy and philosopher appear nineteen times in Strauss's own essay, the central one being in a sentence in this paragraph, which repeats, with a minor modification, what was said a few lines above: "The *Philosophy of Plato* teaches that philosophy is the necessary and sufficient condition of happiness." In the previous statement, happiness was equated with "man's ultimate perfection." The equivalence of happiness and perfection, however, was a major question in Strauss's earlier essay, where it

---

[65] Jonathan Swift, *Gulliver's Travels*, ed. Claude Rawson (Oxford: Oxford University Press, 2008), 223 (IV.4); Allan Bloom, "An Outline of Gulliver's Travels," in *Ancients and Moderns: Essays on the Tradition of Political Philosophy in Honor of Leo Strauss*, ed. Joseph Cropsey (New York: Basic Books, 1964), 255–56.

[66] On the importance of omission as an esoteric technique of writing see Strauss, "Fârâbî's Plato," 372; Strauss, *Thoughts on Machiavelli*, 31; Strauss, "Literary Character of the Guide for the Perplexed," 76; Strauss, *Xenophon's Socrates*, 126.

was argued that by distinguishing between these two, Alfarabi implies that philosophy, which is the perfection of man, only by the addition of the royal art can lead to happiness. The statement on the insufficiency of philosophy for providing man with ultimate happiness, however, Strauss noted there, is later on corrected by Alfarabi through equating the philosopher with the king: Alfarabi's last word is that "[p]hilosophy is the necessary and sufficient condition of happiness."[67] As Strauss explains in his 1945 commentary, the roundabout way in which Alfarabi goes to make his final position known to the careful reader is due to the fact that such a position would clash with the claim of Islam, which argues for the insufficiency of all human endeavors for providing man with happiness in absence of the divine guidance provided by divine revelation. This last claim, Strauss notes, is underlined and prominently present in the *Summary*, which speaks rather frequently of not only the divine but also of the life after death, the subject to whose absence Strauss draws our attention in his earlier essay.[68] It is therefore particularly suitable to describe the relation between Alfarabi's *Philosophy of Plato* and his *Summary* as that "between two entirely different worlds."

The relationship between Alfarabi's *Philosophy of Plato* and his *Summary* is further clarified by saying that the former contains a discussion of "Plato's philosophy" while the latter contains "his art of *kalām*" (¶ 10). That for Strauss the *Summary* is a work of *kalām* is due to the fact that Alfarabi seems to distinguish between the concern of the legislator and that of Plato: while the legislator is concerned with the laws proper as well as the roots of the law, Alfarabi's Plato is concerned mainly, if not exclusively, with "the roots" (*uṣūl*), so much so that he claims the whole first eight books of the *Laws* deal with that question (D 150). Dealing with the roots, in Strauss's perspective, is the proper work of those who practice *kalām*, namely the *mutakallimūn* or the so-called dialectical theologians. Strauss notes that the words derived from the root *klm* appear twenty-six times in the *Summary*. It happens that the English equivalent of such words are used seventeen times in Strauss's own essay.[69] Now it is rather surprising to call the *Summary* a work

---

[67] Strauss, "Fârâbî's Plato," 381.

[68] Strauss, "Fârâbî's Plato," 371, 375–77. In this essay of his too Strauss avoids the words "future life" or "afterlife" and speaks only of "other life" while in the paragraph heading of ¶ 9 he speaks of "future life." For a discussion of this point see pp. 184–85 below.

[69] Here it is worth quoting a letter written to Muhsin Mahdi by Strauss on September 27, 1954, shortly after the date indicated in the notebook as when he finished working on his essay: "I was perhaps slightly unpolite [sic] to your wife because I was so anxious

of *kalām* because Alfarabi is famous for being very critical of the whole enterprise of the dialectical theologians. Strauss points to this problem by drawing our attention to a part of Alfarabi's understanding of dialectical theology, which consists of "the art of defending the laws or religions" (¶ 10). Strauss's description of Alfarabi's view of dialectical theology, however, remains incomplete if one does not add that according to Alfarabi, dialectical theologians employed all sorts of pseudo-arguments, which fall short of true philosophical arguments for defending *their* own particular religion while debating the adherents of other religions. What would be the justification then, for applying the term *kalām* to Alfarabi's understanding of Plato's *Laws*? One understands Strauss's claim better if one considers that Strauss brings up the question of the afterlife for justifying the attribution of the term *kalām* to Alfarabi's *Summary*: it is only in the ninth chapter of the *Summary*, Strauss notes, that Alfarabi does "refer to punishment in the other life." In the previous version of his essay, Strauss actually used the term "allude" rather than "refer," which is a more exact description of the passage he has in mind: Alfarabi does not actually speak of "punishment in the other life," not even of "the other life," but rather of "a future punishment" (*al-'uqūba al-ājila* : D 151). This slight revision of the essay, as well as Strauss's unliteral translation, remind one of the previous paragraph, in which Strauss spoke

to devour your notes. I went over them, and wish to thank you very, very much for the trouble you have taken, although I console myself with the thought that it was *nāfi'* [useful] for you to check on what I said. You are a *hakīm* [a wise man or philosopher] in what you say about the character of your notes – but precisely as ruthless reminders of the literal meaning they are immensely helpful to me, even if, or precisely if, I do not follow all of them. Some of your suggestions I gratefully adopted. I hope you allow me to acknowledge my debt to you in print – except if you think that an article by me on the Father of Defence (what a wonderful stroke of τύχη [chance]) is not a good place to be mentioned in for a *fāḍil* [virtuous]. I am really grateful to you for having helped me overcome my hesitation to write the article; I enjoyed myself very much in study-ing Farabi's *nawāmīs* [Laws] and in writing about them. There is one point which I saw no reason to emphasize, which is of special importance to me – viz. the fact that '26' is important for Farabi. You know perhaps that it is a key number in Machia-velli." The transcription is done by Svetozar Minkov. Strauss refers to the assistance of Mahdi in the first footnote of his essay. The meaning of the playful allusion to "Father of Defence" is not clear to me. Perhaps it is a play on Alfarabi's name (Abū Naṣr) which means "Father of Victory" in Arabic. Another possibility is an Arabic metonymy describing city as Abū Mansūr: See John Richardson, *A Dictionary, English, Persian and Arabic: Vol.* 2 (London: Blumen and Co., 1810), 281; Leonard Chappelow, *Notes, Critical, Illustrative and Practical on the Book of Job. Vol.* 2 (Cambridge: J. Bentham, 1752), 54. For number twenty-six in Machiavelli and number seventeen, see Chapter 2 of this volume.

of Alfarabi's frequent usage of the terms such as "the other life" in his *Summary* (¶ 9). To begin with, as it was mentioned, Alfarabi does not actually use this term in the *Summary*. Furthermore, Strauss's term "the other life," just like Alfarabi's "future punishment" are quite ambiguous: "the other life" does not necessarily mean the life after death, although it is ambiguous enough to remind some readers of that idea too. Strauss's ambiguous terminology seems to point to Alfarabi's ambiguous terminology. Two other passages in Alfarabi's writings, in which the distinction between this life and the other life is mentioned, and to which Strauss refers elsewhere, are also capable of being understood in a nonorthodox manner.[70] The distinction might refer to "this life" as the life dedicated to the goods appreciated by the vulgar such as wealth, honor, and pleasure, and the "other life," which is the life dedicated to higher goods such as virtue or knowledge. In other words, one can also speak of living "the other life" in "this life," to live the life of virtue and knowledge among the vulgar who lives "this life."[71]

It seems that for Strauss, the *Summary* is a work of a specific kind of *kalām*: this unique form of *kalām*, whose existence Strauss principally deduced from Alfarabi and Maimonides's critique of the common form of *kalām*, is elsewhere described as the "enlightened *kalām*."[72] Strauss employs this term for describing Maimonides's *Guide for the Perplexed*, and explains that Alfarabi's critique of *kalām* is of "decisive importance" for understanding the genus to which Maimonides's book belongs. In fact, Maimonides's specific kind of *kalām* as it is found in the *Guide* takes Alfarabi's specific critique of the *mutakallimūn* into account while formulating a new art of *kalām*. What this new *kalām* precisely entails

[70] Strauss, "Fârâbî's Plato," 371n34.
[71] Strauss, "Fârâbî's Plato," 371–72, 374–75, 379; Mahdi, *Alfarabi and the Foundation of Islamic Political Philosophy*, 83–84. See also the explanation of what afterlife means in Alfarabi, "On the Intellect," in *Classical Arabic Philosophy: An Anthology of Sources*, trans. John McGinnis and David Reisman (Indianapolis: Hackett Publishing, 2007), 76 (Bouyges 31); Alfarabi, "Selected Aphorisms," in *The Political Writings: "Selected Aphorisms" and Other Texts*, trans. Charles E. Butterworth (Ithaca and London: Cornell University Press, 2001), 25–26 (Najjar 45–46), 52–53 (Najjar 86–87). See also Alfarabi, "The Attainment of Happiness," in *Philosophy of Plato and Aristotle*, trans. Muhsin Mahdi (Ithaca: Cornell University Press, 2001), 13 in princ. (Hyderabad 2), 133n1.
[72] Strauss, *Persecution and the Art of Writing*, 1952, 40–41, 40n9; Alfarabi, "Enumeration of the Sciences," 80–84 (Uthman Amin 111–13); Moses Maimonides, *The Guide of the Perplexed*, trans. Shlomo Pines (Chicago: University of Chicago Press, 1963), 175–74 (I.71). For a substantial discussion of the "enlightened *kalām*" see also Parens, *Leo Strauss and the Recovery of Medieval Political Philosophy*, 83–95. See also Strauss, *Gesammelte Schriften. Band 3*, 767 (Letter to Gershom Scholem on February 26, 1973).

is not explained here, and even in Strauss's other writings it remains quite obscure. But a few things seem clear: First, the enlightened *kalām* remains a defense of the Law, with the difference that, unlike the vulgar *kalām*, it is not formulated in opposition to philosophy.[73] Second, the enlightened *kalām* occupies a place between the vulgar *kalām* and philosophy proper. What distinguished it from the *kalām* of the dialectical theologians is that it is not anti-philosophic, while what distinguishes it from philosophy proper is its religious elements. "Plato's philosophy" as it is presented in Alfarabi's *Philosophy of Plato* corresponds rather clearly with Strauss's understanding of philosophy as a "*radically* atheistic" enterprise, while the enlightened *kalām* of the *Summary* "speaks rather frequently" of religious themes and the divine.[74] Not that the *Summary* is entirely free of heretical ideas: for instance, Strauss points to the fact that Alfarabi implicitly speaks of God as the final and not as the efficient cause of the world; the idea which Strauss attributes to the "Averroists" in general and other atheist philosophers like Machiavelli in particular.[75] Third, this specific form of *kalām*, although friendly to philosophy, is quite distinct from philosophy, and one can say that it is not *philosophical*, or more precisely, *demonstrative*. One should suppose that the enlightened *kalām* employs inferior and less exact forms of argumentation, perhaps rhetoric, dialectic, or even a synthesis of them.[76] An indication for the lower status of the *Summary* in Strauss's view is also the fact that the *Summary* is described as "more 'personal'" than Alfarabi's *Philosophy of Plato* (¶ 11). What is personal is infinitely less significant than what is truly individual, that is, "the necessarily anonymous truth."[77] Fourth, the arguments presented by the enlightened

---

[73] Strauss, "How to Begin to Study the Guide of the Perplexed," 169–70.

[74] Strauss, "Reason and Revelation (1948)," 146.

[75] Cf. the reference in the central paragraph (¶ 12) to Alfarabi's statement on Zeus as the final cause in D 125 with Strauss, *Thoughts on Machiavelli*, 175; Strauss, "How to Begin to Study the Guide of the Perplexed," 178; Meier, *Political Philosophy and the Challenge of Revealed Religion*, 66n80. See also ¶ 21.

[76] Leo Strauss, "Introduction to Maimonides' The Guide of the Perplexed," in *Leo Strauss on Maimonides: The Complete Writings*, ed. Kenneth Hart Green (Chicago: University of Chicago Press, 2013), 428, 428n17; Strauss, "How to Begin to Study the Guide of the Perplexed," 179–83; Parens, *Leo Strauss and the Recovery of Medieval Political Philosophy*, 24. That Alfarabi is practicing the art of *kalām* and its questionable methods is also implied by the fact that Alfarabi contradicts himself by attributing a thought first to Plato and then to himself, and this in the same context in which he speaks of *mutakallimūn* contradicting themselves (¶ 14).

[77] Strauss, "Fârâbî's Plato," 377.

kalām are of exoteric character.[78] The practitioner of the enlightened *kalām* is more concerned with formulating the rational basis, the rational justification of the Law or "the reason of the Law," by concentrating on the end of the Law, rather than with a discussion of its divine origin (cf. ¶ 21). This is precisely what Strauss describes as the method followed by the Athenian Stranger of the *Laws* in his evaluation of the Dorian laws. Strauss implies this move from the origin of the Law to the end of the Law by inviting the reader to compare the end and the beginning of the opening statement of the *Summary*, which summarizes the beginning of the first book of the *Laws* (footnote 6: "cf. also 5, 4–5 with 5, 2–4"): Zeus is there imperceptibly transformed from the maker of the Law and the one who sets down the Law, to Zeus who is the final cause of the Law.[79]

In paragraph 12, Strauss describes the characteristics of the *Summary* as something between a simple report and a mere enumeration – the title of this paragraph in the manuscript reads: "General characteristics of the Summary: from simple report to mere iḥṣā [enumeration?]." He notes that Alfarabi's "chief concern" in his work is to unveil the "purposes" of Plato in discussing some subjects, the purposes (aghrāḍ) which Plato did not expound himself. In the next paragraph, Strauss underlines Alfarabi's allusion to Plato's discussion of "a law which was famous in his time" without identifying which law is meant or even where precisely the subject is brought up in Alfarabi's *Summary* (¶ 13). He moves

---

[78] Strauss, "Literary Character of the Guide for the Perplexed," 57n64.

[79] Elsewhere Strauss claims that for Maimonides, the study of the origin of the Law has the potential to lead to "Epicureanism." What Maimonides rather recommends is to discover the "reason of the law" which is accessible to human reason: Strauss, "Some Remarks on the Political Science of Maimonides and Farabi," 299 (GS II:145); Strauss, *1971–72 Course on Plato's Laws*, 5 (Session 1); Pelluchon, *Leo Strauss and the Crisis of Rationalism*, 223. One other point worthy of consideration is that there might be a connection between this concern with the end of the Law and the genealogy of the Revelation which Strauss formulated in one of his unpublished writings, the genealogy which has, as one of its objectives, the refutation of the claims of Revelation. See Strauss, "Reason and Revelation (1948)," 165–67; Meier, *Leo Strauss and the Theologico-Political Problem*, xiii–xvi; Heinrich Meier, "On the Genealogy of Faith in Revelation," in *Leo Strauss and the Theologico-Political Problem* (Cambridge: Cambridge University Press, 2006), 29–44. See also Strauss's claim elsewhere that some of the rational *nomoi* composed by the philosophers "served the purpose of undermining the belief in Divine legislation proper." In the footnote attached to this passage, Strauss refers to the opening of Plato's *Laws* and the question of the divine origin of the Dorian laws: Strauss, "The Law of Reason in the Kuzari," 125, 125n96. The "rational *nomoi*" seem to be what Strauss means by "the Greek law" in this essay (¶ 17).

rather swiftly to another theme instead, one which is discussed twice in
Alfarabi's *Summary*, that of "tyranny." In order to have some notion
of what Strauss is doing here, let us begin by noting the "law" to which
Alfarabi is referring. That law is mentioned by the Athenian Stranger of
the *Laws* in the context of his criticism of the divine laws of the Dorians.
When the gentle discussion of an old Athenian with two old Dorian interlocutors risks turning into a bitter conflict born out of criticism of the
divine laws of the Dorians, the Athenian Stranger reminds his companions of the existence of an old law, what Strauss calls the "law of laws,"
supposedly laid down by Minos, the divine lawgiver. This law forbids
the criticism of the laws in front of the youth and commands everyone
to say with one voice that the laws are given by the gods and that they
are good in every respect. The same law of laws, however, permits the
old men to evaluate and criticize the laws when no young person is present.[80] In the case of Alfarabi, the protection against the prying eyes of
the young seems to be provided by esoteric writing; in this context, by
only implying what one should understand by tyranny. Strauss points to
the esoteric meaning of the discussion of tyranny by speaking of it in the
thirteenth paragraph of his essay, the number which in Strauss's thought
is intimately linked with the question of *divine* tyranny.[81] In his discussion, Strauss draws our attention to two statements of Alfarabi on the
necessity and justification of tyranny. Although Strauss intimates that
there are some difficulties in understanding these two statements, the real
significance of his discussion is only revealed by looking up the passages
mentioned in the seventh footnote attached to this paragraph. The footnote has two sets of references, each referring to three passages. The first
set of references are to passages in which Alfarabi mentions, respectively,
the issue of the plurality of traditional laws which must be eliminated
by the legislator, the necessity of imposing one set of laws on all citizens
regardless of their different natural dispositions, and the corruption of
the laws of a city through its conquest by foreign kings and the imposition of some divine law on the citizens.[82] The second set of references turn
out to be an implicit critique of tyranny: they speak, respectively, of the

---

[80] Plato, *Laws* 634d–e; Strauss, *The Argument and the Action of Plato's Laws*, 10–11.
[81] Strauss, *Thoughts on Machiavelli*, 49; Strauss, "Niccolò Machiavelli," 31.
[82] The central passage mentioned in the first set of references, which seem out of place,
draws our attention to a strange remark of Alfarabi which Strauss had mentioned previously, in the central paragraph: "a Platonic expression" which Alfarabi had not used
in summarizing the passage concerned (¶ 12). This Platonic expression happens to be
"children."

superiority of the path of freedom, which creates a spirit of cheerfulness and voluntary obedience among the subjects, censure the legislators who are "envious," mention the corruption and destruction engendered by slavish and coerced obedience, and praise the city founded on affection and intellect. This critique is, however, mitigated partly by the fact that tyranny is a way to convince the good men to accept the laws laid down by those who assimilate themselves to what is divine; this is precisely the synthesis of two different statements of Plato related by Alfarabi; in the first statement Plato has "intimated" the advantage of the festivals which make pleasures divine, while in the second statement he "mentions" that the festivals of gods serve the purpose of reinforcing the attachment of the public to the laws.

The rather tiring repetition of "then" (thumma), characteristic of Alfarabi's exposition of Plato's *Laws*, provides an opportunity for Strauss to draw our attention to a rather surprising observation: "that it is sometimes impossible to say where the alleged report of what Plato did ends and Fārābī's independent exposition ... begins" (¶ 14). The decisive step in Strauss's gradual unveiling of his understanding of Alfarabi's *Summary* is taken when he refers to the enigmatic character of the seventh chapter of the *Summary*. That chapter is supposed to resume the content of the seventh book of the *Laws*. In reality, however, we cannot even speak of an incomplete, inexact, or even a misleading summary: of the content of Alfarabi's chapter "one barely finds a single trace in the alleged source" (¶ 15). This does not mean that the seventh chapter is completely incomprehensible. In fact, Strauss quotes a surprising statement of the editor of the *Summary* – who is above all forms of suspicious interpretation – to the effect that in writing one of the passages of the chapter, "which is not at all found in the Greek text of Plato, it seems that Farabi had before his eyes the judgment of Muhammad himself on the law of earlier prophets."[83] Strauss mentions that the editor also found

---

[83] Strauss does not quote Gabrieli's complete footnote. Next comes the following: "The Arab prophet accused Jews and Christians of changing the genuine law which they have received from their prophets, and [accused them] of denying the congruence [of that law] with Islamic revelation." The footnote is attached to the following passage from the *Summary*: "When necessity prompts a legislator to change a statute of previous laws, let him repudiate instead the alteration made by the inhabitants of those cities in what was brought forth by their legislators and the distortion of the traditional laws and usages" (D 146, Gabrieli 35.22–36.2). For the question of "falsification" (*taḥrīf*) in Islam see Qur'ān 2:75, 4:46, 5:13 and Hava Lazarus-Yafeh, "Taḥrīf," in *Encyclopaedia of Islam*, ed. Th. Bianquis et al., 2nd ed., vol. 10 (Leiden: Brill, 2000), 111.

it reasonable to entertain the idea that Alfarabi must have been aware of the fundamental difference between the Islamic Laws and Plato's laws. In this way, Strauss builds a bridge between the editor's claim and the possibility of an esoteric art of writing practiced in Alfarabi's *Summary*, and proposes a hypothesis: perhaps the discrepancies between Alfarabi's account and Plato's text is due to Alfarabi's awareness regarding "the fundamental difference between Islam and Plato's philosophic politics." In other words, and more radically, Strauss suggests that Alfarabi "may have rewritten the *Laws*" to respond to the requirements of his Islamic context and the changes brought about by the revealed religions. What is conveyed through Alfarabi's *Summary* is not Plato's teaching: Strauss goes so far as to say that Alfarabi has ascribed his "revised" version of Plato's teaching to "the dead Plato." What remains of Plato in Alfarabi's account is rather "Plato's purpose." In order to protect himself and his science, Alfarabi has refrained from openly agreeing with the teaching of "his Plato" and has blurred the distinction between "his mere report and his independent exposition."

Strauss depicts the seriousness of Alfarabi's encounter with Plato's *Laws*, the seriousness which is rarely, if ever, a concern for a mere historian, by reminding us of a major point, a point which must have been a concern of "[e]very serious reader of the *Laws*," including "[e]very Muslim reader in the Middles Ages": "The *Laws* contains a teaching which claims to be true, i.e., valid for all times" (¶ 16). Facing this issue, Strauss notes, those Muslim readers had three options: (1) they could have rejected Plato's philosophy on the basis of and because of its incompatibility with their Muslim faith; (2) they could have begun evaluating their Muslim beliefs by the standard of Platonic philosophy; (3) they could have claimed that Islam is in perfect harmony with Platonic philosophy, nay, it is the realization of the Platonic ideas in deed and can be understood in purely rational terms. Here it is important to remind oneself of the fact that what is the main issue is the relationship between Alfarabi's own thoughts as a man living under the shadow of Muslim revelation and Plato's philosophy. Strauss does not spell out his own view of the debate. One is tempted, however, to conclude that the central statement reflects Strauss's position, while the first position can be attributed to those Muslim readers of the Greek writings like al-Ghazālī, who found the wisdom of the Greeks incompatible with their Muslim beliefs and rejected that wisdom and its representatives among their contemporaries. That the central position is what Strauss attributed to Alfarabi is also confirmed by the title of this paragraph in the manuscript which depicts a movement from the *Laws* to Islam: "Plato's *Laws* → Is Islam true?" Two supplementary points are here of particular importance: First, Strauss clearly supposes that in Alfarabi's perspective, a perfect harmony between Plato's philosophy and Islam is not possible. Second, it is interesting that the third possibility mentioned by Strauss seems rather a good summary of the position often ascribed by scholars to the Falāsifa, the view which has solid textual basis in the writings of the Falāsifa themselves. Would it mean that Strauss took that view *simply* to be the exoteric teaching of the Falāsifa? We will come back to this point on pp. 196–99.

SPECIFIC CHARACTER OF THE *SUMMARY*

Strauss's essay on Alfarabi's *Summary* is in a sense a rejoinder to his earlier writing on Alfarabi's *Philosophy of Plato*. It is therefore not surprising that there are continuities as well as revisions in these two presentations of Alfarabi's thought. Perhaps one of the most remarkable revisions in Strauss's understanding of Alfarabi's thought concerns a passage in *Philosophy of Plato* which presents the content of Plato's *Laws*. In his earlier essay, Strauss began by drawing our attention to the fact that in his *Philosophy of Plato*, contrary to his *Attainment of Happiness*, in which he speaks in his own name, Alfarabi does not assert "the identity of legislator and philosopher," or that the legislator of the perfect city is a prophet-philosopher. In the absence of such a clear statement, Strauss warned us not to presume that the esoteric teaching of Alfarabi is that the ruler of the virtuous city is a prophet. This remark paved the way for Strauss's comment on Alfarabi's description of Plato's *Laws*: Strauss observed that in his description, Alfarabi "conceives of the *Laws*, not, as Plato himself had done, as a correction of the *Republic*, but as a supplement to the *Republic*: whereas according to Plato the *Republic* and the *Laws* deal with essentially different political orders" Alfarabi gives us the impression that "the *Republic* deals with the best political order and the *Laws* deal with the best laws belonging to the very same best political order."[84] This reading of Alfarabi's description of Plato's *Laws* was used by Strauss as further evidence for his thesis, according to which Alfarabi does not claim that the existence of the virtuous city is dependent on the revelation of a divine law, or even more fundamentally, that the foundation of the perfect

---

[84] Strauss, "Fârâbî's Plato," 379–80, 380n55.

political community is the requirement of perfect happiness, the happiness which is only brought about by philosophy. Strauss's new consciousness in his study on Alfarabi's *Summary* regarding what he called the "problematic character of law" leads to a new understanding of Alfarabi's enigmatic description of Plato's *Laws*. While what attracted Strauss's attention to this description in his earlier writing was the fact that, according to Alfarabi, the legislator of the virtuous city is not a prophet, and its laws are not divinely legislated, in his new study he was more surprised by "the silence of that passage about the obvious and guiding theme of the *Laws*, namely, the laws" (¶ 22). To clarify this pregnant silence, Strauss draws our attention to another passage in *Philosophy of Plato* which also refers to Plato's *Laws*. In that second passage, Alfarabi claims that the science and art of Socrates is presented in the *Laws*. Strauss adds another observation from his earlier study, according to which Alfarabi distinguished between "the way of Socrates" and "the way of Plato." From the absence of Socrates in Plato's *Laws* as we know it, and Alfarabi's silence about the laws in his description of the *Laws*, Strauss concludes that Alfarabi's intention is to imply the idea that "if *per impossibile* the *Laws* were Socratic, they would not deal with laws."[85] What Strauss is pointing toward is his understanding of the so-called Socratic turn and its relation with the question of esotericism. To summarize, Strauss claimed that the change in character of philosophy from pre-Socratic to Socratic is of utmost importance for understanding the essential characteristics of the Socratic school and the political character of its teaching. This Socratic turn, as it was reflected in the writings of Socrates's detractors like Aristophanes, as well as his followers like Xenophon and Plato, is depicted as one from deep interest in natural philosophy to political things, to the noble and the just. This political turn is concomitant with discovery of "the doubtful character of the freedom to say everything" characteristic of the pre-Socratic Socrates and his "arrogance and impatience with stupidity" as

---

[85] On this question one might also consult Aristotle's curious remark at the end of *Nicomachean Ethics*, where he claims that his predecessors have ignored the subject of legislation in their political science. Aristotle's claim seems rather perplexing, as one cannot suppose that he has forgotten Plato's *Laws*. Could this have something to do with the fact that Aristotle seems to identify the Athenian Stranger with Socrates? Aristotle, *Nicomachean Ethics* 1181a12–19, *Politics* 1265a12, Strauss, "What Is Political Philosophy?," 33; Strauss, *The Argument and the Action of Plato's Laws*, 2; Carnes Lord, "Introduction," in *Aristotle's Politics*, 2nd ed. (Chicago: University of Chicago Press, 2013), xxxi; Ronna Burger, *Aristotle's Dialogue with Socrates: On the Nicomachean Ethics* (Chicago: University of Chicago Press, 2008), 211n43.

is depicted in Aristophanes's *Clouds*. In Strauss's perspective, one of the pillars of Aristophanes's friendly criticism of Socrates consists of ridiculing "Socrates, not for trying to keep his teaching secret from the uninitiated, but for his ineptitude in this respect." Socrates after his turn is, on the contrary, "the unrivaled master in judging human beings and in handling them"; "he is of infinite patience with stupidity" and for this reason he is superior in wisdom to the pre-Socratic Socrates.[86] In his essays on *Philosophy of Plato* and the *Summary* also, Strauss points towards this change in rhetorical strategy consequent to the Socratic turn by referring to Alfarabi's distinction between "the way of Socrates" and "the way of Plato."[87] While Socrates is "intransigent" and advertises an "open break" with the many, Plato synthesizes the Socratic rhetoric which is only appropriate for dealing with "the elite" and Thrasymachus's art of speaking suitable for dealing with "the vulgar." Platonic rhetoric and the art of writing which Alfarabi follows demand "judicious conformity with the accepted opinions." While in the perspective of "the way of Socrates" the unphilosophical character of the laws makes them unworthy of a philosopher's concern, "the way of Plato" permits "appreciation or legitimation" of the laws as an instrument for dealing with the vulgar, because the *Summary* establishes a connection "between the vulgar and laws" (¶ 22).[88]

Right at the end of *Socrates and Aristophanes*, whose importance in Strauss's oeuvre is attested by him calling it his "real work," Strauss describes Abū Bakr Muhammad ibn Zakariyyā al-Rāzī's short treatise entitled *The Book of the Philosophic Life* as the "clearest and most thoughtful exposition" of the Socratic turn.[89] While al-Rāzī seems to attribute the Socratic Turn, "the profound differences between the Aristophanean Socrates and the Platonic-Xenophontic Socrates" to a change in the

---

[86] Strauss, *Socrates and Aristophanes*, 313–14.

[87] Strauss, "Fârâbî's Plato," 383.

[88] See also Strauss, *The City and Man*, 78; Strauss and Voegelin, *Faith and Political Philosophy*, 63 (Letter to Eric Voegelin on December 17, 1949).

[89] Strauss, *On Tyranny*, 309 (Letter to Alexandre Kojève on May 29, 1962). Strauss mentions, if I am not mistaken, al-Rāzī twice in his published writings: Strauss, "The Law of Reason in the Kuzari," 117n65; Strauss, *Socrates and Aristophanes*, 314. The place and the manner in which Strauss mentions al-Rāzī in the latter book shows also the importance of Islamic political thought for Strauss: his "real work" ends where al-Rāzī's begins. Strauss's knowledge of al-Rāzī owes much to Paul Kraus's groundbreaking work on this figure, to whose edition Strauss refers: Paul Kraus, "Raziana I," *Orientalia* 4 (1935): 300–34. For an excellent English translation of al-Rāzī's treatise see Abū Bakr Muhammad ibn Zakariyyā Al-Rāzī, "The Book of the Philosophical Life," trans. Charles E. Butterworth, *Interpretation: A Journal of Political Philosophy* 20 (1993): 227–36.

character of the *historical* Socrates, Strauss entertains the idea that perhaps the Socratic Socrates, which has gone through a political turn, is a *construction* of his followers as a reaction to the Aristophanean critique of the historical Socrates. That this is a preoccupation of Strauss in his essay on the *Summary* is reflected in the last paragraph. The last paragraph points toward the "'unhistorical' character of the *Philosophy of Plato* and the *Summary*" (see the paragraph heading in the manuscript). The guiding theme is here an understanding of what "Plato's philosophy" is – the term which is used twice in Strauss's essay (¶¶ 10, 23). In both occasions, "Plato's philosophy" points toward the esoteric aspect of Alfarabi's thought as distinguished from its exoteric façade, the exoteric aspect which was previously described by the term *kalām*. The distinction between the way of Socrates and the way of Plato is a way toward understanding the precise meaning of Plato's philosophy as it is presented in Alfarabi's two "historiographical" works. Strauss's main concerns seem to be to overcome a very commonsensical misconception: contrary to what one might reasonably expect, Plato's philosophy is not properly speaking *Plato's* philosophy. In fact, one might perhaps do better by dropping the proper name because, according to Strauss, Alfarabi does not mean "to say that all insights which he ascribed to Plato were peculiar to Plato" (¶ 23). Even this formulation, "insights," prove to be misleading because right away Strauss explains that the "only originality" which Alfarabi attributes to Plato and Plato alone is a remark on the dialogue *Menexenus*. "Plato" is, therefore, here a type of place-holder for some specific kind of individual who is dissatisfied with the state of knowledge at a particular time, and who, like Alfarabi's Plato, "did not find the science which he desired among the sciences and arts which are known to the vulgar" of his time. That desired "science" which Strauss is referring to is not any science, but "the science of the essence of each of all beings," the science which is provided by philosophy. "Plato" is therefore any individual who is dissatisfied with the sciences of his time and begins walking in the footsteps of similar individuals in search of "the science of the essence of each of all beings." The curious description of Plato's *Laws* is just another piece of evidence which points to the unhistorical character of Alfarabi's "historiographical" writings, an example of Alfarabi inventing Platonic speeches.[90]

---

[90] Strauss, "Fârâbî's Plato," 354–65, 376. The last line of Strauss's essay directly refers to his earlier "Fârâbî's Plato." In the manuscript, Strauss has copied the invented quotation quoted in his 1945 essay before changing it with pencil to what appeared in the published version.

ALFARABI AND THE DIVINE LAWS

While Strauss argued for the importance of observing what Alfarabi refrains from mentioning in his summary of Plato's *Laws* (¶ 2), he believed that Alfarabi's secretiveness in his *Summary* is also found in his practice of avoiding speaking of some subjects in some places while mentioning them in other places. In the longest paragraph of his essay, Strauss follows this point particularly regarding Alfarabi's treatment of the divine. Strauss draws our attention to the fact that Alfarabi reserves his mentioning of theological themes to the beginning and the end of his *Summary*, while "there is silence in a central section" (¶ 19). Not that the *Summary* is relatively free of theological reflections: it contains more on those subjects than *Philosophy of Plato* – an exception, Strauss notes, is the sixth chapter which "is the closest approximation, within the *Summary* to the *Philosophy of Plato*," because in that chapter theological subjects are absent. Furthermore, Alfarabi's secretiveness is also observable in the manner in which he goes out of his way to speak exclusively of "gods" rather than "God," even going so far as deviating from Plato's text. One remarkable example of such a deviation is found in two passages in which, when Plato speaks of God and chance, in his report Alfarabi speaks only of chance. In one instance to which Strauss alludes, when Plato's *Laws* speaks of praying "both to the god and to good luck," Alfarabi speaks of availing oneself of "drawing by lots, chance, and what resembles them," implying some kind of identity between the divine and chance.[91] Moreover, Alfarabi's usage of the adjective "divine" in the *Summary* is of an unusual character; Strauss claims that a careful inquiry shows that "divine" in the *Summary* is "a certain quality of human pursuits, namely, their excellence." This is the same conclusion which Strauss reached while studying this point in his earlier study on *Philosophy of Plato*.[92] Finally, Strauss draws our attention to a peculiar deviation from the text of Plato's *Laws* in the central chapter of the *Summary*: the Athenian Stranger of the *Laws* puts the soul below the gods from the point of view of honor. The issue is much more ambiguous in Alfarabi's report, which describes soul as "superior in nobility or dignity to the divine," but also as "inferior to the divine" (¶ 19). What Strauss seems to imply by highlighting this point

---

[91] Cf. Strauss, "Niccolò Machiavelli," 311 ("God is fortuna"); Meier, *Political Philosophy and the Challenge of Revealed Religion*, 75. If there is a similarity between Alfarabi and Machiavelli, it would mean that according to Strauss, perhaps Alfarabi does not follow the classic teleological Aristotelian view which is often ascribed to his Averroist followers.

[92] Strauss, "Fârâbî's Plato," 391.

is the thought which he alludes to in one of his published writings and explains in more detail in an unpublished lecture.[93] The point concerns the seventh book of Aristotle's *Politics*, where six essential functions of the city are enumerated in a descending order. The fifth item turns out to be the "concern with the divine," but Aristotle calls that element "fifth and first" instead.[94] Strauss interprets that statement as Aristotle meaning that no "city is possible without religion, without established religion, a state religion obligatory on all citizens."[95] The concern with the divine is therefore the first among the essential functions of the city, it is even "more necessary even than food," which occupies the first place in the enumeration. Strauss adds, however, that "in another respect it is not the first, therefore he says fifth or first." In other words, the concern with the divine, from a political perspective, occupies the first rank; as it is *political*, however, it does not have the same dignity even as something as low as food, and should be ranked as the fifth.[96]

In the seventeenth paragraph, which numerologically points to nature, Strauss addresses the possibility of Muslim philosophers believing in the perfect harmony between Islamic Law and Platonic philosophy, the possibility which was previously only mentioned without being developed further (¶ 16).[97] He begins by reminding us of Alfarabi's awareness of the conflict between "the Greek laws" and Islamic Law. Strauss gives two examples to establish this point: singing and another "institution" are accepted by one code and rejected by another. He then notes that Alfarabi has explained in which conditions this variety in what concerns the second "institution" is unobjectionable. The "institution" which Strauss has in mind is wine-drinking, and in the passage which Strauss has in mind Alfarabi actually discusses the benefits of wine rather than providing a justification for its prohibition. These two practices, both of which provided

---

[93] Leo Strauss, "The Liberalism of Classical Political Philosophy," in *Liberalism Ancient and Modern* (Chicago: University of Chicago Press, 1968), 27. In this essay Strauss speaks laconically of "the precarious status of religion" in Aristotle's scheme. See also a comparable statement in Strauss, *The Argument and the Action of Plato's Laws*, 63.

[94] Aristotle, *Politics* 1328b11–12.

[95] Strauss also refers to Aristotle's statement on natural right, where "he indicates that sacrificing to the gods, and hence of course also praying, belongs to natural right. It is by nature just that the citizens pray and sacrifice." Aristotle actually only mentions sacrificing; praying is Strauss's addition. I owe this observation to an unpublished lecture by Nathan Tarcov, which he made available to me. See Aristotle, *Nicomachean Ethics* 1134b23–25.

[96] Strauss, "Religion and the Commonweal," 95–96.

[97] For the significance of number seventeen see the discussion in Chapter 2 of this volume.

recourse for the ascetic as an escape, pave the way for a discussion of the quest for the rational justification of Islamic Laws, which seemed to be rejected by Strauss because of its "apologetic" character. It turns out, however, that even this third approach to the relationship between Islam and Plato is as unorthodox as the second possibility. This point is discussed by Alfarabi in two statements. In the first, the self-sufficiency of political virtues is put forward as something common to both Greek and Islamic Laws. The point should, however, be understood as a depiction of the natural limitations common to all human political associations – Greek, Islamic, or otherwise. It is as natural as fire, which burns equally in Athens as in Baghdad, that the highest end of a good political association always falls short of what is needed for the highest perfection of the individual.[98] The second common element turns out to be more complex: it refers to the corruption and restoration of the laws in cataclysms such as universal deluges. Such a perspective on the cyclical movement of things, which Strauss describes as "Plato's natural explanation" of the origin of the laws, be they human or divine, manifests its problematic character for Islamic revelation by being related to the heretical view, according to which world is eternal rather than created: Strauss refers to this problem, rather ambiguously, by mentioning it at the end of a peculiar enumeration consisting of very unequal objections to this interpretation as well as by inventing a quotation which cannot be found in Alfarabi's *Summary*.[99] The question of "eternity or creation" sheds more light on the meaning of Strauss's allusion to "what Plato had said about the natural beginning" of

---

[98] Strauss, *On Tyranny*, 101, 202–3; Strauss, *Natural Right and History*, 121, 150n24, 151; Strauss, *On Plato's Symposium*, 86; Strauss, *The City and Man*, 27; Strauss, *Xenophon's Socratic Discourse*, 161; Strauss, "The Liberalism of Classical Political Philosophy," 57; Leo Strauss, "Introduction," in *History of Political Philosophy*, eds. Leo Strauss and Joseph Cropsey, 3rd ed. (Chicago: University of Chicago Press, 1982), 3–4; Mahdi, *Alfarabi and the Foundation of Islamic Political Philosophy*, 23–25.

[99] In the original version of the essay as well as the manuscript, "eternity or creation" was put in single quotation marks, while in the final edition they were replaced by double quotation marks. The doctrine of the eternity of the world is elsewhere described by Strauss as a "pernicious fruit" of the "wisdom of the Greeks," or "the crucial question" which distinguishes "philosophers" from "the adherents of revelation." See Strauss, "The Law of Reason in the Kuzari," 109n39, 124; Strauss, "Progress or Return?," 252. The connection between necessity and philosophy, which is one of the major aspects of Strauss's thought, is also alluded to by the fact that the term necessity and the terms of the same family appear nine times in Strauss's essay. The central example is found in the statement which also contains the central example of the terms "philosophy" and "philosopher" being mentioned (¶ 9). The connection between necessity and philosophy can be explained as follows: "Creation from nothing is the necessary presupposition

every code, the issue alluded to also by a reference to Alfarabi's *Summary* (¶ 17: "cf. 18, 4"). In the latter passage, Alfarabi speaks of the dual sources of the change of divine laws, one due to the natural corruption of the mores and the other through the imposition of a new divine law by a conquering king. Differently stated, the change of divine laws has two natural sources, one being the cyclical changes which lead to sudden or gradual changes, and the other, the human agency which brings about the establishment of "divine" laws which are actually of "human origin." The connection between the issue of the eternity of the world and the divine or human origin of the laws is established through the fact that the doctrine of the eternity of the world presupposes necessity, which leaves no place for divine omnipotence or for divine intervention in the affairs of the world through the exercise of providence in the form of legislation, appointment of prophet-legislators, or even the performance of miracles.[100] Furthermore, it is doubtful that a god who is obedient to a blind necessity can be "assumed to be capable of such motions as fear, anger or hate, and grief," not to say love, the passions which, at least in some cases, are prerequisites of the idea of providence and legislation.[101] Moreover, the doctrine of the eternity of the world and its concomitant idea of cyclical cataclysms, as in the case of Alfarabi, lead to the idea of recurrent

of talk of omnipotence. But talk of omnipotence means in just as many words that everything is possible and nothing is necessary. And if nothing is necessary, philosophy is impossible." Meier, *On the Happiness of the Philosophic Life*, 250–51.

[100] This connection between the doctrine of the eternity of the world and denial of the divine origin of laws is pointed to in the case of Machiavelli too. See Strauss, *Thoughts on Machiavelli*, 32, 205, 334n72 as well as Meier, *Political Philosophy and the Challenge of Revealed Religion*, 189 ("His allusion to eternity – creation and to human origin of Christianity"). In his earlier study, Strauss says that Alfarabi "substitutes politics for religion." This seems to mean that according to Strauss's Alfarabi, the only providence one can rely on is human providence in the shape of politics in contradistinction to divine providence. Strauss, "Fârâbî's Plato," 378; Strauss, *Persecution and the Art of Writing*, 1952, 15; Parens, "Escaping the Scholastic Paradigm," 215. The doctrine of the eternity of the world rejects in the same breath the possibility of miracles as well as divine legislation. If god, like any other being, is bound by necessity which he cannot disobey, god cannot perform miracles which by definition are the violation of the necessary laws of nature. See Strauss, "The Law of Reason in the Kuzari," 124; Strauss, "Notes on Philosophy and Revelation," 169; Strauss, "On the Interpretation of Genesis," 360; Strauss, "Reason and Revelation (1948)," 145, 158; Strauss, "An Untitled Lecture On Plato's Euthyphron," 17; Meier, *Leo Strauss and the Theologico-Political Problem*, 25.

[101] Strauss, *The Argument and the Action of Plato's Laws*, 150. The quoted passage appears in Strauss's discussion of the tenth book of Plato's *Laws*. This would help us understand Strauss's statement to the effect that some of the peculiarities of Alfarabi's *Summary* make it possible to "see without great difficulty how Fārābī would have

corruption of codes and gradual introduction of new ones. This is while a revealed religion proclaims "only *one* divine law," and demands the complete obedience of man to that law because of its finality, perfection, and its uniqueness to the end of times. The plurality of divine laws born out of cyclical cataclysms is incompatible with the demand for absolute obedience.[102] Finally, the doctrine of the eternity of the world weakens the demand for "*full* obedience to the law" characteristic of divine legislation, because for such a demand to be sustained, "the law must be the source of *all* blessings" and therefore "the god must be *omnipotent*."[103]

One must be wary of Strauss's statement about the "only originality" that, in *Philosophy of Plato*, Alfarabi attributes to his Plato. Strauss writes that according to Alfarabi's report, Plato's investigation in the *Menexenus* "led to the result that the philosophers, as distinguished from the legislators, cannot expect to be deified by the citizens" (¶ 23). This peculiar – one might say audacious – statement of Strauss, which is just mentioned in passing, "by the by," and without any explanation, needs to be understood. Right after this statement, Strauss changes the subject by one of his idiosyncratic expressions which appear in some of his writings as a kind of "pointer" or "warning sign" for a thought which requires special attention: "However this may be."[104] A look at Alfarabi's text shows that the original source does not speak of "legislators" nor of "deifying" but only of "the princes" or "the rulers" (*mulūk*) and "the virtuous" (*afaḍil*) on the one hand, and of "making great" ('*aẓama*; Mahdi's translation: to glorify) and "praising" or "glorifying" (*majada*; Mahdi's translation: to exalt), on the other. One is therefore reasonably led to the question of why Strauss makes these changes and what might be the main purpose behind his movement of thought, or the basis of this statement. I believe this statement points to one of Strauss's most ambiguous ideas implied only, to my knowledge, in three other writings:

---

interpreted the tenth book of the *Laws* had he been in a position to do so" (¶ 10). See also very difficult passages which imply the access of Maimonides to the *Laws* X as a possibility in Strauss, "Some Remarks on the Political Science of Maimonides and Farabi," 310–12 (GS II:153–56).

[102] Strauss, "Reason and Revelation (1948)," 166 (point 5); Meier, "On the Genealogy of Faith in Revelation," 36–37, 40. Cf. "*the* difficulty: how only one perfect *sharia* (given the eternity of the universe)?" in SNA 1.20.

[103] Strauss, "Reason and Revelation (1948)," 166 (point 6).

[104] This expression appears only once in Strauss's essay. I owe my familiarity with the importance of this expression in Strauss's writings to Heinrich Meier. See also a comparable expression in John Locke's usage of "by the by": Pierre Manent, *Le Regard politique: Entretiens avec Benedicte Delorme-Montini* (Paris: Flammarion, 2010), 60.

the possibility of a philosopher becoming the founder of a civil religion disguised as a revealed religion. In two instances, Strauss denies this possibility: When discussing the classical philosophers' understanding of the relationship between politics and religion, Strauss states that none "of these philosophers believed that he could found a religion. Religion is a work of the founders or legislators." Strauss does not exclude the possibility of philosophers trying to "affect or modify religion" which they find existing already in their respective communities; but he categorically states that religion is "not meant to be the work of philosophers."[105] Elsewhere, he goes even further and denies the possibility of any religion being the work of philosophers who as such, Strauss claims, could have understood its basis and principles. In view of the stark opposition between religion and philosophy, Strauss finds it incomprehensible that philosophers might engage in founding a religious code and questions the rationale behind a philosopher's effort in founding "what only an entirely different human type bent on the anti-philosophic possibility could discover or invent."[106] This rationale, however, is implied in another writing of Strauss where he discusses the affinity between books such as the famous *Nabatean Agriculture* and Plato's *Laws*. Although at first Strauss seems careful to make a distinction between the books dealing with superstitious practices and beliefs which he describes as "superstitious *nomoi*" and the works by philosophers properly speaking which he calls "philosophic *nomoi*," the distinction gradually seems to disappear: Strauss ends up claiming that it is a possibility that "the authors of some of the superstitious codes, were themselves philosophers." Why these philosophers would engage in such an enterprise is also implied in Strauss's statement which mentions "addressing the multitude."[107] In other words, although Strauss mentions

---

[105] Strauss, "Religion and the Commonweal," 100.
[106] Strauss, "Reason and Revelation (1948)," 167.
[107] Strauss, "The Law of Reason in the Kuzari," 124. The footnote attached to this paragraph (89) is also of particular interest. Strauss refers to three passages: the first two passages from Halevi's *Kuzari* claim that philosophers found it necessary to employ images for addressing the multitude, and also refer to the idea that philosophers believed that prophets were themselves only wise men who achieved their knowledge through purely human means – this is the central passage. The third passage is from Andrea Alpago's comments on his Latin translation of Avicenna's treatise on resurrection, the so-called *Adhawiyya*. Alpago claims that the doctrine of metempsychosis attributed to Plato and Pythagoras should be understood metaphorically and that these philosophers actually only believed in the immortality of the soul. Alpago then claims that the metaphorical character of these philosophers' doctrine is comparable to the metaphorical nature of the divine law's statements on bodily resurrection, the doctrine which is suitable to the education of the multitude.

that the esoteric intention of these works might have been to serve "the purpose of undermining the belief in Divine legislation proper," they seem to have a mainly or supplementary political purpose also, which is fulfilled by conveying an exoteric teaching to the multitude: these religions act as a supplement to purely political laws "in order to strengthen the people's willingness to obey the purely political laws."[108] But one should not lose sight of the fact that even here, Strauss seems to be persuaded that the enterprise of *founding* such a civil religion is not the work of philosophers but rather of legislators and rulers, while philosophers again seem to be open to working within the confines of the existing religion of their communities.[109] This is also confirmed by the character of Plato's *Laws* and Alfarabi's writings in general, and his *Summary* in particular, which seem to deal with variations on the existing religions of their communities. Be that as it may, one must refrain from categorically denying Strauss's interest in this possibility, especially since one encounters the following rather audacious statement in Strauss's essay: "the divine laws are the work of a human legislator" (¶ 19).[110]

AN UNFINISHED TASK

In the end, one should bear in mind the tentative character of Strauss's interpretation of Alfarabi's *Summary* as it is presented in his essay. The provisional character of Strauss's interpretation in addressing all the difficulties of Alfarabi's *Summary* is reflected in the statement in which he warns us of overstating our capacity to claim that "we are in a position to explain these difficulties." What he particularly finds defective is our knowledge of "the religious situation in Fārābī's age" (¶ 20).[111] This does not mean that Strauss does not believe that he has acquired "a certain understanding of the manner in which such writings need to be read"; his essay reflects that understanding. Strauss gives us "a specimen" of his understanding of the way in which Alfarabi's *Summary* should be

---

[108] Strauss, "The Law of Reason in the Kuzari,"125, 122.
[109] Strauss, "The Law of Reason in the Kuzari,"115, 122.
[110] One should bear in mind that this possibility is mentioned in the twenty-third paragraph of the essay. This number might point toward "the insufficiency of the given revelation" and an invitation to go beyond it. On the significance of twenty-three for Strauss see Behnegar, "Reading 'What Is Political Philosophy?,'" 41n9.
[111] See also the remark in Paul E. Walker, "The Political Implications of Al-Razi's Philosophy," in *The Political Aspects of Islamic Philosophy: Essays in Honor of Muhsin S. Mahdi*, ed. Charles E. Butterworth (Cambridge, MA: Harvard University Press, 1992), 70.

read by concentrating on the first chapter and depicting "the problem of νόμος" (see the title of ¶ 21 in the manuscript). He brings together different elements of his reading of the *Summary* through the idea that the move from Zeus as the efficient cause of the laws to Zeus as the final cause is concomitant with the move from the divinity of the laws toward their agreement with the precepts of reason (¶ 21). This movement has a consequence which one can anticipate: from such an evaluation, one can distinguish between a true legislator and an imposter. As the laws of Zeus did not live up to the standard of reason, one must conclude that Zeus was not a true legislator, although Alfarabi does not say so in so many words. The true legislator intends to guide men toward God, the desire for "the other life," and the highest virtue, which is "above" moral virtues. That highest virtue turns out to be "human virtue," which includes "science." "Human virtue" can be acquired without practicing it according to the prescriptions of the laws; "one can acquire human virtue without obeying the law." The end of the laws is to produce "divine virtue" or to make men "religious." The divine virtue is not necessary for seeking the countenance of God or for desiring "the other life." One must conclude that divine virtue, whose production is the end of the laws, is of a lower status than human virtues, which can be acquired without obeying the law: divine virtue seems to be of more "political" character. Law has for its objective leading "the people" (see ¶ 21: "cf. 16, 14–15"). This should not distract us from the thought that not all divine laws are good. In fact "some older laws" of "the vanquished" contained precepts regarding music and singing which were of "consummate soundness," and they rendered great service, although they were replaced by the laws of "the victors." Here Strauss draws the obvious conclusion: such a view certainly "casts some doubt on the divinity of Zeus and Apollo." The divinity of the lawgiver is further put in doubt by Alfarabi's requirement that the lawgiver himself should obey his own laws, because in the same way that "gods do not pray," they cannot obey their own laws. In fact, by this statement, Strauss refers us to the difficulties of imagining a perfect being who rules human beings "by telling people what they should do, or by issuing commands."[112] But doubts regarding the divinity of the

---

[112] This seems to be the core of Strauss's understanding of Alfarabi's rejection of the idea of a divine law: A perfect being "loves more the people who do what he does than those people who merely do what he tells them to do." A perfectly pious man who imitates the gods would neither pray nor would he obey mere commands. See Strauss, "An Untitled Lecture on Plato's Euthyphron," 14.

divine laws should not lead to forgetting the utility of such laws, because in contrast to "the reasonable individuals" who possess "human virtue in the comprehensive sense of the term," others need the guidance that can only be provided by the laws. The divinity of laws is necessary for those people who are described as "the ignorant and children."[113]

---

[113] For "the ignorant and children" see the first reference in footnote 18. ¶ 21 has twenty-one passages referred to in the body of the paragraph. The central passage refers to the divinity of the musical laws of Egypt. On the utility of the consecration of the laws see Strauss, *The Argument and the Action of Plato's Laws*, 25. In this regard one should mention a passage, missing in our manuscripts but which seems to have been a part of Alfarabi's *Summary*: "Alfarabi wrote in the *Book of Laws* that 'those who possess the perfect divine Law through which people attain eternal happiness in this world and in the world to come do not by nature need philosophy, but there must be among them a few individuals who know it in order to strengthen the divine Law through it and save it from the infidels who arise to do battle with it.'" Quoted in Harvey, "Did Alfarabi Read Plato's Laws?," 66. A comparable passage from Maimonides is the subject of Strauss's next essay in *What Is Political Philosophy?* See Strauss, "Maimonides' Statement on Political Science." One must also add that the one who only obeys the laws and nothing beyond the laws should not be considered the highest type of man, "virtuous and praiseworthy" in the highest sense.

Appendix A

Leo Strauss's Notes on Averroes's Commentary on Plato's *Republic*

Editorial remarks: This text is an edited version of an untitled transcript of fourteen pages found in the Leo Strauss Papers.[1] There are two sets of corrections by hand on the transcript: some are by pencil and some by a blue pen. It seems that Strauss has corrected the transcript at least twice and has been preparing it for an unspecified later use. Strauss used E. I. J. Rosenthal's edition of Averroes's work and refers to the page numbers of his edition.[2] However, all translated passages from Hebrew are Strauss's own, not Rosenthal's. It is therefore tempting to date the transcript sometime after 1956, although there are no dates indicated on the papers. Numbers in curly brackets, inserted by the editor, refer to the page numbers of the transcript; numbers in square brackets, also inserted by the editor, refer to the paragraph numbers of the transcript; numbers in parenthesis are in the original transcript and refer to the page and line numbers of Rosenthal's edition; all handwritten and typed underlinings have been converted to italics; crossed out words and handwritten insertions are mentioned in the footnotes; arrow symbol, used for showing the logical consequence of ideas, is everywhere inserted by hand; Strauss's corrections of typographical errors have not been noted; the abbreviated title of the books and names are everywhere replaced by their full forms. The errors are responsibility of the editor.

---

[1] Leo Strauss Papers, box 18, folder 17, Special Collections Research Center, University of Chicago Library.
[2] Averroes, *Commentary on Plato's "Republic."* The page numbers of Rosenthal's edition are also indicated in the margins of Ralph Lerner's translation: Averroes, *On Plato's "Republic."*

{1} [1] How to approach Islamic (political) philosophy? a. not from a modern point of view b. not from the point of view of Christian scholasticism (e.g., assuming that Averroes is Islamic Thomas Aquinas). Islam[ic] philosophy seems to be a combination of Aristotle and Neo-Platonism (emanation of everything including matter from the One). But 1. Farabi's *The Philosophy of Plato* shows no trace of Neo-Platonism and is much closer to Cicero than to Plotinus 2. connected with this is the great importance of political philosophy, Platonic and not Aristotelian: obvious difference from Christian scholasticism; furthermore, no Roman law and[3] Cicero: no natural law tradition 3. connected with difference between Islam and Christianity? Avicenna on *Republic* and *Laws*: Plato's political science is the clue to the understanding of *sharia*, the prophet as philosopher-king (radically different from Aristotle's *Politics*) cf. Farabi, *Ihsa' al-'ulum* on *fiqh* and *Kalam* as appendages to political science.

[2] Sketch of the prophetology of the Falāsifa according to Maimonides: a strictly natural process – intellect and imagination – *the* difficulty: how only one perfect *sharia* (given the eternity of the universe)?[4]

[3] Averroes on the *Republic*. How to read it? Not on the assumption that Averroes did not have access to the *Republic* but only to some summary. Averroes says that he paraphrased the *Republic* because he didn't have access to the *Politics*; this implies that he did have access to the *Republic*, of course only an Arabic translation. That translation is not accessible to us; we cannot know how good or bad it was; but we have no right to assume that it was bad or unintelligible. We can judge it to be unintelligible only with {2} a view to *our* understanding of the *Republic*; do *we* understand the *Republic*? cf. Farabi's *The Philosophy of Plato* on Thrasymachus.

[4] Besides, even if there can be no question that Averroes presents Plato in a manner which differs entirely from anything Plato says or suggests, this need not be due to incomprehension on his part or on the part of the translator of the *Republic*. The example of Farabi on *Laws* VII: the problem of *Islam* → Averroes too may *use* Plato, he may hide behind Plato, for presenting unorthodox views of the *sharia*.

[5] Summary: before we can make a comparison of the *Republic* and Averroes's paraphrase, one must have understood that paraphrase by itself.

---

3 "in" is crossed out and "and" inserted by hand.
4 "?" inserted by hand.

[6] The problem: *Republic* → al-madīna al-fadīla – the perfect community – communism, equality of the sexes, rule of philosophers; the consequence: Islam is not the perfect community. But perhaps Averroes does not identify himself with Plato: why then did he paraphrase the *Republic*?

[7] In his introduction (21, 5 → 21, 3–25, 9) Averroes sets forth what he regards as the truth as to practical science. Practical science in contradistinction to theoretical science (natural science and divine science) (21, 8–13). Practical science consists of two parts: the scientific and the practical part. Scientific part: the virtues (and vices) simply; practical part: how the virtues are to be established in the young, etc. – the latter requires understanding of the *political ends* of the virtues (21, 21–22, 2; 24, 12–32). (cf. Aristotle's silence in his *Ethics* on the end which courage serves). Both parts of practical science are still theoretical as compared with that knowledge which is required for treating individual cases; for this requires {3} power of judgment which arises from long experience (25, 2–8).

[8] First part of practical sciences: *Nicomachean Ethics* Second part: *Politics* and Plato's *Republic* Averroes will explain Plato's *Republic* because the *Politics* "has not yet come to us." (22, 3–5).

[9] Averroes uses then the *Republic* only for the second part of the theoretic part of practical science. But before he turns to this subject, he gives a summary of the first part of practical science; in that survey he uses, and even explicitly refers to (22, 27 and 23, 31), Plato's *Republic* → the *Republic* contains the two parts of practical science, but Averroes uses it chiefly for the second part. Averroes identifies himself with the first part of practical science as developed within the *Republic* at least to the extent to which he summarizes it (cf. 65, 8–9 and context regarding the whole section up to 74, 14: the teaching of the first part of practical science is not based[5] on Plato). By all this we are led to expect that he regards the practical science as developed in the *Republic* as the true teaching. This would imply a complete break with Islam.

[10] Averroes reassures us at the beginning of the discussion of the second part of political science, i.e., at the beginning of the theme of his work. "*We* say that the beginning with which Plato opened the speech about the emergence of those virtues (i.e., the citizen's virtues) is the virtue of courage." He makes clear immediately afterward that he will

---

5 "best" is crossed out and "based" inserted by hand.

speak first in his own name before permitting Plato to speak: "as *we* have said, the way to the understanding of how it (the virtue of courage) is attained by the citizens and preserved with respect to them in the most perfect manner is that *we* should contemplate what is primarily intended by the actions of this virtue in the[6] city. {4} *We* say then[7] ..." (25, 10–19). He then goes on to present the true teaching regarding the function of courage without ever mentioning Plato. At the end of that presentation he says: "this is what Aristotle holds about the wars of the virtuous city according to the report of Farabi. But what we find about this subject in Plato's book ..." It appears that Plato's teaching regarding the wars of the virtuous city and therewith about the function of the virtue of courage is not simply true (26, 26ff). Averroes does not simply agree with the teaching of the *Republic*.

[11] What is the issue? There are two ways in which the vulgar (≠[8] the elite) can acquire speculative opinions, opinions about matters of speculation, i.e., about the first principle of the whole and the end (25, 24): 1. rhetorical and poetic speeches and, 2. compulsion. The first is applicable generally speaking to people who have been trained in these things from their youth on or to citizens of the virtuous city. The second is to be applied to "the rest of the nations," to the barbarians. The virtuous city – "the city which we describe in speech" (26, 12–13) – makes little use of the second way[9], chiefly in regard to foreign nations. Compulsion → war → virtue of courage.

[12] That Averroes makes these remarks as a Moslem appears from the following statement: "this is the state of things in the *sharia* which go in the direction of the human shariai[10] in this our divine *sharia*, for the ways in it (sc. in our divine law) which lead to God are two: one of them is by *speech* and the other is by war." (26, 16–18). To understand this remark, one has to consider that the true way to "speculative opinion" is demonstration (25, 17–18), demonstrative speech: by saying that our divine law leads to God "by speech" and both by rhetorical or poetic speech[11] Averroes leaves it open that {5} Islam leads the elite to the speculative truth by means of demonstration. Secondly, the quoted statement

---

[6] "this" is crossed out and "the" inserted by hand.
[7] "them" is crossed out and "then" inserted by hand.
[8] "≠" is inserted by hand.
[9] "way" is inserted by hand.
[10] Strauss translates torot (the plural of torah) as "shariai" to remind us of the Arabic term Averroes presumably used in the original.
[11] "and both by rhetorical or poetic speech" is inserted by hand.

implies that there are laws within the law which radically differ from all human laws. This leads to the consequence that the specifically divine ways leading men to God are not speech and war but silence and peaceful action (say, justice, alms giving ...)[12] and: practical science (i.e., philosophy)[13] is perhaps not able to understand those parts of the divine law which have no analogy in human law: only the lower part of the divine law is covered by the *Republic*.

[13] In his exposition of the truth regarding speech and war as the ways leading to God, Averroes does not mention Plato – by name. But he seems to refer to him in the following passage (25, 19–23): "in teaching wisdom to the vulgar he used the rhetorical and poetic ways. For they (i.e., the vulgar) are in this respect exposed to this alternative: either they know them (i.e., the speculative opinions) by demonstrative speeches or they do not know them at all. The first is impossible. The second is possible. For it is proper for every man to acquire the maximum of human perfection which his nature permits and for which he is prepared." It is not certain that Averroes means here Plato – cf. 26, 1 יעשה[14] which may be punctuated in different ways. Apart from this the statement is very strange:[15] it is impossible for the vulgar to know the speculative truth by demonstrations, and it is possible for the vulgar not to know the speculative truth at all; the latter alternative is in perfect agreement with the nature of the vulgar. The conclusion: knowledge of the speculative truth by rhetorical and poetic argument is in fact ignorance of the speculative truth. It certainly is not knowledge but belief which is effected by {6} rhetorical and poetical arguments, and belief appears to be a moral virtue rather than an intellectual virtue (25, 24–26). No other conclusion could be drawn from the premise that the true ways to speculative science are a preserve of the elite (25, 17–18). The passage which contains an *allusion* to Plato, suggests that belief has no cognitive dignity whatever.

[14] Averroes questions in our context not what Plato says about speech – demonstrative or poetic – rhetorical – as a way of bringing men to God. *Averroes on Plato's error* (26, 26–27, 23)[16]. According to Plato war and the art of war and hence courage are needed only because of necessity: Plato implicitly or explicitly rejects the war of civilization and

---

[12] ")" is inserted by hand.
[13] Two parentheses inserted by hand.
[14] "יעשה" is inserted by hand.
[15] "and" is crossed out.
[16] "27-28" is crossed out and "26-27" inserted by hand.

the holy war. He apparently thought that only Greeks are by nature fit
for wisdom (hence wisdom could not be spread to other nations by war).
Yet, Averroes says, granting that the Greeks are most gifted, the men
of Andalus, Syria, Iraq, Egypt are gifted too. (He does not speak of the
inhabitants of Arabia – see Ibn Ḥaldūn). Furthermore, even if one accepts
Plato's premise (regarding the uniqueness of the Greeks) one could *perhaps* say that the nations other than the Greeks are particularly gifted
for virtues other than the intellectual (and therefore that they may be
subjected by conquest to discipline in those virtues). Yet here the important question arises as to whether the highest development of the other
virtues does not depend on the corresponding development of wisdom.
Still, many nations, especially in the two moderate climes, the 5th and
the 4th, are fit for the other virtues. It seems that one could argue as follows: proficiency in those other virtues depends on education from early
childhood on; hence coercion by war comes too late. But it does not
come too late {7} for the small children of the nations concerned. Even
the older generation of nations which have been brought up in a regime
close to the virtuous regime can attain to the virtues *to some extent*. If in
a given case this is not possible, the people concerned must be killed or
else enslaved, i.e., treated like irrational animals.

[15] I conclude: Averroes makes the war of civilization dependent on
natural conditions (whilst the holy war may have to be waged against[17]
the reds and the blacks) – and: in many cases not *conversion* to the true
religion but treating the conquered like irrational animals.

[16] Above all, Averroes argues on the premise that the purpose of the
war of civilization is to spread wisdom.

[17] *Later discussion of compulsion and war*

[18] 1. Plato's guardians must punish such a guardian as is unwilling
to accept the Law (41, 6–7; cf. also the reference to the *sharia* in Plato's
perfect city: 44, 23). [i.e., Plato did not believe that *wisdom* could be
brought about by compulsion but adherence to the *sharia* could; this
means that for Plato wisdom is radically different from the *sharia* whereas
Averroes maintains that wisdom and the *sharia* coincide and hence the
holy war is legitimate, if qualified by the *natural* condition of wisdom].

[19] 2. Discussion of the size of the good city. That size, Averroes,
holds depends on the circumstances (time, place, neighboring nations)
and must be determined by political *judgment* which is distinguished
from political science. Plato was satisfied {8} with 1000 warriors – rightly,

---

[17] "between" crossed out and "against" inserted by hand.

given the circumstances of his time. Yet *we* who assume that the virtuous city must wage war against *all* men, cannot accept that figure, as Plato himself would readily admit (45, 29–46, 12). *Or*, one might say, that the virtuous community would consist of many communities each of which possesses a determinate size. In that case one would have to draw the line between the member societies properly, e.g., according to the natural climes as the[18] Master of the *sharia* has said "I have been sent to the reds and to the blacks." This is not indeed the opinion of Plato but that of Aristotle and it is undoubtedly the true opinion (46, 13–21). [Agreeing with Islam Averroes demands a *universal society* and therewith the war of civilization not limited to a part of mankind – i.e., he retracts the concession to Plato made before – on the other hand, he brings the *conflict_* between Plato and Islam into the open – yet he prevents that conflict from becoming a conflict between Islam and *philosophy* by asserting that the view of the *sharia* is the view also of Aristotle.] He allegedly knows this view only through Farabi (cf. 26, 26–27); *where* does Farabi say this? and if Farabi says it, to what Aristotelian work does he refer? A genuine work of Aristotle? (cf. Pines on 46, 20).[19]

[20] 3. Plato's suggestions regarding limitations of warfare. The citizens must not enslave men of their kind and language. The may call enemies of this kind (their fellows in race and language) men in error but not unbelievers. This opinion of Plato is at variance with what many bringers of *torot* say (59, 20–60, 5). [Here Averroes merely *notes* the disagreement between Plato and many prophets; he does not say here what he thinks to be the truth; nor does he refer *here* to Aristotle's agreeing {9} with many prophets and disagreeing with Plato: *should racial and linguistic unity override religious diversity*? Conclusion: one of the great issues between philosophy and law is religious war, and this is connected with the problematic character of a *universal* society.]

[21] Canon of interpretation: Averroes is aware of the conflict between the *Republic* and the torot[20]; speaking of that conflict he takes the side of the torot[21]; but what about those cases in which the conflict between the *Republic* and the torot[22] is obvious and Averroes does not polemicize against Plato? What does it mean when Averroes says regarding religious

---

[18] "a" crossed out and "the" inserted by hand.
[19] Shlomo Pines, "Notes on Averroes' Political Philosophy," *Iyyun: The Jerusalem Philosophical Quarterly* 8 (1957): 75.
[20] "Laws" is crossed out and "torot" inserted by hand.
[21] "Laws" is crossed out and "torot" inserted by hand.
[22] "Laws" is crossed out and "torot" inserted by hand.

war and universal society that the Islamic view is undoubtedly the truth? Averroes sheds some light on this when he discusses his next great theme: the education of the guardians by music or rather by poetic and rhetorical speeches. The question concerns the use of untruth, of untrue fables. He teaches in his own name that for the education of the young imitative presentation of both speculative and practical matters is required but the imitation must be true. The first principle and the second principles [i.e., God and the angels] must be represented by their analogues in the political principles [i.e., as rulers issuing commands]. True happiness must be represented by imaginary happiness (29, 27–30, 12) but the vulgar cannot help taking the representations as the truth and hence the vulgar is in fact led[23] toward the untruth.

[22] Averroes turns then to Plato. Plato disapproved of untrue tales or untrue imitations. Tacitly imitating the ambiguity of Plato, Averroes presents Plato as disapproving of tales which are untrue and base (30, 20–21), thus leaving room for noble lies. He then explicitly replaces Plato's discussion of untrue and base {10} tales which were famous in Plato's time by a discussion of such tales which are famous "with us"; he explicitly *follows* Plato in doing so. God must not be represented as the cause of good and evil; evil must be traced to a principle other than God, say, to demons; but this has other disadvantages; therefore, evil must be traced to a representation of matter such as darkness [i.e., no teaching of omnipotence] (30, 23–31, 6). Happiness must not be represented as *reward* for actions which are conductive to happiness nor misery as *punishment* but as health of the soul, survival of the soul and eternal life (31, 7–25). This is said by Averroes in his own name.

[23] Then he adds that *according to Plato* the guardians must not be afraid of anything which might happen to them after death. [i.e., there must not be presentations of hell as little as of demons and of the devil]. The he says *in his own name* that "songs of women" like those implying that evil befell a friend through death must be rejected, and that fear should not be ascribed to *prophets* (31, 26–32, 9). Then he reports these opinions of *Plato*: a. much laughter should not be ascribed to *blessed men* [there is no danger that prophets be presented as given to laughter as distinguished from fear, to say nothing of weeping] (32, 7–8) and b. that the guardians must be most eager for truth – for lying does not befit God's rulership nor the angels [cf. opp. cit. ad 32, 14][24] nor the vulgar whereas

---

[23] "led" is inserted by hand.
[24] "31" is crossed out and "32" inserted by hand.

the kings may lie to the vulgar, for *untrue tales are necessary in teaching the citizens*, and there is no bringer of a *nomos* who does not use fictitious stories since they are necessary for the happiness of the vulgar [the vulgar not knowing true happiness] (32, 12–22). Averroes says in a disguised way in his own name what {11} he makes Plato say explicitly; for if the *sharia* represents true happiness by imaginary happiness and the first principles by political principles, the bringer of the *sharia* must use fictitious stories.

[24] (Averroes says "lying does not befit God's rulership" – God is not a ruler; but let us assume that God is a ruler – human rulers must lie because their subjects do not understand the true reasons of the actions demanded by them; yet the distance between God and the most intelligent human beings is infinitely greater than the distance between the most intelligent human rulers and their human subjects; hence if God is a ruler, he *must* lie – or if he does not lie he is not a ruler – cf. the implication of *Republic* II). Above all, Averroes does not criticize Plato's proposition regarding noble lies or untrue fables – he does not make an *explicit* reservation on behalf of the *sharia* (as distinguished from the *nomos*); furthermore, the rulers in the best regime are the philosophers; hence the philosophers may lie to the multitude – or is this superfluous in the inferior regimes? Either Islam is the best regime then the philosophers must lie; or Islam is an inferior regime then the philosophers must lie for another reason – 64, 23–27: the dangerous situation of the philosophers.

[25] Plato's discussion of poetry: frequent application to the censure of Arabic poetry (32, 24; 33, 3; 34, 18) – cf. esp. 34, 13–14: the emphasis on *Averroes's* criticizing Arabic poets; next the demand for *paintings* of virtuous men: almost explicitly in Averroes's own name (34, 21–29); this leads to 35, 11–12 & 19–20: explicit criticism of "our time" by the standard of Plato's time (and not of early Islam) in regard to music.

[26] {12} Averroes *in his own name*: the virtuous city does not need the art of the judges, i.e., *fiqh*, at all; only bad cities need it; this is explicitly applied to "the cities of today" and allusively to "our time and the past" (37, 9–19). cf. 47, 4–28: particular or detailed laws are undesirable; many bringers of nomoi and shariai erred in this respect.

[27] Plato: the details regarding temples, prayers, etc. are to be determined by *prophecy*; this sort of things occur in all nomoi and shariai. [*This* is the superhuman part of the *sharia* (cf. 26, 16–18) – but not only of *this sharia* but of every nomos as well.]

[28] *Rule of philosophers* 81, 1–8 if "the first" is not available [and only then], obedience to his laws → *fiqh* → sep[eration] of political government and lawyers as it exists in many Muslim countries.

[29] *The problem of the exposure of infants and suicide.* People born with incurable defects which make them unfit for being useful to the city or people having become incurably unfit for the city: should they be killed (or kill themselves) as *Plato* says? Averroes knows that the issue is controversial; his decision is obscure (37, 20–38, 18).

[30] Averroes *in his own name no private property for the guardians*; "these cities" condemned with the view to this principle (41, 17–24; 42, 9 & 19–23) – no private property for *anyone* (43, 1–14) → 49, 1–7: manliness (and education in music and gymnastics) required of the *whole* vulgar – but: 49, 14 ff. – but: 60, 7–12.

[31] *Rule of philosophers* (48, 14–29).

[32] *Equality of the sexes,* esp. regarding war, government and {13} wisdom (52, 30–54, 20; esp. 53, 22–23) criticism of "some of the torot" and of[25] "these cities" with a[26] view to this principle (53, 24–26 & 54, 6–13).

[33] Difference between *the sharia* and the shariai or nomoi as well as Plato regarding intercourse or procreation is irrelevant (54, 21–26) – the women common to all men, this is different from "these cities" (55, 9–13).

[34] Incest between brothers and sisters, allusion to contrast to *sharia* (56, 11–12 & 16).

[35] *Absolute communism* is[27] *Plato's* view (57, 4) (but no[28] criticism of it) but Plato *proves* this view (57, 5; 57, 23–58, 14) → Averroes[29] accepts it as evidently sound *in his own name*. In this context he accepts the perpetually fixed number of citizens of the virtuous city without any polemics (56, 23). cf. 57, 6: many virtuous cities side by side. cf. 79, 24–25.

[36] *Second Treatise*

[37] Averroes *in his own name*: philosopher =[30] bringer of *sharia* (60, 22 & 24; 61, 11), i.e., no excess of *sharia* beyond reason and nature. It is left open whether the bringer of *sharia* must be a prophet (61, 17–19). Since rhetoric and practical science is implied in philosophy (61, 1–4), "prophet" can refer only to knowledge of the future (cf. 41, 1) or to details regarding prayers, sacrifices, etc. (47, 26).

---

[25] "of" is inserted by hand.
[26] "the" is crossed out and "a" is inserted by hand.
[27] "in" is crossed out and "is" inserted by hand,
[28] "no" is inserted by hand.
[29] "Aristotle" is crossed out and "Averroes" inserted by hand.
[30] "=" is inserted by hand.

[38] The difficulty: is there no vicious circle? virtuous city *presupposes* perfect philosophers who have been brought up within the virtuous city! No, perfect philosophers may choose that common law which no nation can help choosing and the peculiar {14} torot of the philosophers may not differ greatly from the human torot under which they live; under these conditions wisdom can be completed within the lifetime of the philosophers in question; these conditions are fulfilled in our time and in our torot. If the philosophers would rule for an *infinite* time (cf. 78, 26–29), the best regime would emerge (62, 25–63, 5).

[39] [1. Islam is a human torah not greatly different from the private torah of the philosophers; at the very least there is no significant excess of Islam over merely human laws (cf. 47, 24–28).

[40] 2. Private torot of philosophers essentially[31] different from the human torot.

[41] 3. "common law" =[32] minimum conditions of society ≠[33] human torot ≠[34] private torah of the philosophers (cf. my essay on Cuzari).[35]

[42] 4. best regime not in existence now nor was it ever in existence under Islam at any rate. cf. "now" עתה[36] in 63, 8 & 26.]

---

[31] "assertedly" is crossed out and "essentially" inserted by hand.
[32] "=" is inserted by hand.
[33] "≠" is inserted by hand.
[34] "≠" is inserted by hand.
[35] Strauss, "The Law of Reason in The Kuzari."
[36] "עתה" is inserted by hand.

Appendix B

Leo Strauss's Notes on the *Arabian Nights*

Editorial remarks: The following is the edited version of a typescript of eighteen pages entitled "1001 Nights" found in Leo Strauss Papers.[1] The typescript is corrected by pencil in Strauss's handwriting. There is another version of the same typescript which is a photocopy whose original could not be found.[2] The corrections of the second version are fewer and are by a different hand. Some of the corrections are only present in the first version of the typescript and absent in the second one: these discrepancies are indicated in the footnotes by SNAN 1 and SNAN 2; numbers in curly brackets, inserted by the editor, refer to the page numbers of the typescript; numbers in square brackets, also inserted by the editor, refer to the paragraph numbers of the typescript; numbers in parenthesis are in the original typescript and refer to the page and volume numbers of Littmann's translation;[3] underlined words are replaced by italics; crossed out words and handwritten insertions are mentioned in the footnotes; arrow symbol in the typescript, used for showing the logical consequence of ideas, is everywhere inserted by hand; Strauss's corrections of typographical errors have not been noted. The errors are responsibility of the editor.

---

[1] Leo Strauss Papers, box 20, folder 2, Special Collections Research Center, University of Chicago Library.
[2] Leo Strauss Papers, box 23, folder 13, Special Collections Research Center, University of Chicago Library.
[3] Littmann, *Die Erzählungen aus den Tausendundein Nächten.*

1001 NIGHTS

{1} [1] 1001 = 7 × 11 × 13. If one adds the two stories preceding the stories told by Shahrazad, 1003 =[4] 17 × 59. The overall suggestion: refutation of the nomos regarding inferiority of women; and: indictment of tyranny; and: how *jealousy* of a king[5] is appeased.

[2] *The Introductory story*: it is dangerous to deceive kings; it is not dangerous to deceive demons. The kings deceive the demon out of fear of the demon: they are compelled to deceive him. Both the demon and the kings are *jealous*. The number of deceptions practiced by the demon's wife: 570 (= 19 × 30) and 572 (= 13 × 11× 4).[6]

[3] *The donkey and the seer*: the man with the secret knowledge which he cannot reveal except at the danger of death – he is tempted to reveal it and hence to die but is saved by another piece of secret knowledge: of a rooster and 50 hens – of 51: the secret knowledge is knowledge of the language of *brutes*. The first piece of secret knowledge: the donkey is happy by doing nothing; his happiness is due to his silence on the *reason*[7] of his happiness; he is made miserable by the revelation of his secret. The master of the animals is said to be a peasant – in fact he is a merchant. (27).

[4] *The merchant*[8] *and the demon*: the merchant is saved from the demon who is set to kill him, through story tellers; certainly two of the three story tellers are also merchants. (Merchants are travelers.) The first story reminds of Abraham's sacrifice of Isaac: the *jealous* wife wishes that the father slaughter his own son; the son who is saved goes to India. Cf. 74: Allah is a jealous God. In both the first and second story the [human][9] revenge is much milder than the crime; but the she-demon wished a greater revenge than the brother of the treacherous brothers (the fellow-men); in the third story only the proper punishment of the adulterous wife but not of the slave. The three stories describe the transformation of men into brutes (cf. the language of brutes {2} in the preceding story); both stories of demons and of the transformations of men into brutes gradually disappear.

[5] *The fisherman and the demon*: these stories are told not as the preceding ones[10] in order to appease the demon but after the demon has

---

4   "=" is inserted by hand.
5   "of a king" is inserted by hand.
6   Two "=" are inserted by hand.
7   Underline not in SNAN 2.
8   "merchant" has a double underline, hence it is put in bold characters.
9   Square brackets are in the typescript and are inserted by hand.
10   "as the preceding ones" is inserted by hand.

been brought under control. The fisherman tells the demon the story of the vizier of King Junan to justify his action against the demon; fisher: demon = the sage[11] (who heals the king by his worldly wisdom): the king or the vizier – i.e., the story told parallels the story in which the story teller acts – the fisherman will not make the mistake of the sage. The story is partly told in the form of inserted stories, of the story told by the king and story told by the vizier. In the light of the events the vizier's suggestion amounts to this – vizier in the story : king in the story =[12] king and sage : vizier. The story telling wicked vizier brings it about that the king and the sage kill one another: *nothing happens to the story telling wicked vizier. /→ the vizier becomes the king/.* In the vizier's *story*[13] the wicked vizier tries to destroy the prince but since the vizier's ally betrays the vizier by asking the prince to pray to God, the vizier is destroyed – just as the real vizier wants to destroy the sage (of whom he is jealous). /the real vizier succeeds because he has no ally and the sage does not pray – the king is a fool/. But why does the wicked vizier succeed through telling a story of a wicked vizier and through extolling the virtue of prayer? /the wicked vizier is a prophet who denigrates his predecessors and the foolish king is the prophet's master/. First – fisher : demon = sage : king or vizier[14] (cf. 96). Then – fisher : demon = king : sage.

[6] The demon is a *heretic* (53 top) – through the fisherman who takes the risk of trusting the demon, the demon brings about the salvation of a prince and of a state which had been ruined by the prince's *adulterous wife who had preferred to him a most ugly negro slave,* a *leper-*/that adulterous wife =[15] the wicked vizier in the story told by the fisherman/- the wife believing in the {3} beauty of the ugly slave had transformed the people into fishes, the dumbest of all animals, and the fisherman is the enemy of the fishes.

[7] Whereas the sage refuses to tell a life-saving story because he is not free (69[16] bottom), the demon connects the same refusal based on the same ground with a request to be set free so that he can tell the story (73) and the fisherman sets him free without requiring the demon to tell his story (neither the demon nor the sage tell their stories),[17] to the benefit

---

[11] "=" is inserted by hand.
[12] "=" is inserted by hand.
[13] Underline not in SNAN 2.
[14] "=" is inserted by hand.
[15] "=" is inserted by hand.
[16] "9" is inserted by hand.
[17] Comma not in SNAN 2.

of the fisherman, the demon, and the ruined state. The sage does not *wish* to live /=[18] Socrates – the name of the king is Junan =[19] Greek – cf. 75/ /in Socrates' time the action of the fisherman was not yet possible or necessary/.

[8] The inserted story: the victory of the wicked vizier and the destruction of the king and the sage (Socrates).

[9] The frame story: through the heretical demon, destruction of the adulterous wife who loved the ugly and leprous negro slave and of that slave.

[10] *The porter and the three ladies* – the frame: wine drinking – paradise on earth[20] (105) – beauty and joy – graceful obscenity. Questions are forbidden (109) but the prohibition is transgressed: the three monks (former kings) tell their stories in order to escape capital punishment incurred because they asked the forbidden questions.

[11] Story of the first monk: a terrible divine punishment for incest and: an unpunished, successful act of treachery by a wicked vizier.

[12] Story of the second monk: a justly jealous demon transforms a sage who does not know philosophy and physics, into a monkey; right is on the side of the demon (142f., 155), the monk lies about him (160). In the two preceding stories (merchant-demon and fisherman-demon) the demons were not infinitely revengeful but could be appeased by story-telling or proof of superior cleverness. And: while the lover of the ugly negro slave transforms men into fishes, the demon here transforms the sage only into the external shape[21] of a monkey. The inserted story told originally under duress and now again as part of the whole story {4} under duress → demon : adulterer = envied good man : envious bad man (= monk), i.e., the demon who is a descendant from the devil himself and who denies Islam (157 bottom) is perfectly pious, befriended by good spirits. But in the light of the action: the jealous demon is envious and hence miserable /→ the sage would not hate the jealous God but pity him and forgive him/. The sage regains his human form by an act of treachery on the part of the king's daughter who knows 170 charms (154); that princess kills the demon and the demon kills her posthumously: just as the king Junan kills *the* sage and the sage kills the king posthumously → the demon = Socrates = envied good man – the fight between demon and

---

[18] "=" is inserted by hand.
[19] "=" is inserted by hand.
[20] Strikethrough not in SNAN 2.
[21] "shape" is inserted by hand.

princess to the benefit of the religious sage[22] ≠[23] the fight between king and Socrates to the benefit of the wicked vizier. /alliance between the perfectly just demon and the philosopher to the ruin of the wicked vizier and his master, the ugly negro slave, remains unspoken/.

[13] The story of the third monk: his salvation depends on his not mentioning the name of Allah – he mentions it and is punished for it (165f.) – apart from pronouncing the forbidden name, he raises forbidden questions and opens a forbidden door (176, 181) – the ten half-blind youths who had opened the forbidden door and were like him half-blinded for that reject him /but they had not pronounced the forbidden *name* – they never mention it/. The story confirms the truth of astrology (169ff.) → he is not punished for a killing decreed by the stars – /this is a different *world* than the world described in the stories of the first and second monk – cf. 162 top/.

[14] The story of the oldest sister: the 17th night – Allah's terrible revenge ≠[24] the demon's comparatively mild revenge ≠ the oldest sister has no desire for revenge at all. (Cf. the story of the second man in merchant-demon (41–45): there two brothers changed into dogs, here two sisters changed into she-dogs). A whole {5} city (including children and animals) transformed into stone by Allah's wrath (cf. the prince half-transformed into stone by his adulterous wife, the lover of the ugly leprous negro slave) for its unbelief – (they were[25] fire *worshippers*) – the son of the king of the pagans is the only one to escape thanks to the *treachery* of an old woman who was a Muslim in secret (194) /cf. the story of the treacherous vizier in fisherman-demon and the treacherous princess and the treacherous vizier in the present cluster of stories as well as the treacherous hags or old witches later on/.

[15] The story of the she-janitor: a story of terrible revenge brought on by a slanderess out of unfounded jealousy (cf. Allah's jealousy: 208); the human beings here do not kill nor infinitely punish /God is jealous either because He is not, or does not believe himself to be, infinitely attractive, and the reason for that is his hiddenness: He Himself is the ground of His jealousy./. /The terrible effects of God's jealousy come about through humans who are motivated by human jealousy and may or may not believe in God's jealousy/.

---

[22] "≠ the fight between king and Socrates to the benefit of the religious sage" is crossed out.
[23] "≠" is inserted by hand.
[24] "≠" is inserted by hand.
[25] "are" is crossed out and "were" inserted by hand.

[16] *The three apples*: murder out of unfounded jealousy. In order to save the life of his half-guilty negro slave from the wrath of his ruler, a vizier tells a story which ends happily. A merciful vizier tells a story of a merciful vizier who punishes his nephew senselessly and threatens him (without meaning it) with still greater punishment for something which is in no way a sin (281 bottom – 282 top) in order to find out something (285) which could have been found out without that inhuman threat. In the inserted story, two orthodox demons avert the catastrophe threatened by an angry ruler; through Allah's permission, one of these two demons is destroyed (255 bottom – 256 top) but this has no effect on the following events. /for the benefit of a negro slave who is indirectly responsible for a murder out of unfounded jealousy, a story is told of a merciful vizier and of orthodox demons and of Allah's permission (≠[26] infliction) of death of an orthodox demon – an orthodox version of the earlier story./.[27]

{6} [17] *The hunchback*. A tailor's wife kills a hunchbacked court jester in China ruled by a Muslim; three other men are brought to *believe* to have killed him: a Christian, a Muslim, and a Jew; all three tell stories told to them by Muslims who were mutilated; the most mutilated occurs in the Muslim's story. Only the Christian has acted without any guile (403) – he tells a story of a perfect and happy love; the Muslim: cruel punishment for nothing by his beloved, a slave girl, who thereafter becomes his wife; the Jew: terrible revenge out of jealousy, the revenge followed by life-long repentance – but thereafter a wholly unexpected compensation for the woman murdered out of jealousy (he gets the murdered wife's sister). The Muslim tailor is the socially lowest of the 4: a youth does not get the girl thanks to the loquacity and busybodiness of a barber who acted as a demagogue (360) and hence as a ruler of kings (352) although he belongs to a very low class, like *camel-drivers* (355) – contrary to the obvious fact he claims to be the silent one, a man of few words and unobtrusive, in contradistinction to his six brothers who are all mutilated, talk much and are impolite (363–66) → the barber is not mutilated (has no bodily defect). The stories of the six brothers: 1 | 2,3 | 4–6.[28] The Caliph laughs only at the end of 1, 3, and 6: central stories 2–3 → [the *two* brothers of the barber] [the barber denigrates his brothers just as the wicked vizier denigrated a wicked vizier] [no profession is mentioned in the case of the two brothers: they might have been barbers too].[29]

---

[26] "≠" is inserted by hand.
[27] "/." Is not in SNAN 2.
[28] Two vertical lines are inserted by hand.
[29] Four previous Square brackets are in the typescript and are inserted by hand.

Brothers 2–3 succeed in entering a house; the 2nd brother is called to a house where he is robbed of pleasures of *love*; the 3rd brother goes by himself into a house where he loses the little bit of money he had instead of getting *money*. At the end, the barber *resurrects the dead* court jester (405).

[18] *Nur ed Din*. The open transgression of the *law* in the presence of the Caliph compatible with perfect virtue and happiness.

[19] *Ghānim*: but it is indispensable that one should have the utmost respect for the honor of the *powerful Caliph*.

{7} [20] *Nur* – the son of a perfectly virtuous vizier, hurts the honor of his sultan (427, 446) by living together with a slave girl destined for the Sultan; he escapes to Baghdad, transgresses openly but gracefully the legal prohibition against wine drinking(434f.), his girl even seduces a pious old man into joining them in the transgression (436ff.); the Caliph vanquished by the beauty of Nur and his girl and especially by the beautiful singing of the girl, forgives them and makes Nur the king of his homeland. Nur cannot kill the wicked vizier who has driven him from his homeland, for he is impressed by the wicked vizier's verse to the effect that both he and Nur only acted according to their *nature* (459).

[21] *Ghanim* – a young *merchant* comes into mortal danger through three castrated negro slaves two of whom tell the story of their castration; the 2nd is more wicked than the 1st and the 3rd is the most wicked of all; only the 2nd has nothing to do with sex; his crime is that he is a terrible liar; the 1st is really innocent. Ghanim does not touch the girl, the beloved of the Caliph, out of sacred awe of the Caliph (481) or out of fear (482, 484); the Caliph would not have been able to discover Ghanim and the girl because the Caliph is unable to transgress the law or to overcome the fear of God (485, 486).

[22] *Omar and his sons* – an alliance between the Christian king of Constantinople and the Muslim king of Baghdad against the Christian king Hartub; the Christian seems to plan treachery against the Muslim (533). Sharkun, the son of the Muslim king meets on the campaign the paragon Christian girl Abriza, the daughter of Hartub, whose mother is an old hag whom Abriza loathes. Abriza does not betray Sharkun to the Christian knights, she is free from all religious fanaticism (518) but she refuses to go with Sharkun to the land of Islam because the Muslim men are lascivious (522), she has a perfect command of Arabic culture while Sharkun does not know Greek. Sharkun quotes to her an Arabic poem dispraising the holy war while praising the war with faire women (530; cf. the poem 639 center). She sides with Sharkun in his fight with the Christian knights and reveals to him the treachery of the Christian

king of Constantinople; she follows him to Baghdad where Sharkun's {8} father Omar disgracefully violates her (confirming her view of Muslims); on her flight home she is murdered by a treacherous negro slave.

[23] The adventures of Omar's daughter Nuzzath-as-Zamān, philosophically trained; her lecture on government: the king of faith (≠³⁰ the king who protects the holy – the latter in the center is also concerned with the things of the world, he is not necessarily a believer)(602; cf. the parallel 653 bottom – 654 top); cf. also her praise of a perfect pre-Islamic king of Persia (601, 603); a single truly just man is sufficient for a whole country (607f.) → no need for *many* just men. The account of her lectures takes seven nights – the lectures given by the Christian girls later on take six nights – altogether thirteen nights.

[24] Sharkun marries unknowingly his half-sister Nuzzath; they are shocked by their mortal sin; she bears him a daughter; they separate immediately; no further untoward consequences because the affair is kept secret. The story of the incest, unusually short, is told in the 68th (4×17) night (622f.).

[25] The old Christian witch, Abrizza's grandmother, murders Omar. Ban el nukum (Nuzzath's brother) becomes the Sultan; the old witch brings him five perfect Christian girls who pretend to be Muslims; the girls know philosophy and the stories of the past; the king is interested only in the latter (652); the five girls and the witch lecture on piety (667) (Cf. 662 para. 3 on the problem of piety); the instigator of those pious lectures is the unbelieving witch (700) who plans to ruin the king, the violator of her granddaughter.

[26] Holy war against the Christians; the description is full of savage hatred and invectives (≠³¹ the humane relation of Sharkun and Abrizza); the Muslims march off against Constantinople; marvelous victories of the Muslims but Constantinople is not conquered (which is indicated rather than said); Sharkun is killed through the treachery of the old witch; the king finds no comfort for the death of his brother except through stories (715). The vizier tells him a story into which a story is inserted – both are love stories – the frame story is one of happy love: {9} son and daughter of kings³² – the youth had only *heard* of the princess – the princess originally loathes men on the basis of a dream – the happy ending brought

---

³⁰ "≠" is inserted by hand.
³¹ "≠" is inserted by hand.
³² "a" is crossed out and "s" inserted by hand.

about by a wise vizier (≠[33] the prince and his father) (II 89, 85). Cf. Dan el nukum making a senile former worker the king of Damascus (II 140). The inserted story is one of *unhappy* love: merchant – a youth had *seen* the girl – a[34] girl who loves him but is not loved by him dies from grief – she is of perfect sweetness, overcomes her jealousy completely – does not use force or guile against him she unhappily loves – the youth is eventually castrated – he repents his unfaithfulness to the good girl he had deserted – the alternative would have been the satiety of fulfilled love (II 59) – cf. the praise of love in the poem II 30. Cf. the poem I 83: the complete atheistic loneliness of the unhappy lover (in the 130th night) → the uselessness of religious comfort as underlying the vizier's story telling here.

[27] In an entirely different context the witch who intends to kill the prince, tells him a most ridiculous story of a hashish eater who had a dream of approaching bliss and then a bitter awakening; i.e., she predicts his intended terrible fate to him, but then the witch's plan comes to naught.

[28] The end: the son of Omar and Abrizza who had become a *Muslim* had been brought up by his *Christian* grandfather (Hartub) as a Christian and the *Muslim* king *rule Baghdad jointly – nothing is said of that Christian's becoming a Muslim* – but a certain obscurity prevails (223–24).

[29] This is the first story in which Christianity-Islam is manifestly the theme. At the end of the story the first apparent change in the mood of Shechrazad's husband (224 bottom – 225 top).

[30] The king wants to hear stories of birds, of beings which fly *high* (244) – Schechrazad tells stories of birds, and other animals but no longer of metamorphoses: the stories must have been told by men who know the language of animals. The 1st story describes man from the brutes' point of view: all animals would live in {10} peace and freedom but for man's guile. The most frightened of the animals, the duck, alarms all other animals but is caught and killed by man. According to the she-peacock, the duck perished because alone of all creatures it had not praised God (239). The male peacock mentioned at the beginning of the story has dropped out completely: a female explanation of the fate of beings. The duck [which does not fly high and is the[35] pig among the birds][36] says: our danger comes from man. But the she-peacock says: our

---

[33] "≠" is inserted by hand.
[34] "the" is crossed out and "a" inserted by hand.
[35] "a" is crossed out and "the" inserted by hand.
[36] Two Square brackets are in the typescript and are inserted by hand.

danger comes from God. The story taken literally is nonsense: birds are killed also by other brutes, not only by men. But the story makes sense if retranslated into human terms (birds : men = men : God): the duck says that all evil comes from God and the she-peacock confirms this somehow. The she-peacock's assertion that praising God is sufficient for averting disaster is refuted by the story of the hermit and the doves. The story of the pious shepherd who is perfectly chaste (ascetic) and his male companion who is of extreme charity to beasts and birds (both live in the service to God) (to the jealous God who demands complete surrender to Him) and they do not even die (end of the story): *at this point, the king shows the first sign of repentance for his cruelty and jealousy.* The water bird and the turtle: the water bird sees a human corpse and believes that the man must have been a criminal [only criminals are killed: simple moralism; God is killed][37] – strikes up a friendship with a turtle – develops a doctrine of what befits the true man – *is killed, as it is said because it did not praise God*; the turtle is not killed. The wolf and the fox: the fox (the subject) warns the wolf (the king – 256 bottom) to be gentle to him lest man, the wily insidious being, might control the wolf; but the fox gets rid of the wolf by his own ingenuity. *The inserted story told by the fox to the wolf*: the stronger eats the weaker but *through God's action* dies from it. The mouse and the weasel (the central story) – the weasel arranges that the mouse be killed by man [*tracing* everything to God ~ doing everything through God].[38] The raven and the {11} cat: this edifying story of pure friendship is told at the request of the king; everything is done here by animals; the shepherd [God][39] hardly does more than looking at, whereas in the preceding unedifying story, man [God][40] is the actor.

[31] The animal stories = 146th–152nd nights = 7 nights. The next story (Abu ibn bakkar) = 153rd-169th nights = 17 nights.

[32] The story of a young prince falling in love with an odalisk of the ruler of the faithful and she with the young prince; they meet for a night; they become separated and each dies from grief. The caliph does not become jealous: because he loves the girl so much that he doesn't believe what is reported to him about her misconduct. [*A story of an unfaithful*

---

[37] Square brackets are in the typescript and are inserted by hand.
[38] Square brackets are in the typescript and are inserted by hand.
[39] Square brackets are in the typescript and are inserted by hand.
[40] Square brackets are in the typescript and are inserted by hand.

woman whose unfaithfulness is not believed by her husband, is told to a jealous king.][41]

[33] Kamr az-zamān. In this story 2.65 pages on the average for a night; in the preceding stories 6.42 pages on the average for a night.

[34] A prince who is *very pious* hates women because of their faithlessness; a believing she-demon from the race of the devil but a believer together with a cursed he-demon brings him together with a princess who is less chaste than the prince (391–92) but *very intelligent* (373); she does not wish to marry him because she does not wish to be ruled by a man (375): the *believing* she-demon admires the *pious* prince; the *cursed* he-demon admires the *intelligent* princess. Prince and princess marry and are separated by some accident; the princess must pretend to be a man and marries a princess to whom she reveals her sex. The prince comes to a city of the Magians. They are reunited; the prince marries also princess number 2 and has two wives, gets a son from each; each wife tries to deceive him with a son of the other wife → the prince's view of women was true (480.f, 484, 490) – the two wives behave like Potiphar's wife, the sons are driven into the wilderness, one of the sons falls into the hands of fire-worshippers and the other falls under the spell of a woman who expresses pagan feelings (508f.), is compelled to kill her; son number 1 converts the daughter of the Magian who keeps him prisoner and tortures {12} him, to Islam; eventually he converts that girl's father too and everything is forgiven. But nothing is done to the faithless wives and the Magians are tolerated. *The king is more pleased with this story which includes the account of the unpunished faithless wives (569) than with any previous story.*

[35] The inserted story. The caliph forgives and reunites the young couple, the male part of which had entered his harem to recover the girl who had been spirited away there – the central reason: the lover and the beloved were in his house and in his power (559) [application to God obvious][42].

[36] *Ala ed-din abu esch-shamāt* – twenty-one nights. An unheard of remark of Shechrazad's sister (580 top) at the beginning of the 252nd night. A jealous old wife accused by her old husband of sterility tells him that he is sterile and advises him as to what he should do to improve his semen [she did not wish to have a child nor did her husband hitherto];[43] the child born against all expectations, brought up in strict isolation out of

---

fear of the evil eye – the impossibilities: after forty years of marriage she is still menstruating and the new-born babe looks like a one year old (572f.). The young boy sees how foolish his parents are; owing to his silly upbringing he himself is easily fooled, by a Magian who pretends to be a Muslim, a wicked pederast (581) but[44] is infinitely better than the Arabs of the desert, he does not kill[45] anyone (592f.); the boy's father is opposed to traveling (584). In Baghdad he gets a marvelous wife and becomes a favorite of the caliph; his wife dies but in 625f. the wife seems to be still alive as a mistress of the caliph ?? He is disgraced and condemned to be hanged. But through a ruse a heretic who is also a criminal is hanged in his stead; he flies with a friend, on the flight they kill two Jews; a heretic tries to kill the caliph and is executed for this. Ala el din is captured by Christians and brought to Genoa together with forty other Muslims, the latter are executed by the Christians, he is saved by an old woman for service in the church, but the old woman tells him how he can force others to do the work for him. His wife has lived all the time with a Christian princess who was served by {13} a she-demon who has taken on the shape of his wife (was buried in the latter's stead); the wife herself was brought by a mighty demon to Genoa; the princess was predestined to become the wife of Ala el din; she was a secret Muslim; her father refuses to become a Muslim and is killed by Ala el din who returns with his two wives to Egypt [a stupidly fantastic and very pro-Islamic story – Schechrazad's king does not react].[46]

[[Volume III]][47]

[37] The king expresses his pleasure with the story told and asks her to continue; Schechrazad will tell stories of the men of generosity (84 bottom – 85 top). The 1st story of a *pagan* Arab (sculptures of girls) (85–86); the 2nd story of an early Muslim famous for his generosity; → generosity not specifically Islamic, no reference to anything Islamic in the first two stories. The 4th story has nothing to do with generosity but with the Muslim conquest of Andalus and with the Muslim's *finding* of wealth and *science* in the conquered lands → still less is science specifically Islamic. The 5th story: the moral superiority of a young Bedouin to a Caliph.

---

44 "he" is crossed out.
45 "hurt" is crossed out.
46 Square brackets are in the typescript and are inserted by hand.
47 Square brackets are in the typescript and are inserted by hand.

6th story: the nobility of character of a poor negro and also of a deposed Caliph as well as of the ruling Caliph. 7th story (277th – 279th night – 277th night extremely short) someone believes to have discovered the paradise on earth, an extremely beautiful but uninhabited city; it was built by a ruler of the whole earth who lived more than 300 years and was an unbeliever ruling over unbelievers in imitation of the paradise in the beyond; Allah destroyed that ruler and all the people with him. 8th story: contains a reminder by Schechrazad of the fact that her fate is still uncertain; the Caliph's bride is praised more highly than the Caliph. 9th story: a beautiful wife sleeps out of jealousy with a dirtiest and most ill-smelling man. 10th story: a man who imitates the Caliph perfectly, in some respects superior to any Caliph (136 top), is particularly generous (141), he only played the Caliph in order to reach his goal, i.e., to get back his wife; his wife {14} had revered him like a prophet or more than the prophet (147) but had rejected and tormented him out of unfounded jealousy [a true prophet rejected by his admiring wife had to become a false Caliph, a savage killer or at least threatening with death (151) in order to regain his rank].[48] The stories told in each night here are particularly short. 11th story: two impudent liars, for this very reason scolded as being Manicheans by kadi. 12th story: *parody of fiqh – here for the 1st time the author addresses the reader.* 14th story: the story of a man whom a Caliph had crucified out of jealousy (cf. 195 para. 1 beginning). 15th story: 172 bottom – 173 top. The fate of Schechrazad is still as undecided as it was at the beginning, as the king makes clear → the 15th story is a story of demons and metamorphoses – in order to arouse the king's interest. 16th and 17th story: a generous family of which the Caliph was jealous.

[38] The man from Yemen and his six slave girls: note the change of order, 1st yellow and black and then yellow and brown – change in the repetition regarding the yellow (dropping of the prophet) (293) – special praise of the brown one (294 bottom) who does not refer to the Koran, nor does the slim one whereas the other four refer to the Koran (cf. 284).

[39] P.409: *the counter-religion of love* = a frequently recurring theme. The stories on 526ff. seem to have this connection: asceticism (526–33) – falling in love on hearsay (533–35) – the absurdity of asceticism (536–37) – the fantastic story of the bird Ruch, stories of unhappy lovers. Cf. 589 bottom – 590 top on secrecy; 623 para.2–625 tyranny, human or divine (cf. Machiavelli Disc. I 26).

---

[48] Square brackets are in the typescript and are inserted by hand.

[40] *The slave girl Tavaddud*: a fantastic account of philosophy – at the end (696) a long address of Schechrazad to the king on the liberality of kings which has disappeared.

[41] *3 stories of the angel of death* (697ff.) – 1. Islamic – a pious man longs for death to see God, contrasted with a king 2. Islamic – only a God forgetting king 3. Jewish – a wicked Jewish king goes to hell; the kings are all stupid and wicked. {15} Immediately afterward (704) Alexander the Great confronted by a cynic wise king[49] (≠ angel of death) who teaches hell and paradise after death – Alexander neither stupid nor wicked. Immediately thereafter (706) a wise old Persian king → *the 2nd long address of Schechrazad to her king* to the effect that religion depends on government – followed first by a Jewish and then by an Islamic pious story, then by a story of a wonderfully pious negro slave, then by a Jewish pious story, etc.

[42] For the Queen of Serpents see my references in III 812.

[[Volume IV]][50]

[43] P.115: the beginning of the speech of the narrator is the end of a night's tale of Schechrazad (161).

[44] *Sindbad* – the central story – a pagan people (145) – cannibals; they are apparently Muslim people with the custom of burying the surviving spouse alive together with the dead spouse – Sindbad becomes a murderer.

[45] Messingstadt – preaches unqualifiedly world-denial, meditatio mortis – but cf. 258: Solomon (≠ Mohammed).

[46] Ruse of women – i.e., Schechrazad's own doings (cf. 267 and 297) but ruse of women only in stories # 1, 2, 6, 9, 11, 12, 17, and 22. Note that this story contains harmless repetitions of some stories from the 1st section.

[47] *Dshaudar*: the last and decisive test is incest with mother.

[48] *Adshib and Gharib*: the whole world is made Islamic (Abrahamitic) long before Mohammed by war and with the help of armies of demons. Contrast with the next story (Utba and Raija) which is very short: see the central poem (619), and the story of[51]

[49] *El Mausidi and the devil*: a very attractive description of the devil (645–49).

[[Volume V]][52]

[50] 1st story: the impotence of kings vis-à-vis love; the kings' complete dependence on their servants – these are frequently recurring themes.

[51] 4th story: contains a *non-public* story (225–26) which was *written* in the {16} first place – of a pagan king (228) but: 230 – God's revelation to Solomon (231) the pagans become Muslims (235–237). Contains an account of a vizier (≠ king) who conducts himself prudently like Odysseus with the Cyclops, etc.; the vizier (≠ king) does not have a marvelous ring from King Solomon; the whole adventure of the king and the vizier caused by the thoughtlessness of king Solomon (295) or through his complete indifference (305 bottom – 306 top).

[52] 5th story: it is not said which book Hasan read (316); he is taught the best of all arts, i.e., the art of making gold, a *dangerous* art (319f.), a *non-public* art (321) by a fire worshipper (325) who cheats and torments Hasan.

[53] 6th story: a monkey predicts to a fisherman that if he persuades a rich Jew to say certain things, the fisherman will become very rich and the Jew very poor (510–511) – the rich Jew says the words in question (in this connection: complete indifference of the fisherman to the Jew becoming a Muslim: 515) but nothing happens; by a series of accidents the fisherman becomes incredibly rich but nothing is said about the Jew becoming poor.

[54] 7th story: a married Jewish woman's adultery with a Christian (574, 582); in order to escape punishment for her crime, she pretends to be a Muslim (604); she becomes a Muslim; four kadis promise her their help against the Jew and to marry her; her husband is humiliated and jailed but the woman deceives the kadis who die from sorrow; the Jew is freed from jail; on her way home the woman stops in a monk's convent where all forty monks try to seduce her; she regains her lover who also becomes a Muslim and she arranges that her husband is buried alive [a victory of wicked love presented as victory of Islam].[53]

[55] 8th story: Nur transgresses the Islamic law re wine (639); in his drunkenness he beats his father and deprives him of one eye; he flees to Alexandria where he falls in love with a Frankish slave girl who had become a Muslim and who was the daughter of a Frankish king; while being drunk he sells her to the one-eyed vizier of the Frankish king who takes her back to her father. Nur cannot fight just as he has no brains

---

[52] Square brackets are in the typescript and are inserted by hand.
[53] Square brackets are in the typescript and are inserted by hand.

nor self-control whereas the Frankish princess is a marvelously {17} courageous fighter and killer; she kills her three brothers in single combat and escapes with Nur to Muslim lands; she abjures all connections with Christianity and her people and family [a triumph of Islam, in fact a triumph of love – Islam *used* for such a triumph – the opposite (i.e., the use of Christianity for this purpose) is equally possible].54

[56] 9th story: a Muslim falls in love with a Christian woman in the then Christian Akko but out of fear of hell abstains from intercourse with her (760); after the Muslim conquest of Akko, she is taken prisoner, bought by a Muslim, and becomes a Muslim; her Muslim lover even gets back the money he had spent on her while she was the wife of a Christian knight in Akko. [The whole story presupposes that she did not love her Christian husband.]55

[57] Tenth story: a young Muslim who had become poor, sells his beloved, his slave-girl, to a noble Muslim; he does not commit suicide out of fear of hell; he becomes reunited with her and again wealthy thanks to the generosity of that noble Muslim. [56also a story of a reward for Muslim piety but it also presupposes that the man and the woman love one another passionately57].

[[Volume VI]]58

[58] 1st story: the necessary conflict between this world and the next – men cannot be just while living in this life (49–51); the contradistinction between reason and the Sharia (53–54; cf. 65 top); 135: this teaching of a 12-year-old boy (+ terror of enemies) achieves what the boy's wise father and philosophy did not achieve.

[59] 3rd story: the absurdity of those who believe in another better life and weep when someone they love dies; those free from that absurdity, i.e. who draw the conclusion from belief in better life, live in nakedness and promiscuity (208).

[60] 4th story *from end*: story of *apparent* infidelity of a sultan's mistress.

---

54 Square brackets are in the typescript and are inserted by hand.
55 Square brackets are in the typescript and are inserted by hand.
56 Square brackets are in the typescript and are inserted by hand.
57 "properly" is crossed out and "passionately" inserted by hand.
58 Square brackets are in the typescript and are inserted by hand.

[61] 3rd story *from end*: a dervish who sings very impure songs but proves to be of incorruptible chastity – and: the successful deception and ruin of a husband by his wife with a bitter end for the wife – contrasted with the adulterer's sister who does not even remarry after her husband's death.

{18} [62] 2nd story *before the last* – transformation into *stones* of a *pagan* city by Allah; the single survivor, a most beautiful princess who became a Muslim; transformation into *dogs* of the *treacherous* two brothers by a she-ghost out of gratitude to the 3rd brother who had saved the she-ghost from disgrace; the Caliph demands that the two brothers be no longer punished but restored and that they be forgiven; but they do not deserve to be forgiven. The beautiful princess commits suicide when two brothers throw the decent 3rd brother into the sea.

[63] Last story: a poor shoe repairer who is so gentle that he must run away from his vicious wife; he learns to give away other people's money which he gets by telling the untrue story that his caravan will come soon (589). He believes those untruths in his simplicity (589); he marries the king's daughter and confesses his lies to his wife who for sheer shame helps him with her money so that he can make his lies true; by a lucky accident he finds a ring which makes him the master of a spirit who procures him everything he wants through the ring, yet his wife gets possession of the ring and does not give it to her husband or her father (cf. Schechrazad who is wiser than her father and her husband). The ring is so powerful that its possession endangers the survival of Islam; the princess alone insures the survival of Islam (633, 634). The princess dies. His abominable 1st wife finds him: he *forgives* her and lives to *repent* it (cf. 639) – out of piety (640 bottom – 641 top) he takes off the ring and would have been destroyed by his first wife but for the prompt action of his 7-year-old young son from his second wife.

Appendix C

Table of Concordance of the *Arabian Nights*

The following table of concordance is provided to make Strauss's notes on the *Arabian Nights*, available in this volume as Appendix B, more accessible to the readers. In this table, story numbers and titles are borrowed from *Encyclopedia* and follow Burton's edition. The following abbreviations are used:

Encyclopedia   Ulrich Marzolph and Richard van Leeuwen, *The Arabian Nights: An Encyclopedia* (Santa Barbara, CA: ABC-CLIO, 2004).

Burton   Richard F. Burton, *Arabian Nights with Introduction and Explanatory Notes*, 16 vols. (Beirut: Khayat, 1966).

SNAN   Appendix B.

Mahdi   Husain Haddawy, *The Arabian Nights: Based on the Text Edited by Muhsin Mahdi* (London: W. W. Norton and Company, 1990). References are by page numbers.

Lyons   Malcolm C. Lyons, Ursula Lyons, and Robert Irwin, *The Arabian Nights: Tales of 1,001 Nights*, 3 vols. (London: Penguin Books, 2010). References are by the volume and page numbers.

Littmann   Enno Littmann, *Die Erzählungen aus den Tausendundein Nächten. Vollständige Ausgabe in Sechs Bänden. Zum ersten Mal nach dem arabischen Urtext der Calcuttaer Ausgabe vom Jahre 1939 übertragen von Enno Littmann. Einleitung von Hugo von Hofmannsthal* (Wiesbaden: Insel-Verlag, 1953). References are by the volume and page numbers.

No.	Story	SNAN	Lyons	Mahdi	Littmann
1	Shahriyar and His Brother	1, 2	I.3	5	I.19–26, VI.644–46
2	The Bull and the Ass	3	I.7	15	I.27–29
3	The Merchant and His Wife	3	I.8	18	I.29–31
4	The Trader and the Jinnī	4	I.10	21	I.32–48
5	The First Shaykh's Story	4	I.12	27	I.35–40
6	The Second Shaykh's Story	4	I.15	31	I.41–45
7	The Third Shaykh's Story	4	I.18		I.46–48
8	The Fisherman and the Jinnī	5, 9	I.19	36	I.48–96
9	King Yūnān and the Sage Dūbān	5, 8	I.25	44	I.56–72
10	King Sindbād and His Falcon	46	I.28		I.62–65
11	The Husband and the Parrot	46		50	
12	The Prince and the Ogress	5	I.30	52	I.65–66
13	The Ensorcelled Prince	6,7,9	I.41	68	I.83–96
14	The Porter and the Three Ladies of Baghdad	10	I.50	80	I.97–214
15	The First Qalandar's Tale	11	I.66	104	I.121–31
16	The Second Qalandar's Tale	12	I.76	111	I.131–62
17	The Envier and the Envied	12	I.79	122	I.144–47
18	The Third Qalandar's Tale	13	I.90	138	I.162–85
19	The Eldest Lady's Tale	14	I.106	162	I.187–99
20	The Tale of the Portress	15	I.113	171	I.199–214
21	The Three Apples	16	I.126	181	I.214–91
22	Nūr al-Dīn 'Alī and His Son Badr al-Dīn Hasan	16	I.129	189	I.224–91
23	The Hunchback's Tale	16	I.173	248	I.292–406

No.	Story	SNAN	Lyons	Mahdi	Littmann
24	The Nazarene Broker's Story	16	I.178	258	I.300–18
25	The Reeve's Tale	16	I.189	275	I.318–31
26	The Tale of the Jewish Doctor	16	I.197	287	I.331–43
27	Tale of the Tailor	16	I.205	300	I.343–406
28	The Barber's Tale of Himself	16	I.217	320	I.363–402
29	The Barber's Tale of His First Brother	16	I.219	323	I.366–71
30	The Barber's Tale of His Second Brother	16	I.223	328	I.372–77
31	The Barber's Tale of His Third Brother	16	I.226	332	I.377–381
32	The Barber's Tale of His Fourth Brother	16	I.228	335	I.381–85
33	The Barber's Tale of His Fifth Brother	16	I.231	340	I.385–96
34	The Barber's Tale of His Sixth Brother	16	I.237	349	I.396–402
35	Nūr al-Dīn 'Alī and Anīs al-Jalīs	18, 20	I.244	416	I.406–60
36	Ghānim ibn Ayyūb	19, 21	I.278		I.460–500
37	Tale of the First Eunuch, Bukhayt	21	I.282		I.465–66
38	Tale of the Second Eunuch, Kāfūr	21	I.283		I.467–73
39	'Umar ibn al-Nu'mān and His Sons Sharrkān and Daw' al-Makān	22, 23, 24, 25, 26, 28, 29	I.304		I.500–766, II.7–224
40	Tāj al-Mulūk and the Princess Dunyā	26	I.475		II.7–133
41	'Azīz and 'Azīza	26	I.489		II.25–79
42	The Hashish Eater	27	I.594		II.193–95
43	Hammād the Badawī		I.605		II.211–25
44	The Birds and Beasts and the Carpenter	30, 31	I.613		II.225–39
45	The Hermits	30, 31	I.621		II.239–40
46	The Water-fowl and the Tortoise	30, 31	I.624		II.244–48

(*continued*)

No.	Story	SNAN	Lyons	Mahdi	Littmann
47	The Wolf and the Fox	30, 31	I.627		II.249–68
48	The Falcon and the Partridge	30, 31	I.632		II.257–58
49	The Mouse and the Ichneumon	30, 31	I.639		II.268–70
50	The Cat and the Crow	30, 31	I.640		II.270–71
51	The Fox and the Crow	30, 31	I.641		II.272–80
52	The Flea and the Mouse	30, 31	I.642		II.273–76
53	The Saker and the Birds	30, 31	I.644		II.277–78
54	The Sparrow and the Eagle	30, 31	I.645		II.278–80
55	The Hedgehog and the Wood-pigeons	30, 31	I.645		II.280–84
56	The Merchant and the Two Sharpers		I.647		II.283–84
57	The Thief and His Monkey		I.648		II.284–86
58	The Foolish Weaver	30, 31	I.648		II.285–86
59	The Sparrow and the Peacock	30, 31	I.649		II.286–89
60	'Alī ibn Bakkār and Shams al-Nahār	31, 32	I.650	356	II.289–357
61	Qamar al-Zamān and Budūr	33, 34	I.693		II.357–569
62	Niʿma and Nuʿm	35	I.808		II.530–61
63	'Alā' al-Dīn Abu 'l-Shāmāt	36	I.832		II.569–658
64	Hātim of the Tribe of Tayy	37	I.884		III.85–86
65	Maʿn ibn Zā'ida	37	I.886		III.87
66	Maʿn ibn Zā'ida and the Badawī	37			III.88–90
67	The City of Labtayt	37	I.888		III.90–92
68	The Caliph Hishām and the Arab Youth	37	I.889		III.93–95
69	Ibrāhīm ibn al-Mahdī and the Barber-surgeon	37	I.891		III.96–107
70	The City of Many-columned Iram	37	I.898		III.108–15
71	Ishāq of Mosul	37	I.903		III.115–23

No.	Story	SNAN	Lyons	Mahdi	Littmann
72	The Sweep and the Noble Lady	37	I.908		III.124–30
73	The Mock Caliph	37	I.912		III.130–55
74	'Alī the Persian	37	I.928, II.3		III.155–60
75	Hārūn al-Rashīd and the Slave-girl and the Imām Abū Yūsuf	37	II.6		III.160–63
76	The Lover Who Feigned Himself a Thief	37	II.8		III.164–69
77	Ja'far the Barmakid and the Bean-seller	37	II.11		III.169–72
78	Abū Muhammad Hight Lazybones	37	II.13		III.172–95
79	Yahyā ibn Khālid with Mansūr	37	II.27		III.195–99
80	Yahyā ibn Khālid with a Man Who Forged a Letter in His Name	37	II.29		III.199–204
81	Caliph al-Ma'mūn and the Strange Scholar	37	II.32		III.204–07
82	'Alī Shār and Zumurrud	37	II.33		III.207–58
83	The Loves of Jubayr ibn 'Umayr and the Lady Budur	37	II.69		III.258–80
84	The Man of al-Yaman and His Six Slave-girls	38	II.83		III.280–98
85	Hārūn al-Rashīd and the Damsel and Abū Nuwās		II.96		III.298–304
86	The Man Who Stole the Dish of Gold		II.100		III.305–09
87	The Sharper of Alexandria and the Chief of Police		II.103		III.309–11
88	Al-Malik al-Nāsir and the Three Chiefs of Police		II.104		III.312–17
89	The Story of the Chief of Police of Cairo				III.312–14
90	The Story of the Chief of the Būlāq Police				III.315–16

(continued)

No.	Story	SNAN	Lyons	Mahdi	Littmann
91	The Chief of the Old Cairo Police				III.316–17
92	The Thief and the Shroff				III.317–19
93	The Chief of the Qūs Police and the Sharper		II.109		III.319–21
94	Ibrāhīm ibn al-Mahdī and the Merchant's Sister		II.110		III.321–26
95	The Woman Whose Hands Were Cut Off for Giving Alms to the Poor		II.113		III.326–28
96	The Devout Israelite		II.114		III.329–30
97	Abū Hassān al-Ziyādī and the Khorasan Man		II.115		III.331–35
98	The Poor Man and His Friend in Need		II.118		III.335–36
99	The Ruined Man Who Became Rich Again through a Dream		II.119		III.337–38
100	Caliph al-Mutawakkil and His Concubine Mahbūba		II.120		III.339–41
101	Wardān the Butcher		II.122		III.341–47
102	The King's Daughter and the Ape		II.125		III.347–50
103	The Ebony Horse		II.127		III.350–85
104	Uns al-Wujūd and al-Ward fī 'l-Akmām		II.148		III.385–425
105	Abū Nuwās with the Three Boys		II.177		III.425–31
106	'Abdallāh ibn Ma'mar		II.181		III.432–33
107	The Lovers of the Banū 'Udhra		II.182		III.433–35
108	The Vizier of al-Yaman and His Young Brother		II.183		III.435–37
109	The Loves of the Boy and Girl at School		II.184		III.437–38
110	Al-Mutalammis and His Wife Umayma		II.185		III.439–40

No.	Story	SNAN	Lyons	Mahdi	Littmann
111	The Caliph Hārūn al-Rashīd and Queen Zubayda in the Bath		II.186		III.440–42
112	Hārūn al-Rashīd and the Three Poets		II.187		III.442–44
113	Musʿab ibn al-Zubayr and ʿĀʾisha bint Talha		II.189		III.444–46
114	Abu ʾl-Aswad and His Slave-girl		II.190		III.446
115	Hārūn al-Rashīd and the Two Slave-girls		II.190		III.446–47
116	The Caliph Hārūn al-Rashīd and the Three Slave-girls		II.190		III.447–48
117	The Miller and His Wife		II.191		III.448–50
118	The Simpleton and His Sharper		II.192		III.450–52
119	The Qāḍī Abū Yūsuf with Hārūn al-Rashīd and Queen Zubayda		II.193		III.452–53
120	The Caliph al-Ḥākim and the Merchant		II.194		III.488–89
121	King Kisrā Anūshirwān and the Village Damsel		II.195		III.489–91
122	The Water-carrier and the Goldsmith's Wife		II.196		III.492–94
123	Khusraw and Shīrīn and the Fisherman		II.197		III.494–96
124	Yahyā ibn Khālid the Barmakid and the Poor Man		II.198		III.496–97
125	Muhammad al-Amīn and the Slave-girl		II.199		III.497–99
126	The Sons of Yahyā ibn Khālid and Saʿīd ibn Sālim al-Bāhilī		II.200		III.499–501
127	The Woman's Trick against Her Husband		II.201		III.501–02
128	The Devout Woman and the Two Wicked Elders		II.202		III.508–09
129	Jaʿfar the Barmakid and the Old Badawī		II.203		III.510–11

(*continued*)

No.	Story	SNAN	Lyons	Mahdi	Littmann
130	The Caliph 'Umar ibn al-Khaṭṭāb and the Young Badawī		II.204		III.512–18
131	The Caliph al-Ma'mūn and the Pyramids of Egypt		II.208		III.518–20
132	The Thief and the Merchant		II.209		III.521–23
133	Masrūr the Eunuch and Ibn al-Qāribī		II.211		III.523–26
134	The Devotee Prince		II.213		III.526–33
135	The Unwise Schoolmaster Who Fell in Love by Report	39	II.217		III.533–35
136	The Foolish Dominie	39	II.219		III.536–37
137	The Illiterate Who Set Up for a Schoolmaster	39	II.219		III.537–39
138	The King and the Virtuous Wife	39	II.221		III.539–41
139	'Abd al-Rahmān the Maghribī's Story of the Rukhkh	39	II.222		III.541–43
140	'Adī ibn Zayd and the Princess Hind		II.223		III.543–47
141	Di'bil al-Khuzā'ī		II.225		III.547–50
142	Ishāq of Mosul and the Merchant		II.227		III.550–55
143	The Three Unfortunate Lovers		II.231		III.556–57
144	How Abū Hasan Brake Wind				
145	The Lovers of the Banū Tayy		II.232		III.558–59
146	The Mad Lover		II.233		III.560–62
147	The Prior Who Became a Moslem		II.235		III.562–68
148	The Loves of Abū 'Isā and Qurrat al-'Ayn		II.239		III.568–77
149	Al-Amīn ibn al-Rashīd and Ibrāhīm ibn al-Mahdī		II.245		III.577–78

No.	Story	SNAN	Lyons	Mahdi	Littmann
150	Al-Fath ibn Khāqān		II.246		III.578–79
151	The Man's Dispute with the Learned Woman		II.246		III.579–90
152	Abū Suwayd and the Pretty Old Woman		II.254		III.590–91
153	The Emir ʿAlī ibn Tāhir and the Girl Muʾnis		II.254		III.591
154	The Woman Who Had a Boy and the Other Who Had a Man to Lover		II.255		III.592–93
155	ʿAlī the Cairene and the Haunted House		II.255		III.593–622
156	The Pilgrim Man and the Old Woman	39	II.273		III.622–25
157	Tawaddud	40	II.275		III.626–96
158	The Angel of Death with the Proud King	41	II.321		III.697–99
159	The Angel of Death and the Rich King	41	II.322		III.699–702
160	The Angel of Death and the King of the Children of Israel	41	II.324		III.702–03
161	Alexander and a Certain Tribe of Poor Folk	41	II.325		III.704–06
162	The Righteousness of King Anūshirwān	41	II.326		III.706–07
163	The Jewish Qādī and His Pious Wife	41	II.327		III.708–12
164	The Shipwrecked Woman and Her Child	41	II.330		III.712–15
165	The Pious Black Slave	41	II.332		III.715–19
166	The Devout Tray-maker and His Wife		II.335		III.720–25
167	Al-Hājjāj and the Pious Man		II.338		III.725–27
168	The Blacksmith Who Could Handle Fire without Hurt		II.340		III.727–31
169	The Devotee to Whom Allāh Gave a Cloud for Service		II.343		III.731–36

(continued)

No.	Story	SNAN	Lyons	Mahdi	Littmann
170	The Moslem Champion and the Christian Damsel		II.345		III.736–43
171	The Christian King's Daughter and the Moslem		II.350		III.743–47
172	The Prophet and the Justice of Providence		II.353		III.747–49
173	The Ferryman of the Nile and the Hermit		II.354		III.749–51
174	The Island King and the Pious Israelite		II.356		III.752–58
175	Abu 'l-Hasan and Abū Jaʿfar the Leper		II.360		III.758–62
176	Queen of the Serpents	42	II.363		III.762–823, IV.7–97
177	The Adventures of Bulūqiyā		II.367		III.771–823, IV.7–80
178	The Story of Jānshāh		II.390		III.810–23, IV.7–74
179	Sindbād the Seaman	44	II.453		IV.97–208
180	The City of Brass	45	II.518		IV.208–59
181	The Craft and Malice of Women	46	II.546		IV.259–371
182	The King and His Vizier's Wife	46	II.547		IV.262–65
183	Story of the Confectioner, His Wife, and the Parrot	46	II.549		IV.265–67
184	The Fuller and His Son	46	II.550		IV.268
185	The Rake's Trick against the Chaste Wife	46	II.551		IV.268–71
186	The Miser and the Loaves of Bread	46	II.552		IV.271–72
187	The Lady and Her Two Lovers	46	II.553		IV.272–74
188	The King's Son and the Ogress	46	II.554		IV.274–78
189	The Drop of Honey	46	II.556		IV.278–79
190	The Woman Who Made Her Husband Sift Dust	46	II.557		IV.279–81

No.	Story	SNAN	Lyons	Mahdi	Littmann
191	The Enchanted Spring	46	II.558		IV.281–89
192	The Vizier's Son and the Hammām-keeper's Wife	46	II.562		IV.289–91
193	The Wife's Device to Cheat Her Husband	46	II.563		IV.291–97
194	The Goldsmith and the Cashmere Singing-girl	46	II.567		IV.297–302
195	The Man Who Never Laughed	46	II.570		IV.303–12
196	The King's Son and the Merchant's Wife	46	II.576		IV.313–15
197	The Page Who Feigned to Know the Speech of Birds	46	II.578		IV.316–19
198	The Lady and Her Five Suitors	46	II.580		IV.319–29
199	The Three Wishes	46	II.587		IV.329–31
200	The Stolen Necklace	46	II.588		IV.331–33
201	The Two Pigeons	46	II.589		IV.333–34
202	Prince Bahrām and the Princess al-Datmā	46	II.589		IV.334–40
203	The House with the Belvedere	46	II.593		IV.340–52
204	The King's Son and the 'Ifrīt's Mistress	46	II.601		IV.353–57
205	The Sandal-wood Merchant and the Sharpers	46	II.603		IV.357–63
206	The Debauchee and the Three-year-old Child	46	II.607		IV.364–65
207	The Stolen Purse	46	II.608		IV.365–68
208	The Fox and the Folk	46			IV.369–70
209	Jūdar and His Brethren	47	II.610		IV.371–431
210	Gharīb and 'Ajīb	48	II.648		IV.432–616
211	'Utba and Rayyā	48	II.757		IV.616–23
212	Hind bint al-Nu'mān and al-Hajjāj		II.762		IV.623–26
213	Khuzayma ibn Bishr and 'Ikrima al-Fayyād		II.764		IV.626–33
214	Yūnus the Scribe and the Caliph Walīd ibn Sahl		II.768		IV.633–38

(continued)

No.	Story	SNAN	Lyons	Mahdi	Littmann
215	Hārūn al-Rashīd and the Arab Girl		II.771		IV.638–41
216	Al-Asmaʿī and the Girls of Basra		II.773		IV.641–45
217	Ibrāhīm of Mosul and the Devil	49	II.776		IV.645–49
218	The Lovers of the Banū ʿUdhra		II.779		IV.650–59
219	The Badawī and His Wife		II.784		IV.660–66
220	The Lovers of Basra		II.789		IV.667–73
221	Ishāq of Mosul and His Mistress and the Devil		II.794		IV.674–78
222	The Lovers of al-Madīna		II.796		IV.678–82
223	Al-Malik al-Nāsir and His Vizier		II.799		IV.682–85
224	Dalīla the Crafty		II.801		IV.685–724
225	The Adventures of Mercury ʿAlī of Cairo		II.824		IV.724–76
226	Ardashīr and Hayāt al-Nufūs	50	II.855, III.3		V.7–87
227	Jullanār		III.3		V.87–153
228	King Muhammād ibn Sabāʾik and the Merchant Hasan	51	III.91		V.219–315
229	Prince Sayf al-Mulūk		III.95		V.228–315
230	Hasan of Basra	52	III.145		V.315–503
231	Khalīfa the Fisherman	53	III.261		V.503–56
232	Masrūr and Zayn al-Mawāsif	54	III.293		V.557–624
233	ʿAlī Nūr al-Dīn and Maryam the Girdle-girl	55	III.341		V.624–757
234	The Man of Upper Egypt and His Frankish Wife	56	III.428		V.758–64
235	The Ruined Man of Baghdad and His Slave-girl	57	III.432		V.764–75
236	Jalīʿād and Shimās	58	III.439		VI.7–144

No.	Story	SNAN	Lyons	Mahdi	Littmann
237	The Mouse and the Cat		III.441		VI.10–14
238	The Fakir and His Jar of Butter		III.444		VI.16–18
239	The Fishes and the Crab		III.447		VI.21–23
240	The Crow and the Serpent		III.449		VI.24–25
241	The Wild Ass and the Jackal		III.450		VI.27–28
242	The Unjust King and the Pilgrim Prince		III.452		VI.30–33
243	The Crows and the Hawk		III.454		VI.33–36
244	The Serpent-charmer and His Wife		III.456		VI.38–39
245	The Spider and the Wind		III.458		VI.41–42
246	The Two Kings		III.463		VI.49–51
247	The Blind Man and the Cripple		III.465		VI.52–54
248	The Foolish Fisherman		III.485		VI.86–87
249	The Boy and the Thieves		III.486		VI.88–90
250	The Man and His Wife		III.489		VI.92–94
251	The Merchant and the Robbers		III.490		VI.95–97
252	The Jackals and the Wolf		III.493		VI.99–101
253	The Shepherd and the Rogue		III.495		VI.103–04
254	The Francolin and the Tortoises		III.500		VI.113–16
255	Abū Qīr and Abū Sīr		III.519		VI.144–85
256	ʻAbdallāh the Fisherman and ʻAbdallāh the Merman	59	III.544		VI.186–215
257	Tale of Hārūn al-Rashīd and Abū Hasan the Merchant of Oman		III.561		VI.353–78
258	Ibrāhīm and Jamīla		III.576		VI.379–408
259	Abu ʼl-Hasan of Khorasan	60	III.594		VI.408–32

(*continued*)

No.	Story	SNAN	Lyons	Mahdi	Littmann
260	Qamar al-Zamān and the Jeweller's Wife	61	III.608		VI.432–508
261	'Abdallāh ibn Fādil and His Brothers	62	III.654		VI.509–71
262	Ma'rūf the Cobbler	63	III.690		VI.571–644

Appendix D

Paragraph Headings of "How Fārābī Read Plato's *Laws*"

Editorial remarks: Like some of Strauss's other writings, such as *Thoughts on Machiavelli*, the manuscript of Strauss's "How Fārābī read Plato's *Laws*" has a heading for each paragraph which is carefully numbered. The headings are not reproduced in the published version of the essay but are significant for understanding Strauss's intention.[1] My transcription of the headings was significantly improved by Heinrich Meier and Svetozar Minkov, to whom I am grateful.

¶ 1. F is silent on *Legg.* X.

¶ 2. F' preface: the general statement.

¶ 3. F' preface: the story.

¶ 4. F' preface: the story viewed in the light of the general remark.

¶ 5. F'. preface: the application to Plato.

¶ 6. F. preface: interpretation of remark on Plato in the light of general statement.

¶ 7. F' preface: interpretation of the remark on Plato in the light of the story.

¶ 8. F. adopts Plato' principle of secretiveness: allusive character of his Summary.

¶ 9. F' *Summary* is silent about philosophy – just as his *Plato* is silent about God, the future life and the divine law.

¶ 10. Summary : Aflatūn = Kalām : philosophy.

---

[1] Leo Strauss Papers, box 22, folder 1, Special Collections Research Center, University of Chicago Library.

¶ 11. Summary is personal – Aflatūn is not personal

¶ 12. General characteristics of the Summary: from simple report to mere iḥṣā [?] [Arabic for "enumeration"]

¶ 13. Continuation.

¶ 14. Continuation.

¶ 15. These features are partly due to the problem posed by Islam.

¶ 16. Plato's *Laws* → Is Islam true?

¶ 17. Allusions to the problem of Islam.

¶ 18. Ambiguities re : καλά.

¶ 19. Ambiguity re : θεος.

¶ 20. Transition to specimen

¶ 21. A specimen: the problem of νομος.

¶ 22. *Philosophy of Plato* on the *Laws*: the *Laws*, being emphatically Socratic = non-conformist, are silent about laws.

¶ 23. The "unhistorical" character of the *Philosophy of Plato* and of the *Summary*.

Bibliography

Abbès, Makram. "Leo Strauss et la philosophie arabe. Les Lumières médiévales contre les Lumières modernes." *Diogène* 226, no. 2 (2009): 117–41.

Adorisio, Chiara. "Some Remarks on Leo Strauss's Philosophical-Political Reading of Medieval Islamic and Jewish Philosophers." In *La Philosophie Arabe à l'étude / Studying Arabic Philosophy. Sens, Limites et Défis d'une Discipline Moderne: Meaning, Limits and Challenges of a Modern Discipline*, edited by Jean-Baptiste Brenet and Olga L. Lizzini. Paris: Vrin, 2019, 65–79.

Akasoy, Anna. "Was Ibn Rushd an Averroist? The Problem, the Debate, and Its Philosophical Implications." In *Renaissance Averroism and Its Aftermath: Arabic Philosophy in Early Modern Europe*, edited by Anna Akasoy and Guido Giglioni. Dordrecht: Springer, 2013, 321–47.

Alfarabi. *Alfarabi's Philosophy of Plato and Aristotle*, translated by Muhsin Mahdi. Ithaca, NY: Cornell University Press, 2001.

Alfarabi. *Compendium Legum Platonis*, edited by Francesco Gabrieli. Plato Arabus. London: Warburg Institute, 1952.

Alfarabi. *De Platonis philosophia*, edited by Richard Walzer and Franz Rosenthal. Vol. 2. Plato Arabus. London: Warburg Institute, 1943.

Alfarabi. "Enumeration of the Sciences." In *The Political Writings: Selected Aphorisms and Other Texts*, translated by Charles E. Butterworth. Ithaca and London: Cornell University Press, 2001, 69–85.

Alfarabi. *Kitāb Al-Siyāsa al-Madaniyya, al-Mulaqqab Bi-Mabādi al-Mawjūdāt*, edited by Fauzi Najjar. Beirut: al-Maṭbāa al-Kāthūlīkiyya, 1964.

Alfarabi. "Le Sommaire du Livre des 'Lois' de Platon." *Bulletin d'études orientales* 50 (1998): 109–55.

Alfarabi. "On the Intellect." In *Classical Arabic Philosophy: An Anthology of Sources*, translated by John McGinnis and David Reisman. Indianapolis: Hackett Publishing, 2007, 68–78.

Alfarabi. *On the Perfect State*, translated by Richard Walzer. Oxford: Clarendon Press, 1985.

Alfarabi. "Political Regime." In *The Political Writings: Volume II: Political Regime and Summary of Plato's Laws*, translated by Charles E. Butterworth. Ithaca and London: Cornell University Press, 2015, 27–97.

Alfarabi. "Selected Aphorisms." In *The Political Writings: "Selected Aphorisms" and Other Texts*, translated by Charles E. Butterworth. Ithaca and London: Cornell University Press, 2001, 1–69.

Alfarabi. "Summary of Plato's Laws." In *The Political Writings: Volume II: Political Regime and Summary of Plato's Laws*, translated by Charles E. Butterworth. Ithaca and London: Cornell University Press, 2015, 97–175.

Alfarabi. "The Attainment of Happiness." In *Philosophy of Plato and Aristotle*, translated by Muhsin Mahdi. Ithaca: Cornell University Press, 2001, 13–53.

Alfarabi. "The Harmonization of the Two Opinions of the Two Sages: Plato the Divine and Aristotle." In *The Political Writings: "Selected Aphorisms" and Other Texts*, translated by Charles E. Butterworth. Ithaca and London: Cornell University Press, 2001, 115–69.

Alfarabi. "The Philosophy of Plato." In *Philosophy of Plato and Aristotle*, translated by Muhsin Mahdi. Ithaca: Cornell University Press, 2001, 53–71.

Alfarabi. *The Political Writings. In "Selected Aphorisms" and Other Texts*, translated by Charles E. Butterworth. Ithaca and London: Cornell University Press, 2001.

Alfarabi. *The Political Writings: Volume II: Political Regime and Summary of Plato's Laws*, translated by Charles E. Butterworth. Ithaca and London: Cornell University Press, 2015.

Al-Ghazali. *The Incoherence of the Philosophers: A Parallel English-Arabic Text*, edited and translated by Michael E. Marmura. Provo: Brigham Young University Press, 2000.

Al-Kindi. *The Philosophical Works of Al-Kindi*, translated by Peter Pormann and Peter Adamson. Karachi: Oxford University Press, 2012.

Allard, Michel. "Le Rationalisme d'Averroès d'après une étude sur la création." *Bulletin d'études orientales* 14 (1952): 7–59.

Al-Musawi, Muhsin J. *The Islamic Context of the Thousand and One Nights*. New York: Columbia University Press, 2009.

Almutawa, Shatha. "'The Death of the Body Is the Birth of the Soul': Contradictory Views on the Resurrection in Rasā'il Ikhwān Al-Safā." *Studia Islamica* 113, no. 1 (2018): 56–75.

Al-Rāzī, Abū Bakr Muhammad ibn Zakariyyā. "The Book of the Philosophical Life." *Interpretation: A Journal of Political Philosophy* 20, no. 3 (1993): 227–36.

André, Jean-Marie. *L'otium dans la vie morale et intellectuelle romaine des origines à l'époque augustéenne*. Paris: Presses Universitaires de France, 1966.

Arberry, Arthur J. "Some Plato in an Arabic Epitome." *Islamic Quarterly* 2 (1955): 86–99.

Aristotle. *The Arabic Version of the Nicomachean Ethics*, edited by Anna Akasoy, Alexander Fidora, and Douglas Morton Dunlop. Leiden: Brill, 2005.

Arnzen, Rüdiger. "Plato, Arabic." In *Encyclopedia of Medieval Philosophy*, edited by Henrik Lagerlund. Dordrecht: Springer, 2011, 1012–16.

Arnzen, Rüdiger. "Plato's Timaeus in the Arabic Tradition. Legend – Testimonies – Fragments." In *Il Timeo: Esegesi Greche, Arabe, Latine. Greco, Arabo, Latino*, edited by Francesco Celia and Angela Ulacco. Pisa: Pisa University Press, 2012, 181–267.

Averroes. *Commentary on Plato's "Republic,"* translated by Erwin I. J. Rosenthal. Cambridge: University of Cambridge Oriental Publication, 1956.

Averroes. *Faith and Reason in Islam: Averroes' Exposition of Religious Arguments*, translated by Ibrahim Najjar. Oxford: Oneworld Publications, 2001.

Averroes. *On Plato's "Republic,"* translated by Ralph Lerner. Ithaca: Cornell University Press, 1974.

Averroes. *Tahafut Al-Tahafut (The Incoherence of the Incoherence)*, translated by Simon van den Bergh. 3rd reprint edition. London: Gibb Memorial Trust, 2008.

Averroes. *The Epistle on the Possibility of Conjunction with the Active Intellect by Ibn Rushd with the Commentary of Moses Narboni*, edited by Kalman P. Bland. New York: Jewish Theological Seminary of America, 1982.

Avicenna. "On the Divisions of the Rational Sciences." In *Medieval Political Philosophy: A Sourcebook*, edited by Ralph Lerner and Muhsin Mahdi, 1st edition. New York: Free Press of Glencoe, 1963, 95–98.

Azadpur, Mohammad. "Is 'Islamic Philosophy' Islamic?" In *Voices of Change*, edited by Vincent Cornell and Omid Safi, 5. Westport: Praeger, 2007, 23–41.

Behnegar, Nasser. "Reading 'What Is Political Philosophy?'" In *Leo Strauss's Defense of the Philosophic Life: Reading "What Is Political Philosophy?,"* edited by Rafael Major. Chicago: University of Chicago Press, 2013, 22–43.

Beiner, Ronald. *Civil Religion: A Dialogue in the History of Political Philosophy*. Cambridge: Cambridge University Press, 2011.

Belo, Catarina. "Some Considerations on Averroes' Views Regarding Women and Their Role in Society." *Journal of Islamic Studies* 20, no. 1 (December 6, 2008): 1–20.

Benardete, Seth. *Herodotean Inquiries*. The Hague: St. Augustine's Press, 1969.

Besier, Frederick C. *The Fate of Reason: German Philosophy from Kant to Fichte*. Cambridge, MA: Harvard University Press, 1987.

Bloom, Allan. "An Outline of Gulliver's Travels." In *Ancients and Moderns: Essays on the Tradition of Political Philosophy in Honor of Leo Strauss*, edited by Joseph Cropsey. New York: Basic Books, 1964, 238–58.

Bloom, Allan. "Cosmopolitan Man and the Political Community: An Interpretation of Othello." *American Political Science Review* 54, no. 1 (March 1960): 130–57.

Bloom, Allan. "Leo Strauss: September 20, 1899–October 18, 1973." *Political Theory* 2, no. 4 (1974): 372–92.

Bobonich, Christopher, ed. *Plato's Laws: A Critical Guide*. Cambridge: Cambridge University Press, 2010.

Bodine, J. Jermain. "Magic Carpet to Islam. Duncan Black Macdonald and the Arabian Nights." *The Muslim World* 67, no. 1 (January 1, 1977): 1–11.

Bolotin, David. "Review of The Argument and the Action of Plato's Laws by Leo Strauss." *The American Political Science Review* 70, no. 2 (1977): 668–70.

Bosworth, Clifford Edmund. "The Persian Impact on Arabic Literature." In *The Cambridge History of Arabic Literature: Arabic Literature to the End of the Umayyad Period*, edited by Robert Bertram Serjeant, Alfred Felix Landon Beeston, Thomas M. Johnstone, and G. R. Smith, 1. Cambridge: Cambridge University Press, 1984, 483–96.

Brague, Rémi. "Athens, Jerusalem, Mecca: Leo Strauss's 'Muslim' Understanding of Greek Philosophy." *Poetics Today* 19, no. 2 (Summer 1998): 235–59.

Brague, Rémi. "Leo Strauss et Maïmonide." In *Maimonides and Philosophy: Papers Presented at the Sixth Jerusalem Philosophical Encounter, May 1985*, edited by Shlomo Pines and Yirmiyahu Yovel. Dordrecht: Springer, 1986, 246–68.

Brague, Rémi. "Note sur la traduction arabe de la Politique d'Aristote. Derechef, qu'elle n'existe pas." In *Aristote politique: Études sur la Politique d'Aristote*, edited by Pierre Aubenque. Paris: Presses Universitaires de France, 1993, 423–33.

Brague, Rémi. *The Law of God: The Philosophical History of an Idea*, translated by Lydia G. Cochrane. Chicago: University of Chicago Press, 2007.

Buhot de Launay, Marc. "Leo Strauss et la découverte du classicisme ésotérique chez Lessing." *Les Études philosophiques* 65, no. 2 (2003): 245–59.

Burger, Ronna. *Aristotle's Dialogue with Socrates: On the Nicomachean Ethics*. Chicago: University of Chicago Press, 2008.

Burns, Timothy W. "The Place of the Strauss-Kojève Debate in the Work of Leo Strauss." In *Philosophy, History, and Tyranny: Reexamining the Debate between Leo Strauss and Alexandre Kojève*, edited by Timothy W. Burns and Bryan-Paul Frost. Albany: State University of New York Press, 2016, 15–51.

Burton, Richard F. *Arabian Nights with Introduction and Explanatory Notes*. 16 vols. Beirut: Khayat, 1966.

Burton, Richard F. *The Book of the Thousand Nights and a Night*. London: Burton Club, 1885.

Butterworth, Charles E. "In Memoriam: Muhsin S. Mahdi." *The Review of Politics* 69, no. 4 (2007): 511–12.

Butterworth, Charles E. "New Light on the Political Philosophy of Averroes." In *Essays on Islamic Philosophy and Science*, edited by George F. Hourani. Albany: State University of New York Press, 1975, 118–27.

Butterworth, Charles E. "Philosophy, Ethics, and Virtuous Rule: A Study of Averroes' Commentary on Plato's 'Republic'." *Cairo Papers on Social Science* IX, no. 1 (1986): 1–95.

Butterworth, Charles E., ed. *The Political Aspects of Islamic Philosophy: Essays in Honor of Muhsin S. Mahdi*. Cambridge, MA: Harvard University Press, 1992.

Butterworth, Charles E. "The Political Teaching of Averroes." *Arabic Sciences and Philosophy* 2, no. 2 (1992): 187–202.

Butterworth, Charles E. "Translation and Philosophy: The Case of Averroes' Commentaries." *International Journal of Middle East Studies* 26, no. 1 (1994): 19–35.

Chacón, Rodrigo. "On a Forgotten Kind of Grounding. Strauss, Jacobi, and the Phenomenological Critique of Modern Rationalism." *The Review of Politics* 76, no. 4 (2014): 589–617.

Chappelow, Leonard. *Notes, Critical, Illustrative and Practical on the Book of Job: Vol. 2.* Cambridge: Jeremy Bentham, 1752.

Colmo, Christopher. *Breaking with Athens: Alfarabi as Founder.* Lanham: Lexington Books, 2005.

Colmo, Christopher. "Reason and Revelation in the Thought of Leo Strauss." *Interpretation* 18, no. 1 (1990): 145–60.

Colmo, Christopher. "Theory and Practice: Alfarabi's Plato Revisited." *American Political Science Review* 86, no. 4 (1992): 966–76.

Colmo, Christopher. "Wisdom and Power in Averroes' Commentary on Plato's Republic." *Maghreb Review* 40, no. 3 (2015): 308–18.

Connelly, Coleman. "New Evidence for the Source of Al-Fārābī's Philosophy of Plato." In *A New Work by Apuleius: The Lost Third Book of the De Platone,* edited by Justin Stover. Oxford: Oxford University Press, 2016, 183–97.

Corbin, Henry. *Histoire de la Philosophie Islamique.* Paris: Gallimard, 1986.

Crone, Patricia. *Medieval Islamic Political Thought.* Edinburgh: Edinburgh University Press, 2005.

Davidson, Herbert A. *Alfarabi, Avicenna, and Averroes on Intellect: Their Cosmologies, Theories of the Active Intellect, and Theories of Human Intellect.* New York: Oxford University Press, 1992.

El-Zein, Amira. *Islam, Arabs, and Intelligent World of the Jinn.* Syracuse, NY: Syracuse University Press, 2009.

Fakhry, Majid. *A History of Islamic Philosophy.* London: Longman, 1983.

Fakhry, Majid. *Al-Farabi, Founder of Islamic Neoplatonism: His Life, Works and Influence.* Oxford: Oneworld Publications, 2002.

Fakhry, Majid. "Philosophy and Scripture in the Theology of Averroes." *Medieval Studies* 30, no. 1 (1968): 78–89.

Foley, Helen P. "Women in Greece." In *Civilization of the Ancient Mediterranean,* edited by Michael Grant and Rachel Kitzinger, Vol. 3. New York: Scribner, 1988, 1301–17.

Fudge, Bruce. "Underworlds and Otherworlds in The Thousand and One Nights." *Middle Eastern Literatures* 15, no. 3 (December 1, 2012): 257–72.

Galen. *Galeni Compendium Timaei Platonis aliorumque dialogorum synopsis, quae extant fragmenta,* edited by Paul Kraus and Richard Walzer. London: Warburg Institute, 1951.

Galland, Antoine. *Les Mille et Une Nuits: Contes Arabes.* Paris: Le Normant, 1806.

Galston, Miriam. "A Re-examination of al-Farabi's Neoplatonism." *Journal of the History of Philosophy* 15, no. 1 (1977): 13–32.

Gauthier, Léon. *La Théorie d'Ibn Rochd (Averroès) sur les Rapports de la Religion et de la Philosophie.* Paris: Ernest Leroux, 1909.

Gauthier, Léon. "Scolastique musulmane et scolastique chrétienne." *Revue d'Histoire de la Philosophie* 2 (1928): 221–53 and 333–65.

Goichon, Amélie M. "Ḥikma." In *Encyclopaedia of Islam,* edited by Thierry Bianquis, Clifford Edmund Bosworth, Peri Bearman, Emeri J. van Donzel, and Wolfhart P. Heinrichs, 2nd edition, 3. Leiden: Brill, 1986, 377–78.

Green, Kenneth Hart. *Leo Strauss and the Rediscovery of Maimonides.* Chicago: University of Chicago Press, 2013.

Gunnell, John G. "Strauss before Straussianism: Reason, Revelation, and Nature." *The Review of Politics* 53, no. 1 (1991): 53–74.

Gutas, Dimitri. *Avicenna and the Aristotelian Tradition: Introduction to Reading Avicenna's Philosophical Works.* Leiden and Boston: Brill, 2014.

Gutas, Dimitri. "Classical Arabic Wisdom Literature: Nature and Scope." *Journal of the American Oriental Society* 101, no. 1 (1981): 49–86.

Gutas, Dimitri. "Fārābī's Knowledge of Plato's 'Laws'." *International Journal of the Classical Tradition* 4, no. 3 (1998): 405–11.

Gutas, Dimitri. "Galen's Synopsis of Plato's Laws and Fārābī's Talḫīṣ." In *The Ancient Tradition in Christian and Islamic Hellenism: Studies on the Transmission of Greek Philosophy and Sciences*, edited by Remke Kruk and Gerhard Endress. Leiden: Research School CNWS, 1997, 101–19.

Gutas, Dimitri. "On the Historiography of Arabic Philosophy. Postscript 2017." In *La Philosophie Arabe à l'étude / Studying Arabic Philosophy. Sens, Limites et Défis d'une Discipline Moderne: Meaning, Limits and Challenges of a Modern Discipline*, edited by Jean-Baptiste Brenet and Olga L. Lizzini. Paris: Vrin, 2019, 37–45.

Gutas, Dimitri. "On Translating Averroes' Commentaries." *Journal of the American Oriental Society* 110, no. 1 (1990): 92–101.

Gutas, Dimitri. "Plato's Symposion in the Arabic Tradition." *Oriens* 31, no. 1 (1988): 36–60.

Gutas, Dimitri. "Review of Muhsin Mahdi, Alfarabi and the Foundation of Islamic Political Philosophy (Chicago: University of Chicago Press, 2001)." *International Journal of Middle East Studies* 35, no. 1 (2003): 145–47.

Gutas, Dimitri. "The Study of Arabic Philosophy in the Twentieth Century: An Essay on the Historiography of Arabic Philosophy." *British Journal of Middle Eastern Studies* 29, no. 1 (2002): 5–25.

Haddawy, Husain. *The Arabian Nights: Based on the Text Edited by Muhsin Mahdi.* London: W. W. Norton & Company, 1990.

Harvey, Steven. "Can a Tenth-Century Islamic Aristotelian Help Us Understand Plato's Laws?" In *Plato's Laws: From Theory to Practice*, edited by Samuel Scolnicov and Luc Brisson. Sankt Augustin: Academia Verlag, 2003, 325–30.

Harvey, Steven. "Did Alfarabi Read Plato's Laws?" *Medioevo. Rivista di storia della filosofia medievale* 28 (2003): 51–68.

Harvey, Steven. "Leo Strauss's Developing Interest in Alfarabi and Its Reverberations in the Study of Medieval Islamic Philosophy." In *The Pilgrimage of Philosophy: A Festschrift for Charles E. Butterworth*, edited by René M. Paddags, Waseem El-Rayes, and Gregory A. McBrayer. South Bend: St. Augustine's Press, 2019, 60–84.

Harvey, Steven. "The Story of a Twentieth-Century Jewish Scholar's Discovery of Plato's Political Philosophy in Tenth-Century Islam: Leo Strauss' Early Interest in the Islamic Falāsifa." In *Modern Jewish Scholarship on Islam in Context: Rationality, European Borders, and the Search for Belonging*, edited by Ottfried Fraisse. Berlin and Boston: de Gruyter, 2018, 219–44.

Henninger, Josef. "Mohammedanische Polemik gegen das Christentum in 1001 Nacht." *Neue Zeitschrift für Missionswissenschaft* 2 (1946): 289–305.

Hopper, Vincent Foster. *Medieval Number Symbolism*. Mineola: Dover Publications Inc., 2003.

Horten, Max. *Die Hauptlehren des Averroes nach seiner Schrift: Die Widerlegung des Gazali*. Bonn: Marcus und Webers Verlag, 1913.

Hyman, Arthur, ed. *Essays in Medieval Jewish and Islamic Philosophy*. New York: Ktav Publishing House, 1977.

Ibn al-Nadīm. *The Fihrist: A Tenth Century AD Survey of Islamic Culture*, translated by Bayard Dodge. 2 vols. New York: Columbia University Press, 1970.

Ibn Ḥanbal, Aḥmad. *Al-Musnad*. Beirut: Dar "Ihya" al-Turath al-'Arabi, 1993.

Ibn Majah. *Sunan. Vol. V*, translated by Nasiruddin Al-Khattab. Riyadh: Darussalam, 2007.

Ibn Miskawayh. *The Refinement of Character*, translated by Constantine K. Zurayk. Beirut: American University of Beirut, 1968.

Ibn Tufayl. *Hayy Ibn Yaqzān: A Philosophical Tale*, translated by Lenn Evan Goodman. Chicago: University of Chicago Press, 2015.

Imam Muslim. *Ṣaḥīḥ Muslim: Vol. IV*, translated by Nasiruddin Al-Khattab. Riyadh: Darussalam, 2007.

Irwin, Robert. "Political Thought in 'The Thousand and One Nights'." *Marvels and Tales* 18, no. 2 (2004): 246–57.

Irwin, Robert. "Preface." In *The Arabian Nights and Orientalism: Perspectives from East and West*, edited by Yuriko Yamanaka and Tetsuo Nishio. London: I.B. Tauris, 2006, vii–xiii.

Irwin, Robert. *The Arabian Nights: A Companion*. London: Allen Lane-The Penguin Press, 1994.

Jacobi, Friedrich Heinrich. *The Main Philosophical Writings and the Novel "Atwill,"* translated by George di Giovanni. Montreal: McGill-Queen's University Press, 1994.

Janssens, David. "The Problem of the Enlightenment. Strauss, Jacobi, and the Pantheism Controversy." *The Review of Metaphysics* 56, no. 3 (2003): 605–31.

Kahn, Charles H. and Glenn R. Morrow. "Foreword." In *Plato's Cretan City: A Historical Interpretation of the Laws*, edited by Charles H. Kahn. Princeton: Princeton University Press, 1993, xvii–xxvii.

Kauffmann, Clemens. "'Men on Horseback'. Leo Strauss über „The Argument and the Action of Plato's Laws." In *Platons Nomoi. Die politische Herrschaft von Vernunft und Gesetz*, edited by Francesco Knoll and Francisco L. Lisi, 100. Staatsverständnisse. Baden-Baden: Nomos-Verlag, 2017, 212–46.

Kerber, Hannes. "Strauss and Schleiermacher on How to Read Plato: An Introduction to 'Exoteric Teaching'." In *Reorientation: Leo Strauss in the 1930s*, edited by Martin D. Yaffe and Richard S. Ruderman. New York: Palgrave Macmillan, 2014, 203–14.

Khalidi, Muhammad Ali. "Orientalisms in the Interpretation of Islamic Philosophy." *Radical Philosophy* 135 (2006): 25–33.

Knoll, Francesco, and Francisco L. Lisi, eds. *Platons Nomoi: Die politische Herrschaft von Vernunft und Gesetz*. Vol. 100. Staatsverständnisse. Baden-Baden: Nomos-Verlag, 2017.

Kraemer, Joel L. "The Death of an Orientalist: Paul Kraus from Prague to Cairo." In *The Jewish Discovery of Islam: Studies in Honor of Bernard Lewis*, edited by Martin Kramer. Tel Aviv: Moshe Dayan Centre for Middle Eastern and African Studies, 1999, 181–225.

Kraus, Paul. *Jābir ibn Ḥayyān. Contribution à l'histoire des idées scientifiques dans l'Islam. Vol. 1. Le corpus des écrits jabiriens*. Cairo: Mémoires de l'Institute d'Égypte, 1943.

Kraus, Paul. *Jābir ibn Ḥayyān: Contribution à l'histoire des idées scientifiques dans l'Islam. Vol 2: Jabir et la science grecque*. Cairo: Mémoires de l'Institute d'Égypte, 1942.

Kraus, Paul. "Plotin chez les Arabes. Remarques sur un nouveau fragment de la paraphrase arabe des Énnéades." *Bulletin de l'Institut d'Egypte* 23 (1941): 263–95.

Kraus, Paul. "Raziana I." *Orientalia* 4 (1935): 300–34.

Lahy-Hollebecque, Marie. *Le Féminisme de Schéhérazade: La Révélation Des Mille et Une Nuits*. Paris: Radot, 1927.

Lampert, Laurence. "Exotericism Embraced: 'The Law of Reason in the Kuzari'." In *The Enduring Importance of Leo Strauss*. Chicago: University of Chicago Press, 2013, 32–73.

Lampert, Laurence. "Strauss's Recovery of Esotericism." In *The Cambridge Companion to Leo Strauss*, edited by Steven B. Smith. Cambridge: Cambridge University Press, 2009, 63–93.

Lane, Edward William. *Arabian Society in the Middle Ages: Studies from the Thousand and One Nights*, edited by Stanley Lane-Pool. London: Chatto & Windus, 1883.

Lane, Edward William. *The Thousand and One Nights, Commonly Called, in England, The Arabian Nights' Entertainments*. London: Charles Knight and Co., 1839.

Lazarus-Yafeh, Hava. "Taḥrīf." In *Encyclopaedia of Islam*, edited by Thierry Bianquis, Clifford Edmund Bosworth, Peri Bearman, Emeri J. van Donzel, and Wolfhart P. Heinrichs, 2nd edition, 10. Leiden: Brill, 2000, 111.

Lazier, Benjamin. *God Interrupted: Heresy and the European Imagination Between the World Wars*. Princeton and Oxford: Princeton University Press, 2008.

Leaman, Oliver. *An Introduction to Classical Islamic Philosophy*. Cambridge: Cambridge University Press, 2004.

Leaman, Oliver. *Averroes and His Philosophy*. Oxford: Clarendon Press, 1988.

Leaman, Oliver. "Is Averroes an Averroist?" In *Averroismus im Mittelalter und in der Renaissance*, edited by Friedrich Niewöhner and Loris Sturlese. Zurich: Spur, 1994, 9–22.

Leaman, Oliver. "Orientalism and Islamic Philosophy." In *History of Islamic Philosophy*, edited by Oliver Leaman and Seyyed Hossein Nasr. London: Routledge, 2001, 1143–49.

Leibowitz, David. *The Ironic Defense of Socrates: Plato's Apology*. Cambridge: Cambridge University Press, 2010.

Lenzner, Steven J. "Strauss's Farabi, Scholarly Prejudice, and Philosophic Politics." *Perspectives on Political Science* 28, no. 4 (January 1, 1999): 194–202.

Lerner, Ralph. "Beating the Neoplatonic Bushes." *Journal of Religion* 67, no. 4 (1987): 510–17.

Lessing, Gotthold Ephraim. "Leibniz on Eternal Punishment." In *Lessing: Philosophical and Theological Writings*, edited and translated by Hugh B. Nisbet. Cambridge: Cambridge University Press, 2005, 37–61.

Littmann, Enno. *Die Erzählungen aus den Tausendundein Nächten. Vollständige Ausgabe in Sechs Bänden. Zum ersten Mal nach dem arabischen Urtext der Calcuttaer Ausgabe vom Jahre 1939 übertragen von Enno Littmann. Einleitung von Hugo von Hofmannsthal.* 6 vols. Leipzig: Insel-Verlag, 1953.

London, Jennifer. "How to Do Things with Fables." *History of Political Thought* 29, no. 2 (2008): 189–212.

Lord, Carnes. "Introduction." In *Aristotle's Politics*, 2nd. Chicago: University of Chicago Press, 2013, vii–xliii.

Lutz, Mark J. "The Argument and the Action of Plato's Laws." In *Brill's Companion to Leo Strauss' Writings on Classical Political Thought*, edited by Timothy W. Burns. Leiden and Boston: Brill, 2015, 424–40.

Lyons, Malcolm C., Ursula Lyons, and Robert Irwin. *The Arabian Nights: Tales of 1,001 Nights.* 3 vols. London: Penguin Books, 2010.

MacDonald, Duncan B. "From the Arabian Nights to Spirit." *The Muslim World* 9, no. 4 (October 1, 1919): 336–48.

MacDonald, Duncan B. "Lost MSS. of the 'Arabian Nights' and a Projected Edition of That of Galland." *Journal of the Royal Asiatic Society of Great Britain and Ireland* 43, no. 1 (1911): 219–21.

Machiavelli, Niccolò. *Discourses on Livy*, translated by Harvey C. Mansfield and Nathan Tarcov. Chicago: University of Chicago Press, 1996.

Mahdi, Muhsin. *Alfarabi and the Foundation of Islamic Political Philosophy.* Chicago: University of Chicago Press, 2001.

Mahdi, Muhsin. "Alfarabi et Averroès. Remarques sur le commentaire d'Averroès sur la République de Platon." In *Multiple Averroès: Actes du Colloque International Organisé à l'Occasion du 850e anniversaire de la naissance d'Averroès*, edited by Jean Jolivet and Rachel Arié. Paris: Les Belles Lettres, 1978, 91–101.

Mahdi, Muhsin. "Al-Fārābī's Imperfect State." *Journal of the American Oriental Society* 110, no. 4 (1990): 691–726.

Mahdi, Muhsin. "Averroes on Divine Law and Human Wisdom." In *Ancients and Moderns: Essays on the Tradition of Political Philosophy in Honor of Leo Strauss*, edited by Joseph Cropsey. New York and London: Basic Books, 1964, 114–32.

Mahdi, Muhsin. *Ibn Khaldūn's Philosophy of History: A Study in the Philosophic Foundation of the Science of Culture.* London: George Allen & Unwin, 1957.

Mahdi, Muhsin. "Orientalism and the Study of Islamic Philosophy." *Journal of Islamic Studies* 1, no. 1 (1990): 73–98.

Mahdi, Muhsin. "Religious Belief and Scientific Belief." *The American Journal of Islamic Social Sciences* 11, no. 2 (1994): 245–59.

Mahdi, Muhsin. "Remarks on the 1001 Nights." *Interpretation* 3, no. 2–3 (1973): 157–68.

Mahdi, Muhsin. "The Editio Princeps of Fârâbî's Compendium Legum Platonis." *Journal of Near Eastern Studies* 20, no. 1 (1961): 1–24.

Mahdi, Muhsin. *The Thousand and One Nights*. Leiden: Brill, 1995.

Mahdi, Muhsin. *The Thousand and One Nights: From the Earliest Known Sources. Vol. 1. Arabic Text*. Leiden: Brill, 1984.

Mahdi, Muhsin. *The Thousand and One Nights: From the Earliest Known Sources. Vol. 2. Critical Apparatus: Description of Manuscripts*. Leiden: Brill, 1984.

Mahdi, Muhsin. "Years of Chicago: Forming a Soul." *Alif: Journal of Comparative Poetics* 29 (2009): 171–91.

Maimonides, Moses. "Eight Chapters." In *Medieval Political Philosophy: A Sourcebook*, edited by Joseph C. Macfarland and Joshua Parens, translated by Joshua Parens, 2nd edition. Ithaca and London: Cornell University Press, 2011, 203–5.

Maimonides, Moses. *The Guide of the Perplexed*, translated by Shlomo Pines. Chicago: University of Chicago Press, 1963.

Major, Rafael, ed. *Leo Strauss's Defense of the Philosophic Life: Reading "What Is Political Philosophy?"* Chicago and London: University of Chicago Press, 2013.

Manent, Pierre. *Le Regard politique: Entretiens avec Benedicte Delorme-Montini*. Paris: Flammarion, 2010.

Mansfield, Harvey C. *Machiavelli's New Modes and Orders: A Study of the Discourses on Livy*. Chicago: University of Chicago Press, 2001.

Marzolph, Ulrich. "The Arabian Nights in Comparative Folk Narrative Research." In *The Arabian Nights and Orientalism: Perspectives from East and West*, edited by Tetsuo Nishio and Yuriko Yamanaka. London: I.B. Tauris, 2005, 25–46.

Marzolph, Ulrich, and Richard van Leeuwen. *The Arabian Nights: An Encyclopedia*. Santa Barbara: ABC-CLIO, 2004.

Matar, Nabil. "Christians in the Arabian Nights." In *The Arabian Nights in Historical Context: Between East and West*, edited by Saree Makdisi and Felicity Nussbaum. Oxford: Oxford University Press, 2008, 131–53.

Mehren, August Ferdinand. "Etudes sur la Philosophie d'Averroès concernant son rapport avec celle d'Avicenne et Gazzali." *Le Muséon* VII (1888): 613–27.

Meier, Heinrich. *Carl Schmitt and Leo Strauss: The Hidden Dialogue*, translated by J. Harvey Lomax. Chicago and London: University of Chicago Press, 2006.

Meier, Heinrich. "How Strauss Became Strauss." In *Reorientation: Leo Strauss in the 1930s*, edited by Martin D. Yaffe and Richard S. Ruderman. New York: Palgrave Macmillan, 2014, 13–32.

Meier, Heinrich. *Leo Strauss and the Theologico-Political Problem*, translated by Marcus Brainard. Cambridge: Cambridge University Press, 2006.

Meier, Heinrich. "On the Genealogy of Faith in Revelation." In *Leo Strauss and the Theologico-Political Problem*. Cambridge: Cambridge University Press, 2006, 29–44.

Meier, Heinrich. *On the Happiness of the Philosophic Life: Reflections on Rousseau's Rêveries in Two Books*, translated by Robert Berman. Chicago: University of Chicago Press, 2016.

Meier, Heinrich. *Political Philosophy and the Challenge of Revealed Religion*, translated by Robert Berman. Chicago and London: University of Chicago Press, 2017.

Meier, Heinrich. "The History of Philosophy and the Intention of the Philosopher: Reflections on Leo Strauss." In *Leo Strauss and the Theologico-Political Problem*, translated by Marcus Brainard. Cambridge: Cambridge University Press, 2006, 53–75.

Melzer, Arthur M. "On the Pedagogical Motive for Esoteric Writing." *The Journal of Politics* 69, no. 4 (2007): 1015–31.

Melzer, Arthur M. *Philosophy between the Lines: The Lost History of Esoteric Writing*. Chicago: University of Chicago Press, 2014.

Menon, Marco. "Leo Strauss and the Argument of Natural Theology." *Etica and Politica* 18, no. 3 (2016): 573–89.

Merrill, Clark A. "Leo Strauss's Indictment of Christian Philosophy." *The Review of Politics* 62, no. 1 (2000): 77–105.

Minkov, Svetozar. *Leo Strauss on Science: Thoughts on the Relation Between Natural Science and Political Philosophy*. Albany: State University of New York Press, 2016.

Minowitz, Peter. *Straussophobia: Defending Leo Strauss and Straussians against Shadia Drury and Other Accusers*. Lanham: Lexington Books, 2009.

Montgomery, James E. "Leo Strauss and the Alethiometer." In *Renaissance Averroism and Its Aftermath: Arabic Philosophy in Early Modern Europe*, edited by Anna Akasoy and Guido Giglioni. Dordrecht: Springer, 2013, 285–320.

Morris, James W. "The Philosopher-Prophet in Avicenna's Philosophy." In *The Political Aspects of Islamic Philosophy: Essays in Honor of Muhsin S. Mahdi*, edited by Charles E. Butterworth. Cambridge, MA: Harvard University Press, 1992, 152–99.

Moseley, Geoffrey J. "Arabic Support for an Emendation of Plato, Laws 666b." *The Classical Quarterly* 69, no. 1 (2019): 440–42.

Namazi, Rasoul. "Illuminationist Texts and Textual Studies: Essays in Memory of Hossein Ziai." *Iranian Studies* 53, no. 5–6 (April 14, 2020): 1013–16.

Namazi, Rasoul. "Politics, Religion, and Love: How Leo Strauss Read the Arabian Nights." *Journal of Religion* 100, no. 2 (2020): 189–231.

Nelson, Allan D. "Review of the Argument and the Action of Plato's Laws by Leo Strauss." *Canadian Journal of Political Science* 9, no. 3 (1976): 515–16.

Neumann, Harry. "Review of the Argument and the Action of Plato's Laws by Leo Strauss." *Journal of the History of Philosophy* 17 (1979): 81–82.

Nietzsche, Friedrich. *Beyond Good and Evil: Prelude to a Philosophy of the Future*, translated by Walter Kaufmann. New York: Vintage Books, 1989.

Nöldeke, Theodor. "Review of 'Histoire d'Alâ al-Dîn ou la Lampe merveilleuse' by Hermann Zotenberg." *Wiener Zeitschrift für die Kunde des Morgenlandes* 2 (1888): 168–73.

Novotný, František. *The Posthumous Life of Plato*, translated by Jana Fábryová. Prague: Academia Prague, 1977.

Orwin, Alexander. *Redefining the Muslim Community: Ethnicity, Religion, and Politics in the Thought of Alfarabi*. Philadelphia: University of Pennsylvania Press, 2017.

Ostenfeld, Erik. "Who Speaks for Plato? Everyone!" In *Who Speaks for Plato? Studies in Platonic Anonymity*, edited by Gerald A. Press. Lanham: Rowman & Littlefield, 2000, 211–20.

Palacio, Asìn. "El Averroismo teologico de Santo Tomas de Aquino." In *Homenaje a D. Francisco Codera en su jubilación del profesorado. Estudios de erudición oriental*, edited by Eduardo Saavedra. Zaragoza: Escar, 1904, 271–331.

Parens, Joshua. "Escaping the Scholastic Paradigm: The Dispute between Strauss and His Contemporaries about How to Approach Islamic and Jewish Medieval Philosophy." In *Encountering the Medieval in Modern Jewish Thought*, edited by James A. Diamond and Aaron W. Hughes. Leiden: Brill, 2012, 203–28.

Parens, Joshua. *Leo Strauss and the Recovery of Medieval Political Philosophy.* Rochester: University of Rochester Press, 2016.

Parens, Joshua. *Metaphysics as Rhetoric: Alfarabi's Summary of Plato's "Laws."* Albany: State University of New York Press, 1995.

Pelluchon, Corine. *Leo Strauss and the Crisis of Rationalism: Another Reason, Another Enlightenment*, translated by Robert Howse. Albany: State University of New York Press, 2014.

Perho, Irmeli. "The Arabian Nights as a Source for Daily Life in the Mamluk Period." *Studia Orientalia Electronica* 85 (2014): 139–62.

Peters, Francis Edward. *Aristotle and the Arabs: The Aristotelian Tradition in Islam.* New York: New York University Press, 1968.

Pines, Shlomo. "Aristotle's Politics in Arabic Philosophy." *Israel Oriental Studies* 5 (1975): 150–60.

Pines, Shlomo. "Limitations of Human Knowledge According to Al-Fārābī, Ibn Bājja, and Maimonides." In *Collected Works of Shlomo Pines*, edited by Moshe Idel and Warren Zen Harvey, 5. Jerusalem: Magnes, 1997, 404–31.

Pines, Shlomo. "Notes on Averroes' Political Philosophy." *Iyyun. The Jerusalem Philosophical Quarterly* 8 (1957): 65–84.

Press, Gerald A. "The State of the Question in the Study of Plato." *The Southern Journal of Philosophy* 34, no. 4 (December 1996): 507–32.

Press, Gerald A. "The State of the Question in the Study of Plato: Twenty Year Update." *The Southern Journal of Philosophy* 56, no. 1 (March 2018): 9–35.

Rashed, Marwan. "On the Authorship of the Treatise on the Harmonization of the Opinions of the Two Sages Attributed to Al-Fārābī." *Arabic Sciences and Philosophy* 19 (2009): 43–82.

Reisman, David. "Al-Fārābī and the Philosophical Curriculum." In *The Cambridge Companion to Arabic Philosophy*, edited by Peter Adamson and Richard C. Taylor. Cambridge: Cambridge University Press, 2005, 52–71.

Reisman, David. "Plato's Republic in Arabic: A Newly Discovered Passage." *Arabic Sciences and Philosophy* 4 (2004): 263–300.

Renan, Ernest. *Averroès et l'Averroïsme: Essai Historique.* 3rd edition. Paris: Michel Lévy Frères, 1866.

Richardson, John. *A Dictionary, English, Persian and Arabic: Vol. 2.* London: Blumen & Co., 1810.

Ridgeon, Lloyd. *Morals and Mysticism in Persian Sufism: A History of Sufi-Futuwwat in Iran.* New York: Routledge, 2010.

Robinson, Thomas M. "Review of The Argument and the Action of Plato's Laws by Leo Strauss." *The Classical World* 70, no. 6 (1977): 405.

Rosenthal, Erwin I. J. "Introduction." In *Averroes' Commentary on Plato's "Republic."* Cambridge: University of Cambridge Oriental Publication, 1956, 1–21.

Rosenthal, Erwin I. J. "Maimonides' Conception of State and Society." In *Moses Maimonides,* edited by Israel Epstein. London: Soncio Press, 1935, 191–206.

Rosenthal, Erwin I. J. "The Place of Politics in the Philosophy of Al-Farabi." *Islamic Culture* 29 (1955): 157–78.

Rosenthal, Franz. "Addenda." *Islamic Culture* 15 (1941): 396–98.

Rosenthal, Franz. "On the Knowledge of Plato's Philosophy in the Islamic World." *Islamic Culture* 14 (1940): 387–422.

Said, Edward. *Orientalism: Western Conceptions of the Orient.* London: Penguin Books, 2003.

Saif, Liana. "The Cows and the Bees: Arabic Sources and Parallels for Pseudo-Plato's Liber Vaccae (Kitab al-Nawamis)." *Journal of the Warburg and Courtauld Institutes* 79, no. 1 (2016): 1–47.

Sarrió, Diego R. "The Philosopher as the Heir of the Prophets. Averroes's Islamic Rationalism." *Al-Qanṭara* 36, no. 1 (2015): 45–68.

Saunders, Trevor J. "Review of The Argument and the Action of Plato's Laws by Leo Strauss." *Political Theory* 4, no. 2 (1976): 239–42.

Schimmel, Annemarie. *Mystical Dimensions of Islam.* Chapel Hill: University of North Carolina Press, 2011.

Schimmel, Annemarie. *The Mystery of Numbers.* New York: Oxford University Press, 1994.

Schofield, M. "Review of The Argument and the Action of Plato's Laws by Leo Strauss." *The Classical Review* 28, no. 1 (1978): 170.

Shell, Susan Meld. "Taking Evil Seriously: Schmitt's 'Concept of the Political' and Strauss's 'True Politics'." In *Leo Strauss: Political Philosopher and Jewish Thinker,* edited by Kenneth L. Deutsch and Walter Nicgorski. New York: Rowman & Littlefield, 1994, 175–93.

Shell, Susan Meld, ed. *The Strauss-Krüger Correspondence. Returning to Plato through Kant.* Cham: Palgrave Macmillan, 2018.

Sheppard, Eugene. *Leo Strauss and the Politics of Exile: The Making of a Political Philosopher.* Waltham: Brandeis University Press, 2006.

Smith, Steven B. *Reading Leo Strauss: Politics, Philosophy, Judaism.* Chicago: University of Chicago Press, 2006.

Solmsen, Friedrich. "Leisure and Play in Aristotle's Ideal State." *Rheinisches Museum für Philologie* 107 (1964): 193–220.

Spinoza, Benedict de. *Theological-Political Treatise,* translated by Jonathan Israel and Michael Silverthorne. Cambridge: Cambridge University Press, 2007.

Stern, Samuel M. "Review of R. Klibansky (Ed.), F. Gabrieli (Ed. and Tr.), Plato Arabus, Volumen III. Alfarabius: Compendium Legum Platonis. London: Warburg Institute, 1952, 21s." *Bulletin of the School of Oriental and African Studies* 17, no. 2 (1955): 398.

Strauss, Leo. *1959 Course on Plato's Laws Offered at the University of Chicago,* edited by Lorraine Smith Pangle. Chicago: Leo Strauss Center, 2016.

Strauss, Leo. *1963 Spring Course on Aristotle's Nicomachean Ethics Offered at the University of Chicago.* Chicago: Leo Strauss Center, 1963.

Strauss, Leo. *1963 Spring Course on Vico Offered at the University of Chicago,* edited by Wayne Ambler. Chicago: Leo Strauss Center, 2016.

Strauss, Leo. *1963 Winter Course on Xenophon Offered at the University of Chicago,* edited by Christopher Nadon. Chicago: Leo Strauss Center, 2016.

Strauss, Leo. *1966 Spring Course on Montesquieu Offered at the University of Chicago,* edited by Thomas L. Pangle. Chicago: Leo Strauss Center, 2014.

Strauss, Leo. *1967 Course on Nietzsche Offered at the University of Chicago,* edited by Richard Velkley. Chicago: Leo Strauss Center, 2015.

Strauss, Leo. *1971–72 Course on Nietzsche's Beyond Good and Evil Offered at St. John's College,* edited by Mark Blitz. Chicago: Leo Strauss Center, 2014.

Strauss, Leo. *197l-72 Course on Plato's Laws Offered at St. John's College,* edited by Lorraine Smith Pangle. Chicago: Leo Strauss Center, 2016.

Strauss, Leo. "A Giving of Accounts." In *Leo Strauss, Jewish Philosophy and the Crisis of Modernity,* edited by Kenneth Hart Green. Albany: State University of New York Press, 1993, 457–67.

Strauss, Leo. "A Lost Writing of Farâbî's (1936)." In *Reorientation: Leo Strauss in the 1930s,* edited by Martin D. Yaffe and Richard S. Ruderman, translated by Martin D. Yaffe and Gabriel Bartlett. New York: Palgrave Macmillan, 2014, 255–65.

Strauss, Leo. "An Untitled Lecture On Plato's Euthyphron." *Interpretation: A Journal of Political Philosophy* 24, no. 1 (1996): 5–23.

Strauss, Leo. "Cohen and Maimonides." In *Leo Strauss on Maimonides,* edited by Kenneth Hart Green. Chicago: University of Chicago Press, 2013, 173–222.

Strauss, Leo. "Eine vermißte Schrift Farâbîs." *Monatsschrift für Geschichte und Wissenschaft des Judentums* 80, no. 1 (1936): 90–106.

Strauss, Leo. "Exoteric Teaching." In *Reorientation: Leo Strauss in the 1930s,* edited by Hannes Kerber, Martin D. Yaffe, and Richard S. Ruderman. New York: Palgrave Macmillan, 2014, 275–87.

Strauss, Leo. "Fârâbî's Plato." In *Louis Ginzberg: Jubilee Volume on the Occasion of His Seventieth Birthday,* edited by Saul Lieberman, Alexander Marx, Shalom Spiegel, and Solomon Zeitlin. New York: The American Academy for Jewish Research, 1945, 357–93.

Strauss, Leo. *Gesammelte Schriften. Band 3. Hobbes' politische Wissenschaft und zugehörige Schriften – Briefe,* edited by Heinrich Meier and Wiebke Meier. 2nd edition. Stuttgart and Weimar: J. B. Metzler, 2008.

Strauss, Leo. *Hobbes's Critique of Religion and Related Writings,* translated by Svetozar Minkov and Gabriel Bartlett. Chicago: University of Chicago Press, 2011.

Strauss, Leo. "How Fārābī Read Plato's Laws." In *Mélanges Louis Massignon,* III. Damascus: Institut français de Damas, 1957, 319–44.

Strauss, Leo. "How Fārābī Read Plato's Laws." In *What Is Political Philosophy? And Other Studies.* Glencoe: Free Press, 1959, 134–55.

Strauss, Leo. "How to Begin to Study the Guide of the Perplexed." In *Liberalism Ancient and Modern.* New York: Basic Books, 1968, 140–84.

Strauss, Leo. "How to Study Medieval Philosophy." *Interpretation: A Journal of Political Philosophy* 23, no. 3 (1996): 321–38.

Strauss, Leo. "How to Study Spinoza's Theologico-Political Treatise." In *Persecution and the Art of Writing*. Glencoe: The Free Press, 1952, 142–203.

Strauss, Leo. "Introduction." In *History of Political Philosophy*, edited by Leo Strauss and Joseph Cropsey, 3rd edition. Chicago: University of Chicago Press, 1982, 1–6.

Strauss, Leo. "Introduction." In *Persecution and the Art of Writing*. Glencoe: Free Press, 1952, 7–12.

Strauss, Leo. "Introduction to Maimonides' The Guide of the Perplexed." In *Leo Strauss on Maimonides: The Complete Writings*, edited by Kenneth Hart Green. Chicago: University of Chicago Press, 2013, 417–91.

Strauss, Leo. "Jerusalem and Athens (1946)." The New School for Social Research, November 1946.

Strauss, Leo. "Jerusalem and Athens: Some Preliminary Reflections." In *Studies on Platonic Political Philosophy*, edited by Thomas L. Pangle. Chicago: University of Chicago Press, 1983, 147–74.

Strauss, Leo. "Lecture Notes for 'Persecution and the Art of Writing'." In *Reorientation: Leo Strauss in the 1930s*, edited by Hannes Kerber, Martin D. Yaffe, and Richard S. Ruderman. New York: Palgrave Macmillan, 2014, 293–304.

Strauss, Leo. "Le problème de la connaissance dans la doctrine philosophique de Fr. H. Jacobi (I)." *Revue de Métaphysique et de Morale* 99, no. 3 (1994): 291–311.

Strauss, Leo. "Le problème de la connaissance dans la doctrine philosophique de Fr. H. Jacobi (II) b) Les formes données de la connaissance." *Revue de Métaphysique et de Morale* 99, no. 4 (1994): 505–32.

Strauss, Leo. "Literary Character of the Guide for the Perplexed." In *Persecution and the Art of Writing*. Glencoe: Free Press, 1952, 38–95.

Strauss, Leo. "Maimonides' Statement on Political Science." In *What Is Political Philosophy? And Other Studies*. Glencoe: Free Press, 1959, 155–70.

Strauss, Leo. "Maimunis Lehre von der Prophetie und ihre Quellen." *Le Monde Oriental* 28 (1934): 99–139.

Strauss, Leo. "Marsilius of Padua." In *History of Political Philosophy*, 3rd edition. Chicago: University of Chicago Press, 1987, 276–96.

Strauss, Leo. *Natural Right and History*. Chicago: University of Chicago Press, 1953.

Strauss, Leo. "Niccolò Machiavelli." In *History of Political Philosophy*, edited by Leo Strauss and Joseph Cropsey, 3rd edition. Chicago: University of Chicago Press, 1987, 296–318.

Strauss, Leo. "Notes on Lucretius." In *Liberalism Ancient and Modern*. Chicago: University of Chicago Press, 1995, 77–141.

Strauss, Leo. "Notes on Philosophy and Revelation." In *Leo Strauss and the Theologico-Political Problem*, edited by Heinrich Meier, translated by Marcus Brainard. Cambridge: Cambridge University Press, 2006, 168–80.

Strauss, Leo. " On a Forgotten Kind of Writing. " In *What Is Political Philosophy? And Other Studies*. Glencoe: Free Press, 1959, 221–33.

Strauss, Leo. "On a New Interpretation of Plato's Political Philosophy." *Social Research* 13, no. 3 (1946): 326–67.

Strauss, Leo. "On Abravanel's Philosophical Tendency and Political Teaching." In *Isaac Abravanel: Six Lectures*, edited by J. B. Trend and H. Loewe. Cambridge: Cambridge University Press, 1937, 95–129.

Strauss, Leo. "On Abravanel's Philosophical Tendency and Political Teaching." In *Leo Strauss on Maimonides: The Complete Writings*, edited by Kenneth Hart Green. Chicago: University of Chicago Press, 2013, 579–615.

Strauss, Leo. "On Classical Political Philosophy." *Social Research* 12, no. 1 (1945): 98–117.

Strauss, Leo. "On Classical Political Philosophy." In *What Is Political Philosophy? And Other Studies*. Glencoe: The Free Press, 1959, 78–95.

Strauss, Leo. *On Moses Mendelssohn*, edited by Martin D. Yaffe. Chicago and London: University of Chicago Press, 2012.

Strauss, Leo. "On Natural Law." In *Studies in Platonic Political Philosophy*, edited by Thomas L. Pangle. Chicago: University of Chicago Press, 1983, 137–46.

Strauss, Leo. "On Plato's Apology of Socrates and Crito." In *Studies in Platonic Political Philosophy*, edited by Thomas L. Pangle. Chicago and London: University of Chicago Press, 1983, 38–67.

Strauss, Leo. *On Plato's Symposium*, edited by Seth Benardete. Chicago: University of Chicago Press, 2001.

Strauss, Leo. "On the Basis of Hobbes' Political Philosophy." In *What Is Political Philosophy? And Other Studies*. Glencoe: Free Press, 1959, 170–97.

Strauss, Leo. "On the Interpretation of Genesis." In *Jewish Philosophy and the Crisis of Modernity*, edited by Kenneth Hart Green. Albany: State University of New York Press, 1997, 359–77.

Strauss, Leo. "On the Minos." In *Liberalism Ancient and Modern*. Chicago: University of Chicago Press, 1995, 65–75.

Strauss, Leo. *On Tyranny: Including the Strauss-Kojève Correspondence: Corrected and Expanded Edition*, edited by Victor Gourevitch and Michael Roth. Chicago: University of Chicago Press, 2013.

Strauss, Leo. "Persecution and the Art of Writing." *Social Research* 8, no. 4 (1941): 488–504.

Strauss, Leo. *Persecution and the Art of Writing*. Glencoe: Free Press, 1952.

Strauss, Leo. " Persecution and the Art of Writing." In *Persecution and the Art of Writing*. Glencoe: Free Press, 1952, 22–38.

Strauss, Leo. *Philosophy and Law: Contributions to the Understanding of Maimonides and His Predecessors*, translated by Eve Adler. Albany: State University of New York Press, 1995.

Strauss, Leo. "Progress or Return?" In *The Rebirth of Classical Political Rationalism: An Introduction to the Thought of Leo Strauss*, edited by Thomas L. Pangle. Chicago: University of Chicago Press, 1989, 227–71.

Strauss, Leo. "Quelques remarques sur la science politique de Maïmonide et de Fârâbî." *Revue des Etudes Juives* 100 (1936): 1–37.

Strauss, Leo. "Reason and Revelation (1948)." In *Leo Strauss and the Theologico-Political Problem*, edited by Heinrich Meier, translated by Marcus Brainard. Cambridge: Cambridge University Press, 2006, 141–81.

Strauss, Leo. "'Religion and the Commonweal in the Tradition of Political Philosophy'. An Unpublished Lecture by Leo Strauss." *American Political Thought* 10, no. 1 (2021): 86–120.

Strauss, Leo. *Socrates and Aristophanes*. New York and London: Basic Books, 1966.

Strauss, Leo. "Some Remarks on the Political Science of Maimonides and Farabi." In *Leo Strauss on Maimonides: The Complete Writings*, edited by Kenneth Hart Green, translated by Robert C. Bartlett. Chicago and London: University of Chicago Press, 2013, 275–314.

Strauss, Leo. *Spinoza's Critique of Religion*, translated by Elsa M. Sinclair. New York: Schocken Books, 1965.

Strauss, Leo. *Studies in Platonic Political Philosophy*, edited by Thomas L. Pangle. Chicago and London: University of Chicago Press, 1983.

Strauss, Leo. "The 1965 Preface to Hobbes Politische Wissenschaft." *Interpretation: A Journal of Political Philosophy* 8, no. 1 (January 1979): 1–3.

Strauss, Leo. *The Argument and the Action of Plato's Laws*. Chicago: University of Chicago Press, 1975.

Strauss, Leo. *The City and Man*. Charlottesville: The University of Virginia Press, 1964.

Strauss, Leo. "The Dissertation (1921)." In *Leo Strauss: The Early Writings (1921–1932)*, translated and edited by Michael Zank. Albany: State University of New York Press, 2002, 53–61.

Strauss, Leo. "The Law of Reason in the Kuzari." *Proceedings of the American Academy for Jewish Research* 13 (1943): 47–96.

Strauss, Leo. "The Law of Reason in The Kuzari." In *Persecution and the Art of Writing*. Glencoe: Free Press, 1952, 95–142.

Strauss, Leo. "The Liberalism of Classical Political Philosophy." In *Liberalism Ancient and Modern*. Chicago: University of Chicago Press, 1968, 26–64.

Strauss, Leo. "The Literary Character of the Guide for the Perplexed." In *Essays on Maimonides*, edited by Salo Wittmayer Baron. New York: Columbia University Press, 1941, 37–91.

Strauss, Leo. "The Mutual Influence of Theology and Philosophy." *The Independent Journal of Philosophy* 3, no. 1 (1979): 111–18.

Strauss, Leo. "The Origins of Political Science and the Problem of Socrates." *Interpretation* 23, no. 2 (1996): 127–209.

Strauss, Leo. "The Place of the Doctrine of Providence According to Maimonides." In *Leo Strauss on Maimonides: The Complete Writings*, edited by Kenneth Hart Green, translated by Gabriel Bartlett and Svetozar Minkov. Chicago: University of Chicago Press, 2013, 314–29.

Strauss, Leo. *The Political Philosophy of Hobbes: Its Basis and Its Genesis*. Oxford: Clarendon Press, 1936.

Strauss, Leo. *The Political Philosophy of Hobbes: Its Basis and Its Genesis*, translated by Elsa M. Sinclair. Chicago: University of Chicago Press, 1952.

Strauss, Leo. "The Spirit of Sparta or the Taste of Xenophon." *Social Research* 6, no. 4 (1939): 502–36.

Strauss, Leo. *Thoughts on Machiavelli*. Glencoe: Free Press, 1958.

Strauss, Leo. "What Is Political Philosophy?" In *What Is Political Philosophy? And Other Studies*. Glencoe: Free Press, 1959, 9–56.

Strauss, Leo. *What Is Political Philosophy? And Other Studies.* Glencoe: Free Press, 1959.

Strauss, Leo. *Xenophon's Socrates.* Ithaca: Cornell University Press, 1972.

Strauss, Leo. *Xenophon's Socratic Discourse: An Interpretation of the Oeconomicus.* Ithaca: Cornell University Press, 1970.

Strauss, Leo, and Karl Löwith. "Correspondence between Karl Löwith and Leo Strauss." *The Independent Journal of Philosophy* 5/6 (1988): 177–92.

Strauss, Leo, and Karl Löwith. "Correspondence between Karl Löwith and Leo Strauss Concerning Modernity." *The Independent Journal of Philosophy* 4 (1988): 105–21.

Strauss, Leo, and Eric Voegelin. *Faith and Political Philosophy: The Correspondence Between Leo Strauss and Eric Voegelin.* 1934–1964, edited by Peter Emberley and Barry Cooper. Columbia: University of Missouri Press, 2004.

Strickland, Lloyd. "Leibniz on Eternal Punishment." *British Journal for the History of Philosophy* 17, no. 2 (2009): 307–31.

Stroumsa, Sarah. *Freethinkers of Medieval Islam. Ibn al-Rāwandī, Abū Bakr al-Rāzī and Their Impact on Islamic Thought.* Leiden: Brill, 1999.

Swift, Jonathan. *Gulliver's Travels*, edited by Claude Rawson. Oxford: Oxford University Press, 2008.

Tamer, Georges. *Islamische Philosophie und die Krise der Moderne: Das Verhältnis von Leo Strauss zu Alfarabi, Avicenna und Averroes.* Leiden: Brill, 2001.

Tanguay, Daniel. "How Strauss Read Farabi's Summary of Plato's 'Laws'." In *Leo Strauss's Defense of the Philosophic Life: Reading "What Is Political Philosophy?,"* edited by Rafael Major. Chicago: University of Chicago Press, 2013, 98–116.

Tanguay, Daniel. *Leo Strauss: An Intellectual Biography*, translated by Christopher Nadon. New Haven: Yale University Press, 2011.

Tarrant, Harold. *Plato's First Interpreters.* Ithaca: Cornell University Press, 2000.

Wacker, Bernd, and Jürgen Manemann. "'Politische Theologie'. Eine Skizze zur Geschichte und aktuellen Diskussion des Begriffs." In *Politische Theologie und Politische Philosophie*, edited by Marie-Christine Kajewski and Jürgen Manemann, 1st edition. Baden-Baden: Nomos Verlagsgesellschaft, 2016, 9–54.

Walker, Paul E. "The Political Implications of Al-Razi's Philosophy." In *The Political Aspects of Islamic Philosophy: Essays in Honor of Muhsin S. Mahdi,* edited by Charles E. Butterworth. Cambridge, MA: Harvard University Press, 1992, 61–95.

Walzer, Richard. "Arabic Transmission of Greek Thought to Medieval Europe." *Bulletin of the John Rylands Library* 29 (1945): 160–83.

Walzer, Richard. *Greek into Arabic: Essays on Islamic Philosophy.* Cambridge, MA: Harvard University Press, 1962.

Walzer, Richard. "Platonism in Islamic Philosophy." In *Greek into Arabic.* Cambridge, MA: Harvard University Press, 1962, 236–52.

Wilson, Catherine. "The Reception of Leibniz in the Eighteenth Century." In *The Cambridge Companion to Leibniz*, edited by Nicholas Jolley. Cambridge: Cambridge University Press, 1995, 442–74.

Wirmer, David. "Arabic Philosophy and the Art of Reading: I. Political Philosophy." In *La Philosophie Arabe à l'étude / Studying Arabic Philosophy. Sens, Limites et Défis d'une Discipline Moderne: Meaning, Limits, and Challenges of a Modern Discipline*, edited by Jean-Baptiste Brenet and Olga L. Lizzini. Paris: Vrin, 2019, 179–250.

Yamanaka, Yuriko. "Alexander in the Thousand and One Nights and the Ghazālī Connection." In *The Arabian Nights and Orientalism: Perspectives from East and West*, edited by Tetsuo Nishio and Yuriko Yamanaka. London and New York: I.B. Tauris, 2006, 93–115.

Zhang, Ying. "The Guide to The Guide: Some Observations on 'How To Begin To Study The Guide of the Perplexed'." *Interpretation: A Journal of Political Philosophy* 46, no. 3 (2020): 533–65.

Zotenberg, Hermann. "Notice sur quelques manuscrits des Mille et une nuits et la traduction de Galland." *Notice et extraits des manuscrits de la Bibliothèque nationale et autres bibliothèques* 28 (1888): 167–320.

Zuckert, Michael, and Catherine Zuckert. *Leo Strauss and the Problem of Political Philosophy*. Chicago: University of Chicago Press, 2014.

Zuckert, Michael, and Catherine Zuckert. *The Truth about Leo Strauss: Political Philosophy and American Democracy*. Chicago and London: University of Chicago Press, 2006.

Index

Printed in the USA
CPSIA information can be obtained
at www.ICGtesting.com
LVHW040108051123
763062LV00002B/126